OCCUPATION:
HOUSEWIFE

 *Helena Znaniecki Lopata*

Oxford University Press

London   Oxford   New York

To Dick Teddy Stef

OXFORD UNIVERSITY PRESS

Oxford London New York
Glasgow Toronto Melbourne Wellington
Cape Town Ibadan Nairobi Lusaka Addis Ababa Delhi
Bombay Calcutta Madras Karachi Lahore Dacca
Kuala Lumpur Hong Kong Tokyo

Preface

Occupation: Housewife is based on many different big and small studies. The whole idea began to take shape when we moved out to a suburb near Chicago while I was simultaneously finishing my doctoral dissertation and juggling Teddy, our daughter, on my lap. Having been brought up in Poland and seen America only in university communities and an Air Force base that I viewed as atypical, I had serious reservations about the suburban move. Although not specializing in the sociology of the family, being much more involved in theory and social psychology, I had read enough about American suburbs to dread having to live among non-academic women. The community in which we settled amazed me. The young women simply did not fit any stereotype contained in the literature I had covered. The frankness with which they discussed problems and issues for which cultural patterns were inadequate motivated me to undertake a study of housewives. The original interview was designed with the help of a seventeen-woman pilot group. The respondents were the young and "modern" residents of a row development, containing twenty-four almost identical houses surrounded by fields. The late Pierre Martineau, Director of Research at the *Chicago Tribune,* learned of the project, which at that time consisted of diaries, charts of interaction, and several other forms of data-collecting techniques, and offered to fund an expansion of the study to a sample of housewives in twelve socio-economically divergent suburbs. I narrowed the method down to a single, though very long interview originally called "The Young Suburban Housewife" schedule. The study was written up as a report to the *Tribune* and in several articles, and I returned to child-rearing. However, the many years of sociological training im-

pelled me to begin wondering how different my suburban housewives were from urban women, from working women, and from
those beyond the stage of rearing small children.

With the help of students, several research grants, and many
years of work, two repetitions of the first interview, now renamed
"The Social Role of Housewife" schedule, were administered in
the mid-1960's. This time I did not place any restrictions on age
or working status and was also able to locate some non-white
respondents. Other studies followed in the ensuing years. The
many different interviews and questionnaires which have been
used are described in the Introduction. As usual, the topic became more and more complex, and I ventured into roles other
than that of the housewife. I finally included the major roles of
women except that of employment, although I used the latter as
a factor in attitudes about the former. The original emphasis of
the study remains; I have been interested throughout in the
trends in ideologies and the role definitions of women fully involved in the role of housewife, in the stages of the life cycle
which are called the "expanding circle," the "peak stage," and
the "full-house plateau." The Midwest Council for Social Research in Aging, which gave me two fellowships, was interested
in the older housewife who performs the role minimally, though
my data was focused upon the earlier stages. For this reason I
later decided to study role shifts in widowhood for women fifty
years of age and older. The study of widows will be published
separately.

Although this set of studies deals with Chicago women, many
of its conclusions are undoubtedly applicable to housewives in
other metropolitan regions of America. After all, most Americans
live in such areas, most of these complexes are in the northern
belts of the country, and the mobility of the population through
migration and of its ideas through mass communication have
made new patterns of life increasingly available in all locations.

Interesting problems have arisen as a consequence of the rate
of change of American culture and the huge volume of data upon
which this book is based. For example, the new movement among
leaders wishing to change the identity of "Negro" into that of
"black" posed problems in my writing. I may be dating the book
by using the name "Negro" to delineate that segment of the
American society. Furthermore, my sympathies are with the

movement. My decision to use "Negro" is sociologically interesting. The change in concepts is very new and not fully accepted by all who could change their identity from "Negro," with all its historical connotations, to the equally symbolic, but different in content, title "black." The respondents who are involved in this set of studies identified themselves as Negro, and in the final analysis I do not have the scientific right to change their identity. The name "Negro" thus remains.

The same problem arose at the beginning with the ascription of the term "housewife." Many women object to it, but it is a source of identification by most respondents to identity questions, and it appears on many official forms asking for occupation. Substitution of the word "homemaker" is again a switch supporting new ideology with which many of the women are not identified.

I am very grateful to myself for having had the courage in my second major research project (the work for the dissertation was the first) to start out with such a large subject and with open-ended depth questions. Thanks to the latter and to the willingness of housewives to spend hours explaining their definitions and feelings, I have learned in greater depth more social psychology and more sociological theory than I could have obtained through the library methods I had previously favored. I do not think that I would ever do the same work again; analyzing 571 two-hour or longer open-ended interviews into a variety of codes is a job I would not wish on many people. Nor will I ever write a first book again. The combination of masses of data and the desire to include all eleven years of research into one book produced a painful year and 1084 pages of manuscript. I must admit that, after good advice from Howard S. Becker as to ways of splitting the whole work into several parts and publishing only one book, I began to really enjoy the writing stages that followed.

It has always seemed to me that the acknowledgments are the most difficult part of a book to write. After all, how can one select among all those who directly or indirectly helped the thought and work experiences. The major ones are obvious, but toward them the feeling of gratitude is so personal as to make its public presentation difficult. However, this is part of academic practice, so I shall try.

My strongest debt is to three generations of relatives, my parents, my husband, and my children. I am a Znaniecki, the daughter of Florian and Eileen Znaniecki, and a sociologist, so my debt to them is obvious. In addition to learning sociology in spite of myself—I finally stuck to it after trying to become a chemist—I am grateful to them for the *joi de vivre* and excitement in knowledge processes with which they imbued our home. Whenever they had company, I found excuses to convince my dates that I could not go out. My mother really managed an ideationally international home, and my father was constantly discussing with enthusiasm interesting ideas, his own, his students, or someone else's. The students came to the home and I learned along with them.

I am also a Lopata and grateful for everything this identity has brought me. I agree with Eli Ginsberg that women who become scientists must have married husbands who encouraged them in this rigorous life, but I also know that Alice Rossi is right when she says that we had the initial sense to marry the right man. Dick is that kind of person and I am grateful for all his help and encouragement, and for proving how wise I was at twenty to find him. Teddy and Stefan are beginning to understand what it's like to want to contribute to the world of knowledge, and they have helped me not only with emergency tasks but in understanding and discussion. It is a pleasure to see this.

I was lucky to have learned sociology from both faculty and fellow students at two universities. In the post-World War II years, the University of Illinois was a base for William Albig, E. T. Hiller, Donald Taft, B. F. Timmons, J. E. Hullett, Richard Dewey, Robert Janes, and Bob Bierstedt. The students were few, but very stimulating and always a pleasure to meet. The University of Chicago faculty and student body during the later 1940's has been a source of perpetual gratitude for many of us. Everett Hughes, Louis Wirth, and Herbert Blumer oversaw my dissertation, and I feel myself a disciple of all three in spite of their ranging interests. I also enjoyed William Ogburn, Ernest Burgess, Harvey Smith, and Peter and Zena Blau. The fellow students of that period were, as fact and legend has recorded, something very special. I not only learned from them at that time, especially in the famous "prelim" study groups, but I have continued to do so during my years of academic inactivity and more recent renewed commitment. Those to whom I feel special gratitude for reading my first drafts are Irving Goffman, Joseph Gusfield, Howard S. Becker, and Morris Janowitz. Others who have assisted the process of my becoming a sociologist include Inge and Hans Mausch, Rhoda and Bernard Goldstein, Kurt and Gladys Lang. Special thanks also go to the members and students of the Midwest Council for Social Research on Aging for many opportunities to test my ideas and especially to Warren Peterson for guiding the process. Ethel Shanas and Robert Winch have spent hours helping me formulate interview schedules and research plans.

I also wish to thank Roosevelt University, which gave me a major research grant to do the book and which for years adjusted courses and hours to my expanding interests. Special thanks go to St. Clair Drake for many stimulating discussions and to S. Kirsen Weinberg, Robert Roberts, Ferdinand Kolegar, Arthur Hillman, and the late Rose Hum Lee for sharing the task of teaching the very interesting group of students we had at that time. The students are the life blood of a scholar, and I have been very lucky to have ones with a variety of backgrounds, willing to get excited by research and ideas and to work at all the levels of becoming a sociologist. I already find such stimulation among my new colleagues and students at Loyola University.

I am naturally grateful to Irving Louis Horowitz for his role in the publication of this book. Mrs. Manuela Kruger edited the manuscript as did my mother, Eileen Markley Znaniecki, and Mrs. Patricia Cristol put on the finishing touches. Joan Lichterman and Mary Sherwood slaved to make the manuscript presentable, often with difficult deadlines, and Wanda Jefferson worked throughout, coding, table making, hunting through library sources, plus doing any number of other emergency jobs.

I see that the list of people to whom I want to express my gratitude is large. This is my first book, so this is understandable.

Contents

List of Tables

List of Charts

The accomplish'd housewife or,
the gentlewoman's companion: containing

I. Reflections on the education of the fair sex; with characters for their imitation.

II. The penman's advice to the ladies . . .

III. Instructions for addressing persons of distinction . . .

IV. An easy introduction to the study of practical arithmetic.

V. Directions for copying prints or drawings, and painting either in oil or water colours, or with crayons.

VI. Directions for marketing . . .

VII. A bill of fare for every month in the year.

VIII. Recipes in cookery, pastry, &c.

IX. Instructions for caring and placing dishes on the table.

X. All sorts of pickles, made wines &c.

XI. Remarks on the nature and qualities of the most common ailments.

XII. Recipes in physick and surgery.

XIII. Remarks on the causes and symptoms of most diseases.

XIV. The florist's kalendar.

XV. Familiar letters on several occasions in common life.

XVI. A dictionary serving for the translation of ordinary English words into more scholastic ones.

Concluding with some serious instructions for the conduct of the fair sex, with regard to their duty toward God and toward their neighbours.

Index card in the files of the Library of Congress referring to a volume contained in the rare book collection, published in London by J. Neuberry, 1745.

OCCUPATION: HOUSEWIFE

✼ ✼ ✼

Introduction

THE HOUSEWIFE

This book deals with women who perform the social role of housewife and live in an urbanized region of the United States. A
housewife is a woman responsible for running her home, whether
she performs the tasks herself or hires people to do them. This distinguishes her from an employed housekeeper who maintains a
dwelling belonging to someone else without having final responsibility for it. Many other people may undertake the tasks of housewives, but they are socially recognized as substitutes, assistants,
or deviants. A man or girl can *behave like* a housewife, but in this
society the role is customarily performed by a woman who is, or
has been, married, and who is *the* person responsible for the
dwelling. It is *her* house, in terms of responsibility if not possession.

Thus, all housewives are women. But not all women are housewives. This study focuses upon only those women involved in that
role, particularly within its expanding or peak stages, when the
house is also likely to be occupied by a husband and growing children. The research is not limited to that role, but deals with the
related roles of wife, mother, worker, neighbor, friend, and community participant as the housewife sees them.

SOCIAL ROLES

The basic sociological concept utilized in the study of housewives
is that of "social role" as developed by Florian Znaniecki.[1] He

1. Florian W. Znaniecki, *Social Relations and Social Roles: An Unfin-
ished Systematic Sociology*, San Francisco: Chandler, 1965. This theoretical

defines a social role as a set of mutually interdependent social relations between a "social person" and members of his "social circle." The role's functions are performed through "patterned duties" on the part of the person toward the circle in general or toward any segment of it, and through the "personal rights" its members grant him, in the form of action, facilities, or permission to carry out his part.

Most social roles are based in the culture of a society. Several people may be involved in social roles bearing the same title, like "doctor," and they are assumed by everyone to meet the same function in their separate social circles. The patterns of their relations are recorded by word of mouth or written history. In large societies, most roles are carried out by more than one set of persons, many of whom are aware of the behavior of other sets and usually strive intentionally for a greater similarity of action than coincidence alone would bring about.

Social roles—sets of inter-connected relations—change over time, each adjusting in varying degrees to the personalities of the participants or to the circumstances under which their component relations are developed. If they change greatly, they may be redefined as a new type of role. In American society the role of doctor, for example, has changed dramatically with new knowledge, greater specialization, complex hospitals and expanding staffs, and changes in the general public's view of the profession. The change is evident in the increase of occupations carrying out tasks previously assigned to doctors, including the new paraprofessional jobs, and of subtypes of practitioners differentiated as pathologists, surgeons, internists, and so forth.[2]

Descriptions of social roles contain explanations and justifications of their functions, of the goals they are expected to achieve or strive toward reaching. A mother, for example, is expected not only to give birth to a child but to care for it physically and to

---

framework was a major interest to Znaniecki, who used it in his presidential address for the American Sociological Association: "Basic Problems of Contemporary Sociology," *American Sociological Review,* 19, No. 5 (October 1954), 519–42.

2. The study of the evolution of social roles was considered by Znaniecki to be an important task of sociology because it contributes to the understanding of not only these sets of relations but also social groups and societies. See *Social Relations and Social Roles.*

socialize it to be a human being capable of participating in the ongoing life of the society. It is on the basis of social roles that the total society is able to function. The economic, political, recreational, religious, educational, and family spheres of American life are carried out through roles such as farmer, miner, advertising man, manufacturer, assembly-line worker; President, senator, precinct captain, voter; baseball player, moviegoer, fan, golfer, hippie; rabbi, nun, church councilman, parishioner; teacher, student, dean, fraternity member; wife, husband, mother, grandmother, son. These and many other roles exist in society, each comprising the persons who bear the title and relate to others who grant rights and receive duties. In the case of some roles, only a few such sets of relations are simultaneously involved; in the case of others, there are millions.[3] Some roles encompass the minimum of three people with two of them forming the social circle, as in the case of a lover, his mistress, and the landlord who rents them a room. Others take in great numbers of co-operating and interacting individuals, for instance, the role of the President of the United States. Roles vary in many other features, such as in the degree of precision or determinateness of the rules of behavior governing the participants.[4]

The explanation of what a role should accomplish and the justification of its "division of labor" and "hierarchy of status" form part of the social institution into which it fits.[5] The hierarchy of status is the system of prestige positions assigned to the role's participants. In American society, the doctor is given a higher status than is the nurse, the laboratory technician, and most of the patients. In this sense, the institution is a system of procedures, forming the cultural foundations for social roles and con-

3. A segment of a social role as viewed by Znaniecki is somewhat similar to a single role within Merton's Role-Set. The former conceptualization has the advantage of enabling analysis of the role as a unit of inter-dependent components, whereas the latter focuses upon each section as a more or less isolated relation. See Robert K. Merton, "The Role-Set: Problems in Sociological Theory," *British Journal of Sociology*, 8 (1957), 106–20.

4. Raymond W. Mack, "Occupational Determinateness: A Problem and Hypotheses in Role Theory," *Social Forces*, 35, No. 1 (October 1956), 20–24.

5. Some of the technical aspects about the sociological uses of the concepts of social status and social role are discussed in Helena Znaniecki Lopata, "A Restatement of the Relation Between Role and Status," *Sociology and Social Research*, 49, No. 1 (October 1964), 58–68.

taining the ideological justification of the need for them.[6] The
dating system, the marriage ceremony, the way the wife acts
toward her husband and toward everyone with whom she interacts *because* she is his wife, all tend to be drawn from the norms
or customs of the family institution. The patterns of action and
norms, which we call institutions, are the culture; the people who
carry them out, organized in a variety of relations, social roles,
and groups, are the society.

Each human being is involved in many roles, simultaneously or
in sequences ascribed by others or achieved by himself. Each role
requires only a segment of his personality and calls forth only
those qualities and behaviors which fulfill the set of duties and
rights of the role. The fact that the total individual is not called
forth in each role is signified in the sociological concept of the
"social person." For example, Mary Brown as a "total individual"
relates to people within many social circles, entering each one
with different sentiments and behaving differently. Each circle
sees her through a different set of perspectives, as a mother, a
wife, or a customer. As a total individual she may relate to another total individual through several separate roles, that is, as
several different social persons. She relates to John Brown as a
wife with a quite different set of traits from those she displays
when she interacts with him as a mother of their children. She has
different duties in each role and she receives different rights from
each. She may also be his co-worker, a hostess when he is host, a
fellow Christian Scientist, and a daughter-in-law when he is a son.
In each of these roles she has a different social circle, and John
Brown is not the same person when he is in the circle of Mary
Brown as mother as he is in the circle of Mary Brown as wife. In
the complexity of relations between these two individuals, each
must be careful not to confuse any situation by indicating incor-
rectly within which role he is functioning. Conflict between people often arises when their relations are fitted into a diversity of
roles calling for mutually exclusive behavior, without clear indication of separation and transition. A woman may respond to a
man as the mother of their children at a time when he wants her
to act as his wife, for example. She may refer to herself as a housewife and then list her responsibilities belonging to the role of wife

6. The classic book focusing on social institutions is J. O. Hertzler's *American Social Institutions,* Boston: Allyn and Bacon, 1961.

or mother, confusing in her mind both the inter-connection among the roles and that between them and herself as a total individual.

The concept of social role is basic to the analysis of the sets of relations in which women who are housewives are involved, because it recognizes that each individual performs more than one role. Thus it makes consistent analysis possible. One of the characteristics of American society is an expanding number of diverse social roles available to and participated in by the urban woman before, or at the same time, she has the role of housewife. Mirra Komarovsky and Ruth Benedict among others have found that these roles are often contradictory and mutually discontinuous.[7]

Much of the literature dealing with American women is far from scientific or value-free.[8] Grandiose generalizations camou-

7. Mirra Komarovsky, *Women in the Modern World, Their Education and Their Dilemmas*, Boston: Little, Brown, 1953, and "Cultural Contradictions and Sex Roles," *American Journal of Sociology*, 52 (1946), 184–89. Ruth Benedict, "Continuities and Discontinuities in Cultural Conditioning," *Psychiatry* (1938), 161–67.

8. The books devoted to descriptions of American women are numerous. Many, even supposedly scientific ones, contain one-sided or even highly biased generalizations. A number of social scientists find Helene Deutsch's two-volume *The Psychology of Women* difficult to verify objectively. Even less objective seems Ferdinand Lundberg and Marynia F. Farnham's *Modern Woman: The Lost Sex*, New York: Harper and Brothers, 1947. *The American Woman: An Historical Study* by Eric J. Dingwall, London: Duckworth, 1956, is, in spite of the title, an emotionally charged attack on this group. Finally, Philip Wylie's *Generation of Vipers*, New York: Holt, Rinehart and Winston, 1955, is a strong rejection of mothers in this society. Books sympathetic to women include the famous *The Second Sex* by Simone de Beauvoir, New York: Alfred Knopf, 1953, and Betty Friedan's *The Feminine Mystique*, New York, W. W. Norton, 1963. Morton Hunt's *Her Infinite Variety*, New York: Harper & Row, 1962, has a flattering tone.

The mass communication media have not neglected women either. Periodically, major television networks do "an analysis in depth." *Life* magazine periodically devotes an issue to this subject, the fullest of them, entitled "The American Woman," came out on December 24, 1956. *Life* returned to the subject in a series on "Today's Dilemmas of Love and Marriage," beginning with its September 6 issue in 1961. More recently, *Look* turned over fifty pages of its January 11, 1966 issue to "The American Woman." Magazines aimed at the feminine reading public are numerous and filled with reports of the character and life style of the American woman. *The Ladies' Home Journal* had a special issue in July 1967 on what it feels is a new development in this society, located presently in one of the states, entitled "The California Woman." Many mass communication outlets have responded to the new women's movements, generally called "Women's Lib." *The Saturday Review*

flage the components of the various social roles performed by different kinds of women and the changes within each. The purpose of this study is to examine the ways women define the major social roles connected with their adult life in an American urban area. The analysis is based on a series of investigations which spanned more than ten years and utilized several sociological research tools. The focus throughout is on the woman's conceptualization of the roles she performs as well as on her actual contacts and involvements. Relatively little of the research was devoted to the latter years of women's lives, within which they perform the roles of housewife, wife, and mother at a less intensive level.[9] This report focuses on the woman who is either in the early or "full-house" stage of the social role of wife—that is, the woman who is living with her husband and whose children live at home or have left it only recently. Older women were interviewed to provide information on all stages of the life cycle, but stress is upon fully active housewives who are likely to be experiencing and expressing the newer trends in the role-clusters of women in America.

METHODOLOGY

The first studies which elicited the information in this volume began in the late 1950's with depth interviews of 299 women in 12 of the 147 incorporated suburbs around Chicago having a population of 2500 or more. These communities were selected, with the help of the research staffs of the *Chicago Tribune* and the Illinois Bell Telephone Company, on the basis of two sets of criteria. First, they represent towns of as great a range as possible of traits, such as socio-economic composition of population, size, distance

---

cover story of February 21, 1970 was highlighted on the front page as "The New Feminism," and *Newsweek* was quick to match it with an issue on March 23, 1970 highlighting "Women in Revolt." Few issues of current magazines lack some comment about the "modern woman" or the "revolutionary," and FBI lists are commented upon because of the prominent part played by young radical women.

9. A study of role shifts in widowhood, entitled *Widowhood in an American City*, soon to be published by Schenkman Publishing Company, was facilitated by an Administration on Aging, H.E.W. grant, and by Roosevelt University.

and direction from the city, and historical past.[10] Second, only towns with a high rate of expansion or newly developing sections of older communities were selected, because hypothetically they were more likely than the more settled areas to be the home of the American housewife of the newly emerging life styles. The final selection of blocks within each suburb drew upon as wide a range of housing types, sizes of lots, and general features of the area, including free space and distance and direction from the center of the town, as all sources could make available. Interviews were conducted only with women who met the criteria of being full-time homemakers—those who owned their homes and had pre-high-school children. Some women pregnant with their first child were included. The interviewing took place in late spring and summer.

In addition to background data, the first interview, called the "social role of housewife" schedule, contained open-ended questions asking for the woman's perceptions, conceptualizations, and actions in the following areas of her life:

1. The characteristics of the social role of housewife; contrasts between this role and those of work outside the home; contrasts between the life of the modern homemaker and that of her grandmother; changes during her life; definitions of relations with other persons in major social roles; and general evaluations.

2. The social roles and role changes of the man of the family and the influence a wife is assumed to have upon his occupational achievement.

3. The community in which she lives, her reasons for moving there, and the relations she maintains with neighbors.

4. The other social roles and relations she had undertaken in the past, in which she was presently involved, or which she anticipated for the future, including a ranking of the importance of these roles.

The analysis of these interviews led to an expansion of the

10. The Northeastern Illinois Metropolitan Area Planning Commission has produced the *Suburban Factbook* (1961). Evelyn M. Kitagawa and Karl E. Taeuber have continued a long history of research in Chicago demographic characteristics in *The Local Community Factbook: Chicago Metropolitan Area*, Chicago: The University Community Inventory, 1963. Estimations of the 1968 figures came from the Hospital Planning Council of Chicago, Illinois.

group studied to include married urban women of all ages, with as wide a range of background characteristics as were available in the Chicago area. Urban working women were included. Most of these interviews were conducted in 1964 and 1965 by Roosevelt University students, who had access to a heterogeneous population, including people not often reached by researchers. The content of the open-ended responses gave insight into the ways in which different groups of women approach their various roles— insights which pre-coded schedules cannot convey. These interviews served as a source for a constant flow of new hypotheses, of new ways of looking at material developed from prior analyses.

Each response was coded in a variety of ways as new ideas developed. The vocabulary used in the responses contributed to the elaboration of a social psychology of role involvement and to a deeper understanding of differences among women in approaching a role. Several coders and judges were used and mutually checked to ensure consistency. The total of more than 1000 interviews was finally culled down to 279 with suburban housewives, 192 with non-working housewives, and 100 with working wives. For brevity's sake these are called "suburban housewives," "urban housewives," and "urban working women," although the last category obviously consists of women who are also housewives, even if not full time. More interviews were occasionally used to meet special needs.

The information and insights derived from the "social role of housewife" interviews led to a testing of some specific hypotheses in several additional studies. The major one, the "interaction patterns" interviews, was mainly pre-coded. The responses of 205 women that have been analyzed for this book provide details about the types and frequencies of social interaction, particularly those involving services used both inside and outside of the home in order to maintain it. The only part of the interview which was not pre-coded asked for a list of the ten most important past events in the life of the women interviewed and of five predicted for the future. These responses provided more detailed explanations of role shifts of different types of women than those provided by the early interviews.

The relation of urbanites to persons living in the same apartment building was investigated in detail in a questionnaire given to women in some new high-rise buildings. Other, shorter studies investigated the future role expectations of Negro high-school students in the upper part of the lower class; the attitudes of club women toward full-time educational efforts of married students older than average; shopping habits of urbanites and suburbanites; and several other features of life of women who were at least part-time housewives. Participant observation in several communities and analysis of the content of mass communication media directed to women, such as newspapers, magazines, and daytime television programs, provided supplementary data. Thus, the book is a result of the contributions of many people.

BACKGROUND CHARACTERISTICS OF THE RESPONDENTS

A detailed analysis of the demographic characteristics of all the women whose interviews, questionnaires, and observations that have been used for this volume would be extremely lengthy. Therefore, only a brief description of the respondents to the "social role of housewife" schedule is included. All but 19 of the 571 informants are married, 10 being widowed and 9 divorced. Half of the women were reared in Chicago, another 15 per cent in other towns over 25,000 in population and located north of the Mason-Dixon Line outside of metropolitan Chicago. Only 6 per cent were reared in the Chicago suburbs. Only 2 per cent of the suburbanites, but 16 per cent of urban housewives, and 19 per cent of the urban working women were born south of the Mason-Dixon Line. This distribution can be explained partly by noting that no women in the suburban sample are Negro, whereas 26 per cent of the housewives and 38 per cent of the working women in the city are. The numbers in the last two groups are not meant to be proportionate to the Negro population of Chicago (22.9 per cent in 1960); we attempted to obtain a sample large enough to gain more substantial knowledge about this segment of the population. Recent migrations of Negroes into the city and of whites out of it make our figures more representative.

The husbands of the respondents tend to have been brought up in the same kind of community as the women, but both sets of parents came from different areas than their children did, indicating generational mobility. Only 17 per cent of the interviewees' mothers and 16 per cent of their fathers were born in Chicago, but the younger the respondents, the more likely they are to be at least second-generation residents. Very few of the parents were born in the Chicago suburbs. The mothers of the older suburban respondents (forty years of age or over) were born in many parts of this country and abroad. One-quarter of them came from Europe. The older suburbanite (in her forties or older) generally experienced the following mobility pattern. Her mother, and usually also her father, were born outside the Chicago metropolitan area but moved to it in time for the respondent to be reared in the city. The typical "older" suburbanite moved out of the city in the post World War II years. The Chicago suburban ring also contains a relatively high percentage of young housewives who came to the suburbs directly from another part of the country, without having lived in the city. Those still living in the urban center at the time of the study are more likely to have been original migrants from other areas of America or from Europe. Many came from the same community in which their mothers had been born. Both the urban housewives and the urban working women are heavily over-represented by people coming from the South of the United States and from Europe in this or the prior generation.

The religious preference of the respondents is: 42 per cent Protestant, 31 per cent Catholic, 16 per cent Jewish, and 6 per cent "none." The relatively large percentage of respondents of Jewish identification is due to the fact that two of the twelve suburbs selected for the sampling happened to be experiencing a rapid influx of Jews during the study time. The women of the various religious identifications are not evenly distributed by place of residence or by age because of the history and direction of migration in the Chicago area. The highest Protestant percentage, 68 per cent, is among the older suburbanites. This means that the suburbs are now drawing a higher proportion of Catholics and Jews than in the past.

The suburban women interviewed have reached a relatively high educational level compared with that of the nation as a whole and with that of the Chicago Standard Metropolitan Statistical Area in particular. Only 3 per cent of the full-time housewives who own their homes in the suburban areas and have pre-high-school children have not finished grade school; 57 per cent have completed high school, and 41 per cent have attended college. The urban women are much more likely to be at the extremes of educational achievement. Those who are very young are apt to have gone to college, 60 per cent of the housewives and 74 per cent of the working women in that age category having gone beyond high school as compared with 33 per cent of the suburban housewives and a much lower percentage of older urbanites. Working women are more likely to have reached high educational levels than are housewives, in both the white and the black sub-groups. The fact that women in the middle class who work are more likely to have a higher education than women who do not work reflects a national trend in this direction. This is particularly true of women with professional or especially complex training.

More husbands than wives have done at least some college work, and 30 per cent of them have obtained at least a college degree. Most of the highly educated men are in the youngest age group and live in the city or "prestige" suburbs. Proportionally, the older working women, particularly Negroes, have less educated husbands.

All but 4 per cent of the respondents have worked at paying jobs sometime in their lives, whereas another 4 per cent claim to have "always worked." One per cent gives no employment history. Twenty-three per cent of the suburbanites and 27 per cent of the urban housewives worked only before marriage, another 66 per cent of the former group, and 48 per cent of the latter worked both before and after marriage. An additional 3 per cent of those living in the suburbs and 7 per cent of those living in the city have an "off and on" working history. Women currently working are more likely to have had an uneven, rather than a steady, employment history. Twenty-three per cent of them have not worked before or during the early years of marriage. Of the 471 women not working now, 46 per cent have no intention of seeking a job in the future, whereas 25 per cent would do so under special circumstances or have not ruled out the possibility. Few express any identification with work as a career or source of identification. Most of the respondents who have worked held clerical positions, ranging from private secretary to file clerk. Teaching and nursing were the next most frequently held occupations, followed by a range of white- and blue-collar jobs.

One-fourth of the husbands of suburban housewives and of working women hold professional jobs. Fewer of the urban housewives are married to men in such positions. Eight per cent of the suburban husbands are in semi-professions, such as consulting, advertising, or real estate. Eighteen per cent of the respondents are married to men in managerial positions, 5 per cent in clerical jobs, 17 per cent in sales, and 24 per cent in skilled or semi-skilled labor. Only 5 per cent of the husbands of urban house-wives are in semi-professions, 15 per cent in managerial occupations, 9 per cent in clerical jobs, 13 per cent in sales, and 19 per cent in skilled or semi-skilled labor, whereas 5 per cent are in personal service. Among working women, 7 per cent of the husbands are in managerial, 11 per cent in clerical, and 23 per cent in labor jobs above the unskilled level. Ten per cent of the husbands are not working or not supporting their wives for other reasons.

The occupational ranking of the husbands of the women interviewed is generally higher than that of their fathers; thus the women had experienced upward mobility. Thirty-three per cent of the fathers of the suburban housewives were blue-collar workers, 10 per cent were farmers, and only 9 per cent were in the professions. About the same percentage of urban housewives as of urban working women were reared in homes headed by professional or managerial fathers. Twenty per cent of the fathers, as compared with 10 per cent of the husbands, of working women were said not to have supported their families. The dramatic difference between the two generations of men in the lives of working women is that 20 per cent more husbands than fathers are in the professions.

The family income of the suburban women interviewed is concentrated in the range of $6000 to $10,999, the median for American urban areas; 64 per cent declare it in that range. Urban incomes show a much greater spread, only 46 per cent of the housewives and 49 per cent of the working women having family incomes that fall in the median level. Eight per cent more of the urban working women declare their family income above the median than do suburban housewives. The age factor somewhat accounts for that distribution, however, since income tends to rise with age, and the suburbanites are younger.

The age distribution of the respondents must always be kept in mind when comparisons between the three populations of suburban housewives, urban housewives, and urban working women

are made. Since the post World War II housing boom, the suburbs have drawn predominantly young adults with children. This
is true of rings around most American cities. Young people usually start married life in a city apartment. After they have one or
two children and their income rises, they move to the suburbs. In
1960, the median age for the suburban population in northeastern
Illinois, which means around Chicago, was 29.2 or 3.7 years lower
than the median age of Chicago's residents. Only 7 per cent of
the people living in its suburbs were sixty-five years of age or
older, with 12.4 per cent under five years of age and 37.4 per cent
under eighteen years of age. Thus, the bulk of the suburban residents consists of adults with children at home. Many couples have
recently returned to the city because their children left home for
marriage, school, or work. The "social role of housewife" interviews, in addition, are drawn from the newer areas of the mushrooming suburbs so the result is intentionally skewed in favor of
the new and young suburbanites who represent the movement.
Other age groups—that is, the very young and the middle-aged
and older women—are included among the urban housewives and
working women. As a result of all these factors, 31 per cent of the
suburbanites are in their twenties, compared with 24 per cent of
the urban housewives, and 27 per cent of the urban working
women. In addition, the suburbanites are the most likely to be
between twenty-five and twenty-nine years of age, 87 per cent of
those in their twenties being in this range. The three populations
are even more unevenly represented in the age group of women
in their thirties: 57 per cent of the suburbanites and only 9 per
cent of each type of urbanite are in that age group. Twelve per
cent of the suburbanites, 39 per cent of urban housewives, and 36
per cent of urban working women are in their forties. Finally,
none of the suburbanites but 38 per cent and 28 per cent, respectively, of the urban women are in their fifties or over. The
oldest respondent is eighty-four years of age, the youngest nineteen.

THE TWELVE CHICAGO SUBURBS

The women who responded to the "social role of housewive" interview live in a great variety of urban and suburban areas. The
urbanites are drawn from so many different neighborhoods that a

description of each of them would amount to a description of the entire city. The twelve Chicago suburbs chosen to represent the newly expanding communities or newer areas of more established towns also vary considerably, and their description is included as an aid toward visualization of their residents.

Highland Park

Highland Park is the highest in socio-economic rank, based on median income, median education of adults, and percentage of adult workers in white-collar jobs, of the twelve communities. It is not the highest for the Chicago area, however, because of the heterogeneity of its population. It is located about twenty-six miles from the center of the city, along the prestigious North Shore of Lake Michigan. Its median family income was $13,007 in 1960, or almost double that of the city families, and 63 per cent of its families were then living on $10,000 or more. The median number of school years completed by those twenty-five years of age or over was thirteen, and 28 per cent had completed four years of college. In 1960, the occupational distribution of the men shows that 42 per cent worked in professional or managerial occupations or as officials and proprietors; 25 per cent in clerical or sales jobs; 2 per cent as non-farm laborers, and 5 per cent in services outside of private households. All others comprise 14 per cent of the working males. As typical for suburbs a distance from the central city, most of the men work outside Chicago; in 1960, some 49 per cent worked in Lake County, where Highland Park is located, only 37 per cent in Chicago, and 12 per cent in other places in Cook County.

Highland Park was incorporated in 1869. It had a population of 14,476 in 1940 and changed little during the next decade. By 1950 there were only 16,808 residents; by 1960 the town had 25,-532 people, with a very low density of 2093 people per square mile, and in 1968 its estimated population was 31,462. In 1960, the median age of residents was thirty-three, with only 10 per cent under five years of age and only 37 per cent eighteen or under. These percentages are the second lowest within the twelve suburbs studied, reflecting the fact of its high socio-economic status. Young couples with young children are not likely to have the income to move to Highland Park.

The expansion of Highland Park in the 1950's is reflected by the fact that only half of its 1960 residents lived in the same house in 1955. A relatively high percentage, 50 per cent, of the houses existing in 1960 were built before 1940, and 39 per cent were built after 1950. This pattern is typical of the North Shore suburbs which have an old and established pre World War II nucleus and expanded rather late in suburban development. The median housing value was $31,300 in 1960, a figure almost twice the Chicago median and the highest of the twelve communities. The building permits issued in 1960 averaged, however, only $26,615, a drop from the value of older buildings. As is often the case with prestigious communities with room for expansion, Highland Park is drawing a more heterogeneous population in development-type housing. The ethnic background of residents is also surprisingly diverse. In fact, all the figures point to the fact that Highland Park is a more heterogeneous community than expected from its high socio-economic standing.

Glenview

Glenview has a slightly lower socio-economic standing than Highland Park. It lies about twenty miles north and a bit west of the city, bordering on the North Shore. The old, established core of the town became surrounded by new homes in the 1950's. It was incorporated in 1899 and its 1940 population was merely 2500. By 1950, it more than doubled to 6142, then sharply increased to 18,132 by 1960. In that year, the density per square mile was 3555 people, higher than that of Highland Park and Hazel Crest but very low compared with that of the other towns. By 1968 the population had increased to an estimated 24,678.

The average age of the population of Glenview in 1960 was thirty; 13 per cent were under five and 42 per cent were eighteen or under. The average family income was $11,706, second highest of that of the chosen towns, and 60 per cent of the families earned $10,000 or more. The median of school years completed by persons twenty-five years of age or over was 12.9. Seventy-six per cent of its employed males were in white-collar occupations in 1960; 44 per cent as professionals or managers and 32 per cent in clerical and sales jobs. Fourteen per cent of the males were working as craftsmen or operatives, 1 per cent in non-farm labor, and

4 per cent in other than private household service jobs, with 5 per cent falling in the "all other" category. Only 47 per cent of the 1960 population lived in the same house in 1955. Fourteen per cent of the houses were built before 1940; 68 per cent were built between 1950 and 1960, indicating the newness of this community in comparison with Highland Park. The median value of the homes was $29,600 at the time of the last completed census, but the average value of building permits issued that year fell below that figure to $23,419. The town contains many different types of neighborhoods, some with large houses on expansive lots along winding streets, others restricted to small row houses, with areas in between displaying combinations of housing styles and costs.

Park Ridge

Park Ridge and Park Forest are close to each other in socio-economic rank, but they are quite different in character. The former town has a higher income but a lower educational median than the latter, one of the most famous builder-developed communities in America. Park Ridge is eighteen miles northwest of the Chicago Loop, bordering on the city's outer limits. Incorporated in 1910, it was well established in 1940, with a population of 12,-063. This increased to 16,602 by 1950, and then doubled to 32,659 by 1960. In that year, the density of the town was 5103 persons per square mile. There were an estimated 40,587 residents within this suburb by 1968.

The 1960 median age of Park Ridge community members was thirty-four years, which is relatively high. As in Highland Park, only 10 per cent were under five years of age and 37 per cent were under eighteen. The median family income was $11,187 in 1960, and 57 per cent of the households were run on incomes over $10,-000. The educational median was 12.6 years of schooling. Seventy-five per cent of the men worked in white-collar jobs: 43 per cent in professions or as managers, 32 per cent in clerical or sales jobs, 17 per cent as craftsmen or operatives, 1 per cent as non-farm laborers, 3 per cent in service but not in private households, and 4 per cent in other occupations.

In 1960, 58 per cent of the men in Park Ridge worked in Chicago, compared with the 37 per cent figure for the men in Highland Park, a clear indicator of the comparative closeness of Park Ridge to the city. Sixty-nine per cent of the workers drove or shared a car pool, with only 19 per cent using the train. Fifty-three per cent of the residents who were, at that time, five years of age or over lived in a different house in 1960 than they did in 1955. A very high percentage of the residents are native-born Americans with native-born parents, higher than most of the other communities.

Thirty-four per cent of Park Ridge housing units had been built by 1940, and 53 per cent were built after 1950. The median value of the houses was $28,000 in 1960 and more expensive units were being built, as reflected by the fact that the median value for building permits in that year was $29,506. The houses tend to be built by developers in whole tracts surrounding the older core of the town. This is a "ranch house" community.

Park Forest

Park Forest has been studied by many observers of the American scene because it was one of the first communities to have been developed by a single builder and located in virtual isolation from other established towns. The builder intentionally designed both the rental area and that of several waves of owner-occupied houses in a manner facilitating social contact and community participation. Because of its "farm-field" location at a great distance from the city, Park Forest in its early years was jokingly referred to as Siberia by Chicagoans.

The town did not exist in 1940. When its population came, it came in waves; 8138 were settled by 1950, and 29,993 were there by 1960. The estimated 1968 population was 31,813. The houses and apartments were placed together on a small area of land, so that the density was 7141 per square mile in 1960, the highest of all the towns in this study. It originally attracted the young "organization man," especially to the rental area. Every statistic supports Whyte's description of those who rent there.[11] In 1960, the average age in the town was twenty-one, lower than that of any town in the Chicago area except Rolling Meadows, another farm-field development, with an average age of eighteen. Nineteen per

11. William H. Whyte, Jr., *The Organization Man,* New York: Simon and Schuster, 1956.

cent of the Park Forest population was under five years of age and 45 per cent was eighteen or under at the time of the 1960 census. The median income was relatively low, $8946, and was exceeded by that of eight towns in the study, a factor of the youthfulness of the population. The educational level of 13.5 years, however, was greater than that of all the other towns, including Highland Park where the median income was more than $4000 higher. Eighty-eight per cent of the men were in white-collar occupations. No other town in the study group matches that percentage, although several North Shore and similar high-status communities do exceed it. Thus, Park Forest drew to it a unique population, young, highly educated, on the way up, but still relatively non-affluent.

Since only 6 per cent of the women with children six years of age or younger were employed in 1960 and since most families had at least one child in that age bracket, the Park Forest occupational distribution refers essentially to men. Forty-nine per cent of the workers were professionals and non-farm managers or officers and 34 per cent held clerical or sales jobs. Eleven per cent of the men worked as craftsmen or operatives, less than 1 per cent were non-farm laborers, almost 3 per cent were in service occupations excluding private household help and 2 per cent were in other occupations. Only 56 per cent of the workers went the thirty miles to Chicago, the remaining commuting to other Cook County towns. Sixty-two per cent traveled to work by private car or a car pool and 30 per cent by railway.

Of the 68 per cent of persons aged five or over who lived in a different house in the United States in 1955, most had not lived in Chicago. Only 11 per cent came from there but a high of 22 per cent came from other towns in the same Standard Metropolitan Statistical Area. The mobile organization executive is well represented in the 36 per cent of residents who came to Park Forest from other parts of the United States. Only 4 per cent of the population were foreign-born and only 15 per cent were descendants of foreign or mixed parentage. Thus, 82 per cent are at least third-generation Americans, a percentage similar to that of Park Ridge.

The fact that only 28 per cent of the 1960 residents of Park Forest lived in the same house in 1955 is not surprising in view of the town's character. None of the 1960 houses had been built before 1940, and 71 per cent were erected in the 1950's. The median value of the privately owned houses, which must always be separated from residences in the rental area in descriptions of life style, was $17,500. The set being built in 1960 had a median cost of $11,770. The median cost of the houses is low compared with that of houses in towns which have the same or even a lower socio-economic rank. This is another of the unique features of Park Forest. The town has, however, been decreasing slightly in both income and education medians with the entrance of recent migrants. It is possible that it will not maintain its uniqueness for long, and that, like the Levittown described by Herbert Gans, it will become a lower-middle-class community after going through a period of increased heterogeneity.[12] The home-owning segment is already heterogeneous, as indicated by the women who were chosen at random for the interviews included in this study.

Skokie

In this varied collection, the town ranking fifth from the top in socio-economic prestige, out of fifteen levels into which Chicago suburbs have been divided, is Skokie. This community borders on Chicago, is thirteen miles from the Loop and has had an interesting history. It was incorporated in 1888, but in 1940 had a population of only 7172. It doubled in size to 14,832 by 1950 and then rapidly increased to 59,364 by 1960. Its density in that year was a relatively high 5878 persons per square mile, but it has added even more people into a limited geographical area, reaching an estimated 70,948 in 1968. Its development contradicts the patterns of early growth by most towns close to the city and was due to a historical accident which tied up property titles for decades.

The median age of the Skokie population was thirty in 1960, with 12 per cent under five years of age and 39 per cent eighteen or under. Thirty is a relatively high average age for such a new town. The median family income was $9703, and 47 per cent of the households were living on more than $10,000 a year. The median school years completed by persons twenty-five years of age or over was 12.6. Nine per cent of the women whose children were under six years of age and whose husbands were present in the home were working. The men, 73 per cent of whom worked in white-collar jobs, had the following occupation distribution: 40 per cent were in the professions or in managerial positions, 34

12. Herbert Gans, *Levittowners,* New York: Pantheon Books, 1967.

per cent were in clerical and sales jobs, 16 per cent worked as craftsmen and operatives, 1 per cent were in non-farm labor, 4 per cent were in non-private service, and 5 per cent were located in other types of jobs.

In 1960, Skokie had a higher percentage of managers than professionals and a relatively high concentration of sales workers, exceeded only by Park Forest. Fifty-six per cent of the men who were then employed worked in Chicago and 42 per cent worked in other parts of Cook County outside of Skokie. Seventy-five per cent drove to work in a private car or in a car pool, with only 4 per cent using the railway, 8 per cent the elevated or subway, and 6 per cent the bus.

Sixty per cent of the 1960 residents of Skokie aged five years and over had lived in a different house in 1955, a high percentage having moved from the central city. Forty-one per cent, compared with Park Forest's 10 per cent and Highland Park's 15 per cent, had previously lived in Chicago, and an additional 14 per cent lived in other suburbs, leaving only 6 per cent who came from outside the Standard Metropolitan Statistical Area. This distribution helps to clarify the distinctiveness of Skokie, which, in spite of a relatively large white-collar group, does not draw its population from nationally mobile young business executives but from city-bred and locally connected proprietors, business managers, and salesmen.

Nine per cent of Skokie's population is foreign-born and 35 per cent are native-born descendants of foreign or mixed parentage, a relatively high percentage among the different suburbs. Only 57 per cent are third (or later) generation Americans. The place of birth of 27 per cent of the foreign-stock residents was Russia, of 13 per cent Poland, and of 12 per cent Germany. A high percentage of these residents are Jewish, as the community has become an area of secondary or third-wave settlement of this ethnic group.

Only 11 per cent of the housing units were built in this community before 1940, whereas 78 per cent were built in the 1950's. The median value of the homes was $27,300 in 1960, but the average value of the building permits in that year dropped to $19,201. A number of co-operative apartment buildings were developed near the center of town in the late 1940's, and large apartment units were constructed in the late 1950's and early 1960's.

The town has become quite urban in appearance, with a relatively large number of manufacturing and commercial enterprises. Some tract housing exists, and lots tend to be relatively small throughout the town. Skokie declined considerably in income and education in the 1950's.

Mount Prospect

Mount Prospect is unusual because of the degree to which those interviewed expressed open hostility toward fellow residents and toward the town. Its foundation was a small village, incorporated in 1917, and containing only 1720 people in 1940. Located twenty-four miles from the Loop, along the Northwest Highway and a railway line, it drew the attention of developers during the 1950's. The population, 4009 in 1950, grew to 18,906 by 1960, although the developers did not add many shopping or related facilities. The density per square mile at that time was 5110. Its 1968 population increased to an estimated 31,134. Its population in 1960 was young, with a median age of twenty; 14 per cent were under five years of age and 44 per cent eighteen and under. The median income was $10,398, and the median years of schooling completed by those twenty-five years of age and over was 12.7. Seventy-three per cent of the men worked in white-collar occupations, 42 per cent in professions and as managers, 31 per cent in clerical or sales positions, 18 per cent as craftsmen and operatives, 1 per cent as non-farm laborers, 3 per cent in non-domestic service, and 5 per cent in other occupations.

Thirty-six per cent of the 1960 Mount Prospect residents lived in the same house in 1955. Two-thirds were newcomers to their area, a very high ratio. Only 9 per cent of its housing units were built before 1940, and 79 per cent were constructed during the 1950's. The median value of the houses, as of 1960, was $25,000, and the average value of building permits issued that year was somewhat lower, $21,901. Several of the women interviewed indicate a strong prejudice against the neighboring farm-field community of Rolling Meadows (which is socio-economically low), feeling that Mount Prospect is losing prestige and declining as a result of its proximity.

Wheaton

Wheaton does not show many of the characteristics of a suburb. It is more like a small, independent town. Located twenty-six miles from the Chicago Loop, it was incorporated in 1859 and was a flourishing community of 7389 in 1940. New developments started circling the old central part of town, and the population rose to 11,638 by 1950, 24,312 by 1960. Its density was then relatively low, 4675 people per square mile, and it has expanded little since, an estimated 29,419 by 1968. The median age was twenty-five in 1960, 12 per cent of the population being then under five years of age, 39 per cent under eighteen. The youth of the expanded area is indicated in these figures. The median family income was $9227, with 42 per cent living on $10,000 and over. It is ranked third on the prestige level of the socio-economic scale devised for the suburbs in the Chicago area. Sixty-six per cent of the men worked in white-collar jobs. Fewer of them (37 per cent) were in professional or managerial jobs than the men of the previously discussed towns. Twenty-nine per cent were in clerical or sales occupations, 16 per cent worked as craftsmen, 3 per cent as laborers, 7 per cent in the service field (excluding private households), and 8 per cent in other jobs.

Thirty-six per cent of its houses, a relatively high percentage, had been built before 1940. Forty-three per cent of its 1960 population was in the same house in the year 1955. The town has a college, many churches, and a strong emphasis on religion. It has a rather stable, small-town atmosphere, especially in the central sections. The median value of the houses, $21,200, is somewhere in the middle of the various towns, and it is one of the few communities in which the average value of the building permits in 1960 is higher than the median value of existing houses ($23,357).

La Grange Park

La Grange Park has the same socio-economic status as Wheaton. It has absorbed many second- or third-generation offspring of Berwyn's and Cicero's Czech and Bohemian residents. It is fifteen miles from the city and it was incorporated in 1892. Its 1940 population was 3406; it increased only to 6176 by 1950, and to 13,793 by 1960. One of the reasons its population has not expanded more is its limited space. Its density per square mile was very high, 6270, second only to that of Park Forest. These facts are supported by its estimated 1968 population figures of 6240, which presents an unusual decrease for Chicago's suburbs. Some apartment buildings and most homes are built on small lots. The average age of the residents was thirty-six in 1960, the highest of all our towns, with only 9 per cent of the population under five years of age and only 33 per cent eighteen and under. The median income was $10,501, with 53 per cent of the families living on $10,000 or more, a relatively high income. The educational median was then 12.6 years, also relatively high. Seventy-one per cent of its working men were in white-collar occupations, 40 per cent of them having professional and managerial jobs and 31 per cent clerical and sales jobs, and 20 per cent were craftsmen and operators. There was only a sprinkling of other fields, with 1 per cent in non-farm labor, 4 per cent in non-household service, and 4 per cent in other fields. Eleven per cent of its mothers of children under age six were employed.

Forty-six per cent of La Grange Park's 1960 population lived in the same house in 1950. Twenty per cent of the housing units were built before 1940, and 65 per cent were built during the 1950's. The median value of the houses was a high $25,200, and the average value of 1960 building permits was $25,000.

Hazel Crest

Hazel Crest appears as the next town on the socio-economic ranking scale, being within the fifth level of prestige from the top. Located twenty-three miles from the Chicago Loop, it was incorporated as late as 1911. The population was only 1299 in 1940. It rose to 2129 by 1950 and to 6205 by 1960. In other words, it is and has been a very small community, the smallest of our collection, with a density in 1960 of only 3103 people per square mile. Its population was only an estimated 9825 in 1968. It has the not unusual two-class pattern. One side of town has winding roads, houses built on rolling land with large lawns. The rest of town can be identified as working class. Its median age was a young twenty-seven in 1960, with 15 per cent under five years of age and 44 per cent eighteen years or under. The median income was $8613, lower than that of the people in most of the suburbs in this study. Its population twenty-five years of age or over had a median of 12.3 years of schooling. Fifty-seven per cent of the employed males were in white-collar occupations, only 30 per cent of them being in professional or managerial positions (compared with Park Forest's 49 per cent). Twenty-seven per cent were in clerical or sales jobs, 32 per cent worked as craftsmen and operatives, 3 per cent as non-farm laborers, 5 per cent as non-domestic service workers, and 3 per cent in other kinds of jobs.

Twenty-one per cent of Hazel Crest's houses were built before 1940, and 68 per cent were built in the 1950's. The median value of the 1960 houses was a relatively low $16,700, as the more expensive houses came to be outweighed by those less expensive, and the average value of building permits issued that year was even lower, $14,573.

Oak Lawn

Oak Lawn is in the sixth socio-economic rank of fifteen levels, and it is located fifteen miles southwest of the Chicago Loop. It was incorporated in 1909 and developed from a 1940 population of 3483 to 8751 in 1950, and then shot up to 27,471 in 1960—a very strong expansion accompanied by a medium increase in density to 4226 people per square mile. Thus, the expansion followed the average pattern of land use for this urban region, in terms of lot size. Its estimated 1968 population numbered 56,516. Most of the residents live in small houses. The median age of the population was twenty-seven in 1960, with 15 per cent under the age of five and 43 per cent eighteen years old or under.

Forty-one percent of the 1960 residents lived in the same house in 1955. Twelve per cent of the housing units had been built before 1940, and 70 per cent were built during the 1950's. The median value of the houses was $19,800 in 1960, when the average value of building permits was $17,537.

Lansing

Lansing is a workingman's suburb, with most of its men working in the nearby Indiana or Illinois steel mills. Located twenty-six miles south of the center of Chicago, it was incorporated in 1893 and had a population of 4462 by 1940. By 1950, it had doubled to 8682, and in 1960 it had increased to 18,098, with a density of 4022 per square mile. Its estimated 1968 population was 23,815.

Its median density is 4022 people per square mile. Most of the town consists of builder-developed small white houses with greenery around, and it has a lived-in, though quiet, look. The average age of the population was twenty-seven in 1960. Twelve per cent were under five years of age and 43 per cent eighteen or under. The median income was $8028 in a narrow range; only 28 per cent of the families lived on $10,000 or more. It ranks seventh on the fifteen-level socio-economic scale. Forty-six per cent of the employed males worked in white-collar jobs, 21 per cent as professionals and managers and 25 per cent in clerical positions, whereas 41 per cent were craftsmen or operatives. Four per cent worked as non-farm laborers, 5 per cent as non-private household service workers, and 4 per cent in other fields. Ten per cent of the mothers of children under six years of age were in paid full-time employment.

Fifty-nine per cent of the 1960 population lived in the same house in 1955, the highest percentage for any town in the study. This indicates geographic and social stability. Twenty-three per cent of the houses had been built before 1940 and 54 per cent after 1950. The median value of the houses was $16,200 in 1960, and the average value of the building permits was much lower— $10,665.

North Lake

North Lake is located sixteen miles west of the city. It did not exist as a town in 1940—and its population was 4361 in 1950 and 12,318 in 1960, with a density of 4562. By 1968, it had increased in size to an estimated 14,273. The average age of the population was twenty-three in 1960, 13 per cent were under five years of age and 45 per cent eighteen or under. The median family income was $8167, and only 28 per cent of the families earned $10,000 or over. The socio-economic rank of North Lake was tenth out of the fifteen available levels and it falls below that in its educational and occupational distributions. The median educational level was a low 10.5 years. Thirty-one per cent of the working males were in white-collar jobs, only ten per cent of them in professional and managerial positions, the remaining 21 per cent in clerical and sales jobs. Fifty-two per cent of the men were craftsmen or operatives, 4 per cent non-farm laborers, 7 per cent in non-private household service, and 6 per cent were in other occupations in 1960. The community thus contains a high percentage of craftsmen.

ONE ❧ ❧ ❧

The Life Cycle
of Role Involvement

BACKGROUND

The American woman, who eventually becomes a housewife when she undertakes the responsibility for running her own home, has been leaving the household of her family of orientation —the family into which she was born and within which she was basically socialized—for increasingly long periods of time since she was at least six years old. Home socializing contributed to the development of her human sentiments, self-awareness, the ability to take the role and understand others, the capacity, built upon speech and thought, to analyze situations abstractly and to plan action, and complex behavior patterns. Her schooling, added to this store of knowledge, prepared her to live in a complicated society. Although most formal educational programs are supposed to be transmitted to children of both sexes in the same way, home, self, peer, and teacher tendencies to differentiate between boys and girls result in great differences between the sexes in most behavior patterns. Ruth Hartley concluded, on the basis of many studies, that feminine behavior is directly socialized into and observed by the child, assisted by a variety of home and school procedures.[1] However, the main occupational role of most women— that of housewife—is not evaluated by girls as an exciting and

1. Ruth E. Hartley, "Current Patterns in Sex Roles: Children's Perspectives," *Journal of the National Association of Women Deans and Counselors,* 25 (October 1961), 3–13; and "Sex-Role Identification: A Symposium," *Merrill-Palmer Quarterly of Behavior and Development,* 10 (1964), 3–16.

desirable life goal. According to James Coleman, girls do better in the early years of formal schooling than their restless brothers, but they become directed away from study during adolescence and turn toward popularity contests among themselves. Girls' attention becomes focused on general manner or demeanor,[2] while boys become increasingly achievement-oriented.[3] Although unprecedented numbers of young girls are currently in college, they restrict themselves to a limited number of fields culturally approved for their sex and rarely go on to graduate work or even develop strong involvement in their subject matter of study. Arnold Rose found that University of Minnesota coeds placed their primary interest in marriage, while men were much more concerned with the need to finish their education or to become established in an occupation.[4] Most studies show that concern with marriage does not, however, lead to specialization in homemaking knowledge.

The tendency of women to limit their involvement in occupational training to superficial study of approved fields is shown in a study of those who majored in education. The figures indicate that, although most women who go to college major in education —and they predominate in primary education—and although most undergraduate degrees in this subject are attained by women, graduate degrees are awarded predominately to men. Graduate training is rarely entered into by women, as indicated by the fact that the degrees awarded in all fields during a twelve-month period ending June 30, 1962, were given mostly to men and that the proportion increases greatly as higher levels of accomplishment are reached: men outnumber women five to three in receiving B.A. degrees, seven to three in M.A.'s, and twenty-five to three in Ph.D.'s.[5]

Alice Rossi has found that almost half of female college students express "traditionalist" tendencies, that is, interest in fields

2. The concept of demeanor is developed sociologically by Erving Goffman in "The Nature of Deference and Demeanor," *American Anthropologist* (1956), 473–502.

3. James Coleman *et al.*, *The Adolescent Society*, New York: The Free Press, 1961.

4. Arnold M. Rose, "The Adequacy of Women's Expectations for Adult Roles," *Social Forces*, 30 (October 1961), 69–77.

5. *National Education Association Research Bulletin*, 42 (May 1964), 45–46.

in which women predominate, while one-third state that they have no career goals other than being housewives. Only 7 per cent of female students could be termed "pioneers" with long-range career goals in predominately masculine fields—those with a low proportion of women.[6]

Young American women are thus limiting their definition of feminine behavior to a concern with popularity; they work in traditional fields without strong commitment to them, and a career is viewed only as an intermediary state between education and homemaking. Simultaneously, they are not preparing for the social roles of housewife-wife-mother, as Chapter Three will demonstrate and as statistics concerning subjects studied in high school and major fields in college testify. Living in a highly vocationally oriented society, women have not developed a strong vocational orientation toward such future roles.

In spite of their low commitment to fields of knowledge or work, or for that matter to other spheres of societal life, young women do engage in a complex of social roles away from home, roles requiring large stores of information, skill, and relational ability. Whether taking a job after finishing a course of education, or without completing it, most girls work before marriage and often extend the period of employment until their first pregnancy. The organizations within which they hold jobs are usually large, the knowledge required of them specific and precisely measured, and the pattern of their work integrated into a complex of relations. Not only at school and at work, but in all her youth, the American urban woman is being provided a variety of types of knowledge and skills enabling behavior in complex social systems. She learns to interact with many categories of people in circumstances calling for a great range of actions, feelings, and levels of involvement, requiring understanding of complicated situations. She must learn to use different sources of information and to modify her behavior frequently. She participates in a multiplicity of groups within many spheres of societal life, thus learning and acting out multidimensional involvements. Friendship relations, church and clubs, organized recreation, and even politics are im-

6. Alice Rossi, "Barriers to the Career Choice of Engineering, Medicine or Science Among American Women," in Jacquelyn A. Mattfeld and Carol G. Van Aken, eds., *Women and the Scientific Professions,* Cambridge, Mass.: The M.I.T. Press, 1965.

portant to most young women who simultaneously hold down jobs and often take additional school courses. As Robert Winch points out, even the process of dating, extended over many years in the life of a middle-class child, serves many personality expanding and testing functions.[7]

Thus, however strong her interest in marriage, she manages to carry on a great diversity of other social relations, requiring bodies of knowledge each quite different from the other and taken from many areas of a vast culture. Yet there is a gap between the complexity of life led by the American girl and the flatness of her definitions of "feminine" behavior and role involvements.

Nor does her life prior to marriage prepare her for life after she settles down to the complex roles of wife and housewife.

THE LIFE CYCLE OF THE ROLE OF HOUSEWIFE

Becoming a Housewife[8]

The process of dating usually culminates in the mutual selection of a girl and a boy for marital roles. The ceremony takes place, the couple isolates itself from friends and relations for an intensely emotional and personally demanding honeymoon, and then the young bride takes over the responsibility of maintaining her own home. Entrance into the role of housewife is often accompanied by continued involvement in paid employment and/or student roles. The girl has not been prepared, with years of training common in earlier times, to be a homemaker, nor was she selected for that role because of her abilities measured by specific competence tests. Rather, she must train herself, initiate her own action, and build around herself the social circle which will bene-

7. Robert F. Winch, *The Modern Family*, New York: Holt, Rinehart and Winston, revised edition, 1963.

8. I am using the concept of "becoming" as developed by Howard S. Becker in "Becoming a Marihuana User," *American Journal of Sociology*, 59 (November 1953), 235–42. The process of becoming involves learning not only to carry out appropriate behavior patterns, but also how to interpret sentiments and experiences through a new framework. See also Helena Znaniecki Lopata, "The Life Cycle of the Social Role of Housewife," *Sociology and Social Research*, 51 (October 1966), 2–22. The concept of life cycle is a major contribution of Paul Glick in several articles and in *American Families*, New York: John Wiley, 1957.

fit from her duties and assist her in their performance. She has usually looked forward to having her own apartment, and she derives pleasure from bringing objects into it and converting them into products for use, but she speaks of the process somewhat as of a game.

The role of wife is neither automatically learned nor easily performed, owing to cultural differences between the spouses, a lack of training of both partners, the emotional and behavioral individualism into which both have been socialized, and an absence of guidelines. In addition to undertaking the roles of wife and housewife and placing them in central positions, a young woman is expected to add several other roles, such as that of daughter-in-law. She must modify her role of daughter, push into the background that of friend, change her relations at work, and generally relate to all from the new perspective of "Mrs." or "married woman." In a society lacking formal *rites de passage* between youth and adulthood, marriage, at the average age of twenty, often serves as the dividing line, and the expected personality changes are dramatically strong.

Thus, the first stage of becoming a housewife includes for American women a major shift of the whole role-cluster and modifications in all roles. She not only learns the relations and identities involved in being a wife and housewife, but she changes in other ways as well. Symbolic is the change in domicile and in name, indicating a break with the past. A great many of these changes, both voluntary and enforced, are undertaken without the support of traditional formulas, or supportive and predictable behaviors, and are done in isolation from community or kin help and protection.

The Expanding Circle

The next stage of life an American woman experiences usually comes soon after the first, and it too necessitates major shifts in the total role-cluster. Many of the women interviewed explained that the greatest change in their lives was created not by marriage but by the birth of their first child. The shift is abrupt because this society insists that the person who gives birth to the child be directly involved in its care, and because this woman is usually isolated from other adults into a neo-local residence, that is, one containing the nuclear unit of mother, father, and child. The isolation has a dual effect: her life is changed because she was previously involved in many sets and levels of relations, and her role of mother is complicated by the assignment to her of total responsibility for child care. Traditional families contained many adults within the household or nearby who shared in maintenance and socialization of the young. Small infants require a great deal of physical care and their susceptibility to illness has the effect of keeping the mother within the home and away from other social roles and relations. Thus, the young woman is suddenly restricted to a very limited number of contacts within a single social space and institutional framework. The contrast is great and imperfectly understood by society and by the woman. She finds her personality affected and her relations with the remaining few people she continues to see strained. Having left her job, she experiences most of the difficulties of absence of work rhythm and relation maintenance that upset newly retired men. Most occupations provide automatic association with other people who share at least some of the same interests. Friends retain their full round of life, but she now finds herself excluded. Income decreases and expenditures increase. The husband is likely to be highly involved in his career and to lack understanding of the problems of transition his wife is experiencing. Society itself observes some of her difficulties, but usually evaluates them as a consequence of her "neurotic" tendencies, "unfeminine" attitudes, or "selfish" traits. Sometimes she questions her personality, blaming herself rather than understanding the factors contributing to vague or inarticulated discontents.[9]

Many of those interviewed stated that the transition in their lives was dramatic and often difficult, but they did not suggest modifying the education of women. They would not change either stage of life, before or after the birth of a child, in spite of problems of role discontinuity. Nor is total submersion in the family

9. At least three major studies support these conclusions: E. E. LeMasters, "Parenthood as Crisis," *Marriage and Family Living*, 19 (1957), 352–55; Everett D. Dyer, "Parenthood as a Crisis: A Re-Study," *Marriage and Family Living*, 25 (May 1963), 196–201; and Daniel Hobbs, Jr., "Parenthood as Crisis: A Third Study," *Marriage and Family Living*, 27 (May 1965), 367–72.

throughout life a solution which they find welcome or necessary.[10] Their suggestions are that the society, and women themselves, develop more realistic transitions without cutting out the prior richness of life. The currently popular "instant motherhood" ideology seems to be an ineffective way of dealing with discontinuity, just as "instant wifehood" has failed to help romantic love or marriage ideals. Both assume that becoming a mother or a wife is instinctual so that it requires no preparation.

Although women state that they are "tied down" by the responsibility of small children, they also experience satisfaction with several aspects of their role. In the first place, becoming a housewife impresses them by the very openness of the role and by the freedom they now have *from* constraining supervision and the need to integrate their own work to other rhythms. The right to make decisions affecting their lives as well as those of others is a frequently mentioned source of pleasure. "A homemaker is not responsible to anyone higher up. She makes her own decisions on her own," and "Making decisions, on the job, you do what they tell you," are some of their statements contrasting their current life to their working days. "Not meeting a clock or calendar" for the first time since the age of five or six is a major form of freedom. Most women were employed, as most men have been, in subordinate positions, so that "being one's own boss" within the role of housewife is an important feature. Such freedom from constraint is particularly available to the modern woman, who has the right to set up her own home.

Satisfactions also come from interpersonal relations with children and husband. Increasing competence in performance of role-related duties brings pleasure. "You get satisfaction seeing anything you accomplish look nice. Each thing you do is an improvement," says a mother of three, all under the age of four. Finally, anticipation of satisfaction with the children's future is often listed by women in the "expanding circle" stage, for they are very aware of having "created" new human beings. Sometimes there is worry that the children may not turn out so perfectly or may not be acceptable by modern American standards. The young mother, however, seldom expresses deep concern with the behavior of

10. Mirra Komarovsky, *Women in the Modern World: Their Education and Their Dilemmas*, Boston: Little, Brown, 1953.

children, being thus very different from mothers of offspring who have reached adolescence.

On the other hand, women at this stage mention a number of frustrations and problems. Some feel that the whole shift from a work role into that of a housewife increases responsibility, which is not necessarily welcome. They miss the time and work controls and systems of the job, and women not accustomed to being self-motivating or initiative in their behavior have to undertake major personality changes in the way they handle themselves, their duties, and their relations with others. Passive stances, awaiting the initiative of others, may be effective and even desired of secretaries to charismatic and ever-present bosses, but the modern housewife generally cannot afford such an approach to her roles. This stage requires a great deal of work to be planned, organized, and executed by the same person. Interestingly enough, some young women speak of role responsibilities and of the ideal housewife in managerial terms. They present the woman as "seeing to," or "insuring that," as if she were not the same person who is carrying out the work.

As babies are added to the family and social circles increased in several ways, the young mother feels that time is a problem: "Work is never done"; "there are no set hours"; "it's a twenty-four-hour job." The over-worked mother, as described by Mirra Komarovsky, is most likely a woman within this stage of life.[11] The major problem is "Not knowing when and how to do things which may affect the home and the family," as a twenty-one-year-old woman says, but the major consequence of the problem seems to be a dramatic decrease in opportunity for self-expression: "Time for myself," "mental stimulation," and "adult companionship."

There is greater similarity in the lives of women in this stage than in any other stage of adult life. Variations are found in the length of time devoted to this period, and in the size of the social circles within both the role of mother and the role of housewife. The circles can include relatives, friends, neighbors, nurses, maids, and a variety of other service personnel; some women build these into complex systems, others interact with only a few other people. The number and spacing of children are obviously important

11. *Idem.* The "over-worked mother" whom she describes is not explained in life-cycle terms.

factors. Education and socio-economic situation influence the sources from which assisting segments of both social circles are drawn. The less highly positioned women do all the work of caring for the house and children virtually by themselves and without many labor-saving devices, while others have nurses for newborn babies, diaper service, servants, washing machines and other appliances, and help from family members. Some are overwhelmed by their current life and see no continuity between it and the past or future, while others combine various sources of knowledge and help in order to cut down or change the nature of work. Trained in general problem-solving, such women form babysitting clubs, exchange services with neighbors, and utilize the household hints transmitted by mass communication media. Some young mothers are lonely, isolated from kin, and lack skills or even a geographical location facilitating the building of relationships with peers. Many choose to move from the institutionally non-interactive city areas, discussed in Chapter Five, which met their needs when they were busy in many roles away from home, to the strongly neighboring communities occupied by women in similar situations.

The Full-House Plateau

The next stage, that of the "full-house plateau," when new family members are no longer likely to be born, but before children completely move away, rather than just being gone part of the time, is one of an increasing diversity of life styles among the housewives interviewed. Traditionally, this stage was the pinnacle of a woman's career. She was ideally portrayed as surrounded by several offspring of varying ages, pleased to be the center of the house, sewing and baking, and knowing that the rest of her life would bring a gradual and gentle decline in roles and status. The decrease in family size and the number of years during which children live at home, combined with the increasing span of hours the young spend away from their mother, have diminished both the length of this period and its intensity. In the meantime, the average length of active adult life has grown, and women whose children decreasingly need them are left with a great deal of energy and no traditionally acceptable way of using it. Of course, some women are learning to transform past competency of involvement in many areas of societal life into new means of opening boundaries between home and "outside activities." Even during the peak period of the role of housewife they manage to bring the larger world into full contact with themselves and their homes, joining their husbands and children in such ventures.

Often the young mother makes the new contacts contributing to such a life through the activities of her children outside of the family, within peer groups, school voluntary associations, religious clubs, and community projects. In return, many of the projects of American children which expand their abilities, awareness of the world, and identification with its people are a direct product of the time and effort of their mothers. For some interesting, though historically not surprising reason, such efforts are often met with derogatory comments which attempt to make women feel that they are truly "the generation of vipers" and "overprotective mothers." Chauffering children is seen as only a means of meeting the exploitive or other neurotic needs of mothers, while a child's interest in some competency-building activity is sarcastically explained as a consequence of the prodding of a domineering matriarch. The women interviewed are aware of such evaluations of their efforts and feel vaguely guilty over doing things which in the long run will make their children aware and highly develop their abilities. So few observers recognize their activities as anything but an attempt to fill empty time that the mothers themselves do not defend what they are doing with any culturally satisfactory explanation.

Several types of women can be found in the full-house plateau stage of the social role of housewife. Some become settled in the role, on the assumption that they will spend the rest of their lives totally involved with home-based relations. The role of grandmother is assumed by them to flow naturally out of the role of mother. This traditional view is most often expressed by older urban and lower-middle-class women, who are somewhat hesitant about becoming involved in society.

The working woman returns to paid employment during this time, often sporadically and with complicated rationales, as she shifts from one style of life to another. Most "club women" first join the PTA or a church group and gradually expand their activities as their interests and skills lead into a variety of fields. Upper-class women never fully disengage, even during the "expanding circle" stage, and now they extend their involvement. Neighboring developed during the prior stages of home-bound existence may continue, but generally with selective contacts and controls. Friendship becomes less geographically constricted. The husband-oriented woman is not likely to remain so vicariously involved in her husband's job, but usually changes her activities to direct action, such as bookkeeping or entertaining, or from passive listening to opinion giving.

Most women continue modifying their lives, much as a kaleidoscope changes in sequence, refining roles they already perform by adding or subtracting new relations as the "full-house plateau" progresses. Because of the modern scientific orientation, middle-aged women develop different responses to their major roles: a feeling of increasing competence in the role of housewife, task-orientation or routine-orientation in the role of wife, and questioning uncertainty in the role of mother. Motherhood is a source of many problems and frustrations to modern women because they have an increased awareness of the psychological and developmental needs of children, while suffering from a lack of guidelines. At the same time, motherhood is a major source of satisfaction whenever worries turn out to be unfounded and children measure up to expectations. Rewards are often experienced as small scenes of pleasure from relational changes, as when children suddenly express an interest in subjects of interest to parents. Patience is considered by many respondents to be the most important virtue of the ideal housewife in this stage.

Increasing experimentation with a variety of roles and life patterns is clearly discernible in all statistical accounts of American women in their thirties and forties. Their children are already in school for the major part of the day or they are leading their own lives elsewhere. The return to work or to school by women of this category of housewives is numerically dramatic.[12] In fact, formal

12. Women with young children are beginning to re-enter the labor force, and married women are forming a dramatically larger proportion of it than ever before, according to the Manpower Development Council. (*Womanpower,* New York: Colombia University Press, 1957.) A similar pattern is evidenced in other societies, according to Viola Klein, "Women Workers: A Survey of 21 Countries," Organization for Economic Cooperation and Development, 1965.

training and education in organized schools are being made available to American adults in great numbers because of a redefinition of knowledge from a closed unit learned in childhood to a continuing process.[13] Females, who in their teens were quite contented by limiting themselves to competitions in popularity and appearance, and who then turned to marriage and motherhood with no plans for later years, have found creative outlets within and outside the home. Too filled with energy to retire into repetitive and minimal household maintenance, they are changing the content of every role and entering many sets or relations—work, school, organizations, friendship, and neighboring, often inventing new means of meeting societal needs.[14] Breaking the traditions of the culture, they turn to the arts and culinary aspects of the role of housewife, learning to perform creatively services such as sewing and dress designing for themselves and others, an opportunity they ignored early in life. Middle-aged respondents have become involved in a great variety of learning combinations, as full-time students, student-workers, or specialty retrainees. Middle-class women are often re-entering work roles not at their minimal level, but with new skills. They are even creating new roles, supplying services or objects which were previously unavailable. Often their search for some solution to a homemaking problem turns into a source of occupational or artistic endeavor. The number of businesses founded and managed by women—in their homes, as in the early years of industrialization—has expanded dramatically in recent times.

Even though they were eager to leave jobs in order to become full-time housewives, returning workers speak positively of employment. Some enter routine and relatively unrewarding jobs for money, or to increase contact with people, or to get away from the home. The tendency to seek "interesting" work is, however, increasing among those who can afford to experiment, as many can. Justification by the culturally approved explanation that women work for money only, whether for basic necessities or luxuries, is

13. John W. C. Johnstone and Ramon J. Rivers, *Volunteers for Learning*, Chicago: Aldine, 1963.

14. Adele R. Lewis and Edith Bobroff describe many business and other employment ventures of middle-aged women in *From Kitchen to Career*, Indianapolis: Bobbs-Merrill, 1965.

used less often by respondents in career and in self-created jobs than by those re-entering more traditional occupations.[15]

The Shrinking Circle

Many housewives are no longer waiting to re-enter society till the last child moves out of the home, leaving an "empty nest." They are increasingly anticipating such a life situation by becoming involved in roles opening connections between home and society. Such actions require initiative behavior, and sufficient self-confidence to relinquish old habits and the traditional frame of mind during the second half of life. The basic tasks of womanhood, as defined by American society, those of bearing and rearing children, are completed within a relatively short period of time, thus leaving those who limit their definitions of such roles to very narrow boundaries with empty lives. Entrance into other spheres of social action is not culturally valued, except as an artificial "keeping oneself busy."

One of the problems of women in both city and suburb is the automatic drop in status which accompanies the unpreventable "shrinking of the social circle" stage in the role of housewife. Their contribution to society has not been defined as sufficiently significant for women with young children who do not belong to the very numerically limited upper class. Most of the female population of American society is treated as rather valueless, once it has produced at least one child and reared it to pre-adulthood. Thus, most women are left in a situation similar to that of retired men, for thirty or more years of their lives. Actually, the self-descriptions of women interviewed show that they, or at least the more trained and educated among them, are solving the problems of "retirement" by becoming competent in new areas of life and by enjoying their expanding horizons. It is only the climate of opinion, or the "feminine mystique" as Betty Friedan calls it, which prevents them from feeling the lack of a justification for existence. "I'm just a housewife" is a transitional self-concept, possibly leading in the future to either satisfaction with that role

15. Various aspects of the role changes with return to work are discussed by the contributing authors to F. Ivan Ney and Louis Hoffman, eds., *The Employed Mother in America*, Chicago: Rand McNally, 1963.

defined in creative terms or the use of another identity. As Bernice Neugarten points out, middle-aged women are one of the segments of the population neglected by social scientists.[16] Observation of American life indicates that this may be the "revolution generation." Even the aged, until recently the silent members of this society, are now receiving attention; and the woman in decades after her role of mother is no longer vital to the child, but whose husband is still involved in his occupational career, is simultaneously developing an individual life style.[17]

The second phase of the "shrinking circle" stage occurs with widowhood. In modern society, the probability of reaching this phase increases with age, although it can precede the departure of children from the home. Widowhood results in very dramatic changes in social roles and relations. A number of factors, including, of course, the manner in which she accomplishes what Eric Lindemann calls "grief work," complicate the effect it will have upon a particular person.[18] Role shifts are connected with the form and degree of dependence she had on her husband and on his role involvements, as well as on the kinds of relations available in widowhood. Contacts with former friends become strained for a variety of social and psychological reasons. Financial, housing, recreational, sexual, and sentimental problems result in redefinitions and in attempts at solutions which meet with varying levels of success.

The last stage of life has been called by Cumming and Henry "disengagement." [19] According to their description, the process in-

16. The collection of essays in Bernice L. Neugarten's *Personality in Middle and Late Life*, New York: Atherton, 1964, and her later paper, "Adult Personality: Toward a Psychology of the Life Cycle" (presented at the American Psychological Association meetings, New York, September 1966, mimeographed), all point to the lack of research in this field.

17. One of the few articles referring to this stage of life is Irwin Deutscher's "The Quality of Postparental Life," *Journal of Marrage and the Family*, 26 (1964), 52–59.

18. Eric Lindemann, "Symptomology and Management of Acute Grief," in Robert Fulton, ed., *Death and Identity*, New York: John Wiley, 1965.

19. Elaine Cumming and William E. Henry, *Growing Old*, New York: Basic Books, 1961. A number of critics have pointed to the variations in styles of aging among Americans which contradict the assumed inevitability of the process of disengagement, but the concept has been very popular among the various scientific personnel dealing with aging.

volves a voluntary, mutual withdrawing of the person and of society from each other. Some individuals never reach this stage, remaining actively involved in many relations which are carried over from the past or developed anew after changes in the components of life.

In summary, the social roles and role-clusters of modern urban American women undergo at least six major life changes:

1. From home-based infanthood, in the circle of personality developing and sentiment-bound family members, to the school and work situations in which performance is measured by impersonal, increasingly rational and competency-demanding standards.

2. From the multidimensional, non-family focused life of the adult young woman to one changed by the addition of the roles of wife and of housewife, and by modifications in relations to her family of orientation, friends, work contacts, housing, and personal interactions ("becoming a housewife").

3. From the modified, but still multidimensional life of the young wife, to the geographically and institutionally confining role of new mother, requiring a change in personality, interests, behavior, and attitudes without supportive or transitional mechanisms ("expanding circle" and "peak stage").

4. From a total immersion in the physical care of several small children to a situation combining increasing competence in the role of housewife, problems in the role of mother, habituation in the role of wife, and class-varied participation in community and societal roles. This stage continues over a period of almost twenty years, and it is accompanied by the gradual movement of the role of mother into the background, with increasing child involvement outside of the home ("full-house plateau").

5. From a full participation in family life, culturally defined as ideal for the woman, to one restricted by the departure of children and later by the highly dramatic event of the death of the husband, often accompanied by a complete transformation of most relations and social roles ("the shrinking circle").

6. From being the sole member of a household to one of several lines of life style until death: gradual "disengagement," involuntary loneliness, strong dependency on others, concentration upon a limited number of relations or active involvement in many roles.

Several sub-stages are possible here, as during the other phases, and the woman can move out of one into another as her circumstances or personality changes.

RANK ORDER OF IMPORTANCE OF WOMEN'S ROLES

Throughout the life cycle of family roles the woman and her household are located in a society which carries on a complex system of action by many social roles and groups. Her relation to this world outside of her home has varied in time and place as human culture has varied. All known societies of the world have developed a division of labor between sexes. Most, if not all, have assigned the function of home maintenance to women. However, they have developed a wide range of forms by which their female members directly contribute to life outside the home. Moreover, all the women in the same society are usually not assigned or allowed the same level of participation in the functioning of the total social unit. The most frequent division of women's involvement in life away from home has been along class lines. Lower-class women have generally been allowed the freedom of geographic movement needed to carry out their economic tasks facilitating family maintenance, but they have not been expected to understand or become involved in the social structure in leadership roles. Neither, for that matter, were lower-class men, and most societies have, until very recently, consisted primarily of the rather passive and restricted lower classes. They have been run by a small minority of elites, highly trained in the responsibility of managing internal and external power and the economic relations of the whole unit. The wives of patriarchally organized elites —and most societies of the world have been organized in this manner—also carried their share of obligations in helping the society function. Some societies even encouraged their education in political, philosophical, and literary knowledge to such an extent that they became highly competent women. Western Europe also developed patterns of polite companionship interaction which depended upon highly informed participants, be they men or women. Private tutors reinforced the knowledge obtained through literary sources. The "noblesse oblige" ideology which inculcated in each child of noble birth the obligation to care for the society as a whole, within, of course, the definition of the culture as to the content of such care, applied to both sexes.

The industrializing, urbanizing, and increasingly democratic societies of the world began changing the class restrictions of their participants.[20] Such expanding social groups could not afford to have uneducated and passive members. Therefore, modern societies developed mass education in their national cultures, motivated by a desire for the active support of their citizens. They aimed at encouraging full involvement and a feeling of obligation to the unit by all adults. Women were caught up in these movements, gaining the same types of knowledge as men and internalizing the concepts of democracy. In some societies this trend has increased their active participation in social life at all levels and throughout their life cycle.

American society, highly oriented toward the theory of democracy and toward mass education as a means of training people into self-motivated, that is, voluntary involvement in its complex life, realizes that it faces a strong dilemma between that set of attitudes and the one surrounding the home as the "rightful place" of women. The combination of sentiments is historically very interesting and is reflected not only in the literature about "the American woman" and "the American family" but also in the definitions of the life of those caught on the horns of this dilemma. Instead of accepting the upper-class European image of women as obligated to make the society function according to its ideal standards and to maintain the home as a vital part of its whole life, Americans restrict the woman to a concern with her home only, and confine the idea of "home" to its four walls. This highly limited view of the home as a "castle" with the bridge drawn against any stranger or new ideas is not even typical of the actual situation of the increasingly educated middle-class American woman. The image is thus in disharmony with the major part of the American cultural heritage and the actual behavior of its more

20. Robert F. Winch and Rae Lesser Blumberg, "Societal Complexity and Family Organization," in Robert Winch and Louis Goodman, eds., *Selected Studies in Marriage and the Family,* New York: Holt, Rinehart and Winston, 1968. See alsto William J. Goode, *World Revolution and Family Patterns,* New York: The Free Press, 1963. These theories relate the social structure of the family and the function and position of women to the means of subsistence and to the social complexity of the system within which the family exists.

educated members. It is difficult to determine why American women and men have so consistently limited half of the societal population to passive stances, when the society strongly needs more committed and actively participating members. Even less understandable is the lack of cultural awareness of the expanded life cycle stages now available to healthy and long-lived women for increased involvement in the social system. The contradictions include a strong societal conviction that its members should be competent and that its problems be solved voluntarily, held simultaneously with an equally powerful belief that any woman active in "outside activities," meaning ones outside of the home, is neglecting her family, even when she has no one at home to neglect, owing to the natural configuration of the family cycle. The conflict existing between home and society makes for an ideological, if not a behavioral, constriction of the image of feminity, a constriction reminiscent of lower-class European attitudes.

Most of the educated women who were interviewed or observed for the series of studies on which this book is based are active in the life of the community and society. All but a few housewives and working women, regardless of educational achievement, have led multidimensional lives in the past and belonged to a variety of groups and sets of relations. Most keep up their knowledge of world events, and a high proportion increase their involvement outside of their homes in the middle years of life, following the decreasing intensity of family demands. The role of friend is important to most women at some time, such relations being achieved rather than ascribed, and neighboring is increasing in importance in suburban communities, in the urban fringe, and even in some high-rise apartment buildings. Student roles are increasingly entered by adult women for varying periods of time. More women of all ages than ever before work for money. Participation in voluntary associations by American women supports many important activities which would otherwise be discontinued or converted into recognized occupations or professions. All American social indicators show that an increasingly higher proportion of modern women are expanding their involvement in political, economic, religious, recreational, and educational roles and in relations of great variety and influence upon social structures.

Non-familial Orientations in Answers to
Open-ended Questions

These facts have not altered the value hierarchy and ideology of American housewives—not even those of working women. The cultural lag between role evaluations and behavior is large. Women interviewed who are involved in life outside of the home in the past, present, and probable future restrict the roles women are "supposed to play" to the family institution. Few mention societal, community, religious, neighbor, friend, work obligations, or relations, when asked: "What are the most important roles of a woman, in order of importance?" When forced to rank thirteen roles, including those involving participation in life outside the home, they consistently place obligations to the society at the bottom of the scale. There are exceptions, mostly highly educated and affluent women, but four-fifths of our 568 interviewees, one hundred of whom are currently working, do not feel the importance of female participation in the life of the society sufficiently to remember such obligations in answers to open-ended questions. They limit women to home roles, regardless of their age or actual involvement in the family institution. An overwhelming majority do not even qualify their role-order statements by references to the life cycle, or by separating women who are married and have children from older, younger, single, or childless females. The judgment is that every woman should be married, that she should have children, and that none but family roles should be of even secondary importance to her before, during, or after the time that she is intensely involved in these relations by virtue of the life cycle.

Most of the 268 suburban housewives, 200 urban housewives, and 100 working women who answered the question, "What are the most important roles of a woman, in order of importance?" focus their complete attention on roles within the family of procreation, neglecting even their family of orientation. Most refer to only three roles: mother, wife, and housewife. Often only a segment of a role or a set of duties is given instead of, or in conjunction with, a full set of relations. For example, a Highland Park resident answered the question with: "Raising children, training, education. Homemaker, cleaning, planning meals, social

Table 1: Percentage distributions of total references to different roles in answer to "What are the most important roles of a woman, in order of importance?" by residence and working status.

Role	Suburban Housewives	Urban Housewives	Working Women	Total
Mother	80	83	41	74
Wife	57	67	64	61
Housewife	60	64	37	58
Family, care of	9	9	1	8
Community member, society	26	17	14	21
Friend, neighbor	4	3	7	4
Daughter, other relative	0	3	1	1
Self, duties toward	25	6	5	8
No. of respondents	268	200	100	568

entertaining." The various processes she mentioned can be summarized under the two roles of "mother" and "housewife."

Only 21 per cent of the 568 women even mention social roles connected with being members of social, community, work, or religious organizations. Although no limit was placed on the number of roles they could mention, only 4 per cent mention obligations involved in being a friend or a neighbor. Prodding by interviewers usually elicited only details describing components of the three major roles—mother, wife, and housewife. Table 2 contains more details of the hierarchial location of *societal* roles in a ranking of what is important to half of the population.

Obligations to society are usually assigned to third-place rank, if they are mentioned at all. The least oriented toward such roles are working women, only 14 per cent of whom even mention them, compared with 26 per cent of suburban housewives. The hypothesized percentage for this group prior to the study was much higher; we had assumed them to be much more conscious of the part women play, or should play, in society rather than as full-time housewives. After all, they participate in some form of social life for most of their waking hours. But only one-seventh of the working women make any reference to such roles. Only one worker places any obligation to a group outside of the home in first rank of importance; three women give it second position, and eight women assign it third place. It is possible that working women are actually more supportive of the traditional role conceptions of non-upper-class women than the newly expanding housewives are, in their voluntary involvement, either because of guilt about leaving the home or because of their work schedules, which may exclude the time necessary to take a better view of the world in which they function.

Interest in societal roles is highest for women in their thirties and early forties rather than for those who are older and probably more traditionally oriented or for the very young with small children. Women deeply involved in the wife-mother-housewife sub-cluster are prone to have restricted views of the rest of the world and a flat, that is, institutionally restricted, life-space of interest. Societal roles, for example, are mentioned in first or second place in rank of importance by 1 per cent of suburban women in their twenties, 6 per cent in their thirties, and 9 per cent in their forties. Thus, the women whose children are now in school, but who have not found a place for themselves outside of the home, are more likely to be conscious of their relation to it than are younger women deeply engrossed in family life or older ones who have already resolved their life direction.

The two most influential factors in the way those interviewed evaluate women's roles in society, community, work, and religious institutions are education and income. The level of achievement of both husband and wife is important; the higher the

Table 2: Percentage distributions of the number of respondents assigning ranks to roles in the society in answer to "What are the most important roles of a woman, in order of importance?" by residence and working status.

	Ranking Source			
Rank Given to Societal Roles	Suburban Housewives	Urban Housewives	Working Women	Total
1	1	0	1	1
2	4	3	3	3
3	14	10	8	11
4	7	4	2	7
Total	26	17	14	22

income, the larger the proportion of respondents who think of obligations to the society in an open-ended listing of important social roles. Those with lower levels of schooling, who are also married to men without a high educational achievement, have the traditional lower-class view restricting the woman's responsibilities to those within the home.

The more personal roles of friend and neighbor are mentioned as of importance by only twenty-four women. These roles are not considered a basic part of the woman's set of obligations. Lower-class women are less concerned with people outside of their various family levels than are other groups, but even those among the suburbanites who are involved in high levels of neighboring do not mention it as an important part of the role-cluster of females. These two roles are so far below in importance to what are considered the basic trio of mother-wife-housewife that they do not even come to mind in an interview. Working women are more likely to mention obligations to friends and neighbors than are housewives. One reason may be the fact that several of them are divorced or widowed, so that these relations are of significance to them.

Women with small children—that is, with more than one off-spring the youngest of which is less than nine years of age—are most likely to mention the importance of friend and neighbor relations. Another group that often mentions these roles is that made up of women with no children or with fully grown off-spring. Not having to focus upon the role of mother, these categories of women are perhaps more likely to concentrate their interpersonal emphases upon peer-group relations. Respondents with adolescent children are low in their reference to friendship and neighboring, as are those with little education.

Non-familial Orientations in Forced-choice Answers

Initial analyses of the roles mentioned and ranked by housewives in response to open-ended questions led to a second study using a structured, forced-choice format. The two features of the first set of answers which prompted the use of a list of specific roles to be ranked by the "interaction patterns" respondents were: the omission of certain roles from the roster and the actual ranking system. We feared that women simply mentioned roles

Table 3: Frequency distributions and percentages of total listings of roles, and percentages of respondents giving the four top positions and the four bottom positions to social roles outside the family.

| | Extremes of Ranks, out of 13 | | | | | |
| | Top Four Ranks | | | Bottom Four Ranks | | |
Role Outside Family	No.*	A**	B***	No.*	A**	B***
Artist, self expression	11	2	6	81	18	47
Career woman	13	2	7	67	15	39
Friend	18	3	10	28	6	16
Member of a religious group	18	3	10	52	12	30
Member of the community	14	2	8	56	12	32
Worker	16	2	9	59	13	34

   * Number of respondents
  ** Percentage of responses
*** Percentage of respondents

which came to mind first rather than deliberately evaluating them. The list of roles the second sample of respondents were asked to rank included, in the order in which they were presented: woman, daughter, worker, wife, mother, grandmother, sister, member of a religious group, member of the community, housewife, career woman, friend, and artist (or another self-expressive role).

A very high percentage of women devalue most social roles outside of the family (see Table 3). This fact is particularly evident when the top four and bottom four listings are given, the middle five being ignored. The respondents assign the least importance to participation in the community, religious organizations, careers, work roles, artistic expression roles, and friendship relations. Only eleven respondents place the role of artist in one of the top four categories; one ranks it first. Only two women each list the role of career woman, worker, or friend in the top rank. Each of the following roles receive only one listing in the first rank of importance: member of community, member of a religious group, and worker. In all, only 2 or 3 per cent of the responses put these societal roles in the top four positions. Strong disapproval can be seen in low rankings. For example,

81 respondents list the role of artist among the last four of thirteen ranks. This shows a strong convergence of judgments, representing 18 per cent of the 450 bottom four placements, made by 47 per cent of the women interviewed. The role of career woman is next least important. Only 11 women place it within the top four slots, while 67 respondents, or 39 per cent of the total group, place it among the last four positions. The third least popular role is that of worker, drawing 16 mentions in the top four ranks and 59 in the bottom four. Thirty-four per cent of the women thus find it one of the least significant roles a woman can play, while many do not bother to rank it at all. The fourth role judged unimportant to women is "member of the community," with 14 placements in the first four ranks, most of them in fourth position, and 52 in the bottom four ranks, as seen by 30 per cent of the women. The fifth role from the bottom is that of member of a religious group, with 18 in the top four placements and 52 in the bottom four assignments, by 30 per cent of the women.

The role of friend fares better than any of those already discussed, not so much in being considered more important, but in drawing fewer last-place rankings. It is most frequently assessed in the middle ranks, its highest single concentration being in slots five, six, and seven, along with the role of sister. Relations with siblings draw 78 placements in these positions, those of friend draw 67.

A final indication of the rejection of out-of-the-family roles is the fact that some women simply refuse to rank them at all. Only 84 out of the 205 respondents rank all the roles, 174 ranking at least two out of the total of 686 placements. All but one woman rank the role of wife, but only 129 rank that of artist, 132 rank career woman, and 124 rank worker. Community and religious participation enjoy slightly greater favor, drawing 150 and 146 evaluations, respectively. Thirty-seven women do not rank the role of grandmother. Other family roles have more chance to be included in the ranking system than non-familial ones.

The rejection of non-familial roles is not uniform in the respondent population. In addition to education and income, which operate consistently, the presence and age of children are important factors. Respondents without living offspring are less likely to have strong objections to the career or artistic involvements of women than mothers, particularly when their children are under twenty years of age. Such women see the world from an ethnocentric point of view, feeling that all women should refrain from putting any outside roles above familial ones, regardless of their involvements. Forty-four per cent of childless women place self-expressive roles in the bottom four ranks, compared with 65 per cent of mothers of children under twenty years of age. Career roles are ranked in the top four slots by 24 per cent of women with no children, and only 46 per cent of them assign these roles to the bottom four ranks. Fifty-five per cent of the mothers of younger children likewise devalue career roles. Obviously, these categories are not completely exclusive, but the contrasts are significant. Working women are more tolerant of roles outside of the home than are full-time housewives, although they do not mention them more frequently in answer to open-ended questions.

The respondent's stage in the life cycle has an important influence on the degree of her multidimensionality in assigning roles to women. Mothers of young children are likely to focus on family relations. The next important factor is social class, as reflected in the educational achievements of the woman and her husband and in their family income. However, it is only the very highly located woman in the class system with a relatively stable background who willingly expands the horizon of social involvement for members of her sex. The least educated and poorest women do not feel an interest in, or assign importance to, participation in the broader community or society. The majority of the remaining respondents, some now in the middle levels of socio-economic stratification, reflects the cultural background of this generation of Americans, not in behavior as much as in ideology. Most of the respondents came from a lower background than the status they currently occupy, judging by their father's and their husband's father's occupational identity, their childhood residence, ethnic identifications, and education. Their answers to the role choice of women reflect this background. They have not yet absorbed the traditional upper-class feeling of responsibility toward, and identity with, persons and groups outside of the immediate family, but retain instead the more constricted view of the world typical of the lower social classes.

Of course, this ideological non-involvement in societal roles may be a consequence of the "feminine mystique" posited by Betty Friedan and others, which is being fought by the National Organization of Women and similar groups.[21] Middle-class American urban women may be afraid of being called masculine or of being accused of rejecting feminine life if they express an interest in the world outside of the home. But this explanation overlooks the equally traditional, but upper-class, definition of femininity as containing an awareness of, and a participation in, activities extending beyond the home. It also does not cover the stated rejection of such roles as neighbor, friend, and member of a religious group. Nor does it account for the significant variations among respondents by social class factors. The indication of this study is that traditional class attitudes are very likely to be operating in restricting women to the home, although the "Freudian ethic" may have provided an additional justification for its retention.[22] That is, the Freudian view of the nature of women may be used to support the lower-class attitude toward participation in society, and even toward the role of homemaker itself.[23] Restriction to home roles does not, after all, result in a positive evaluation of these sets of relations as creative, worthy of prior and continuing education, and demanding complex abilities. The restriction placed by women on themselves is thus dual: limitation of roles to home-based ones and devaluation of others in a hierarchy of roles.

It must be reiterated that the judgment of non-familial roles as unimportant to women does not deter women from participating in them. The majority of the middle-class respondents are, have been, or will be actively involved in sets of relations which they ideologically list as unimportant. They work, belong to voluntary associations without which their children's schools, the community, and even the society could not continue to operate as they do, engage in complex and competent action away from home, develop neighboring relations, and enter into non-ascribed friendships. Many of them vote, help in political activities, and

21. Betty Friedan, *The Feminine Mystique,* New York: W. W. Norton, 1963.

22. Richard La Pierre, *The Freudian Ethic,* New York: Duell, Sloan and Pierce, 1959.

23. Helene Deutsch, in *The Psychology of Women,* New York: Grune and Stratton, 1944, defines women as naturally passive and masochistic and the active woman as a masculine type.

contribute to informed public opinion. This actual involvement in societal life even includes many lower-class Negro women who are active in work roles and in church groups. Thus, behavior and ideology either contradict each other, or all the activities women are entering mean little to them. If the ideology is actually believed, then even women without children, widows, and those whose offspring have already developed a life and home of their own are not expected to be committed to any of the societal life processes to which they are contributing.

Richness of the Family Dimension

The fact that family-related social roles take precedence over those requiring involvement outside the home in the rank order of importance of roles of women does not mean that all of them are given equal value. A major distinction between these roles separates those belonging to the family of orientation and those belonging to the family of procreation.[24] In the former the person is born and socialized, in the latter he establishes himself with a spouse and children. Societies differ in the significance they assign to each set of relations and to changes expected in the roles at different stages of the life cycle. For example, in patriarchal families the wife is expected to shift her allegiance from her own family of orientation to that of her husband upon marriage, while he retains a closer tie with his blood relatives than with her.

American society, particularly within its urban centers, expects the woman to concentrate her life focus upon the roles in her family of procreation, de-emphasizing her allegiance to her parents and siblings upon marriage. The process is supposedly duplicated in the life of her husband, although popular literature stresses the fact that such a shift is difficult. Both the forced-choice and the open-ended interviews with housewives indicate the eventual disregarding of obligations to the family of orienta-

24. Talcott Parsons has provided much of the terminology for the sociology of the family. Of particular significance are his "Age and Sex in the Social Structure of the United States," *American Sociological Review*, 7 (October 1942), 604–16; "The Kinship System in the Contemporary United States," *American Anthropologist*, 45 (January–March 1943), 22–38; and, with Robert F. Bales, *Family, Socialization and Interaction Process*, New York: The Free Press, 1955.

tion on the part of married women. At least, most of them consistently give the highest ranks in a listing of importance to roles within the procreational unit, ignoring or giving subsidiary importance to the roles of daughter, sibling, and grandmother. In fact, the whole interview, which provided opportunities for listing many sets of relations, drew very few comments about these social roles. These relations are not of primary consideration in the life of a woman who has a husband and children.[25]

Table 4 documents these comments. The role of grandmother is pushed into the background of all home and kin sets of relations, perhaps explaining why sociologists have neglected this role.

The forced-choice question reminded respondents of the importance of the role of daughter, although few had mentioned it spontaneously in answer to the open-ended question. When placed in a context of thirteen social roles, it is judged as more important than that of sister, 47 per cent of the respondents listing it in the top four positions, compared to the 15 per cent who so list the latter. The role of daughter has the highest convergence of placements in the fourth rank, that of sister in the three ranks immediately below. Sibling and grandmother roles have no first-place assignments. Obligations to parents are most likely to be mentioned by very young women and by those whose children are around twenty years of age. One senses a difference in the vantage points from which they are approached by these two groups.

One role which receives positive attention in the forced-choice selection, but which is ignored in open-ended responses, is that of woman. In spite of a great deal of literature supposedly describing or analyzing the role of women, particularly in American society, and the recent attention it has been receiving from the various "liberation" movements, this role is hard to classify

25. This does not mean that the extended kin group lacks interaction or even an exchange of gifts and services. There is a whole set of studies which has established the fact of continued kin contact, including Marvin Sussman's classic "The Isolated Nuclear Family: Fact or Fiction," in Robert Winch, Robert McGinnis, and Herbert Berrings, eds., *Selected Studies in Marriage and the Family*, New York: Holt, Rinehart and Winston, revised edition, 1962. The most comprehensive collection of all this research is contained in Ethel Shanas and Gordon Streib, eds., *Social Structure and the Family: Generational Relations*, Englewood Cliffs, N. J.: Prentice-Hall, 1965.

Table 4: Frequency distributions and percentages of respondents and listings of the top four positions and the bottom four positions given to rolls within the family dimension.

| | Ranks Assigned by Respondents | | | | | |
| | Top Four Ranks | | | Bottom Four Ranks | | |
Role	No.*	A**	B***	No.*	A**	B***
Grandmother	22	3	13	34	6	20
Daughter	81	12	47	8	2	5
Sister	26	4	15	16	4	9
Wife	165	24	96	3	1	2
Mother	146	21	85	5	1	3
Woman	109	16	63	6	1	3
Housewife	47	7	27	35	8	20

   * Number of respondents
  ** Percentage of responses
*** Percentage of respondents

sociologically.[26] Comments of the women indicate the possibility that it is a *status role,* whose only function is to delineate interaction with persons in the same or in the companionate status role of man.[27] As such it would be much like the status role of "nobleman" in interaction with colleagues, peasants, and the aristocracy. Other women use it as a general identity more than as a specific social role. In either case, it is the third most popular identity in the ranking of roles deemed appropriate to members of this sex. Most women actually place it in fourth position, although it is ranked relatively frequently in third or even second position. Only 3 per cent of the respondents place it at the bottom of the list.

The second peripheral social role to familial sets of relations is that of housewife. Its lack of definite location in any institu-

26. An attempt to develop cross-cultural research on "images of femininity" under the leadership of P. Chombart de Lauwe in Sweden, England, Italy, Poland, France, India, Togo, Austria, and Canada failed to reach agreement on an interview schedule and became restricted to obtaining attitudes about working women. "Images of Women in Society," *International Social Science Journal,* 14 (1962), 7–174.

27. See Helena Znaniecki Lopata, "A Restatement of the Relation Between Role and Status," *Sociology and Social Research,* 49 (October 1964), 58–68.

tion resulted in three different forms of placement assigned it by the women interviewed. One segment of this population deals with it as a vocational role, a separate one lying within both the economic and the familial institutions. A second form of response is to ignore its existence as a separate role, dividing its duties and rights among the roles of wife, mother, and so forth, ignoring all others. The final set of respondents refers to it in identity terms. There "the housewife" is explained as functioning in several other roles, in the same way as "the woman" is sometimes defined. In such use, the title becomes a generic term identifying the total individual in the same way as Mary Jones identifies a specific case.

Twenty-five women ignore completely the role of housewife, 7 rank it thirteenth in order of importance and a total of 20 per cent locate it within the bottom four places. At the other end of the rank of importance scale, only 27 per cent give it honor within the top four spots, most limiting it to the fourth position. Open-ended answers focus more on the duties of that role. When asked, "What are the most important roles of women, in order of importance?" 60 per cent of the suburbanites, 64 per cent of the urban homemakers, and 37 per cent of the urban working women mention housewife as one of the four basic roles. At least, they refer to some segment of this role. It is possible that so few women give it high-rank importance when faced with the term "housewife" because of the word itself. Such a tendency would reflect the general societal prestige scale. Not allowing themselves to identify with roles outside of the home, many women nevertheless cannot bring themselves to assign high status to the title of "housewife" as an identity or vocational designation. One clearly recognizes the "I'm just a housewife" chorus.

The family dimension is thus limited primarily to roles in the family of procreation, especially those of wife and mother, with some additional spontaneous emphasis on home maintenance. Other sets of relations are not mentioned or are listed below this central cluster.

Role Focus Within the Family of Procreation

Although most respondents stress the importance of the wife-mother-housewife trio of roles for members of their sex, to the exclusion of societal participation and with a secondary stress on kin roles, they do not agree upon the primary focus within that kinship-cluster. Their answers reflect the fact that American society has not developed a hierarchical list of family roles or prevented role conflict within it. Conflicts in the family of pro-creation can develop between the roles of wife and mother and between either or both of these and the role of housewife. One basic factor contributing to such conflict, as well as to role strain within each set of relations, is the highly romanticized idealiza-tion of all three roles. The ideal of romantic love implies not only "instant love" "across the crowded room," but exclusive and perpetual love. The young married couple is pictured as sur-rounded by a bubble of mutual attention to the exclusion of other roles and relations. A second, but not necessarily less glamorized role, is that of mother. The child-orientation of our society is subject to much comment in popular literature, re-corded by sociologists and psychologists, and caricatured by Philip Wylie.[28] It portrays the basic unit of relations as that of mother and her small child, and the main obligation of adults as directed toward that child. The role of "homemaker" is even romanticized, especially in terms of the product: a house always immaculately maintained, objects in perfect and static spatial relations to one another. This product-orientation stands in con-flict with the developmental goals of modern child-rearing and the informal comfort ideal of the man in his castle.

The cluster of roles of wife-mother-housewife is also in con-flict with some of the components of the first role. The wife is valued as a sexual object whose responsibility is to make herself attractive and available.[29] This is difficult to synchronize with

28. Phillip Wylie, *Generation of Vipers,* New York: Holt, Rinehart and Winston, 1955, and in a number of other articles by the same author. Bruno Bettleheim feels that some of the child-orientation of American middle-class mothers is dysfunctional to their healthy growth. See "Does Communal Education Work: The Case of the Kibbutz," *Commentary,* 33 (February 1962), 117–25.

29. Bernard Farber feels that the decrease in importance assigned to the procreative function of the family is modifying the relations between men and women into ones of permanent availability as potential mates. Such an emphasis would increase the importance assigned to the recreational and sexual functions of sex status roles. Bernard Farber, *Family: Organization and Interaction,* San Francisco: Chandler, 1964, 103–12.

many features of the role of mother and housewife. Another dilemma in the family institution arises out of the fact that the individualistically reared young woman is expected to become totally submerged in the home-bound trio of roles, while her husband, though selected for personal relations, is expected to be primarily concerned with his career.[30]

An easy solution to role conflict is the hierarchical ordering of different sets of relations by their importance.[31] As indicated before, most women have achieved this partly by separating obligations to the family of procreation from societal roles and even from those to the family of orientation. Within the family, however, women vary considerably along three basic lines: some become husband-oriented, others child-oriented, and a third category develops a home-orientation.[32] There is a segment of the population which generalizes all relations to the family as a total unit, which they see themselves as servicing; but this is not as definite a stance as the three basic ones. Most women questioned at a particular time in their life cycle select one of the three basic roles as a focus, locating the remaining sets of relations around it. Indications are, as we will later detail, that many may actually change their focus with different stages in the life cycle, but most are not aware that there will be such modifications. Young brides and college students in what Kephart calls a "love experience" become indignant when informed that, in all likelihood, the content of their marital relation will change and that they will not remain husband-oriented.[33] Young wives without children experience some anticipatory socialization toward the role of mother, but not enough to move the role of

30. Robert Dubin, in "Industrial Workers' Worlds: A Study of the Central Life Interests of Industrial Workers," Social Problems, 3 (January 1956), 131–42, found workers not involved highly in either the task or the relational aspects of their work.

31. Margaret Mead predicted that by the year 2000 only a segment of the population will produce and rear children, while both men and women of the remaining societal members engage in other social roles. "Toward the Year 2000, Work in Progress," Daedalus, 96 (Summer 1967).

32. Helena Znaniecki Lopata, "Secondary Features of a Primary Relationship," Human Organization, 24 (Summer 1965), 116–23.

33. William M. Kephart, "Some Correlates of Romantic Love," Journal of Marriage and the Family, 29 (August 1967), 470–74.

wife to the side until pregnancy or the birth of the first (or sometimes the second) child. Only about one-fourth of suburban housewives with small children locate the role of wife in the first rank of importance, though a few ranking motherhood first explain that this is a new orientation or that the hierarchy is dependent upon the life cycle.

Many factors contribute to the original role focus, to variations or absence of them in the stages. Some women never return to their original concern with husband-wife relations, even after the children are grown, because of disenchantment with the marriage,[34] the husband's involvement in his work-segregated sphere of life, habit, placement of the focus upon children, other activities, continued occupation with children even after they leave home, etc.

An extremely important factor offsetting the usual life-cycle trends is the dependence of the whole style of existence upon the husband. Those housewives who remain husband-oriented marry a different type of man, who continues to be outstanding, than the women who slide into other role-focus orientations.

The ranks assigned the roles of wife, mother, and housewife by respondents in the "social role of housewife" interview are given in Table 5, by the percentage of the women in the three categories who make such judgments.

The social role of housewife is less important to working women than to women who perform it full time (see Table 5). Only one-third mention it at all, but they tend to give it first or second rank. Moreover, working women are much less interested in the various components of the homemaker's obligations than are the full-time housewives. Many of the non-working urban women interviewed are older and more traditionally oriented toward the role of housewife than their younger suburban counterparts. That is, the urban homemakers are more apt than the suburbanites to rank this role first or second in importance. Moreover, the older urban women are more likely to list the role of wife than that of mother in the first place, in contrast to the more child-oriented suburbanites. The contrast is sig-

34. This conclusion is reached by Peter C. Pineo, in "Disenchantment in the Later Years of Marriage," in Bernard Farber, ed., *Kinship and Family Organization,* New York: John Wiley, 1966, 229–39.

Table 5: The rank assigned the roles of wife, mother, and housewife in answer to "What are the most important roles of a woman, in order of importance?" by residence and working status.

Rank of Role	Suburban Housewives			Urban Housewives			Urban Working Women		
	Wife	Mother	House-wife	Wife	Mother	House-wife	Wife	Mother	House-wife
	Per Cent	Per Cent	Per Cent	Per Cent	Per Cent	Per Cent	Per Cent	Per Cent	Per Cent
1	28	46	14	39	29	20	42	26	14
2	23	31	18	20	44	21	20	38	17
3	6	3	22	7	9	21	2	1	6
4	0	0	6	1	1	0	0	0	0
Total who mention role	57	80	60	67	83	64	64	65	37
Total number	268			200			100		

nificant, and it covers all urbanites whether working or not. Suburban housewives list obligations to themselves as individuals more often than the other two populations.

Analysis of responses led to the conclusion that women interviewed in their homes during the day simply are not thinking of their husbands then, particularly if there are small children around. Forty-three per cent of the suburbanites, 33 per cent of urban housewives, and 36 per cent of working women do not mention them at all when listing the most important roles of women, while only 28 per cent of the first group, 39 per cent of the second, and 42 per cent of the third consider the role of wife as the most important. Forty-six per cent of suburban housewives, but only 29 per cent of urban housewives, and 26 per cent of working women give the role of mother first place, but 80 per cent, 83 per cent, and 65 per cent, respectively, of the three groups make at least some reference to it. The role of mother is often not so important to working women, even though most of them have offspring, perhaps because the latter are generally past childhood. The figures reinforce the image of suburbia as child-oriented.

Forced-choice Ranking of Family Roles

The forced-choice question asking for a ranking of thirteen roles produced a much greater emphasis on the role of wife than the open-ended question did. Ninety-six per cent rank it within the top four slots and only 2 per cent within the bottom four (see Table 4). Sixty women consider it the most important role; the proportion of this response (30 per cent) is close to that of the suburban housewives in the first study. More women, 87, rank it in second place, often following the role of woman, which draws the highest number of first-place assignments. Eighty-five per cent of those who took part in the "interaction patterns" interviews mention the role of mother in the first four ranks, most giving it second- or third-place location. This distribution reinforces the hypothesis that women simply do not think of their husbands during weekdays, unless reminded of their role of wife.

As mentioned before, the role of woman is ranked in first place more often than that of wife or mother, although it is not a specific role mentioned in the "social role of housewife" inter-view. The first study, however, draws many references to the self, to obligations directed toward self-identity. Respondents repeatedly state that it is necessary to have "time for myself," "the opportunity to be creative," "self-expression chances," and "to be myself for a few hours," in answer to questions aiming to elicit the most important roles of women.

This emphasis upon the pervasive self-identity of woman and upon her self and her sentiments, even above the traditional roles of wife and mother, may be a consequence of three trends. The new expansion of women into fresh aspects of life before marriage may lead to a feeling of personal disruption when they enter upon the roles of housewife, wife, and mother which are client-focused. Such a state of mind becomes transformed into the need for a self-identifying role. It is possible that this indi-cates an attempt of the house-bound homemaker to move back into the society in which her minimal non-familial identity card is that of "woman," at a time when other identities as "secre-tary," "beauty queen," and so forth, are unavailable. Or it is possible that constant references to the self and to "being a woman" simply reflect the socializing culture, which insists that girls be self-oriented, concerned mainly with the impression they make on others and the desire for popularity, a certain amount of which is guaranteed by being a woman. All three possibilities imply that traditional roles camouflage the undercurrent of con-cern with self-identity.

A Typology of Women

Our research has suggested a typology of women within the family dimension.

1. The *husband-oriented woman* sees her basic role as that of wife, grouping other sets of relations around it. She is a young, newly married woman or one who is working and in her late forties. If she works, she has no children or only adult offspring; if she lives in the suburbs, she has one very young child. The husband-oriented suburbanite has a high degree of education. The working woman may be a high-school or college graduate,

but not a drop-out. A woman is particularly likely to be husband-oriented if her spouse has a Ph.D. or a professional degree, or if their family income falls between $16,000 and $20,999. In other words, husband-oriented wives have successful husbands.

2. The *child-oriented woman* believes that the basic unit of the family consists of herself and *her* children. The husband is considered relatively external to this unit, someone who provides for it, performs tasks which further its existence, and must be "serviced" by it. If this woman works, she is typically in her late thirties or early forties, with four children, the youngest in his teens, and separated or divorced from a husband who has no more than twelve years of schooling and a relatively low-status occupation. If she is a suburban housewife, she is in her late twenties or early thirties, with an increased orientation toward her children as their number increases, but the offspring may be of any age. She has a relatively low level of education, but her husband may have average schooling, and their family income is average or even slightly above.

3. The *house-oriented woman* establishes her major area of interest in her home and its maintenance. She often feels that people impinge upon this relation, upsetting her equilibrium by disarranging the house. Her husband is a high-school drop-out, and her academic achievement is low or seems to be an unimportant factor. She is an older urbanite rather than a suburbanite or she refuses to give her age. If she works, she has a low family income and older children.

4. The *life-cycle woman* decreases her concentration on the role of wife after the children are born, but returns to it in later years, either when her life changes with the maturity of her children or when the retirement or work disengagement or "phasing out" stages are reached by her husband. She is aware of such shifts in emphasis, explaining it in terms of her own or family needs.

5. The *family-oriented woman* blends all roles related to the home, those of wife, mother, and housewife, into a single "family care" package. She is either aware of this lumping process, like the college graduate who states that she "can't separate wife and mother," or she is the traditional housewife who sees herself as servicing the whole unit. The latter type is found more frequently than the former, being particularly prevalent among

older and lower-class women. She often calls her husband "father," relating to him as father of the children and the originator of the family whose needs she meets.

6. The *self-directed woman* refuses to focus upon any of these roles as basic to her. She is more concerned with herself as a total individual and with satisfying what she defines as her needs than with any role. She is much more likely than the others to speak of generalized obligations to herself "as a woman" and to explain the uniqueness of her involvement in other roles. Often she is a young mother of young children or a sympathizer with the "Women's Liberation Front" or similar groups.

7. One more category of woman exists, but she is very rare and was almost totally missing from our roster of housewives and married women. She is *career-oriented* or *society-oriented,* focused upon a role or set of roles outside of the family institution. Very frequently she is young or no longer married and has a professional or artistic identity or an ideological commitment.

SHIFTS OF ROLE FOCUS DURING THE LIFE CYCLE

The typology of women according to their role focus given above is based on their orientation at a particular time. As stated before, the life-cycle woman is the only one who specifically expects her current focus to shift, following changes in role stages. Contrasts among the respondents naming different roles as the most important indicate that these stages have a greater influence upon the value hierarchy than they realize. Young brides are much more likely to be oriented toward husbands and the self than other women are. They shift to an emphasis on relations with children when they become mothers. After children grow out of infanthood, women develop several different types of orientations, and only one category of mothers continues to focus on that role. The convergence upon certain roles at given periods of the life cycle does not negate the constant influence of education and social class.

The very new wife tends to be husband-oriented and also very aware of the changes in herself as a result of her new experiences. When asked for major events in her past life, she concentrates on emotional states, her response to responsibility, or learning to live with another person. In answer to "What are the most important roles of a woman, in order of importance?" a nineteen-year-old typically lists obligations to her husband: "Good wife —housekeeping, wifely tasks, bearing children. Husband's social obligations—entertaining and organization. I think religion is part of a home." Interestingly enough, she subsumes bearing children under the role of wife. A twenty-two-year-old explains her choice in life-cycle terms: "At this point of my life the most important role is being the best wife and best companion to my husband. In later years these roles will include being the best mother to my children." A nineteen-year-old, pregnant with her first child, places obligation to the self in the first rank of importance. Her statement implies, however, a view of the self as the carrier of another being: "(1) self-care; (2) to make the husband's home a pleasant place; (3) good wife; (4) good mother." She is anticipating the role of mother, but the gist of all her comments, even those pertaining to being a housewife, is husband-oriented. Stronger self-involvement is stated by a young respondent: "Maintaining the home, trying to fix things up the way you'd like to live, go out, have fun." A conflict is implied in the answer of a twenty-year-old Negro mother of a six-month-old child: "Primarily that of wife and mother. However, her individuality expressed as a wife and mother is just as important. A woman's place isn't just in the home. She should invest her time outside of home in other interests. Being a wife and mother isn't the only thing." This statement is not typical, because it lists the wife first and is strong in its outside orientation, but it is representative of the way women approach their involvement. The "outside" is seen not as a source of obligations to society, but as the locus of self-expression and recreation. Another form of self-orientation is shown by a twenty-one-year-old, married over a year but without children: "Immediate family, intellectual indulgence, friends." The significance of self-awareness in the development of mother and wife roles is explained by a twenty-four-year-old: "The most important thing is to be a woman—this sounds silly, but not too many girls know that. They play all kinds of games. Women shouldn't. They have to be a woman to be a good wife and mother. Having a good husband and children helps make a girl a woman. A wife shouldn't fool with other men, either, specially when she's a mother. It's also important to know your man well enough to know what makes him happy, so you know what to do. I'm a good cook, too, although I don't cook a lot." This respondent has two children, aged two and four, and all four of them live in her parents' home.

Yet, not all young married women are husband-oriented. A twenty-one-year-old with no children lists the roles of women as: "(1) taking care of the house; (2) having children." Mothers of two children are more likely to respond this way than newlyweds are. A typical statement by a twenty-three-year-old mother is: "Mother—child care; wife—beside her husband; keeping a clean, well-kept and organized home."

Women in the same stage of the life cycle vary not only in the role upon which they focus, but in the manner in which they perceive their obligations. Some women are oriented toward the process of role fulfillment. Young working women tend specially to be action directed. For example, one who is in her twenties defines the roles as follows: "Taking care of the family if she has one; her duties toward her home; taking care of the children; keeping up the house and herself." These are obligations requiring initiative and action. Many a young suburban woman, on the other hand, defines the same roles as "being" states. "Being a good Christian and a good mother," "being a wife to her husband," and so forth, suggest an essence rather than a problem-solving series of actions. A third category sees her roles in product terms. "Have a clean house," "one with happy children," are the role definitions of such women.

Three Highland Park residents exemplify different ways of perceiving the roles of women during the full-house plateau, when variations stabilize: "Wife, mother, homemaker—doing all that is necessary for the physical, mental and spiritual needs of the family" (a college graduate); "mother, wife" (twelve years of schooling); "homemaker, mother, keeping husband happy" (fourteen years of schooling). A similar difference in rank order and role definitions is demonstrated in the answers of two Negro women. A mother with ten years of schooling and a background of work on a farm and in unskilled factory jobs answers: "Be home and raise your children; keep house well; such as prepare meals." No mention of husband, and the task orientation within a strict schedule are characteristic of one type. In contrast, another Negro woman with seventeen years of schooling gives a more relationally oriented response: "Companion to her husband, mother to their children, teacher, adviser, housekeeper, cook, manager of finances, playmate, etc." This is a broad definition of relations in terms of their main functions.

The qualitative descriptions of some of the roles, particularly of mothering, change with modifications in the life cycle of the child. Mothers of young children speak of "taking care" of them, those with older offspring of "guiding" or "being there when needed." A woman the youngest of whose three offspring is fifteen explains: "Not only like a mother, but like a pal to her kids. Understand and never be shocked by anything." The degree of control decreases according to these statements, particularly in reference to male children.

"Outside activities" enter the role list in the form of associations connected with children; this is accompanied by decreasing concern with self-expression. A Wheaton mother of three, ages one to six, is anticipating some outside involvement, although she does not yet belong to any groups: "Motherhood and being a good wife are equal; striving for a good job as mother and wife; teach the spiritual phase, tend to social obligations, have outside interests." Mothers of older children sometimes find outside activities rather hectic and complain about what their younger counterparts wish they could do. Not all explanations of such involvement are in relational terms: "Keep up your house, send the children to church, belong to the PTA and community affairs." This response avoids interactive terms, listing such involvement as a set of duties and ignoring completely the role of wife. It is likely that this woman carries out relational activities with her children besides sending them to church. Another Wheaton woman lists these roles: "Good mother, caring for physical and emotional needs of the children; good companion to her husband; carry share in community activities: Scouts, church, PTA."

In fact, an interesting tendency was found to exist among Wheaton respondents, although they were randomly chosen in a great range of residential locations. The proportion of those interviewed who mention obligations to the community is higher in Wheaton than in any other place but Park Forest. In addition, the Wheaton women are more likely than those of any other community to mention religious participation. The town does have a strong religious character and the responses support conclusions reached in the chapter on the role of neighbor that the consciousness of involvement in the community is culturally influenced, with each community developing its own ethic. In addition, the Wheaton respondents are predominantly in the stage of the life cycle oriented toward increasing involvement in the community.

The importance of religious roles is greater for older urban residents than for most younger women. A Negro teacher with sixteen years of education whose younger child is twenty-one says: "To be a Christian wife, mother, and church worker, religious worker in the area and in the state" is most important. A Catholic woman, age fifty, with eleven years of education and with grown children, states this interest somewhat differently: "First duty is as a mother—to see that the children are provided for, clothes, food; that I was home when they were home. Being a good manager. Taking part in outside work as church work. Social life comes last." This is a very "virtuous" set of duties, a strict set of self-expectations.

As the full-house plateau stage unfolds, more frequent references to work roles are found: "Mother, housework; I enjoy doing it, but I would like to go to work to help my husband." By most American standards this woman's children are still too young (eight and five) for easy transition into work schedules. "It's good to be a mother, but if you must work, you must work," states a forty-seven-year-old who returned to paid employment and who seems to feel that this prevents her from being a proper mother.

The role of daughter occasionally enters the roster of roles for women in their fifties: "(1) wife; (2) a mother; (3) a daughter, if she has parents living; (4) a friend." The role of friend also increases in frequency of reference in statements by older women.

Women in their fifties tend to respond to the "shrinking circle" stage in a manner suggesting that they are concerned only with backward glances. One states that the roles of women are: "To make a good home for the children and family; good cooking and keep the house clean. Have a good life together, go out once in a while, go to church." This is a task-oriented and lower-middle-class conception of marriage, supplied by a woman who no longer has children at home to eat the food. The husband is often subsumed under "family" by women of this generation. Many of them stress the role of housewife in the first rank of importance: "(1) caring for the home, keeping it straight—housework; (2) the health of her family, keeping them well; (3) preparing the food—that would be the same as taking care of the house. What else is there? That covers it, I guess." When questioned about the role of wife, which she ignored, she answers: "Taking care of her husband, also, picking up after him, trying to make him happy." [35] Such women use cooking as the basic way to sustain relations with family members.

Respondents in their late fifties, many of whom are first- or second-generation Americans, tend to describe the roles of women in an almost matriarchal manner: "Taking care of the family, her children, to take care of her husband; she is responsible for her home." "Taking care of," "looking after," and "keeping the family happy" are phrases frequently used by this age and cultural sub-group. They suggest the strongly initiating, possessive attitudes of a mother hen protecting her brood from hunger, danger, and unhappiness; a mother figure ensuring protection and health, even happiness. Even though the American stereotype pictures women as becoming increasingly matriarchal, especially in the suburbs, younger women do not see themselves as having as much control over their families as the older women do. Their aura of strength is combined with a tendency to speak of the children as if they were still within the home: "Training the children—good manners. Teach the children basic religious principles, take care of the house," was the action-oriented response of a woman no longer active in this phase of the role of mother. No reference is made by her to current roles or to husband-wife relations. Of course, so many life experiences and personality traits differentiate these women from younger mothers that it is impossible to attribute their differences to a single cause. Altering of memory over time, social-class influence, the generation gap in a society undergoing great cultural change,

35. Lee Rainwater, Richard P. Coleman, and Gerald Handel, *Workingman's Wife: Her Personality, World and Life Style*, New York: Oceana Publications, 1959.

all play an important part in the strong contrast between the women quoted above and the modern suburbanite with young offspring.

Some of the women in their fifties express a very protective manner to their husbands, possibly because of the modern concern over the male death rate and as an example to their peer group.

Unless she is a member of the three upper social classes and involved in societally active roles, the woman sixty years of age or over focuses strongly upon the role of housewife: "(1) keep house; (2) see that the husband and children are fed and clean; (3) see if the children are raised right; (4) see them off to school and help them with school work; (5) help them know right from wrong." This respondent is sixty years old, her children are forty-two and thirty-seven, she is not an active church participant, and her values reflect the rigidity imposed by a five-year education. The only currently involving set of duties which she lists are connected with the role of housewife. "Keeping the house clean and cooking" is all another sixty-one-year-old who had reared four children could state, even when prodded for other roles. An orientation toward a role which was meaningful only in the past is contained in the answer of a sixty-year-old mother of three grown children: "Well, a woman is a mother, I took care of the kids, and cooked, and cleaned and helped them all I could. A wife has to help her husband and keep him happy. I try. I do my best."

Widowhood comes to many women in their sixties. A sixty-six-year-old mother of two adult children does not, however, indicate in her answer that her husband has died: "Building a home—prepare yourself through education for this; mother; housewife; be interested in husband's work." Of course, it is possible that she is reflecting on her husband by limiting the role of wife to an interest in the work, not the man. Another urban widow, sixty-three years of age, speaks in terms of her own life: "Since I had no children, my role toward my husband was important to me."

TWO 🌺🌺🌺

Becoming and
Being a Wife

BACKGROUND

American marital roles are undergoing dramatic changes. It is possible that over the long run they will become more functional for personality development and fulfillment, but currently they reflect and contribute to many forms of individual and relational problems. A major part of the change is a direct consequence of rapid industrialization and urbanization. These two processes have separated work from home, training from work and from home, friendship from kinship, and neighbor from co-worker and friend.[1] Mass education and the democratization of American ideologic and social structures have added to the diversification of social contacts, producing and demanding multidimensional involvement of members in a wide range of behaviors. Home socialization and formal education of boys, and—even more—of girls have not caught up with societal needs, and family institutions often hamper the behavior which society requires. Education in schools prepares women for abstract thinking and problem solving; traditional feminine roles require passive stances. The view of the home as an isolated unit facilitating peaceful withdrawal from the ongoing life conflicts with the demand of a democratic nation for full participation by all adults and world aware-

1. Robert F. Winch and Rae Lesser Blumberg, "Societal Complexity and Familial Organization," in Robert Winch and Louis Goodman, eds., *Selected Studies in Marriage and the Family*, New York: Holt, Rinehart and Winston, 1968 and M. F. Nimkoff and Russell Middleton, "Types of Family and Types of Economy," *American Journal of Sociology*, 66 (November 1960), 215–25.

ness of parents. Modern social systems require that wives be business managers, maids, mothers, dieticians, decorators, chauffeurs,
PTA members, and wage earners, but these roles are less valued
than most male roles. Child rearing has become more complex
than in prior generations because of the realization of home influences on personality and even intelligence, yet former "mother's
helpers" in the persons of kin and servants are gone. Traditional
behavior is impossible, yet new standards are not consistent or
available to many women. Cultural shock accompanies the transition from girlhood to marriage, but society treats the American
woman as a neurotic for feeling it. Although both marital partners
experience these changes, the inconsistency is strongest in the life
of the modern woman, because so many of her roles are imbued
with emotionally charged norms.

Another set of factors complicates American marriages. The
ideological emphasis on individual happiness, the assumption that
an event or social relation has happiness as its major function, and
the belief that withdrawal is warranted if it fails to meet this re-
quirement pose problems. These attitudes reflect a belief in "romantic love," although this is a separate aspect of life. People
today expect marriage to be completely satisfying relation, meeting all the personality needs of both partners.[2] The combination of these demands places on marriage a burden heavier than
ever before and heavier than it can now carry. No social relation
between only two people can provide constant and full satisfaction for multidimensional and dynamic individuals unless the
partners are totally adjusted and mature and they are willing to
sacrifice other relations and forms of action. Modern life demands
involvement in other social roles by each partner, and these
require at least some sentimental attachment. A wife is also a
housewife, a mother, a daughter, a friend, and so forth; a husband
is also a member of his occupational group, a participant in a
work organization, a son, a father, a friend, and so forth. Their
needs may not always fit nor their sentiments mesh. The culture
and the social structure do not provide means for satisfying the
expectations raised by the idealized images of marriage.

In addition, the traditional form of family life upon which mar-

2. This is the central theme of Ernest W. Burgess, Harvey J. Locke, and
Mary Margaret Thomes in *The Family: From Institution to Companionship*,
New York: American Book Co., third edition, 1963.

riage is inconsistently grafted is in opposition to the concept of romantic love between the partners. The ideology underlying American culture views the family unit as of primary importance and the individual simply as a link maintaining it. Individual happiness was a concept completely foreign to the system, which built identity through group accomplishments. Relations within the familistic unit were regulated through strongly authoritarian, patriarchally based lines, and marriage was a formalized union for the purpose of the orderly replacement of generations. Known norms of definite clarity surrounded contact between husbands and wives and reminded each of their duties to the whole. Work was sex-segregated, and only upper-class families enjoyed the luxury of intellectual and artistic contact between men and women.[3] Relatively few women ran complex households requiring a variety of skills and a knowledge of the society. Most traditional families thus consisted of members relating formally through institutionalized roles, and female passivity was idealized as a virtue.

The two patterns of marital relations, traditional and modern, are highly contradictory and the newer has not replaced the older completely. Each individual is likely to hold ideas which are mutually inconsistent, and the likelihood of two persons agreeing in their definitions of husband-wife roles is very small. The society is heterogeneous, but women are more apt than men to favor egalitarian and companionate relations which offer more freedom and opportunity to utilize the multidimensional traits into which they have been socialized. This is particularly true of the younger and more educated women of this society, who are joining or sympathizing with the Women's Liberation Movement and who are increasingly experimenting with new roles, including professional careers. Men are the objects against which the movement is directed. Hostility between the sexes is high, whether expressed directly, in humor, or in restrictive ideologies. The new image of marriage is difficult to achieve, even without resistance from a traditional partner, because there are no patterns for it. Each marital team has to work out its own pattern, meeting individually defined needs and requirements. The negative consequence of the changes and inconsistencies is easily visible not only in hos-

3. Thorstein Veblen, *The Theory of the Leisure Class,* New York: Modern Library, 1934.

tility among even the "happily married," but in divorce, desertion, "disenchantment in later years," [4] conflict, and tension. These are the subject of frequent comment, partly because they are psychologically threatening to the observer. The creative components of modern marriage are often ignored.[5] They are evidenced in the excitement over the possibility of full relational development, the satisfaction with dynamic life, and the deep love available when the personalities are fully involved. The relations between some of the women we interviewed and their husbands may be pointing the way to a new range of marital interactions, a range less constricted and more open to human potential for more people than was formerly believed to be possible.

The data provided by our interviews indicate that housewives handle in many different ways the strain which is present in their marriages because of cultural inconsistencies in their own belief and action systems. Some, bound by the tradition of lower-class passivity, continue to handle their world in such a manner, although illness, accident, and juvenile delinquency are often the consequences. Society is no longer organized to cope with such a lack of ability in handling situations, except by means of charity or police control. Other wives become rulers of the roost, even early in life, adding authoritarian behavior to traditional matriarchal actions removed from the husband's province of control, although they are not always satisfied with the right to do this—authoritarian personalities often prefer to be subjected to control by others. A third group of wives flounders through life, being uncertain and inconsistent in what it expects from marriage and from husbands. These women often decide to act in a certain way, only to have the husband respond negatively and violently, causing reaction and withdrawal. The whole life pattern becomes one of push and vacillation, with constant uncertainty, hostility, and a pervasive sense of confusion. At the extreme from both the passive and the authoritarian wife is the woman who, jointly with her

4. Peter C. Pineo, "Disenchantment in the Later Years of Marriage," in Bernard Farber, ed., *Kinship and Family Organization*, New York: John Wiley, 1966, 229–39.

5. Eugene Litwak, Gloria Count, and Edward M. Haydon found that creativity in problem-solving is a vital component of successful marriage. See "Group Structure and Interpersonal Creativity as Factors Which Reduce Errors in the Prediction of Marital Adjustment," in Farber, ed., *Kinship and Family Organization*, pp. 22–228.

husband, strives to build a dynamic relation uniquely fitting their situation and personalities. Of course, many responses to the societally and self-imposed changes in husband-wife relations fall between these four clearly visible types.

BECOMING A WIFE

In order for a person to become involved in a social role, he must develop functionally integrated relations with at least two people, who then form parts of his social circle.[6] The process of "becoming" a ———— (doctor, wife, mother, etc.) includes several stages. In the first place, some contact must be made between the would-be social person and the candidates for his social circle. This contact must be for the purpose of, or have as its consequence, the creation of social roles. Secondly, there develops a mutual testing of future role partners for the qualities assumed to be needed in the performance of their roles. This testing is based on established procedures, on the traits found present in similar roles assumed to be desirable or in newly created ones. It depends on definitions of the duties and rights and on the actions of the social person and of circle members which are assumed to be part of the set of relations between them. Of course, compromises are made whenever one cannot obtain the ideal partner, and bargains are reached when expectations differ—both frequent occurrences resulting in role variations and modifications.

If the testing results in mutual acceptance, such decisions must be announced to all those who are, or will be, involved in the new roles. This sequence of announcements is the third stage. If the person and his social circle members do not have all the knowledge and skills needed to carry out their parts, a fourth stage will contain some method of acquiring them. Of course, the announcement may be delayed until after the training is completed. The fifth stage of the process often (but not inevitably) calls for the acquisition of some material objects to be used as symbols or facilities of action. Finally, the individual and the

6. I am using here the concept of "becoming" as Howard S. Becker develops it in "Becoming a Marihuana User," *American Journal of Sociology*, 59 (November 1953), 235–42.

members of his social circle incorporate the role's behavior and its identities into their personalities. Social roles and those connected with them vary considerably in the depth and pervasiveness of personality change which they involve, but all require some minimal adjustments; part of the change they bring is one of self-identification. The person, assisted by those "in the know," develops definitions of what he is feeling as part of the role. He learns the stages of the procedure and how to identify himself with the process. In addition to this sequence, an individual learns to "see himself" in the role, to become identified with its requirements in past, present, and future scenes. He gradually symbolizes part of himself by the title of the role. Thus, he finally declares, "I am a ———," accepting the official title as one of his identities. "Role distance" occurs when a person refuses to be identified with some or all of the supposed traits of the typical role performer.[7] The dislike of the title "housewife," expressed by many of the women we interviewed, is an instance of role distance—not wanting to be identified as housewives because of the image they have of the typical person bearing that title. The name "wife" does not carry such a negative connotation. One of the aspects of role distance is the opportunity it offers to modify the image. "I am a good cook, but a lousy housekeeper" is one explanation of specialization within the role of housewife.

"Becoming a ———" affects the personality in another way besides identity formation. All other social roles and relations in which the person is engaged are modified, in varying degrees, by his entrance into a new role. As new behaviors are learned, there is a tendency to carry them over to other interaction scenes. Time and space, sentiment and thought, are modified by the new patterns, and they in turn affect other sets of involvements. The self judges itself in the role and these judgments affect the hierarchy of identities.

The six stages of the process of "becoming a ———" are evident in the role of wife. The social circle includes, minimally, the man who marries her and the society's representatives who perform and witness the marriage ceremony and who officially recognize

7. Erving Goffman introduced the concept of role distance in the essay by that title which is part of *Encounters*, Indianapolis, Indiana: Bobbs-Merrill, 1961.

the existence of the new unit. Societies differ in the size of the total social circle of the wife, and variations exist within the American social system owing to many social and idiosyncratic factors.

Contact with the future husband is made by most candidates for the role of wife through a complex of voluntarily undertaken procedures, including the dating of those members of the opposite sex in the category of eligibles. Dating performs many functions and lasts for an extended period of time.[8] It finally leads to the development of a love relationship with the one man who eventually "proposes" marriage. The concept of proposal is traditional in European societies. The man asks the woman to be his wife, rather than waiting for her initiative or for mutual decisions. This institution is connected with the patriarchal system of matchmaking in which the girl awaited male selection or the decision of parents. The self-selection procedure has changed many of the traditional qualities by which potential wives were chosen and the procedures for testing for these. When this role involved familistic obligations to the whole male unit, her abilities to contribute to *it* were of primary importance.[9] The criteria by which a prospect was measured by representatives of the family included what she brought to the unit in economic goods, in work skills appropriate to his family class position, in ability to bear children, and in potential for fitting herself into the ongoing life of the group. Her family, in turn, evaluated his for status matching and for benefits to be derived from the combination. Current testing procedures are based on the concept of romantic love and ignore past criteria, focusing upon the personal and sexual magnetism between the couple. Task-focused traits and kin-relevant standards are not con-

8. Robert Winch, *The Modern Family,* New York: Holt, Rinehart and Winston, revised edition, 1963; and *Mate Selection: A Study of Complementary Needs,* New York: Harper, 1958.

9. William J. Goode, *World Revolution and Family Patterns,* New York: The Free Press, 1963; Barbara Ward, ed., *Women in the New Asia,* Paris: UNESCO, 1963 (including especially S. C. Dube, "Men's and Women's Roles in India: A Sociological Review," 174–203); Denise Paulme, ed., *Women of Tropical Africa* (translated by H. M. Wright), Berkeley: University of California Press, 1963; or Arthur Phillips, ed., *Survey of African Marriage and Family Life,* London: Oxford, 1953. All these works contain details of the relation between mate selection and forms of family organization.

sidered significant in the establishment of a marriage. However, some controls upon the selection remain, even in modern society's system.

All communities are interested in each marriage unit and in the offspring it is expected to produce; thus, they retain the right of deciding who is unfit for forming a new family of procreation, in individual or in matched-couple traits. Caste systems forbid inter-marriage—that is, marriage across most caste lines.[10] Incest taboos prohibit marriage with those whose family roles are considered primary and vital for group survival. Other restrictions, on health or age at marriage, are designed to prevent marriage from ocur-ring among a large number of potential partners. Since regulations are incorporated into a culture and passed down to the young, they often become internalized and influence even self-selection sys-tems. Most marriages occur between those whom society judges as appropriate mates. Even in the United States, where many traditional formal restrictions have broken down, girls and boys tend to select only those partners of whom the societal caste and class system approves. American incest restrictions operate as laws preventing marriage of an ego to his grandparents, aunts, uncles, parents, siblings, children, nieces, nephews, and grand-children. Twenty-nine jurisdictions forbid marriage of first cousins on either the maternal or the paternal side.[11] In this society the legal minimum age at marriage is eighteen for girls, but officially given parental consent can lower it to sixteen. Some Southern states used to forbid the marriage of persons labeled "Negro" to those defined as "white" and, although the legal barrier to such unions has been declared unconstitutional by the federal govern-ment, the norms remain. Finally, many states demand a medical test of future wives and husbands to guarantee the absence of venereal disease.

Marriage is possible in American society with only the groom the bride, the clergyman or civil official, and two witnesses, but most ceremonies take place with a great deal of co-operation on the part of a larger group of people. The usual procedure calls for a gradual involvement of the actors and the audience in the ritual.

10. As late as 1953, twenty-nine states in the United States had laws against miscegenation or marriage across racial lines. See Ray E. Baber, *Marriage and the Family*, New York: McGraw-Hill, second edition, 1953.
11. *Idem.*

The boy and girl who decide upon marriage usually observe the etiquette of informing first their parents and then, or simultaneously, their closest friends. The approval of the families of orientation remains, at least ritualistically, important in this society. The larger community, composed of less intimate friends, acquaintances, and, usually, church co-members, is informed of the planned marriage through institutionalized procedures. Eight out of ten Americans have a religious ceremony involving the cooperation of the minister and church personnel and at least the tacit approval of congregation members. Social class varies the formality of the announcement as well as all stages of the ceremony, but at all levels it is considered an important event designed to change dramatically the lives of the partners. Remaining elements of the patriarchal family pattern result in greater life changes, expected and experienced, on the part of the woman than on the part of the man. This is symbolized by her dropping her former identity in title and group name—she trades the status of "Miss" for that of a married "Mrs.," leaves behind her last name, held in common with her family of orientation, and takes the name of her husband's family of orientation. Only her first name, used in primary relations, is carried by her from one stage of life into the other. The man's identity remains unchanged, as far as his symbolic title and name are concerned.[12]

Marriage as an Event

In American society, lacking official "rites de passage" by which a youth reaches adult status, marriage serves as the main transition event. As such it is composed of many incidents in which the roles of "bride" and "groom" signify the intermediary position between girl and wife, boy and husband. As an event designated to have a deep effect upon these two participants, it contains all the characteristics of any major occurrence in the life of societal members. It is like birth, graduation from school, the birth of children, and death, in that it contains: (1) a ritual composed of many incidents and segments; (2) a definition of the condition of participants "before" and "after"; (3) an identification of "typical stages"; (4) prescriptions as to the appropriate ways in which the

12. Simone de Beauvoir objects strongly to this practice. *The Second Sex*, New York: Alfred Knopf, 1953.

event and its effects are to be handled by those involved; (5) an explanation of the meaning of the event in various levels of ideological abstraction; and (6) an announcement to the community that it will, or did, happen. The title of the event, such as "marriage," camouflages its many facets. The more components that are fully developed, the greater the societal stress upon the importance of the event to the unit and to the larger society. Such evaluations are often related to the assigned importance of the participants. Weddings of the upper classes are much more complex than those of the working classes, unless subcultures stress such events. Within each ethnic community, however, the leading families feel obliged to provide more complex weddings for their offspring than do those who are not necessarily poorer, but less subject to societal attention. By the same token, weddings are an important part of the "conspicuous consumption" society, and many families go into debt to produce a large and showy wedding.

The American girl entering marriage tends to speak of it in highly idealistic terms, with special emphasis on personal relations with, and duties toward, the husband. The event is surrounded by a glow of romantic love, which functions both as a tide-over during the time when conflict is inevitable, as each learns to build a husband-wife relation, but as a detriment in future years, if absent but deemed necessary. Interestingly enough, many intimates of the bride still cry at weddings, though this emotion was more appropriate in times when she literally severed her connection with them upon entering her new husband's family. It is possible that the crying is a mild form of grief for "carefree" childhood, forming part of the "rites de passage."

There is no well-organized way by which a girl learns to be a wife, since traditional methods of training have been replaced by emphases on other areas of competence, such as preparation for economic roles away from the home. The assumption of "instant wifehood" is part of the romantic ideal of marriage, even though a few scenes of imperfection during early months are built into it.

We asked the housewives we interviewed to list past events which importantly changed their lives, and they did refer to marriage. The older they are, however, the more likely they are to forget to mention it in response to open-ended questions. Instead they combine it with a whole series of events and stress the process of becoming a mother more than that of becoming a wife.

The "interaction patterns" respondents, asked to list ten specific events of the past, are more apt to single out their own marriage. Ninety-four per cent of the women in their twenties, 97 per cent of those in their thirties, 73 per cent of those in their forties, and 80 per cent in their fifties or older at least list their own marriage, although not necessarily in the same rank of importance. Some go through a list of major events which skip marriage, but return to it when striving to complete the whole list of ten.

The definition of what entrance into marriage means for the woman varied considerably among respondents. Some perceive it as a *change in patterns of life*, without qualitative or descriptive explanation:

> Marriage has been the biggest change—women have a much more distinct change in their lives at marriage than men do. I wanted to be a nurse so badly, and I still resent my mother not letting me. As the children grow older, I find my duties at home easier and easier. I hope my husband and I stay active and do things together when the children are grown. I want the children to get married to men like their daddy and be on their own.

This thirty-four-year-old woman is definitely husband-oriented; her children are only six and eleven.

The very young often see the effect of "becoming a wife," as a *change in themselves*. One form of such change is increasing maturity. "Met my husband—I grew up a little and learned to govern myself."

> I had a happy, close family in my childhood so I know what I want for my family. I went into marriage spoiled and opinionated, and I had a great adjustment to make to a mate. I have learned to be more tolerant, patient and to expect less of myself and others.

That answer comes from a woman, aged twenty-nine, who has only one five-year-old child. She seems to have expected an automatic "happy, close family," but her way of handling reality is passive. Rather than working toward the establishment of a unit similar to the one she idealized in the past, she treats marriage as an adjustment *to* less acceptable conditions.

The concern with maturity is not surprising in this society. The discontinuity in behavior expected of a girl of twenty (the average age at marriage in America), before and after marriage, has been subject to sociological comment. The traditional bride moved into a household run by an older woman, the mother or sister of her husband, and it took years before she was granted the responsibility of making decisions or expected to behave as an adult. No new systems of training have been developed in modern America to prepare the bride for the sudden set of unshared responsibilities requiring judgment and knowledge, although the kin group which formerly helped to handle them has been removed from close contact.

While some women see "becoming a wife" as a call for new skills or demeanor—"had to learn to act like a wife" or "had to adjust to it, living with a husband, I mean"—others explain the changes in *relational* terms. Several young respondents speak of marriage having the effect of creating an object of care, although they do not necessarily agree on who is that object: "having someone take care of you" and "someone to take care of besides myself."

Consequences of the marriage event are also seen in different ways along a continuum of dependence-independence. For example, a young woman states:

> Since I have been married, I've had to adjust and make a few changes. You have to learn to share. It's different from when you're home with your brother and sister. You have to learn to give as well as take; to learn to be more independent. I don't depend on my folks as much as I used to.

She does not define her relations with her husband as a transference of dependence tendencies to him, contrary to the traditional view of the young woman. A different respondent, a thirty-five-year-old mother of four children, does feel that marriage places her in a dependent position: "Life has gone from independence to dependence. Before marriage, I did what I wanted. Now, I am dependent on my husband. In the future, I will become more and more dependent as the kids grow up and move away." The passive view of the self contained in this definition is reflected in her explanation of what she would like to change if given a choice: "I would manage my money better—we would have a home today if I had been a good manager." Certainly this view of past and present is very different from the one cited earlier, reflecting the style of life each woman led before marriage and her response to the "expanding circle" stage.

The concept of independence is often tied to that of *freedom*. The latter is also contrasted to responsibility—a quite opposite direction. Nor do housewives agree over whether marriage brings more or less freedom. "Oh, before I was married I had freedom. Could come and go as I please, had own money, wasn't tied down. Now I have to budget for the benefit of all the family." This woman identifies the need to control expenditures as the main consequence of marriage, feeling that it is tantamount to a lack of freedom. "I feel much freer than before marriage," is a directly opposite view of marriage, given by a twenty-nine-year-old mother. She adds that "when the house is paid for we will be even freer." She also says that she does not wish to change anything in her life. The interviewer asks if she would like to have the house paid for right away, "No, we are enjoying the struggle; we find it real fun," is her response. This housewife is not the only one to feel that marriage brings freedom or independence. "I have gotten married and am experiencing the greatest amount of independence that I shall ever know," states a newly married twenty-five-year-old who is working full time and maintaining an apartment. The variations in the definitions of life changes brought through marriage depend on whether the duties and rights are regarded as a burden of responsibility or an opportunity for independent action.

Another definition of the consequence of marriage is stated in terms of a *shift-of-status*. One respondent, aged twenty-two, explains: "I went from an unmarried college student to a married one. In the future I will have to resign myself to the fact that I will become a medical student widow since my husband will be in medical school and I won't see much of him." She adds, however, that she is very happy and would not change anything. A complex shift-of-status view of marriage is given by a thirty-eight-year-old housewife: "I have been four different people since I am married. (1) traveling wife; (2) career wife with husband traveling; (3) combination of mother and career with hired help; (4) just completely in home with music as a hobby. I am going back into professional music when the children are older." A task-focused status shift is expressed by a girl who seems to be pushing the role of student slowly out of its prior focal position, to be replaced by the role of wife or that of housewife: "I went from being single to married. Not only do I have the added responsibility of cleaning and doing everything myself, I also have to do things for my husband. Before I was mainly a student, now I am a wife and a student." The new role balance does not seem to be as yet stabilized in her case.

Some respondents list several events without mentioning their husbands or their relations with them. A bride of only five months limits the change she experienced to the statement: "From single to married and having a responsibility of a home." "From child to school work to homemaker. As you get older, your outlook broadens," states a twenty-five-year-old (with a toddler son), who fails to mention any social relations. "Lived in a small town, one of ten children, got more active in church affairs. In the future, more school affairs and more responsibilities. I'll slow down when the children are married." This thirty-one-year-old is married and has gone through the events of childbirth, yet these are not mentioned. "It was a big change from working girl to housewife. I guess in the future I'll just age; get older and crankier," states a respondent who has two small children. Other segments of the interview indicated that she is not unhappy, although she fails to mention her family. For example, she answers the "What would you change if you had a free choice?" question with: "Nothing, I'd like a whole lot of money, but as far as being happy or satisfied, I couldn't expect more than I have." It is surprising that she can define so much of her life without mentioning another human being.

Most often, particularly with increased years of marriage, that event is seen as simply a part of *a sequence of events*. All changes are grouped together, although several different roles have been taken up and left during the time.

> I had a very happy childhood. Marriage, until this past year when I no longer have babies, was a trial sometimes. We look forward to vacations with our children, military school for the boy. I want to keep my mind active after the children are grown—I have parents with young ideas, which is an inspiration to us.

None of these comments really speak of the relation with the husband. Marriage is considered as a condition of motherhood more than as an interpersonal exchange.

Older women mention parenthood more often than marriage, perhaps partly because the former can occur more than once. The birth of each of the first three children is frequently listed as a separate event. In American society, the first offspring is likely to come fairly soon after marriage, and memory fuses these events together.

> Since I got married, I worked first. Second, my husband went into business, children came close together, everything happened at once —on a tight budget. Now I feel comfortable and the children are older; I feel more or less a lady. In the future, we want another child or more, want more, but would settle for one. Not too much financial change—I'll be harried again.

This mother of five children, herself still in her mid-twenties, wishes only that "my husband were home more and less tied down, so that we can take a vacation."

Some of the circumstances surrounding the event of marriage produce unusual consequences which stand out in a person's memory even more than this shift itself. "I was married; I wasn't happy at first, my husband was in the army." World War II and the following "smaller" wars have complicated the process of entering into, and living within, the role of wife. A forty-seven-year-old Japanese mother of three explains her past life: "We were married during the war, and this caused great disadvantages and disorganization in our lives; but after the war things settled down." It was not the marriage, but the fact that the family had been in a relocation camp, which produced the most memorable change.[13] The settling-down process now seems complete. When asked what she would like to change, she does not refer to the past, but responds in terms of the current situation: "I don't think I would change anything, for I am very content. I might drop some of my extra activities. I might stay home more; but everything else is fine." Little reference is made here to the husband-wife relation.

Thus, the event of marriage can be seen as part of a sequence of related events, or as having definite effects upon the self in general attitudes and in relation to others. The concept of marriage covers a spectrum of changes. The details of dating, courtship, and final selection, as well as the actual ceremony, were not

13. Leonard Broom and Ruth Riemer, *Removal and Return: The Sociological Economic Effects of the War on Japanese Americans,* Berkeley: University of California Press, 1949.

spelled out by the housewives we interviewed. Being a bride was not an event which called for specific comment, even when an opportunity of listing ten separate occurrences is offered to the respondent, and this in spite of the great amount of attention this traditional role was given when it took place. The events which were listed produced major life changes, but generic terms were used for many sub-events, such as "I got married."

BEING A WIFE

The wedding ceremony officially converts the "girl" into a "married woman." It serves both as "rites de passage" and public announcement of change in status, a fact which is expected to be reflected in changes in the self. As we have seen, in American culture marriage roles are endowed with many strongly dissonant components. The romantic love ideal, on the basis of which wives and husbands are selected and tested as future mates, demands strong sentiment and a relational focus. It is idealized as the highest form of human involvement, competing only with the feelings expected of a mother toward her child. This ideal pushes into the background all other sentiments and responsibilities. Anger, with flashes of hatred, is assumed to be automatically excluded if people are "in love." Attachments to other people are deemed no longer significant. The relation is to satisfy all human needs, replacing parents, friends, colleagues, kin of all generations and both sexes, and all other social contacts of meaningful depth.

The ideal of romantic love is imperfectly grafted upon the traditional view of marriage as highly formalized, even institutionally regimented for economic and procreative purposes. Much of European tradition assumed marriage to be affectively neutral or only mildly involving sentiments of pride, loyalty, duty-fulfillment, and honor. The man was to feel that his main sentimental ties were with the consanguine or blood line. The woman was expected to shift her identity to that of her husband's family and her offspring belonged to it. Other patterns of family relations include those observed by Elizabeth Bott and other sociologists on the London scene, where neighborhood-bound, working-class wives maintain basic sentimental ties with their "mums" and sisters, and later with their daughters.[14] Husbands work and spend leisure with life-long male friends. The tight sex-segregation of their world makes close and multifaceted marriage impossible. Many other societies assume that intimacy and companionship can only be achieved within same-sex relations, often further limited to family members, although certain roles have been developed by the upper classes which negate that picture in exceptional cases. The mistress, the Greek "hetaera," the "geisha" girl, and the "salon" hostess have existed for centuries side by side with the other tradition. For the most part, the lower classes have been likely to live in a sex-segregated world.[15]

Marriage is now, however, not only procreationally functional, it is expected also to be "fun." It is envisioned as stimulating the personality, sharing activity and interest, and involving the whole self. It is also expected to push kin and past friendship relation into the background. In fact, kin are often portrayed in popular musical comedies and romantic tales as villains interfering with the progress of "true love." [16]

Another feature of romantic love marriage is that its focus is expected to be on the relation rather than on its tasks. It underplays the activities necessary for the survival of the unit, thereby conflicting not only with tradition but with other inevitable circumstances and relations. American society officially imputes total, though sudden, economic self-sufficiency to the newly married couple. Although recent studies indicate assistance to the unit from the families of orientation under the guise of gifts or services, the young husband is expected to provide economic means for the existence of himself and his family.[17] The young wife can-

14. Elizabeth Bott, *Family and Social Network,* London: Tavistock Publications, 1957; Peter Willmott and Michael Young, *Family and Class in a London Suburb,* London: Routledge and Kegan Paul, 1961; and especially Michael Young and Peter Willmott, *Family and Kinship in East London,* New York: The Free Press, 1957.

15. Joel I. Nelson, "Clique Contacts and Family Orientations" *American Sociological Review,* 31 (October 1966), 663–72.

16. The in-law is a traditional villainous figure in this society but only Evelyn Duvall has attempted a sociological analysis of them. *In-Laws: Pro and Con,* New York: Association Press, 1954.

17. Marvin B. Sussman and Lee G. Burchinal, "Parental Aid to Married Children: Implications for Family Functioning," in Farber, ed., *Kinship and Family Organization,* pp. 240–54.

not neglect duties of transforming his income from work outside of the home into the consumer goods like meals and clean clothing which enable him to continue working, being a father and a husband. She performs the role of housewife, being a father and a earner, as minimal side roles to the marital relation, although neither is supposed to select the other for the potential ability to carry them out successfully. Often these tasks interfere with the relational aspects of marriage, as when the husband has to work late or the wife must iron at night. In addition, in spite of the fact that marriage is supposed to satisfy all relational "needs," each partner must maintain contact with other human beings, contact which often leads to role conflicts. The satisfaction of all needs by any one set of relations is in itself a very difficult goal. Ideally, the role of wife encompasses not only the sub-relation of complete sexual compatibility, according to the new standards of achievement, but also the personality and affectual support which was formerly derived from many other sources. The fact that outside relations continue to be important is sometimes hidden in a marriage, or at least judged as detrimental to it, rather than as a way of diminishing some of the excess demands upon it. Husbands and wives are ideally expected to be each other's main companions, concerned with all aspects of life and feelings. They are supposed to have a very strong personal influence on each other, not only in their direct relation, but in behavior carried on outside of it. Thus, although some recognition exists that they still engage in some sex-segregated role specialization, it is expected that they will be involved at least vicariously in each other's spheres.

The possibility of a gap between the ideal of romantic love marriage and the day-by-day life of American housewives, as well as between it and more traditional views of such relations, led us to formulate several sets of questions. The "social role of housewife" interviews contained many related queries, including: "What are the roles, in order of importance, of the man of the family?" "Does the wife have a great deal of influence on her husband's job? How and Why?" and "What have been the changes in the roles of the family man in the past three generations?" The "interaction patterns" questions asked very specifically about the extent of help women received from their husbands in several main areas of family life activity. This was based on the hypothesis that variations in the level of husband involvement in home

Table 6: Percentage distributions of answers to "What are the roles, in order of importance, of the man of the family?"

Roles, in Order of Importance	Urban	Suburban	Working	Total
Breadwinner (total)	84	91	86	87
1st place	63	64	54	64
2nd place	7	12	15	10
3rd place	13	12	17	12
4th place	1	1	0	1
Father (total)	61	70	61	65
1st place	7	12	9	9
2nd place	34	43	36	38
3rd place	19	14	15	17
4th place	1	1	1	1
Husband (total)	45	47	51	46
1st place	16	13	20	14
2nd place	17	14	16	16
3rd place	11	17	13	14
4th place	1	3	2	2
Family member (total)	34	17	19	26
Home-owner or maintenance of residence (total)	13	29	12	20
Community member (total)	0	5	8	2
Duties to self (total)	9	10	3	10
Roles equal in importance	0	3	0	1
Number of respondents	323	299	100	722

maintenance reflect other changes in their relation and are the consequences of the same set of factors as her form of involvement in his occupational role.

THE RANK ORDER OF ROLES OF THE MAN OF THE FAMILY

The romantic love ideal of marriage receives a jolt when women are asked: "What are the roles, in order of importance, of the man of the family?" Even husband-oriented women tend to respond with traditional answers: His main role is that of breadwinner or provider for the family unit (see Table 6).

Eighty-four per cent of the urban housewives, 91 per cent of the suburban housewives, and 86 per cent of the working women mention the role of breadwinner, while 61, 70, and 61 per cent, respectively, mention the role of father and only 45, 47, and 51 per cent mention the role of husband. The role of man as provider is mentioned more often than is the role of woman as mother. The importance of the breadwinner function is further demonstrated by the fact that 64 per cent of the housewives put it in first place, with only 10 per cent assigning it second rank, 12 per cent third, and 2 per cent fourth. Working women, although not ignoring this function, are less likely to think of it as being of primary importance (54 per cent give it first place). This may indicate that a woman's increased economic independence, rather than contributing to family disorganization, can assist in the development of more personally oriented husband-wife relations more than the traditional financial dependence. The emphasis upon the provider function of the man of the family may be incongruous with the romantic ideal, but it indicates a realistic adjustment to life and broadens the concept of familial roles to include task orientations.[18]

Second place in the rank order of roles for men is more likely to be that of father than of husband. Most suburbanites have pre-high-school age children and thus are inclined to list obligations to children as second in importance, but the differences among the three populations are below the level of significance. Many women are beyond the honeymoon stage of marriage; this is reflected by the fact that only 14 per cent of the respondents rank the role of husband in first place. Working women are more hus-

18. Ever since the publication of Talcott Parsons and Robert F. Bales's *Family Socialization and Interaction Process,* a number of studies have tested task versus emotional specialization. See George Levinger, "Task and Social Behavior in Marriage," *Sociometry,* 27 (December 1964), 433–48; Jerold S. Heiss, "Degree of Intimacy and Male-Female Interaction," *Sociometry,* 25 (June 1962), 197–208; and Robert K. Leik, "Instrumentality and Emotionality in Family Interaction," *Sociometry,* 26 (June 1963), 131–45. My studies indicate a great range in task orientation among women, within any social role or in divergent sets of relations depending upon social class. The higher the social class and, particularly, the higher the woman's educational achievement, the less task-oriented she is and the more concerned with social relations in family and home-based roles.

band-oriented than suburban housewives, as we have seen. A major contributing factor is that many of them do not have young children and, as we shall see, other attitudinal variables are present.

Urban housewives tend more frequently than other women to generalize or combine men's obligations to both wife and children under the concept of "family." One-third of them, compared with only 17 per cent of suburban housewives, feel that the man has obligations to the family at large, beyond providing for it. Home-ownership duties are mentioned by almost a third of the suburban respondents. On the other hand, obligations to the society and to its sub-groups are not mentioned frequently, even by the middle-class suburbanites. Working women are more likely than house-wives to refer to community participation as a male role, but even here the total is only 8 per cent. No urban housewife thinks of roles outside of the home. One-tenth of the housewives add that a man has obligations to himself, but only three working women out of a hundred make such a comment. The pattern is consistent with the rank order assigned by·women to members of their own sex, as far as societal roles are concerned.

Thus, most homemakers, whether working in outside jobs or devoting themselves full time to running their houses, are deeply concerned with the husband's function as provider for the unit. The romantic love ideal also would lead to the assumption that the means by which the man earns for the family should be of great interest to a person involved in a primary, personal relation with him. Such a relation is supposed to be multileveled and personality inclusive, not segmentalized. If the occupational role is important to the man, and to the woman because of her depend-wife.
ence upon it, the ideal marriage makes its content important to the

The hypothesis of a wife's strong and direct involvement in her husband's life outside of the home is not borne out by the statements of most of the women we interviewed. Few mention any roles in the community or connections with the occupation or profession in which the man is involved. He is usually pictured as leaving the home, as "out of sight, out of mind"; frequently he is not thought of until he returns.

In spite of this over-all tendency, variations of attitudes toward the man's career are great, reflecting the educational background and the social class of the wife, as well as the type of job held by the husband.

THE WIFE'S INFLUENCE ON THE HUSBAND'S JOB

Many depictions of America contain generalizations about the strong influence the women of this society have upon their husband's career.[19] The image of the actively involved wife has permeated the ideology of the housewives and working women we interviewed. Most of them are careful to explain that, although "some women" have such influence, they themselves do not. Others state the degree of influence depends either on the job the man holds or on his personality. Over one-fourth of the 568 respondents whose answers were analyzed specifically uphold the idea that certain wives have a great deal of influence on their husband's career. Those so involved are classified as married to an "organization man," a professional, a businessman in general, or "an executive." The judgment that some women are influential reflects the social class of the speaker. Lower-class wives imagine upper-class wives as teamed up with their husbands, participating in their occupational role or influencing their career through entertainment and personal charm in business situations. The presence of such personal influence is assumed by lower-class women more frequently than it is acknowledged by those persons whom they are presumably describing. "The wife is more important than the husband in the case of executives; I hear some firms don't hire a man until they see his wife. Getting ahead is a family affair." This is a typically exaggerated interpretation of the influence of upper-class wives on their husband's career, as given by a woman who has not experienced such a relation. Many women claim that "other women" have a very strong influence: "If the job is such that a wife's place is beside her husband in front of his business associates; this is true of the executive's job"; "In some jobs she does; if a man has a professional job, her influence would be more"; "Not when he works in the factory; would be more if he were in business"; "In my case, no, because he is not a profes-

19. The most famous book devoted to this thesis is William H. Whyte's *The Organization Man*, New York: Simon and Schuster, 1956.

Table 7: Percentage distributions of answers to "Does a wife have a great deal of influence on her husband's job?" by selected groups of respondents.

Answer	Urban Housewives			Working Women	Suburban Housewives
	Negro Protestant	White Catholic	White Jewish		
Yes	60	52	48	50	
No	17	14	25	28	
Not I	4	25	17	6	
Depends on job	6	5	2	10	
Depends on man, woman	0	4	5	6	
Total	—	102	97	100	
No. of respondents	48	57	59	100	270

sional man, so I can't say anything." These statements are made from a considerable social distance, which isolates the speaker from actual cases of influence, and they are reminiscent of many an American's assumption that the country is being run by a small "power elite." [20] They include assumptions about general influence drawn from rumors of interview situations, about active participation drawn from mass communication sources, and about control over the behavior of the man himself drawn possibly from wishful role-taking.

Thus, both the forms of influence assumed to emanate from the wives of men in "other positions," and the categories of women who describe the ways a wife can influence her husband's career, are varied (see Table 7).

Among urban housewives, Jewish women are much more definite than any other group in stating that *no wife* should influence her husband's job. Many of them also disclaim their own significance in this area of the mate's life. This ethnic group is least likely to acknowledge direct or even indirect influence. Negro Protestant women are the most likely to claim that wives *do* influence their husband's job. White Catholic women feel that other wives have such an effect, but that they themselves do not. Suburbanites of any religion explain at great length occasions and forms of influence; they are also the most likely to recognize its

20. C. Wright Mills, *The Power Elite*, New York: Oxford, 1956.

existence. Working women often state that a wife cannot influence her husband in this area of life or tend to qualify their answer by saying "that depends on the job" or "that depends on the man." In general, the types of influence assumed or acknowledged to exist vary from highly directive to very indirect (see Table 8). These forms can be divided into three major types: direct involvement in the social circle of the husband's job, direct influence upon the husband himself, and indirect influence by providing a "happy home" from which he ventures out to work.

The first type, containing all forms of direct help, is explained as either assistance in task performance or relational activity. Nine women, eight of them living in the suburbs, assist their husbands in the first manner, mostly through bookkeeping or similar work which would be otherwise carried on by a paid employee. Fifty-eight respondents, all but eleven of whom are suburbanites, refer to their contribution as hostesses of colleagues or clients. "Yes, if someone needs to be entertained, my husband knows I'll always say and do the right thing, make the right impression." This woman has her function clearly in mind. A Wheaton woman is less certain what she is expected to do, although the contact was direct: "I was interviewed when he took the job; big companies do that; I must have some influence on the job, then."

The second major type of influence is on the husband himself, on his decision to undertake or continue training or a specific job, or on his manner of dealing with it.

One of the ways of personal influence is in the choice of a particular occupation:

> Yes, I absolutely had on my husband's taking the garbage job. He was studying to be a dentist when I got pregnant. He gave that up to support us better and became a line man [for the telephone company]. Then father talked him into the garbage business. Neither of us like it, but it will be his and then he can wear white shirts again. I had a great deal to do with his decision.

An opposite direction of influence is described by another woman:

> I can't think of any cases where they either do or don't; in my case I don't interfere with my husband's work at all. The only time I ever did was when he was in law school. The children were here and he was holding down a full-time job and school and almost gave it up as too hard and costly, but I told him he would be foolish to waste the time and money already put into it and told him to stick it out.

Table 8: Frequency distributions of activities describing wife's influence used by suburban and urban respondents in answer to "Does a wife have a great deal of influence on her husband's job?"

	Residence		
Form of Influence	Suburban	Urban	Total
Directly, work with	8	1	9
Entertain, be seen, socially, personal contact	47	11	58
In selection of job	10	14	24
Push him, make or break	14	5	19
Assist with decisions, help decide	9	1	10
Give opinion, advise	16	7	23
Discuss issues	24	10	34
Avoid doing things and interfering	11	3	14
Nagging, complaining	11	9	20
Add pressure, avoid, prevent,	8	3	11
Avoid pushing	4	0	4
Encourage	32	21	63
By her attitude toward his work and earnings	24	9	33
Show interest in his work	10	3	13
Listen	17	3	20
See that he goes off to work happy, relaxed	10	4	14
Provide a happy home where he can relax	35	18	53
Give him food, clothing	4	2	6
Total respondents	294	124	418

This respondent defines direct influence as an "interference" necessary only in emergency situations. Most middle-class women see themselves as more involved in the life of the husband at work than through such sex-segregated perspectives which specify the job as "*his* work."

Changes of jobs in the course of his career may also be affected by the wife. One woman explains: "In moral decisions, not technical; I had to help my husband give up a wonderfully paying job where he was asked to OK materials which were dangerous and harmful." A Hazel Crest respondent represents several others who did not want to leave old ties or their families and who convinced their husbands to turn down job offers involving moving. "I don't push my husband. In fact, I try to curb him because his ambition is so strong. I want security and my husband home, not

traveling. He has turned down several good offers because I don't
want him to take a chance."

A number of women, of all classes but reflecting the matriarchal
attitudes of older European immigrants, feel that they are "the
power behind the throne"; "I don't think I have any influence. I
don't know. I stay in the background. That way I can help and
can push him, but can stay out of the limelight outside of the
house. I'm a silent partner." She does not sound as if she is very
silent within the home. Lower-class women are particularly likely
to feel that they must "push" the man, who is pictured as inher-
ently lazy and easily satisfied with minimal jobs, in terms of pay.
"She has little influence if she is satisfied with his type of work or
pay; but if she is not satisfied then she will spur him to take some
other, better paying job," is a rather lower-middle-class position.
A lower-class statement is: "Not unless he ain't making enough
and then she can bitch at him until he does something." "If she
wants him, for example, to work on a different shift every few
months, she won't stop biting at it until he does what she proposes." Pushing a man to change his job because the pay is not
enough is a frequent definition of influence by women having a
strong concern over the breadwinning function and little interest
in the type of job involved. The staging of woman *against* man is
typical of less educated women and highest among Catholics, who
in Chicago are often immigrants or their immediate descendants.

Influence upon the work itself, through the process of assisting
in decision-making or in adjustment to its frustrating features, is
rather typical of more educated women who regard husband-wife
interaction as a two-way street and who define a job as involving
choice situations. The part played by the wife in helping her husband solve problems on the job can range from strong suggestions
to opinions, discussion, encouragement of decisions he makes, or
acting as a "sounding board." A husband-oriented woman who
sees her function in very personal terms states: "Yes, I make him
see the other point of view. He comes home dejected, I pick him
up. Every now and then I tell him to quit his job. I watch his face;
if he fights back, I know he is happy. A man must be happy at
work as well as in the home." One respondent who feels especially
competent in helping her husband explains: "Yes, by discussing
problems; my social-work background gives me special ability to
suggest ways of handling personnel," while another disclaims the

suggestion of influence: "Not a question of influence. He does consult me on a number of things and there are times when I have influenced his decisions." While some wives are afraid of encouraging the husband in risk ventures, others have a strong entrepreneurial tendency: "Yes, she encourages him to take chances when things are rough. She helps him make decisions."

Assistance in decision-making is a complicated process, often involving advice or opinions on the basis of which the other person forms his own conclusion. These are two separate forms of exchange in social interaction: advice is given by experts or specialists, opinions by anyone who has formed them. A different level of knowledge as well as a distinct aspect of social relations is implied by these two forms of decision-making help, although they are often used interchangeably: "I think so. Her opinion can sway him about the people he is working with," "Her interest in her husband's work and knowledge makes her opinion important to him," "Yes, my husband changed jobs not long ago; we discussed it together for weeks; he seems to value my ideas; does not make decisions without consulting me; although the final decision is his."

The most passive form of influence is listening or being a "sounding board." Discussion of a problem implies much more active participation of all partners in the process. "I have learned enough to discuss the job with him," states a respondent reflecting the upper-middle-class suburbanite or urbanite. North Lake or Lansing women whose husbands are in skilled or semi-skilled blue-collar occupations do not talk this way. "Encouraging him in his ventures" or "taking an interest in his problems" are responses of wives of upper-level non-clerical white-collar workers. For example, a Glenview woman states: "Yes, by proper interest, giving him a boost, if he needs it, or listen and give advice." A wife of a professional wrestler explains: "There are very few friends in my husband's work; I listen to him as if I were his friend." "I imagine a lot, in a round-about way; we talk over the big things; other than that I would not try to influence him, he is at work all day. He knows what is best; of course, if he wanted to spend a very large amount of money, that might be different." These answers indicate a multileveled involvement between husband and wife. One woman attempts to perform an additional role to that of wife, the role of professional friend, while another tries to limit herself to decisions impinging on family life style, but implies greater involvement. A much more passive level of participation is contained in the following statement: "The wife should be there to listen, be interested, be there at company picnics. It is not necessary to entertain." A more initiative stance comes from another: "Not too much, be a good listener and try to encourage him to keep his job. He likes it."

Encouragement is a major concept in the discussion of the influence a wife has on her husband's job or career, although the level of sentiment and involvement contained in even this single word varies. "His striving for advancement and over-all happiness at his job will be determined by whether or not she nags him or is not concerned with the content of the job." "Yes, she encourages him in his work; if she feels there is room for progress, she encourages." These statements define encouragement as a form of pushing. "She has a lot of psychological influence on him, in that she shows him that she appreciates and that she is satisfied with his job. If difficulties should arise on his job, she should talk things over with him and comfort him." The meaning assigned by this respondent to the role is one of almost maternal protectiveness. "A wife must give her husband confidence and encouragement. It is unwise for a wife to discourage her husband when the opportunity presents itself, when he wants to take a chance. She must give him complete faith and trust his decisions. She must never become complacent where she would disagree with him when he makes a decision." This is certainly a different view of the male than contained in most statements of lower-class women, although it does not imply a depth of mutuality or of role-taking identification. The stance is one of constant wariness, an avoidance of negative action, but not an involvement in the husband's initiative. A similar position, but one based on a rather different sentiment, is expressed by a middle-aged suburbanite: "It is up to a man if he likes his job; if he does not, he can change. She should encourage him in whatever feeling he has for himself. Just encourage; wife telling the husband to ask for a raise, that's strictly in the comics." Encouragement is here expressed as support, enlarging already present sentiments. The helping function of encouragement is seen as involvement by a college graduate: "If she does not encourage or appreciate him, he would think things did not matter; she should help him over the hump when things go bad and be happy with him when good things come."

Avoidance of certain actions on the part of the wife is differently defined as a form of influence by varied social classes. Lower-class women speak of nagging: "He has to be in a good frame of mind when he comes to work, and a nagging wife does not help." "She should try and help him and not nag him that he should get another job that pays more." The last statement explains why wives want to nag—to get their husbands to change jobs, because "the grass is greener on the other side." This recommendation is in direct opposition to the one discussed before and implies a different relation with the husband. The distinction between nagging as a contribution to family welfare and as a detriment is attempted by one respondent. "I think that she has, because she can make him happy or very unhappy with her talking or nagging and that could influence his job. A woman can push her husband and this can be good or bad for him, depending on what the situation is." Again, this is a one-way street in which the wife moves the husband. A policeman's wife cautions against "interference." "I don't, and those wives I know don't interfere with their husband's choice of work. I don't think she has any influence on his performance of the job. The danger involved in my husband's job worries me, he has caught his share of criminals already." "Some do, I never interfere, some are always after the husband to change. I feel if he likes to do the job, he should stay." Comments about interference or avoidance of nagging usually refer to projected changes in jobs rather than to relations within it.

Middle-class women also explain a wife's influence as avoidance of certain actions, but their emphasis is different. Some recommend that the wife refrain from criticizing colleagues or making the husband dissatisfied with his work. "Indirectly, if he is enthused, and she does not approve she says little; interested in what he has to say. Her attitude toward superiors and co-workers; even her frame of mind; her physical health and not complaining leave him free of mind."

The last statement in the quotation above exemplifies a form of influence the woman can exert on the man which is very different from participation in the occupation itself or exerting a direct influence upon his decisions in relation to it. This influence can be summarized as "providing a happy home," and it includes not only the atmosphere but also specific services. According to this definition, a woman influences a man's performance on the job by ensuring his physical and psychological comfort through the way she handles her own social roles. This very indirect influence avoids all involvement in what the man does. "I'm not the ambitious kind; I don't think the woman has any place in the man's work; just keep him happy and content." This woman separates the two phases of her husband's life; she will relate to him at home, but she will not have anything to do with his relations or actions outside of the roles in which she is directly involved. Many respondents, particularly of the lower three social classes, isolate themselves completely from their husband's occupational role. This is a different view of marriage from that expressed in the explanations of the other two types of influence. It is a traditionally lower-class view of the world as sex-segregated, and makes clear the relation between the two levels of involvement, direct and "happy home." Although many women claim that other wives are directly involved, while disclaiming any such influence on their own part, no respondent reverses the situation by claiming "some wives influence their husbands by making sure their home life is happy, but I entertain the clients."

"Even if she does not know what he is doing, home life is reflected in his work." Here is a strong statement of non-involvement in the husband's occupational life. "Even if she is not known by the employer, if he is happy at home, that is reflected at work," is another feature in the same position. "If he is content at home, he will do a good job at work." These are typical statements involving a clear agreement as to a stance different from that of direct participation. Sometimes it is stated in the negative, "unhappy at home, wouldn't do a good job," rather than in the positive version.

The general "happy home" definition of influence is occasionally made more specific; rather than referring to a whole life sequence, it selects a time or an activity. Maintaining a good atmosphere just before the husband leaves home for work in the morning is of special significance. Having him go out in a "good frame of mind" is important to many women, who also worry about his mood upon return. "If she sends him off mad, he takes it out at work; a wife should go along with him; should give in, if there is a disagreement; he should go off to work well-fed and happy. This "peace at any cost" attitude portrays the wife as in complete control over the situation and over her own emotions. It treats the man in a rather patronizing manner. "If he gets breakfast and no argument, he does not go off to work grumpy" and "If home life is not happy, he would be crabby and not take interest in the job; many husbands do not have anything to come home to, work late hours and drink. It is her job to plan ahead so he is more interested in the house." The respondents, most from working-class background, portray the wife as a manipulator of emotionally immature husbands who must be catered to. Individuality and freedom of interaction between two human beings are missing in such statements.

Others besides the older, lower-class respondents explain their influence in manipulative terms and their areas of control as not only the moods of husbands, but their actions and interactions. Although some respondents define the wife's influence in only servicing terms—"seeing him well-fed and dressed"; "she is influential as far as appearance"; "if she has no interest or cleaners for his clothes, no ideas on clothes and different colors, then he looks bad"—others broaden the home influence to the creation of a total environment. A doctor's wife explains at length her contribution to her husband's career:

> I waited until he finished medical school—four years; until I married him. A great deal of trouble with couples is due to the wife not knowing financial obligations. It is hard in med school. Now my primary influence is this: if he has a complicated life at home, his mind is not at ease. The wife has the obligation to leave his mind at ease so that he can give his best to work. Added with help in social contacts she should not pester him at the office or to bellyache. She must give him a chance to get together with fellows to exchange ideas [medical colleagues]; give them the right to spend time as they want. She must uphold the social ends of their obligations. The woman, if she has outside interests, does not begrudge time for her husband to have the same. Husbands should have time to go out with the boys and exchange ideas—they will appreciate home more if away from it sometimes.

This respondent is highly husband-oriented and involved in many aspects of his life. Yet, she seems to be holding back from sentimental involvement, feeling that she must control the situation in order to meet those needs which she defines her mate as having. Her statement also exemplifies the multiplicity of levels of influence on a husband's job which a wife can define as part of her interaction with him. Most respondents have a more restricted view of the flow of such influence.

A woman's definition of the type of influence a wife has on the husband in his occupation depends upon the image she has of men and of her mate in particular. Many wives do not trust their husbands to function competently in the outside world, but the lower-class woman does not involve herself in male roles and is very suspicious of that part of the world. A middle-class woman may consider her husband or men in general as clumsy in social relations and may pride herself in guiding him. A third type of wife may not understand what her husband does, but may respect his ability to do it. A fourth type of wife may attempt to understand the complexities of her husband's job, and a fifth may really become involved in its intricacies.

The more highly educated woman who has herself worked in complex organizations tends to be interested in her husband's job, its problems, and social relations. She does not separate the world into "his" and "hers" to the same extent her lower-class counterpart does and she participates, if only vicariously, in what he experiences away from home. She represents an expanding segment of American wives, one reversing past limitations of interaction between sexes and increasing the "breadth of perspectives" derived from an ability to "take the role of the other," even if he performs different roles.[21]

CHANGES IN THE ROLES OF FAMILY MEN IN THE PAST THREE GENERATIONS

Although many wives are becoming at least indirectly involved in their husband's work role, this trend is a consequence of the expansion of interpersonal relations within marriage rather than of an awareness of the sociologically relevant characteristics of such

21. "The role of the other" is a concept used by symbolic interactionists, based upon George Herbert Mead's, *Mind Self and Society*, Chicago: University of Chicago Press, 1934. It refers to the process by which a person imagines himself in the position of another individual and perceives the world through the other's frame of reference. If done accurately, role-taking enables the understanding of the other's behavior and sentiments in any situation.

occupations. Although the role of breadwinner is the one judged most important for the man of the family by the respondents, few mention this aspect of his life when asked, "What are the changes in the roles of the family man in the past three generations?" Most men are in occupations sharply differentiated from those of their grandfathers, yet neither this fact nor the changes in the occupational structure of society draw the attention of the respondents.[22] Even the seventy-one interviewees who are Negro did not "take the role of the other" to explain male role changes from the point of view of work.

There are exceptions, usually stated in personal terms. "My mother's father owned a little farm in Europe, raised everything right there. My father's father was a laborer in the mill and brought home the paycheck." This is one of the few respondents who speak of the changes in the types of occupations which men have developed, whereas the following points to the statistical distribution of jobs: "Fewer small businesses now; so more men work at large companies." [23] Many women are concerned with the effects of work on their husbands, although they come often to contradictory conclusions. Five respondents think that men's work is "easier," while six feel that "He works a lot harder now. It used to be physical. His obligations are greatly increased." "More tension in the business world; grandfather died at ninety-two, now men die at fifty of heart attacks," explains another who uses personal experience to contradict national statistics. Another comment as to men's work refers to its end result or benefit. "Work less for money" is a brief summation of one set of changes. "Things have changed in the past fifty years. Now a man has time to enjoy the fruits of his labor because he doesn't work as hard or as long for his money. Most people own their own homes by the time they are in their forties or so. My father didn't own his until he was over sixty."

The competition of men for work roles drew several comments. "Their work, their job is the biggest change. It's a competitive world now, and getting more so. There are too many people for each job," explains a fifty-one-year-old urbanite with a ninth-grade

22. Robert Dubin, *The World of Work*, Englewood Cliffs, N.J.: Prentice-Hall, 1958.

23. C. Wright Mills found this to be true. See his *White Collar*, New York: Oxford, 1951.

education. Another answers, "The hardest change is the competition in work; fifty years ago the man had no one bucking him, he had his own business; competition is a full-time job for a man today without having to meet any worries at home." Younger women speak of job opportunities, older ones of the threat from other workers.

These few comments notwithstanding, most wives who described the three-generational changes in the roles of men in occupational terms limited their interest to the way the job is related to family roles, although there was no agreement regarding the consequence of this connection. "Now he often puts business before the family," states a Wheaton woman, while eight other suburbanites conclude that "He has more interest in the family, less in work." Some respondents feel that men "Do less at home and more on the job; they don't have any time for their family," while others say that "He has more leisure time to spend home since they work less." Fourteen suburbanites and twenty urbanites point out that the man is often not the only breadwinner, so that more than one family member has to work out the relation between work and family roles.

In all, only 29 per cent of the urban and suburban housewives mention changes in the working roles of men, although almost all of the respondents feel that this is their most important obligation to the family. Most of the comments deal with personal effects of work changes rather than with work relations or tasks of the jobs themselves.

The degree of involvement in other aspects of societal life is mentioned even less often by women as a major change in the roles of men. Lack of interest in a man's participation outside of the home reflects the same lower-class tradition which minimizes female responsibility to the society. It neglects modern American life, which is heavily dependent upon the voluntaristic contributions of its members, and also the actual involvement of a high proportion of the husbands who have left the passive peasant stances of their ancestors.

Nine women speak of the modern man's involvement in outside activities without specifying what it is, and eighteen more state that his "social responsibilities" and interests in sports and hobbies have increased. Five state that men have more leisure time, without explaining what they do with it. Since women list many of their own voluntary association memberships or mention them in contrast to those of a hypothetical "grandmother," and since middle-class men belong to even more voluntary associations than do housewives, this lack of reference is striking. When the same women are asked to list associations to which their husbands actually belong, the urbanites and working women somewhat underestimate and suburbanites dramatically under-represent such participation. Even unions and professional organizations are forgotten by wives of carpenters and doctors. Women highest on the socio-economic scale report more actual memberships than the lower-class women do, but even they forget to mention most of their husbands' affiliations. Thus, not only does an obligation to belong to community groups fail to be listed as a change in the roles of most men within the past three generations, but actual membership is ignored by wives.

The largest number of responses to the question "What have been the changes in the roles of the family men in the past three generations?" concentrates on shifts in his relation to the whole family. Undoubtedly, this overwhelming emphasis has some connection with the way the question is asked. Explanations of these changes are highly divergent in sentiments and relations, although there are similarities among women of the same age and socio-economic status. Women in their twenties were interested in changes in the amount of time the man spends with his family and in the degree of help he gives in the care of children. This concentration is not surprising, because the housewife and mother roles are prominent at that age and the duties are demanding. Women in their thirties and older, however, emphasize three lines of supposed changes in the relations of men to their families. One segment simply states that he is no longer "lord and master." These respondents tend to be lower class and less educated. The mood is one of glee or hostility over the changes, which is limited to "freedom from ———" aspects. The second transitional group of respondents speak's of the democratization of relations within the family, seeing the change in authority as a rebuilding, not just a stripping-away, process. The third segment of the population, consisting mainly of more educated women with higher-class backgrounds, devotes itself to a description of the quality of the relations which are evolving. Sentiment-expressive comments, such as "closer," "more understanding," "friends with," "more interest in the family," tend to be used by these women. Throughout, whatever the age, housing, or residence, *the higher the education of the woman, the more positive her attitude in describing the change in the relations of the man to his family.*

Those women who see the change in families as a loss of power by men define the male of three generations ago as "king," "czar," "lord and master," or "ruler." They do not explain how or why man lost this status, nor do they indicate whether he has been replaced by a new figure of power. The consequence of this status drop is regarded as freedom for former "slaves." The effects on the women are usually judged to be beneficial. "Father was the boss; when he said 'step,' you asked 'how far'?" (urban, aged forty-three); "Ruler of the family went out to work, now home more and can help more" (urban, aged forty-six); "More and more away from being king" (urban, aged forty-two); "He isn't home as much and isn't the big boss anymore" (urban, aged fifty-eight); "He isn't master of all he surveys, he shares the financial responsibility of the home and is a greater part of the family scene than at an earlier stage. My father did not look at me until I was two years old" (urban, young Negro). Sometimes the comments mention a specific "other" over whom the man was ruler: "Not such a king to children; enjoys them, they enjoy him" (urban, aged thirty-eight); or "Before man owned most everything and a woman was some sort of slave to him; without getting much gratitude and help from him" (urban, aged fifty-six). These are rather grim pictures of family relations in the generalized "three generations ago."

Usually the "lord and master" statements do not imply that the woman is trying to perpetuate the feudal system by taking the man's place as the new ruler.[24] The most frequently expressed change is of a shift away from a kingdom structure. Women who do see the change in terms of "from patriarch to matriarch" hasten to add that such a transfer is not taking place in their family: "I don't think Papa wears the pants as he did at one time—this is not

24. Modern sociologists have been very interested in the distribution of authority within the family. Robert O. Blood, Jr. and Donald M. Wolfe's study of Detroit families, *Husbands and Wives,* New York: The Free Press, 1960, gave impetus to a large number of such research projects. The family sessions during the 1966 World Congress of Sociology in Evian, France, focused upon reports of similarly interested studies in a number of other countries.

applicable to my family." The authority-pants connection is a frequent and significant use of a symbol. "The general idea seems to be that he is no longer the head of the household. But it isn't so here—Daddy is still boss." There is a feeling of security in that last statement.

Although most women imply satisfaction with the loss of power by the man, some are highly hostile, seeming to wish that the position of "lord and master" be filled by "its rightful owner," either because they feel a vacuum or because they resent a perceived take-over by women. Hostility is certainly expressed in, "Trying to be pals—looks ridiculous"; "Man has lost control over children's actions"; "Men are not men anymore, they are mice."

Women concerned less with the stripping away of authority from men, and more with the relation which replaces the former one, focus upon a democratization process. The concept of "partnership" is used to describe a *rights-focused* emphasis by some women whose answers fall into this general category. "Fathers spend more time now with wives and children; are not as domineering and treat wives like partners." "His part taken away from him a little bit; is head of the house, but no longer rules; has given 50 per cent to the wife and now they work together; husband used to rule wife, today it is a partnership." These statements seem to show uncertainty about the reason the man lost half of his power to the woman.

The fifty-fifty partnership ideal portrays marriage as a formal authority structure similar to a business arrangement.[25] A less *rights-conscious* statement comes from a Lansing working-class wife. "Were too stern, expected too much; woman was slave, men more considerate now in every respect." "Men held the strings— wife did the work, she had nothing to say. Today mothers are real people." This last statement shifts identity from the role of wife— "Wife did the work"—to "Mothers are real people"—a significant transformation. Other women speak of the change as one of increased co-operation. "The man takes a more active part in the housework and in the care of the children; more adaptable to housework; went from absolute authority to more co-operation

25. Mary Merryfield devoted a number of issues of her "Talkback" in the *Chicago Tribune* in the early part of 1963 to reports on marriage contracts.

with the wife; takes more interest in the education of the child and will become more of a pal." This statement, by a woman in her twenties with small children, is still authority-focused, but much more relation-conscious than those earlier.

A number of respondents give reasons for the perceived change in man's authoritative relation to the family. Some assume it to be an inevitable consequence of the absence of the man from the home during the daytime hours. An angry explanation by a fifty-two-year-old high school graduate who is still fighting the authority battle, demanding rights rather than building a partnership, is: "Since the wife is working, the husband has sort of lost his role as head of the house. If he expects her to help earn the living, then she should be allowed as many decisions as he. He is not actually the head of the house." Other changes in the woman's personal or social roles are given as reasons. "Man has a less dominant role because of the woman's changing role, due to education." A third source of change is located in the man himself. "Men are more educated, now there is more of a partnership between a man and wife; in the past, the man had more authority in the home, now he is a partner." A very paternalistic definition comes from an Oak Lawn resident with a high school education. "They are more lenient now with wives, they give us more luxuries and try to give us better living by providing us with more conveniences." Undoubtedly, many of the other respondents would bristle at that statement.

The more educated woman is less concerned with the distribution of authority and devotes her attention more to the quality of the developing relation between man and wife or father and children. She refers to an increase in companionship and in pleasure in the sexual relation or to a decrease in the formality of interaction. "My grandparents were Pennsylvania Dutch, called each other Mr. and Mrs.," explains a Park Ridge woman who attended graduate school. The modern father is seen as having: "More interest in his children," "More time to spend with his children," and as being "More involved" with them. He is portrayed as concerned about their education, as companionate and more willing to carry the responsibility for their welfare.

More educated women usually separate relations with the wife from those with children. They see modern man as interacting individually with family members. Working-class women still feel that the "man of the family" is not fully within it, but almost external to its basic core, similar to the way some respondents describe the woman as, "Taking care of the family." The family is the unit for which one performs duties or which one controls; individuals are those with whom one has social relations, according to the distinctions made by various respondents. The male part of family life is almost inevitably portrayed in terms of authority, with the man separated from the group he controls; the female part in nurturant terms, with the woman seperated from the group she takes care of.

A fourth area of change mentioned by at least some respondents is stated in personality terms, without reference to the relations within which they are expressed. Sixty-five women describe three-generational modifications in the male personality or life style, rather than in roles or status. Eleven women state that men are now better educated; four that they live longer than before. Half of the comments (39), made mostly by older urban women, are very negative: "He has lost his male image"; "Emasculated"; "Less self-sufficient"; "More materialistic"; "Irresponsible"; "Neurotic"; "Insecure"; "Deteriorated"; these are some of the adjectives by which they describe the modern man. Those who are obviously pleased by the change use terms such as: "Thoughtful," "Kind," "Fair," "Warmer," "More understanding," "More lenient," "Not as harsh," "More recognized for his individuality." It is possible that similar forms of behavior are placed at both ends of the evaluation continuum, depending upon the vantage point.

Many more of the suburban women speak positively of the three-generational changes in men than the urbanites do. There are several reasons for this. In the first place, positive attitudes are related to education. The higher the academic training of the wife, the more positive her judgment of the male personality. This factor is related, of course, to her husband's education; and the more educated men are likely to be less traditional and particularly less harsh in their relations with their families than the less educated men. The same holds true about the prestige of occupations. In fact, class differences in husband-wife relations can be expected to result in class differences in evaluations of the male personality. The suburbanites have a higher average education and are married to more educated men than the urbanites. The second factor is age. The urban respondents are older than the

suburbanites, because of the recency of the suburban expansion
and its relation to socio-economic factors. Finally, all reports indicate that the self-selection of suburbanites and the style of life
developed among them focuses on family life.[26] Families which
regard themselves as stable and as child-oriented may be more
willing to invest money and work in house and garden. The husbands become more leisure- than work-oriented, and the leisure
tends to be companionate. Even the work of home maintenance
comes to be shared. Thus, all indications are that the American
ideal of democracy in the family gets large support from suburban
styles of living and that it is definitely connected with assimilation
away from ethnic subcultures. Women pleased about these
changes and willing to compliment their husbands are thus more
apt to be found in the newer suburbs than in the older urban
areas. The importance of the social class factor is supported by
variations in the definitions of modern males among the suburban
respondents. The lower-class North Lake wives are more negative in their descriptions of men than the more educated Park
Ridge respondents are.

The combination of factors indicates the possibility of a new
trend in male-female relations with increased urbanization, industrialization, and mass education taking place all over the
world and in the lives of recent generations. The first stage is traditional rural or lower-class urban relations, which are usually
patriarchal and harsh. Stage two involves the redistribution of
power in the family unit and is experienced by women with mixed
emotions, but mostly either glee or frustration over the inability of
the male to retain his high level of authority. The third stage is
one of insistence on "equality," "partnership," and so forth. The
final stage then becomes one of decreasing concern over authority
and increasing attempts by both partners to build a co-operative
unit utilizing to as great a degree as possible each other's unique
skills and personalities. As the relations change, so do the definitions of the opposite sex and vice versa.

26. David Riesman has particularly commented on changes in husband-
house orientation in suburban communities in "The Suburban Dislocation,"
The Annals of the American Academy of Political and Social Science, 314
(November 1957), 123–46. See also his work with Nathan Glaser and Reuel
Denney, *The Lonely Crowd*, New Haven: Yale University Press, 1950 (also
in Doubleday Anchor Books in 1956).

THE DIVISION OF LABOR
AND HUSBAND'S HELP IN THE HOME

An area of change in the roles of the husband which suburban housewives tend to stress in his "help with," or sharing of, home-maintaining functions. Many other observers of the American scene have characterized changes in husband-wife relations in terms of the increase of man's activity in home tasks. In middle-class homes, this change is partly accounted for by the increasing scarcity of domestic servants, accompanied by a large number of household objects and higher standards for their maintenance. The democratization of relations and the increased leisure of men are held partially accountable for the expansion of their help in this area. The change goes very deep and has been the object of much comment, both positive and negative, as an unwelcome blurring of sexual ego identities. Traditionally white-collar men have not done physical work in the home, but their involvement and its definition seem to have been modified. One of the women described changes in one of her neighbors, a doctor who was a refugee from a very class-conscious European society. When he and his wife first moved into their new home, he would never appear outside of the house without a white shirt, and his contribution to the home involved organization and direction of whatever labor he could commandeer, including his wife's. Gradually, the neighbor reported, he started doing more and more of the work himself. She then pointed out the window to show the interviewer the now-Americanized husband, mowing his own lawn in a bathing suit.

Home and garden ownership in American society takes on many traditional upper-class styles, but without the servants which formerly made them possible. The work is divided among the wife, her husband, and various professional service men. Children do not take much responsibility, except when a growing boy takes over his father's task of mowing the lawn or a daughter starts doing the dishes. Sometimes work traditionally performed by male servants is now performed by the man of the house: caring for the lawn, repairing, digging, etc. On the other hand, the husband does not polish the silver, although this was the butler's job. Nor is he responsible in most homes for marketing, which was often part of that servant's task. The man in many families is responsible for the grass, the woman for the flowers.[27] Although 289 suburban housewives did make 136 references to their husband's responsibility for outside greenery, these are almost exclusively limited to grass.

The division of previous servant tasks into sex-appropriate domains is based upon an often unpredictable mixture of criteria. According to many respondents, women are judged "weaker," so men handle the tasks considered "heavy." A second set of criteria used for the new division of labor within the home is "logic." That is, respondents explain that they handle finances or that their husbands perform certain tasks as a "natural" or "logical" function. A woman "naturally" must do most of the tasks involved in day-by-day care of the children, "Because my husband travels and he just isn't home." The husband does most of the marketing or they share this task, "Because I don't have the car during the week." However, many aspects of the division are not defended by criteria of either strength or logic, and it is often difficult to determine their origins. Washing clothing and washing dishes seem to be traditionally "women's work"; male servants and husbands are not connected with them. Yet, in many households, sharing the task of doing the dishes has become a big "togetherness" activity. Cooking has been done by both men and women in past centuries, and professional chefs are almost always men. Outdoor barbecuing seems to be a male activity; indoor cooking a female task. Men often prepare their specialties, although American husbands reputedly "leave the kitchen a mess."

The new division of work does not seem to be sufficiently comprehensive to prevent constant references to "maids," "cleaning women," and other services as well as to conflicts over the various provinces of labor.

The 205 women who answered the "interaction patterns" questionnaire were asked specific questions about the help given by others in cooking meals, washing, drying, and putting away the dishes; cleaning and straightening the house; laundry; shopping; care of the children; handling of money; and other jobs to be listed by them (see Table 9). In order to relate the areas and the activities in which help comes from the husband to the responsi-

27. Nero Wolfe, however, a character in a mystery series by Rex Stout, is a hot-house flower power; and there are men's garden clubs.

bilities of the woman and to other sources of assistance, a complex "level of responsibility" format was used.

Only 46 of the 205 interviewees do all the cooking in their homes, with no help from their husbands, and an additional 13 get help from people other than their husbands. Some of the thirteen are widowed or divorced. Ten per cent of the women who feel responsible for the cooking get regular help from their husbands. Twenty-eight per cent of the males undertake the major consequence of lack of servants and disappearance of kin from the conjugal home: help in emergencies, with 19 per cent taking over completely and 7 per cent assisting them, although none help regularly. All in all, 41 per cent of the husbands help their wives with cooking in some way. An almost equal proportion of men give some help in handling dishes after meals. Five per cent less of the women do the dishes alone than cook, not so much because more men help, but because of greater assistance from others.

Forty-seven per cent of the women state that their husbands never help in household tasks such as making beds, straightening, or dusting; and an additional 14 per cent refer to help from others than the husband. Thirty-nine per cent specify some assistance from the spouse, with 11 per cent claiming it to be a regular feature and 18 per cent as an emergency pattern. Laundry and other forms of clothing care draw help from 34 per cent of the husbands, 19 per cent of whom assist only in emergencies. Fifteen per cent carry out the needed actions as a couple, often by dropping off soiled things at professional services.

Modern home maintenance requires a great deal of purchasing and the use of many services in locations owned by others. The frequency of use will be discussed in the following section; of interest here is the amount of participation by husbands in this process. Sixty-four per cent of the women receive assistance with shopping from their husbands, while 33 per cent of the men take no responsibility for it. Thus, this is the area of the greatest amount of housekeeping help from husbands. Four per cent of the men do all the shopping and 12 per cent help always or often. An additional 20 per cent of the men go together with their wives, and 19 per cent assist or take over only in emergencies. In all, two-thirds of the men of the family assist in making the purchases needed to run the house, and only 27 per cent of the women carry on this function by themselves.

Table 9: Percentage distributions of persons giving designated levels of help to the "interaction patterns" interviewees, by activity area and helper.

Frequency by Activity	Husband	Child	Relative	Friend	Neighbor
Cook the Meals					
Their responsibility, not mine	0	0	0	0	0
Mine, they help often, always	10	14	2	1	0
Both do, each part of it	1	2	0	0	0
Take turns, shift	0	1	1	0	0
Do it together	0	0	0	0	0
They help in emergencies	7	3	5	2	2
Mine usually, they do in emergency	19	10	13	7	9
Usually help, emergency take over	2	3	1	1	1
I do it, no help	46	44	50	59	59
Not I, not they, other, no response	13	22	26	30	30
Total	98	99	98	100	101
Wash, Dry, Put Away Dishes					
Their responsibility, not mine	0	4	1	0	0
Mine, they help often, always	10	12	2	0	0
Both do, each part of it	2	3	2	0	0
Take turns, shift	1	3	1	0	0
Do it together	3	1	0	0	0
They help in emergencies	7	5	5	4	4
Mine usually, they do in emergency	16	10	9	7	6
Usually help, emergency take over	2	4	2	0	0
I do it, no help	41	35	46	56	56
Not I, not they, other, no response	16	23	30	32	33
Total	98	100	98	99	99

Beds, Straighten, Clean House

Their responsibility, not mine	0	3	1	0	0
Mine, they help often, always	11	18	1	0	1
Both do, each part of it	3	5	2	0	0
Take turns, shift	1	1	0	0	0
Do it together	3	2	0	0	0
They help in emergencies	3	1	4	2	1
Mine usually, they do in emergency	15	6	8	6	5
Usually help, emergency take over	2	4	0	0	0
I do it, no help	47	34	49	56	56
Not I, not they, other, no response	14	25	33	35	37
Total	99	99	98	99	100

Laundry, Care of Clothes

Their responsibility, not mine	0	1	1	0	0
Mine, they help often, always	5	7	1	0	0
Both do, each part of it	4	2	1	0	0
Take turns, shift	1	0	0	0	0
Do it together	5	3	0	0	0
They help in emergencies	2	2	2	1	0
Mine usually, they do in emergency	15	9	10	4	4
Usually help, emergency take over	2	2	1	0	0
I do it, no help	49	43	48	57	57
Not I, not they, other, no response	16	29	34	38	38
Total	99	98	98	100	99

Table 9 Cont'd: Percentage distributions of persons giving designated levels of help to the "interaction patterns" interviewees, by activity area and helper.

Frequency by Activity	Husband	Child	Relative	Friend	Neighbor
Shop for Food, Other					
Their responsibility, not mine	4	0	0	0	0
Mine, they help often, always	12	10	3	1	0
Both do, each do part of it	6	0	0	0	0
Take turns, shift	1	5	1	0	0
Do it together	20	5	1	0	0
They help in emergencies	5	6	4	4	5
Mine usually, they do in emergency	14	12	10	7	8
Usually help, emergency take over	2	2	1	0	0
I do it, no help	27	40	50	56	56
Not I, not they, other, no response	9	24	28	31	31
Total	100	99	98	99	100
Care of Children, Feed, Bed					
Their responsibility, not mine	2	6	1	0	0
Mine, they help often, always	14	5	2	1	1
Both do, each do part of it	6	0	1	0	0
Take turns, shift	2	1	0	0	0
Do it together	4	1	0	0	0
They help in emergencies	4	1	5	4	5
Mine usually, they do in emergency	6	4	8	5	5
Usually help, emergency take over	2	3	2	1	0
I do it, no help	19	31	30	34	34
Not I, not they, other, no response	40	47	51	54	53
Total	99	98	100	99	98

Care of Money, Bills, Finances					
Their responsibility, not mine	37	0	0	0	0
Mine, they help often, always	3	0	0	0	0
Both do, each part of it	14	2	1	0	0
Take turns, shift	2	0	0	0	0
Do it together	15	2	1	0	0
They help in emergencies	0	2	0	0	0
Mine usually, they do in emergency	2	2	3	3	3
Usually help, emergency take over	0	0	0	0	0
I do it, no help	21	44	45	46	46
Not I, not they, other, no response	5	48	48	51	51
Total	99	99	98	100	100

Other Help, Family Only	Garden	Heavy Cleaning
Their responsibility, not mine	12	5
Mine, they help often, always	4	7
Both do, each part of it	8	10
Take turns, shift	2	1
Do it together	8	14
They help in emergencies	4	4
Mine usually, they do in emergency	3	1
Usually help, emergency take over	0	15
I do it, no help	11	38
Not I, not they, other, no response	52	
Total	100	99

Total No. of Respondents 205

Child care patterns within the last several decades have changed dramatically. Upper-class European families often utilized nurses, governesses, and tutors responsible for much, if not most, of the care of offspring. Older children and kinfolk have provided the mother with assistance in many societies, and sometimes they take over total responsibility for the newborn. The development of the formal education of post-babyhood children has removed a former source of help at home, as the modern school system does not allow a mother to keep her older children away just to care for younger offspring. In spite of these trends removing servants, adult kinfolk, and older children as major sources of help in child care, only 19 per cent of the "interaction patterns" interviewees feel that they have no assistance in the care of their offspring. The 40 per cent who are listed in the "Not I, someone else" category are women who have no children at all or whose families are already grown and do not require care, as evidenced by the other figures. Thirty-nine per cent of the husbands, or 66 per cent of those who have young children needing care, assist in the process. Only 2 per cent take over the whole responsibility, and these four fathers are divorced and have custody of the child. Fourteen per cent of the fathers help always, but 10 per cent only contribute during emergencies.

The whole area of "help" or "help with" needs greater research. Additional clues come from the suburban participants in the "social role of housewife" interview who mention help in child care in answer to the general question. They refer to this area of male assistance more frequently than any others do, 75 per cent out of the 299 making such comments. This fact is not surprising, since they have pre-high-school age youngsters in the home. Twenty-seven per cent of the women answer generally without reference to a specific activity; 13 per cent list baby-sitting, 11 per cent "putting to bed," 8 per cent "bathing," 5 per cent "feeding," 4 per cent "playing with," and 2 per cent "dressing." An additional 17 per cent state that the husband helps in these areas "if necessary." We assume that more than thirteen fathers actually play with their children, but that these responses indicate situations in which the women feel husbands are being a *help to them* in their role of mother. If the father keeps the child happy by playing with it in order that the wife finish another task, or even relax, he is doing it in order to assist her. This is different from playing with the child as a father, or simply because he enjoys it.

The fact that so many respondents feel that their husbands "help with the children" is significant, even when stated as a form of praise. It suggests that child care is not part of the role of father and is done as a favor to the wife rather than being a source of enjoyable interaction.

Another area of husband-wife interaction within the family involves the handling of finances. Of course, when all the property was passed on in the male line, women rarely, if ever, were allowed the management. The disability was often officially tied to a status of legal minority. However, this pattern has changed considerably. When asked in detail the degree of responsibility in this area, only 37 per cent of the women explain that this is the husband's province, and 21 per cent that it is theirs with no help from others. The remaining 37 per cent handle money, bills, and other expenditures as a joint project, 15 per cent doing it together, 14 per cent having a division of labor, and the rest a variety of systems. The answers of suburban housewives to the question "What are the financial rights and obligations set up in your family?" indicate a higher proportion of women handling money. Forty-one per cent of the 299 respondents consider payment of bills and handling of money to be their responsibility, while only 27 per cent feel it is entirely their husband's. The matter is handled through joint checking accounts or other common arrangements in the remaining families. Twenty-four per cent of the women explain that they plan or discuss all large expenditures, 21 per cent that both partners have a free use of the money in the bank account. Sixteen per cent mention specifically that they do not have a budget, another 16 per cent that they do. Seven per cent of the husbands are defined as being on an "allowance."

A further analysis of the relation between financial responsibility within a family and the income which is to be handled indicates a hypothesis needing further testing, but having some support outside of these studies: the higher the income and the more of it which is derived from "entrepreneurial" or "self-employment" sources, the more likely the husband is to manage it. In such cases, the wife is put on an allowance to cover specified areas of expenditure. Almost half of the sixty-one women whose family income is over $10,000 report that the husband manages the money, while only one-third of the wives state that they do so alone. The relation between a high income and male control is not too surprising, since it requires investment outside of the home. When the paycheck is at the level of bare necessities—whatever that may be defined as being by the family in question—so that most of it goes for steady expenditures such as housing, food, clothing, and children's needs, the woman takes care of these needs. Often women who are receiving an allowance list the things it must cover. Less frequently they tell what expenditures fall into the province of the husband.

Some respondents explain the reasons for the financial arrangement in their families. A Skokie woman who is in charge of the $26,000 her husband earns states that "Frequently the reason for the wife's handling of money is the fact that the wife has worked and is therefore experienced in handling of money." A Hazel Crest wife says apologetically that her husband asked her to handle the finances, and a lower-class North Lake woman resentfully declares that she *has* to handle it, although "It should be fifty-fifty." Another North Lake resident is bitter because she never "gets" enough money to "feed and clothe my family," as if this were a problem of distribution rather than of income, which totals less than $5000. Other respondents generally see income management as a function requiring a "natural" division of labor, although there is quite a range in what is defined as natural.

A Special Case of Husband-Wife Relations: The Black Marriage

Both old and new tendencies in marital relations are often embodied in certain population sub-categories which face unique cultural and life situations. For example, lower-class Catholic women more frequently express hostile sentiments toward men in general or their own husbands than any other group does. Lower-class black women come close in frequency of hostility but, in spite of family disorganization indices, they are second to the Catholic respondents of the same class. The most complex and creatively interactive definition of husband-wife relations in this whole set of interviews came from a middle-class Negro woman.

The responses to the "social role of housewife" interviews indicate that some features of urban Negro populations need special comment. Much of the current sociological and related literature dealing with lower-class patterns focuses on "the culture of poverty" and relates specifically or by indirection to those who now live in the ghetto areas of the inner city, the blacks.[28] Many of the family-related comments elicited by this study point to a basic difference between this segment of the Negro population and its white counterpart.

Urban ghetto, near-ghetto, and transitional neighborhood life incorporates a great deal of institutionalized hostility among family members, along both generational and sexual lines. Lower-class attitudes and patterns of action brought to the city from other areas combine hostilities produced by life in disorganizing neighborhoods with negative feelings for past and present social relations. This frustration is accentuated by knowledge of other styles and conditions and is turned to hostility against spouse, parent, even child. Open expressions of such feelings are societally and locally tolerated, allowed, and uncontrolled; the rewards for sublimation are often dim; and middle-class sanctions favoring self-control of temper are absent. The life of the underprivileged worker is precarious, and the world is experienced as a dangerous place, filled with personal tragedy in the form of death, desertion, and victimization. White working-class women also perceive the world negatively. They consider themselves lucky if their husbands are "good to them," do not use physical violence, and bring home the paycheck.[29] They did not really expect to be so fortunate, however, and they passively wait for the next blow from "outside" or from the family.

Lower-class white women in Chicago come from immigrant Catholic families, being first or unsuccessful second-generation members of ethnic minority groups. Many of the women we inter-

28. As many observers have noted, there are very few good studies of the Negro community. The most controversial has been Daniel Patrick Moynihan's *The Negro Family: The Case for National Action*, Cambridge, Mass.: The M.I.T. Press, 1967, as mentioned by Lee Rainwater and William L. Yancey in "Black Families and the White House," *Trans-ACTION*, 3 (July–August 1966), 6–11 and 48–53. A review of past literature is contained in Jessie Bernard's *Marriage and Family Among Negroes*, Englewood Cliffs, N.J.: Prentice-Hall, 1966.

29. One of the best descriptions of lower-class marital relations is contained in Mirra Komarovsky's *Blue Collar Marriage*, New York: Random House, 1962.

viewed are in this category, and their world definitions correspond
to this general picture. Middle-class Catholic women use middle-
class definitions of the social role of wife, as do middle-class
blacks. The attitudinal package is not always perfectly integrated.
For example, two North Lake women who have moved somewhat
up the socio-economic ladder nevertheless state: "Perhaps I
would be better off if I had not married; several women in the
family who never married are much better off than I; my husband's very temperamental; works too hard, too easily aggra-
vated." Asked what she would change in her life, another responded: "Make 'daddy' different, have him finish what he starts.
I enjoy the kids so much; my husband does not bother with them
at all; I feel he is missing so much."

The comments of black women, at the bottom of the class ladder and even in the lower-middle class, are similar but with a dis-
tinctive flavor, as is evident from the sixty-two interviews taken
from the total group for separate analysis. Thirty-one of them are
with persons employed full time and an equal number with housewives generally matching in age. The interviews themselves had
been conducted by black Roosevelt University students, using a
personal referral system to increase rapport. However, several of
the interviews with lower-class women had to be conducted by
non-students, because black students are highly middle class in
their value orientation and this fact interferred with their rapport
in some cases. The interviews represent those with and those without college experience.

The thirty-two who have some higher education are not statis-
tically representative of the Chicago black population, which is
heavily weighted to the bottom of the socio-economic ladder due
to recent migration from the South. They were chosen because
they represent the middle-class segment of the population, a
newly expanding group which is trying to work out new patterns
of husband-wife relations.

One of the unusual facts of the Negro community comes out
when the educational achievement of wives and their husbands
is tabulated; that is, the lack of status crystallization, which
means dissimilarity of rank between husband and wife (see Table
10). Couple non-crystallization is frequent, particularly of black
working women, half of whom have more schooling than their

Table 10: Number of black respondents and their husbands having designated years of completed schooling, by working status.

| | Sex and Working Status of the Wife | | | | | |
| | Full-Time Housewives | | Working Women | | Total | |
Education	Self	Husband	Self	Husband	Self	Husband
Less than 8th grade	3	1	0	2	3	3
8th grade	2	3	1	2	3	5
9 to 11 grades	4	5	3	4	7	9
12 finished	5	7	12	8	17	15
Total, 12 or less	14	16	16	16	30	32
13 to 15	11	8	7	7	18	15
16, finished college	3	3	3	2	6	5
Graduate work	3	4	5	5	8	9
No response				1		1
Total	31	31	31	31	62	62

Educational crystallization of the marital unit:

Wife has more education than husband	= 14	Wife has more education than husband	= 16
Husband has more education than wife	= 9	Husband has more	= 10
Both have equal education	= 8	Education equal	= 4
		Husband education not given	= 1

husbands, but twice as many non-workers do not surpass their husbands. Four patterns are represented: (1) traditionally crystallized, with both husband and wife without much education and falling generally within the lower class; (2) non-crystallized, with the wife having a higher educational status than the husband; (3) non-crystallized, with the husband reaching a level above his wife; (4) crystallized, in high levels of achievement, a pattern still rare among the women we interviewed.

Within the white society, generational upward mobility of descendants of farmers and immigrants is usually accomplished through the achievements of the husband. Often he ascends by increasing his educational level beyond that of his parents. Proportionally few white marriages contain a wife with more education than the husband. In the Negro community this is much more common: more women within the mobile portion of this population are better educated than their husbands. This sharp contrast to the white population and to the patriarchally based dominant culture makes interaction between sexes often difficult. Matriarchal traditions of pre- and post-slavery are accentuated by educational and occupational factors favoring women, in the same way as they themselves are buttressed by asymmetrical discrimination against black men and women: poverty which does not allow female withdrawal from the labor market, the scarcity of educational opportunities, and the difficulty in finding appropriate employment for educated males in comparison with females with the same schooling.

The difference in marital status-matching in the black and white communities can be compared with the case of the Poles in America. Thomas and Znaniecki found them undergoing family conflict and disorganization during the first decades of their immigration as a result of culture dissonance and of ghetto life in a society in which they had minority status and a deviant family pattern.[30] Most of the family conflict occurred between two generations: the Polish-cultured parent and his children who were learning American values which disparaged that heritage. Husband-wife relations, tense as they may have been, did not lead to a desire for withdrawal from the family unit on the part of the male nor domination in other than traditional ways by the female. There are several historical factors contributing to the continued male domination of the Polish family in America, which are very divergent from those of the black community. In the first place, traditional Polish culture was highly patriarchal and monogamous. The circumstances of migration and settlement in the new country tended to accentuate the importance of all aspects of the heritage, and the ability of this group to create an ethnic community facilitated its preservation. Acculturation was experienced by the different members of a Polish-American family variously, and in a manner quite divergent from that faced by the Negro families. The Polish male went out into American economic organizations faster than the woman; he got the better paying job, leaving the home each day to become more rapidly acculturated than the female. The children attended schools which, even when they were run by teachers educated in Poland and determined to re-

30. W. I. Thomas and Florian W. Znaniecki, *The Polish Peasant in Europe and America*, New York: Alfred Knopf, 1918–19.

produce its culture, were unable to do so in the new environment. The women were the ones who remained dependent on the men for their status in the community and in the society at large, and they had no emotional support from their offspring of either sex. These facts are not true of black women. As many sociologists have pointed out, the Negro women of all but the top social classes had greater opportunity for contact with the dominant culture for acculturation and for higher status in that part of society than had her male equivalent, who has been intentionally kept in isolated and subservient positions in relation to the white male and female, with an insurmountable social distance between him and the whites of both sexes.

Poles in America surrounded the female with a set of strong sanctions against leaving the male through divorce or separation. Catholicism reinforced this, as did the patriarchal family structure and the isolation of each woman from all but her kin and female friends. As a result, lower-class hostility against the social system developed and reinforced the traditional anti-male attitudes of peasant life. Some of the Polish-American women we interviewed contributed to the hostile scores on the subject of men and marriage which we have described as traits of lower-class Catholic women.

The black community has a different history of marital relations. Slavery destroyed many of the cultural norms which made marriage stable within various African nations and tribes. Matriarchal loyalty and authority became the only feasible means of maintaining family continuity and protecting the young. During slavery women were more likely to be accepted into closer social distance by the dominant society than men. In the years since the Emancipation Proclamation the various social structures and behavior patterns of American society have continued to discriminate against the black male to a much greater extent than against the female, and poverty increased the probability of the woman's working outside the home. Much of the behavior of the Negro woman thus went against the dominant culture's values. The black community, however, has become increasingly heterogeneous, with regionally and vocationally specialized mobility lines; its great range of educational, occupational, and life-style achievements is reflected in a lack of consistency in the definitions of family roles.

Lower-class black women express hostility toward men, but not because of authoritarian behavior, which is often the cause of bitterness among whites. Rather, they complain that husbands do not take enough responsibility for providing money and help in the home, that they make it necessary for the woman to work, and that they are sexually promiscuous. Unaware of the social and socio-psychological justifications for unemployment among black men, lower-class black women simply place the blame for all their problems upon the other sex: "They don't care to work and share the responsibility with the wife and mother"; "He has gotten lazier over the last three generations"; "Men just think women are work horses"; "Want women to work for them. Men these days don't like wives, they go from woman to woman. Men these days aren't satisfied at home." One respondent, when asked if her husband helped in the house, said: "That thing doesn't do anything in here."

A high proportion of the black women work outside of the home, though they do not agree about the value of such behavior. Lower-class women are very likely to feel that they are working only because the man does not want to work or because he does not bring in enough money. Many did add that their own contribution should result in greater rights within the home. One of the respondents, a woman in her thirties, would, if she had had a free choice, never have gotten married. She objects to using her own paycheck to "buy the groceries and pay our whole family bills," and explains that "My mother worked hard, but she did not have to work to pay bills." The whole interview was filled with resentment and anger.

Another woman seems surprised that she has survived the process. She lists as a source of satisfaction: "Seeing the job is well done, such as seeing children grown and that I and my husband are still together." She explains her past as follows: "I have had to make adjustments that I didn't expect." An equally unenthusiastic definition of life is contained in several comments by a woman married twenty-seven years: "I have been adjusting to my mate. As long as you are married there are always changes of some kind. Your values and the things you want in life change." This statement sounds very developmental but, when asked if she leads the type of life she visualized as a teenager, she replied: "No, I thought of magazine love with my husband and children, and that life would be wonderful. I was shocked when I finally realized 'this is it,' that this would be my mode of living."

Many statements imply unfairness, such as that women "Shouldn't have to work"; that they "Should not be asked to work, they should be at home"; and that the combination of job and home duties results in a situation where "Everything falls on the shoulders of the modern woman." A twenty-nine-year-old has her own explanation for the disintegration of husband-wife relations: "I think that women are getting less respect. They say it's because women are competing with men in jobs, but I don't think that's the reason. Men have been told the ratio is 2:1 in favor of women, and I think this makes men cocky." She feels that the male is making unreasonable demands and not meeting marital obligations because he knows that he can always find another woman. Lee Rainwater and his associates found the lower-class female desired to keep her husband, but was fearful about accomplishing this and rather powerless in controlling his behavior.[31] This feeling was evident in many of our interviews.

Yet, a woman's contribution to the family income is expected to bring power. A young housewife, who wants to go to work but feels that she cannot because of a small child, is very bitter of the gap she experiences between her ideal of marriage and its actuality. In answering the questions contrasting the "modern woman" to "her grandmother," she states: "I think in my grandmother's day she was more humble and not as independent as you find them today. They have more jobs, more of an income, more responsibilities which the husband expects of them, and I think when you really boil it down, the women of today make more of the decisions in the home." She feels a lack of such an equality in her own home because of the attitude of her husband, who recently returned from a stint in the armed forces. "He is inconsiderate, quick-tempered about my personality. Around the children he thinks I'm clumsy and he criticizes. He is too observant and much too quick." She adds: "Since his return home from the army, he spends his time around his friends. I do not see much of him." Implied throughout the interview is the conviction that she might have more power over his actions and attitudes if she were working.

31. Lee Rainwater, Richard Coleman, and Gerald Handel describe such women in *Workingman's Wife,* New York: Oceana Publications, 1959.

Another full-time housewife feels that only working women have the equality which she wants. When asked for a contrast to the role of the grandmother, she said: "Because the modern woman is more independent, financially and emotionally, and she desires independence, her roles are conflicting. At home with the family she is subject to the mother and wife role; outside of the home, she must assert independence." This picture of familial roles does not contain independence as part of life for family women. Independence is believed to exist only outside the home. Conflict in a wife's life is explained by this woman in other statements: "A husband tends to underestimate the wife role, because I'm not working. If working, you can work on a more equal basis with your husband." The shift from generalizing about modern woman to one's own position is frequent in many interviews. In another place this respondent criticizes black women as not being trained for the role of housewife: "No, particularly among blacks, because money is so important. A woman is asked 'How much do you make?' before she is asked to be married. Inadequacy of mothers today is due to their little orientation in the home themselves, so they can't train anyone." This statement bridges the problems of several generations. If given the job of editor of the woman's section of a newspaper, this twenty-year-old wife would include writing about "Ways to handle her husband; ways to make the husband more husbandly." The lower-class background of her life is expressed in the way she disagrees with her friends: "Most of my friends are modern, thinking in terms of their privileges. They believe in retaining more of their single independence, which my husband doesn't believe. They believe it's OK to have other fellows in." Thus, this young married woman feels constrained in her life, wishing by implication to be "more modern" and to have more authority, independence, and power in her marriage. She assumes that working and having her own money would provide her with such freedom.

The more educated, lower-middle-class or middle-class woman understands much better the problems growing out of the life patterns of the Negro in urban areas, including her own feelings about "equality." A twenty-seven-year-old church pianist, with relatively little education, explains some of the difficulties of the modern wife in answers contrasting her to a hypothetical grandmother: "Women in grandmother's time made everything they needed. Their ideas were different. The outside was a man's world, the home was a woman's world. Today, we don't know where we belong. It makes us feel equal to men. This is confusing, as men don't really accept women in this role and we don't know where we stand." Roles of the past are viewed as ideally clear-cut; those of the present as confused. This woman defines the past as do many other women—in a patriarchal tradition. It may be that, although the sociologists studying this population feel that it has been matriarchal for many generations, the ideology by which its members define the world is one of patriarchal control. Black women are constantly talking about equality with men, as if their present and past relations were ones of subordinate position to the members of the opposite sex. The same women define the modern female as having problems in family roles owing to the fact that: "She has guilt because she has to work. The husband doesn't like to have his wife working and this creates frustrations. A woman can become frustrated by not being able to stop work when she wants. Grandmother did not have to work." The reason women work is not analyzed in this answer but it is seen as creating strain for the person and difficulties in marital relations. Its personal relevance is evident, since this working wife mentions conflict with her spouse several times in the interview. She hopes that, in the future, "As I become more accustomed to living with someone, I will be able to accept someone else's ideas." She has been married three and a half years. "On TV, we see the wife dressed for her husband, and this gives the husband the idea that his wife should do the same, but the woman has so much to do that she doesn't have the time. Conflicts can be brought about with conflicting interests." She is, in addition to working and being a wife, the mother of a small child. The feeling of underlying frustration is summarized in the way this woman explains the difference between her ideas on the woman's role and those of her parents: "They believe that it is a woman's role to help and encourage the man, but I feel it is very important for the man to encourage the wife all he can in his role, as well as she encouraging him. Men have to accept women as equals in all fields."

The conclusion that equality may not be a simple solution to all problems is expressed by another respondent (housewife): "Modern woman can make decisions in the home and regarding the family equally with her husband. Her relationship with the family is more or less on an equal basis with her husband. In grandmother's time, the woman's role was in the home. I believe she was more honored and cherished by the family than the woman of today." The problems of equality are explained in answer to the question: "Is the modern woman's life more satisfying than her grandmother's?" "Yes and no. Women wanted equality with men, but I believe they wanted it more outside of the home than within. I believe they are finding it difficult to be on an equal basis without and submissive within. I think women want to look up to their husbands, but they are having problems." In predicting the role of women in "our children's generation," this housewife, expressing middle-class values, states: "I think her role will become more complex. I believe more will be expected of her. However, I do believe she will be able to make a better adjustment than we have. Our change was a bit too rapid and drastic."

Another respondent who has a middle-class level of education is aware of the same type of problem arising from changes in the life of the Negro wife. Asked if women are expected to perform conflicting roles, she states: "Definitely. She is expected to be aggressive outside of the house and bring in as much money as possible; but as soon as she gets food in the house, she is supposed to be submissive to her husband. She is expected to be self-sacrificing to the needs of her family, but self-centered in developing her own personality to the greatest extent." She realizes that the male is also experiencing role strain: "He has more pressure to succeed and to go to greater heights now. He is also losing his place as the head of the household for various reasons, the main one being the working wife."

The predominant interest of middle-class black women, and even of those on their way up, focuses on equality in male-female relations. It is justified by the fact that women perform competently in employment roles outside of the home and thus help to maintain it. These respondents imply greater solidarity in their marriages and less passive, though hostile, helplessness over their inability to control the male than is true of lower-class black or white women. Comments of middle-class black women are similar to those of middle-class whites, except that they often show deeper insight into relational dynamics. It is possible that the discrimination against this social race has made the black wife more insightful about social relations and the strains in her own roles than dominant group women are. One of the most discerning explanations of the meaning of being a wife in a modern urban black community is given by a twenty-three-year-old who sees its main difficulty as follows: "Dividing each thing into its proper place and trying to be able to give your man the type of warmth or consolation he needs when he feels that he is not being treated fairly outside of the home." She explains this in greater detail in answer to the questions comparing the life of the modern woman to that of her grandmother. "The modern woman, particularly the black woman, is different from her grandmother in that she is not as dependent on her husband and more opportunities are open to her. However, in comparison to the age in which they lived, limitations are imposed on both. The modern black woman, perhaps as her grandmother, has to be an exceptionally strong figure in this society to keep going herself and to push the men in her life. The black man in this society is almost completely stripped of his dignity. I know of many cases where men can't find work and their wives carry the whole load. This puts a load of pressure on the woman." "Is it easier or harder?" "Although she does not have to work as hard—there are so many modern devices—people are becoming more aware of these problems. This idea of the laughing, happy Negro is a myth. As Langston Hughes said, 'He's laughing to keep from crying and even now he doesn't laugh or cry. It's something that is building and some day he will explode. When a man isn't aware of his problem, he doesn't have a problem, so maybe in this respect grandmother's life or role was easier, since grandfather wasn't always aware of, or willing to face, his problems." There is some of a "women are wiser than men" sentiment of matriarchal role definitions in this whole set of answers, but it is insightful.

The effect of discrimination upon husband-wife relations is explained by another respondent, twenty-five years of age. When asked about problems in the role of housewife, she says: "Men are a problem because your husband will come in and say someone insulted him. Children will come home and say, 'Why did this one say something about you and daddy?'" This indicates the depth of her worry about the future, for she does not as yet have any children who could be experiencing prejudice.

The result of modern education and work experiences upon the woman can be seen in terms other than, or in addition to, those of equality. "Definitely a woman's world has expanded. She works outside of the home. She is on an equal level with the man. So her role has changed *quite* a bit." This respondent sees the change not merely in rights but also abilities. "She can make good, logical decisions in family matters without being dependent on 'papa.' She can also pursue her own goals or ambitions. Before she could do neither of these nor was she capable of having these." This statement was one of the very few to stress that the modern woman is changing in her own personality, not just in relation to others.

Although marriage may encompass problems for a high proportion of blacks because of background and recent urban and upward mobility, many women feel they are working out new patterns even within the limitations of the ghetto. A respondent living on the South Side of Chicago states: "My life has changed because my husband and I really work together and try to understand each other. In the future, I expect us to grow more compatible. Although the role of man in the past has gotten less important, in the future I think that it will change."

Thus, the lives of Negro men and women in American society have experienced some of the same strains as upwardly mobile white husbands and wives, but the content and many features are very different. A major cause of the divergence is that black communities contain women who are more educated and more able to obtain good jobs than their husbands. Existing in a society with a strong patriarchal past and an uneasy transition into more companionate relations, this tendency places an additional burden upon the black male, the female, and the relation between them. The "working wife" within the black community often has a higher status and makes more demands for independence than her white counterpart, whose culture does not favor such behavior for women, and than the Negro housewife, who feels a lack of power to control her spouse. The black working wife is more competent and active in all spheres of life than the non-working woman and often than the Negro man in all but the socio-economically highest groups. The middle-class member of this population is attempting to build new connections across sex lines and to help her husband meet the heavy demands and difficulties which face him. She is much more aware of the complexity of her own position and of her husband's needs than her white counterpart is. The lower-class black woman feels highly frustrated in her life and turns her conflict with poverty, multiple role and relational strain, and general hopelessness into hostility against the male. He is regarded as simply lazy and unwilling to even share the great burden she feels she is carrying.

Modern American marriage is facing a greatly expanded set of expectations, insufficiently reinforced by cultural tools and by the social structure. Romantically defined as the most important primary relation for adults, seconded by or second only to the parent-child interaction, it lacks husbands and wives able to meet their own and each other's demands. Transition from authoritarian into democratic and even companionate interaction has been difficult and imperfect. The shift is portrayed by the lower-class woman, still close to the patriarchal and sex-segregated world, as a dethroning of the male and as an increase of *freedom from* controls for her.[32] The middle-class wife tends to see the shift as one of greater equality and of democratization of relations. The higher her education, the more likely she is to focus her attention upon the *freedom to* create new relations with a more personally perceived husband.

Entrance into marriage can be seen by a woman as an event changing the pattern of life, the self, relations with others, and social status. Some wives feel that marriage brings greater individual freedom and independence, others that it is restrictive and dependency creating. In retrospect, it may be perceived as simply one of a whole sequence of events. The main function of the men of the family is considered to be providing for the unit. The role of father is defined as the next important one of his role-cluster; few women point to the role of husband as his most significant role. Thus, later in marriage the romantic ideal comes to be modified because of the need of the family to be maintained. Women vary considerably in the influence they assume a wife has upon the way the husband earns the family "bread." The more

32. Eric Fromm distinguishes between *freedom from* constraints and *freedom to* do what one wants, which is a positive attitude. See especially his *Escape from Freedom,* New York: Farrar and Rinehart, 1941. Relevant to this chapter is also his *The Art of Loving,* New York: Harper and Brothers, 1956.

educated women whose husbands are in high-income professional or business roles feel that they contribute directly through specific actions as part of the work social circle or through assistance in the decision-making process. The wives of blue-collar workers are more likely to speak of only indirect influence through the "happy home" effect of the performance of their own roles. They are not apt to share vicariously or directly in the life of the husband away from home. Different degrees of influence upon the husband's choice of work or behavior on the job are contained in a great range of wife involvement, including that of pushing, avoiding negative action, assisting in decision-making, advising, giving opinions, discussion, encouragement, and listening. The expectation that the wife of the "Organization Man" has a high level of direct influence is rejected by more women who disclaim its applicability to their own case than is claimed by women because of their own involvement.

The more education a woman has obtained, the more she feels involved in a multidimensional relation with her husband, including a concern for his occupational roles, and the more positively she evaluates men and interaction with them. This conclusion applies not only to the white woman but to the black woman, although the background and content of marriage is different in flavor and focus.

Modern husband-wife relations include not only the wife's involvement in the husband's roles away from home, but also his participation in activities within their dwelling traditionally assigned to servants or to the housewife. The large areas of work are likely to be broken down into smaller units, some of which become the province of the husband; new activities are taken over by him, or else he serves as the main emergency assistant, replacing often unavailable kin. As other studies have pointed out, the nature of such a division of labor and the ease of transition depend on the social class level of the husband and of the wife, on the creativity of their relation, and on the alternative sources of help available to them.

THREE ❧ ❧ ❧

Becoming and
Being a Housewife

BACKGROUND

The social role of housewife, as we have seen, is performed by a woman, currently or previously married, who is responsible for running her own home in co-operation with all those people who benefit by her maintenance of it or who contribute to the process. In American urban society the social circle of a housewife usually includes the man of the house, the children who live in it, the friends who are guests within it, the neighbors and anyone else who utilizes the results of her work as a housewife. Besides these clients, the circle includes the suppliers of services or products who enter her home or allow her to enter their businesses in order to obtain the things she needs to keep the home functioning.

The social role of housewife can be graphically portrayed as a circle, whose segments roughly represent people with whom she interacts (see Chart 1). Each housewife has the obligation to her social circle to maintain herself in health and skill so that she can meet her direct responsibilities to them. In addition to these duties, the housewife has general obligations to all her role partners: keeping the household and its surroundings safe and clean and supplying it with items having specified characteristics. Finally, each housewife has specific duties to each segment of her social circle and they to her: for example, she washes and irons the clothes of her husband and of her children, but not those of visiting guests.

CHART 1: The social role of housewife.*

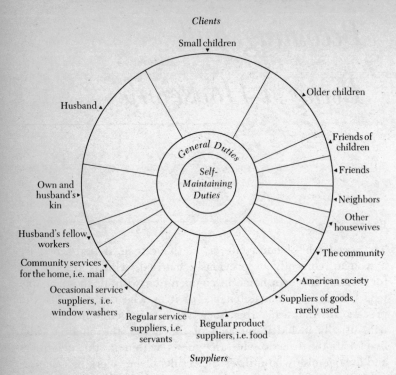

* The size of the area represents its relative significance to the role.

The way the role of housewife is performed by any particular woman depends on many factors, such as the presence of children in the household and the financial resources she has to obtain goods and services. Ideal standards of performance are available in all cultures.

STAGES IN "BECOMING A HOUSEWIFE"

According to the outline of stages by which an individual becomes involved in the set of relations which form a social role (see Chapter Two), he must establish contact with potential circle members, test and be tested with positive results for required qualifications, acquire the knowledge needed to perform the duties and to receive the rights, and acquire the tools for work. The experience usually has at least some effect on the personality, changing perceptions of the self, modifying behavior, and shifting the other roles within the cluster into new configurations.

Most occupational roles in American society involve organized social circles into which the person enters after being found qualified. A firm or factory needing a worker advertises for a person with certain very specific qualifications (age, sex, skill, knowledge, etc.); the candidate is tested through formalized procedures; and is hired or rejected. If accepted, he is given routinized additional training enabling him to fit into the already operating system. Fellow workers initiate him into the informal system of relational norms.

The girl entering the role of housewife faces a completely different situation. One of the role's characteristics is that American girls do not "apply for it." There is no organized social circle which tests a candidate and then admits or rejects her on the basis of proven skills. She enters the role "sideways," as an adjunct to the role of wife, and only then does she pull a social circle around herself. In addition, the role is not easily located in the occupational social structure. Most Americans are not even sure whether it belongs there: it lacks the basic criteria of most jobs. It has no organized social circle which judges performance and has the right to fire for incompetence, no specific pay scale, and no measurement against other performers of the same role or against circle members. It is vague, open to any woman who gets married, regardless of ability; it has no union and belongs to no organizational structure.

On the other hand, what kind of a role could it be, if not an occupational one? All family roles are located within a kinship organizational structure, but it clearly has no place on a family tree. It can be performed by a widow with no children or other family members who directly benefit from it. Only humorists label it as a recreational role. The counterpart male role is always a specific occupation.

This state of affairs results in the role's devaluation, conflict with other roles, and psychological strain for performers. One of its major problems is its lack of high social rank in any ranking system.[1] As an economic role, it is immediately placed low in that status hierarchy, because of a lack of wage or salary scale.[2] As an occupational role, it lacks many traits of the more prestigious jobs. As a family role it seems merely an adjunct to the more important sets of relations of wife and mother. The answer, "I'm just a housewife," in response to the question, "Who (or) what are you?" implies such a devaluated status.

The role of housewife over a complex household did not always have such low status. As Ariés pointed out, the manor homes of Europe, which continent is a source of much of American culture, were centers of societal life, especially in areas which had not developed important public meeting places for the transaction of the political and economic aspects of life.[3] A variety of people lived within these dwellings or came often into them from the outside, and common rooms contained simultaneous and sequential patterns of activity reflecting a great deal of the culture. During the eighteenth century, Ariés says, homes of many nations underwent dramatic changes. They be-

1. A number of commentators conclude that other aspects of the role of housewife give it low status. Eve Merrimen states in *After Nora Slammed the Door*, Cleveland: World, 1964, that "The woman finds her dependency role unbearable and yet does not know how to live otherwise" (p. 32); Judith Hubback feels that "Domestic work, even in its more creative forms, is a check on major creativeness, which demands a single focus," in her report on English college graduates, *Wives Who Went to College*, London: Wm. Heinemann, 1957.

2. Pearl Buck in *Of Men and Women*, New York: John Day, 1941, states that the American housewife has become a parasite, compared to the pre-revolutionary Chinese woman, owing to the decrease of home work groups and of the labor required to maintain a house. The same conclusion that a lack of hard physical work diminishes the contribution of the worker is implied in Hannah Gavron's *The Captive Wife: Conflicts of Housebound Mothers*, London: Routledge & Kegan Paul, 1966. Robert Weiss and Nancy Morse Samelson report in "Social Roles of American Women: Their Contribution to a Sense of Usefulness and Importance," *Marriage and Family Living*, 20, No. 4 (November 1958), 358–66, that only some of the activities carried out within the housewife role make women feel useful and important. Margaret G. Reid felt she had to point out "The Economic Contributions of Homemakers" in *The Annals of the American Academy of Political and Social Science*, special issue, edited by W. Wallace Weaver, devoted to "*Women's Opportunities and Responsibilities*," 251 (May 1947), 61–69.

3. Philippe Ariés, *Centuries of Childhood*, New York: Vintage Books, 1965.

came closed off into private places of residence for family members; they were segregated from the rest of the world and cut off from involvement in the important institutions of the society. Work and politics moved to specially designated physical spaces: the man and children judged old enough to participate in a less restricted life than the one available in the home went to them. Only the woman remained at home, if she was a member of the less educated segments of the several social classes. A tiny minority of women became educated, by tutors or interested male relatives, and they too went out to participate in various aspects of societal activity and continued to bring some of the life back into the home through dinner parties, soirées, or salons, for example. Although they were not able to reproduce the full range of public life in the home, such women prevented it from losing all of its prior involvement in the outside.

In homes other than those of highly educated upper-class women, life became rather barren, closed off from ideas as well as from social contact with the rest of society. The functions of the house diminished: people returned to rest, to shed the cares of a world often judged wicked and full of temptation to evil. According to Ariés, the home was assigned the function of being a man's castle in a very limited and medieval sense— with drawbridge raised and moats filled to prevent an infiltration of strangers or foreign ideas. It became a haven of peace for those who had full lives outside, and a locus of the totally non-involved women who ideally existed only to meet its needs.

Rather than picking up the upper-class image of the European woman, Americans seem to have been influenced by the home and housewife-restricting trend. The homemaker is typically portrayed as someone who needs little intelligence, since the duties are routine and narrow in scope and since her home is not part of the societal life.

The Education of Housewives

A woman now becomes a housewife without much training. In the past, in those cultures upon which the American culture is largely based, the family of orientation provided a girl with extensive training in skills required for running a home of her own. Such education varied greatly in content, depending on the society and particularly on the social class, but her family and their assistants were responsible for and controlled the future housewife. Restricted to the home in her youth, the girl either participated directly in its work or was provided with abstract lessons in all the housewifely skills. She was taught, over many years, how to interact with those people she was likely to contact in her role as mistress of her own home. In fact, she was not likely to enter that stage of the role immediately at marriage; she often first entered the home managed by her mother-in-law or other adults who preceded her into it.

As education for most social roles moved out of the home into generalized or specialized schools, it acquired definite training patterns and performance measures. The knowledge and skills which were taught in schools and which prepared for specific occupations acquired prestige; the number of years of education and the prestige of the role to which the preparation led were interconnected. The knowledge required for maintaining a home was not built into the curriculum as a complex and valued area of specialization. Much of it has been developed into social roles carried out away from the home. Now the school educates future dietitians for hospitals, fabric buyers for stores, and interior decorators who offer professional advice to housewives. However, although specialties in "home economics" can provide entrance into occupations with relative prestige, few girls enter this branch of the university,[4] and even fewer take the courses in preparation for their own entrance into the role of housewife. In fact, an occupational identification with the role of housewife is absent from the adolescent subculture, and girls

4. The attempt to make the knowledge needed in maintaining a complex home more prestigious is witnessed by the enormous collection of volumes under the former title of "Domestic Engineering" or "Home Economics" within the Library of Congress. The movement can be exemplified by the card catalogue description of Mrs. Mary Stranahan Pattison's book, *The Business of Home Management,* New York: R. M. McBridge, 1918: "The principles of domestic engineering; or the what, why and how of a home; an attempt to evolve a solution to the domestic 'labor and capital' problems —to standardize and professionalize homework—to reorganize the home upon 'scientific management' principles and to point out the importance of the public and personal element therein, as well as the practical."

continue to select major fields without vocational goals or those leading to employment appropriate for women in organizations outside the home. Nursing and teaching are prime examples, but they are fields of temporary employment for women who soon withdraw into running a home, a role for which they had not prepared. Instant "housewifehood" is assumed to result, though to the popular mind a few burned dinners show the lack of training. Many tasks have been removed from the home and are performed by business organizations; thus the unprepared homemaker can say, "But I can buy it cheaper than I could make it."

In spite of these trends, other tendencies are visible in America. Vocational orientation to the role of housewife was implied in the supermarket boycotts of 1966 which crystallized group insistence on the right to judgment of services. Mass communication media and adult education programs have dramatically expanded the dissemination of knowledge for the homemaker. "Consumerism" is spreading among educated women, as a search for the best products at the least cost with the help of expert knowledge. Colston Warne, President of the Consumers Union of the United States, sends *Consumer Reports* to 1,800,000 families, as well as other periodicals presenting precise information about various popular products on the market.[5] Women who never prepared for the role of housewife in their teens are turning to all these sources of information and skill in making themselves more expert and creative in the home. Reversing the trend toward buying commercially prepared foods, they are becoming more experimental and knowledgeable about cooking, often building upon partially prepared bases. More confident in their ability to decorate a home and having the economic means to experiment with materials and colors, they are becoming their own interior decorators. The trend is evidenced not only by national sales figures, but by the popularity of the media which offer the housewife professionally prepared and rationally presented knowledge.

Evidence of the trend toward increased professionalism in

5. Colston E. Warne, "Consumerism—A Menace to the Business Community?" speech given before the Harvard Business School Club of Chicago (April 1970), p. 3.

the role of housewife is contained in answers to a whole series of questions in the "social role of housewife" schedule.[6] These were designed to uncover assumptions regarding the form and sources of knowledge necessary for this and related roles, and the sources from which they obtained their own training. The queries included: "Is the modern woman properly trained for her role as a homemaker?", "What training which you received before marriage are you using now?", and "Where have you gotten help in learning to perform your homemaker role?" In addition, several questions elicited the specific ways in which different types of women use the newspaper as a source of knowledge.

The answers show that women do not agree on either of two basic features of role preparation: one, what should be taught future housewives; and two, who is responsible for transmitting such knowledge.

> The modern woman is not properly trained for her role as a homemaker. The schools are not doing their job. They teach Latin, French, and chemistry, not sewing and cooking. Home management should not be an elective (Park Ridge resident, aged thirty-three, college educated).

> Most modern women are properly trained for the role of housewife. High school gives cooking, child care. You don't pay attention, but some sticks (Park Forest housewife, aged twenty-eight, high school graduate).

> They are poorly trained. Can't cook, clean, market or buy anything but clothes. Parents should teach these things (Highland Park resident, thirty-one years of age, thirteen years of education).

> You don't have to be trained. It comes naturally (a frequent comment of the less educated woman, here a twenty-six-year-old Oak Lawn high school drop-out).

These four women certainly view the role of housewife from different perspectives. Two refer only to formal education,

6. The role of housewife is still far from being professionalized, since it lacks an even minimal degree of most of the basic criteria: "the unstandardized product, degree of personality involvement of the professional, wide knowledge of a specialized technique, sense of obligation (to one's art), sense of group identity, and significance of the occupational services to society." Edward Gross, *Work and Society,* New York: Thomas Y. Crowell, 1958, p. 77.

limiting housewifely knowledge and skills to a few clearly delineated areas, capable of being ideationally transmitted, like chemistry or psychology. The perspective which they share approaches the role vocationally, as similar to business management or at least to a high school typing course. Neither of these speakers refers to home training, and they do not agree on the effectiveness of school education.

The second view of the training needed for the role of housewife implies that each generation duplicates prior procedures followed within the home; it is more traditional. Schools teach the rational analysis of object and process composition, showing the reasons for, and consequences of, alternative ways of handling materials or social relations; home personnel tend to teach by example the accepted modes of carrying out patterned actions. The respondents, expecting homemaking to be traditionally based, are likely to look to the home as the basic source of training. They, too, do not agree on the adequacy of preparation given to young girls in the family.

The view that the role of housewife "comes naturally" is the most traditional; it rejects experimental and scientifically based ways of running a household. It is most frequently expressed by women with little formal education who do not identify with the ideational aspects of American culture and who are unfamiliar with the adult training function of mass communication.

American society lacks an integrated set of procedures for the training of housewives before they undertake this role, and over half of the respondents feel that available sources fail to prepare the woman adequately. Schools do not demand a choice of homemaking subjects, and most girls do not elect to take them. The family of orientation lacks many features for adequate training in new styles of life, among them the ways of transmitting knowledge to offspring accustomed to a school system and the power to force the child to learn skills valued by the prior generation. As knowledge becomes expanded, abstracted, and subject to constant change, the home serves less and less as the basic source of preparation for new roles, unless it contains members with specific skills which they continually update. The very popular phrase "generation gap" reflects the attitudes of younger generations toward the knowledge of older ones.

An interesting difference in the attitudes of housewives

emerged in a cross-tabulation by residence and by working status (see Table 11). Suburbanites, living in their own homes, are the most likely to feel that women are not prepared for this role. They blame the school rather than the home. Working women, who are not deeply concerned with the role and who tend to perform it minimally, feel that no special skills are needed. However, even their respect for the knowledge required of housewives increases as their level of education achievement increases (see Table 12). The same trend is noticeable among suburban housewives. The higher their education, the more likely they are to feel that modern women are not adequately trained to be housewives. This indicates the possibility that women who are performing the role of housewife in a complex and creatively competent manner see it as requiring many different areas of knowledge, while women who perform it minimally with little interest or originality assume that it does not require much skill.

The respondents who feel that housewives are adequately trained for this role include older women and those who live in urban apartments. The non-working urban apartment dweller does not show much concern about the education received for the role of housewife. She tends to be older than the suburbanite and to be identified with ethnic sub-groups. Most of the subcultures in American society view the role of homemaker as a "natural" one, requiring no special training or only practical training at home.

The respondents who feel that housewives need more training than they receive include those having a family income of $16,000 or above and those with several relatively young children. Again, this indicates that women who are not satisfied with maintaining their home in a minimal manner think that the role requires a great deal of knowledge. The income bracket of those demanding much knowledge and skill is likely to result in the possession and maintenance of many goods and the need for complex actions in their care, organized management of money, purchasing plans, and synchronization of specialized services. Having a high level of education, these women are leading lives in which they and others demand the rational use of time and money and full life patterns.

The fact that working women tend to undervalue the complexity of the role of housewife and the knowledge which can

Table 11: Percentage distributions of answers to "Is the modern woman properly trained for her role as a homemaker?" by residence and working status.

	Category of Respondent			
Answer	Suburban Housewives	Urban Housewives	Urban Working Women	Total
No	59	46	44	58
It depends	20	16	24	19
Yes	18	37	31	23
No answer	1	1	1	1
Total percentage	98*	100	100	101*
Total persons	279	192	100	571

* Rounding off of percentages causes imperfect totals.

Table 12: Percentage distributions of answers to "Is the modern woman properly trained for her role as a homemaker?" by residence, working status, and education.

	Education					
Anwer, by Population	8 Grades or Less	9 - 11	12	13 - 15	16	Over 16
No						
Suburban	50	50	55	52	66	67
Urban	57	48	45	60	47	67
Working women	0	50	36	48	58	50
Depends						
Suburban	50	28	20	20	16	0
Urban	8	4	26	17	35	11
Working women	33	33	21	34	8	36
Yes						
Suburban	0	22	25	23	19	33
Urban	31	44	29	24	18	22
Working women	67	17	39	28	33	14
No Answer						
Suburban	0	0	4	5	0	0
Urban	4	0	0	0	0	0
Working women	0	0	4	0	0	0
Number of People	39	52	201	129	61	29

The populations are suburban housewives, urban housewives, and urban working women. Sixty interviewees did not answer one of the two questions.

be used to perform it raises interesting questions. Do women who return to work after devoting some time to being full-time housewives consistently maintain a different attitude toward the role from that of women not interested in employment, or do they form this opinion only after returning to work? Most women of this older generation did not work during the early years of their children's lives, and the return to employment is usually a gradual and uneven process. It is possible that variation in the evaluation of the role of housewife among working women partly reflects the degree of their involvement in the outside job. At one end of the continuum, we may find women recently returned to work who resemble their housewife counterparts, because their attitudes have not fully changed. At the other end of the continuum, we would then find women who have always been employed and who have never paid much attention to the role of housewife. We can also ask if the non-working housewives with a restricted view of the role always had this opinion or if they are in the process now of redefining it in anticipation of the need to justify leaving the home in the near future. There are four possibilities accounting for a low evaluation of the knowledge required for the role of housewife in relation to working experience: that women who work are the ones who always held a minimal view of the role of housewife; that some housewives perform this role at a minimal level and thus devalue it; that women planning to return to work in the near future downgrade it; and that the actual process of handling both work and home necessitates the under-evaluation of the latter (maybe of both). The discovery of a close relation between attitudes toward the role of homemaker and orientation toward employment would be of sociological and even societal significance, but it must be based upon more intensive research than that contained in this broader study.

Training for the Role of Housewife Before Entrance

Although those interviewed do not consider the modern woman to be properly trained for the role of housewife, they feel that they themselves are using some of the knowledge gained before marriage. Only one-fifth of the 571 women state flatly that the training acquired before they became housewives is of no value. One-fourth list a few major sets of skills and their sources, and there are 335 scattered references to a wide range of other skills (see Table 13).

Several factors contribute to the prominence of formal education as a remembered source of knowledge and skill. In the first place, a formalized course having a clear beginning and end and a labeled subject matter is more likely to be recalled as a specific contribution than is the rather vague and diffused form of learning experienced as part of family life. In addition, the kinds of activities mentioned are self-contained units which can be isolated for specific content. A person remembers learning to sew through a formalized course. Such subjects are offered, and labeled, by the school so that they form part of a repertoire, but the general foundation upon which they are placed has no name and may be simply taken for granted as "living" or "taking care of the family." Finally, many a woman in this study is living a life very different from that experienced in her childhood, and most of the knowledge with which she is experimenting has been developed and systematized for presentation within recent years. For example, recipes are standardized and cooking increasingly experimental; while interior decorating reflects shifts in fashion requiring skill in the use of new materials or work tools. Many a woman does not see herself as the kind of housewife her mother was—as defined by the daughter through interpreted memory. This is particularly true of the younger suburbanite, who is accustomed to handling herself and her world in problem-solving, action-planning ways rather than through routinized sets of procedures.

"On the Job Training"

When we find that many of the respondents feel that American women are not properly trained for this role and that they themselves did not receive complete preparation prior to marriage, we can assume that most of them experienced "on the job training." Many social roles encourage learning only after entrance, because of the assumption that the skills are so easy to learn that prior training is not necessary, because there is no

Table 13: Percentage distributions of women listing specific sources in response to "What training which you received before marriage are you using now?" by residence, working status, and age decade.

Source	Suburban Housewives				Urban Housewives					Urban Working Women					Total
	20	30	40	Total	20	30	40	50	Total	20	30	40	50	Total	
Mother	17	25	21	22	13	12	24	28	17		11	19	7	10	18
Home, folks	12	13	3	11	7	6	4	8	6	7		3	7	5	9
Experience	7	5	8	6	4	6	2	3	3						4
School course	40	24	32	30	16	18	17	11	15	22	22	14	32	22	23
Other	2	1	12	3	4		4	4	4	4	11			3	3
None	18	20	21	20	24	24	21	12	19	11	44	22	7	17	19
No. of respondents	87	158	34	279	45	17	66	64	192	27	9	36	28	100	571

other method, or because alternative sources are not available to the candidate. Such roles often divide the period between initial acceptance and full status into several testing units. Many candidates may be accepted, with the assumption that all but those finally granted full status will be easily weeded out. Social circles often feel that training centers operating outside of their boundaries are supplying wrong or inadequate training and testing. All circles assume the need for some time to "learn the ropes," during which they forgive the novice mistakes in action, timing, or judgment.

The social role of housewife in American urban areas lacks such legitimated training and testing segments of the social circle. The housewife must pull her own circle around her by actually carrying out the duties of her role. No one is responsible for training her, no one controls the amount of knowledge that she acquires nor the sources from which she draws it, and there are no segments of the circle who can test her, pass her on to the next stage, or "fire her." This does not mean that every person with whom she interacts in order to manage her house lacks standards of judgment of performance and of adequacy in relations but that there is no institutionalized means by which she can become trained, tested, and acknowledged as no longer a novice. The most frequent single test, applied informally, is the first meal she plans, prepares, and serves. American humor abounds with stories of failures by brides in meeting even minimal standards of edibility. Yet the range of performance of the role of housewife is enormous, and social circles vary in the actions they deem necessary for even average performance. All the respondents state or imply that the skills needed to prepare food and to keep the house and its objects in a certain condition of cleanliness and "beauty"—especially objects visible on the outside—are expected of women who are no longer brides. Yet the range of objects and conditions varies from a single room equipped with fifteen objects to a home containing numerous items of "beauty" and "comfort." The knowledge demanded by the housewives themselves may range from simple skills of washing and dusting to interior decorating, wood refinishing, furniture upholstery, design and sewing of household furnishings or personal clothes, and meal preparation. A suburban home, as Dobriner points out, may be a very visible and public space, easily entered by neighbors and service personnel, and seen into through expanses of glass.[7]

Few roles are similarly dependent upon the self-motivation of the social person to acquire knowledge and skill which society makes available to the voluntary seeker. Unlike the traditional system, the level of accomplishment is dependent upon the initiative rather than the passive or reactive actions of the woman, requiring familiarity with sources and a great deal of choice among alternatives. The role is indeterminate, and modern society is supplying a great deal of freedom to the social person to choose the content and source of knowledge with which to change herself from a factory worker, secretary, or teacher into a housewife.[8] By the same token, it places a heavy burden of responsibility upon women who by their cultural past and background social class are not accustomed to such action. As a consequence, the role can be minimally and passively, or even apologetically, carried out. Role strain in the transitional stages of "becoming" a housewife is frequent. On the other hand, this complex of possibilities of the role is a contributing factor to the development of a new type of housewife: one who works competently and creatively in the role and opens the home to societal participation. Whenever a role's circle trains specifically, it tends to demand close conformity. Housewives do not have to cope with such stifling control, unless they slide far below the minimal level of performance.

One member of the social circle does possess more detailed standards of role behavior: the man who supplies the means by which the house is run. At least in urban white families the man is still seen as the basic breadwinner and the woman as the basic housekeeper.[9] However, the American mate-selection system pre-

7. William M. Dobriner, *Class in Suburbia,* Englewood Cliffs, N.J.: Prentice-Hall, 1963. See also his collection *The Suburban Community,* New York: Putnam's, 1958. The relation between privacy, space, and location of residence has also been studied by Charles Madge and presented in "Private and Public Spaces," *Human Relations,* 3, No. 2 (June 1950), 187–99.

8. Raymond Mack, "Occupation Determinateness: A Problem and Hypotheses in Role Theory," *Social Forces,* 35 (October 1956), 20–25.

9. The discriminatory educational and occupational practices against the black male in America have frequently resulted in the woman being the breadwinner or at least contributing a major part of the family income.

vents too strong a task orientation by the man concerning his wife's housewifely duties during the first years of marriage. The romantic love ideal ignores the importance of secondary or work features of their relation. The patrilineal family, which was much more apt to be task-oriented, which supplied constant training and criticism, is absent from daily life and often prevented from voicing judgment.[10] Thus the housewife has been freed from most external constraints upon her work, particularly in urban areas in which neighbors do not undertake this function.

The rate of cultural change in American urban life and the relative independence of the newly married unit from constant supervision by either kin group led us to hypothesize that modern housewives are not likely to use the traditionally oriented older generations, or even their own backgrounds, as major sources of "on the job training." Study of American society indicates that young marrieds of the 1950's and 1960's were deliberately changing life, revolting against the past. "Old fashioned" experts or trainers in many roles became rejected in a *freedom from* ———— movement, and the new middle class turned away from ethnic subcultures. Although there is some tendency to increased, though selective, enjoyment of parts of ethnic cultures, spurred undoubtedly by the "black is beautiful" movement, it is still insufficient to offset the trend rejecting the parental generation's advice on how to live. Many of the respondents are maintaining new homes in the suburbs or in the outer fringes of the city, although they had been brought up either in dense apartment areas or on farms or in provincial communities. Older relatives are hypothetically less usable in the present than in prior centuries, due to mobility and the relatively high value given formal schooling, which separates the young from childhood's primary influences. After all, 40 per cent of the suburbanites, 35 per cent of the urban housewives, and 38 per cent of the working women have at least some college (although only 6 per cent, 14 per cent, and 26 per cent of them, respectively, received a B.A. or B.S. degree). On the other hand, this education is so recent on the part of women as not to provide a complete foundation for

10. Bernard Farber concludes that a major function of the kin group is to provide criticism and controls upon each nuclear unit. Bernard Farber, *Family Organization and Interaction,* San Francisco: Chandler, 1964.

a *freedom to* ———— trend which, unlike the revolt of *freedom from* ————, enables the chooser to use any source, even the past, if it meets the purpose.[11]

All these factors contributing to discontinuity in the way three generations have maintained their homes are evident in the answers to the question "Where have you gotten help in learning to perform your homemaker role?" given by the women interviewed. The prediction of dependence upon abstract and depersonalized sources is supported: the majority of respondents lists secondary materials, in preference to older generation members, as sources of learning to run their homes competently and creatively. The 571 women list 1006 sources of knowledge, and 547 of these are secondary: courses, books, magazines, newspapers, and radio-TV. Less than half of the answers refer to primary or personal sources, including peer group members and husbands. Of these only 35 per cent refer to "mother," 9 per cent to "home," and 4 per cent to other relatives.

Magazines are mentioned as a source of help in learning the role of housewife almost as often as is "mother" (185 to 196). The urban housewife is disproportionately likely to use these. As several respondents explain, magazines focus on specific areas of activity of interest to women, and picture decorating, cooking, or sewing ideas. Newspapers are mentioned by only 52 women, although the latter part of the interview shows that they are used by many more women. We infer that, although newspapers are interesting or useful, they are not a major source of training. The most frequent specific reference is to cooking help, in the form of purchasing information and recipes. Books serve as training means for 53 women; mass communication in general for 38; radio and TV specifically for 60; "school" for 30; and the combination of printed materials for 46. The other secondary sources, mentioned by 42 respondents, are work and church. The subjects most frequently listed in which training has been gained from these sources include: sewing and fashion (152), cooking (72), child care (40), housework (21), and budgeting (7). Very young urban housewives are most likely to mention fashion and sewing. Those concerned with child care here blur the boundaries between the role of housewife and that of mother.

11. Erich Fromm, *Escape from Freedom,* New York: Farrar and Rinehart, 1941.

One of the dramatic surprises emerging from Table 15 is the infrequency with which the suburban woman lists her mother. Only one-fourth of the women refer to their mother as a source of knowledge after entrance into the homemaking role, compared to almost half the working women and two-fifths of the urban housewives. As we have said, the life style of a suburban family is likely to be more different from the mother's than that of an apartment-dwelling family is. The upwardly mobile suburbanite may even repress any memory of help obtained from persons connected with her prior life, owing to a wish to feel herself as different from the past. Whatever the reason, the references to mother and home are very low. All three populations, in addition, decrease with increased age in frequency of reference to "mother" as a source of "on the job" training, a pattern not present in the case of secondary sources other than magazines for urban housewives. Since there is a likelihood that the mother is still alive, the decreased reference to her as a source of knowledge implies that she has a stationary fund. Once what mother knows has been learned, new sources are used. In sum, it seems that the contribution of the mother is considered relatively insignificant compared to the learning obtained from secondary sources.

Younger urban housewives, the ones who turn so often to magazines, are also much more likely than their counterparts to refer to the husband as a source of training. Our assumption had been that working women would learn more from the spouse. The suburbanites turn to friends, neighbors, and the doctor. The last named is usually a pediatrician, and he advises in the designing of meals and the physical care of children, which combine the roles of housewife and mother. Surprisingly, working women make no reference to the doctor as a supplier of knowledge, although all but 17 per cent have offspring. One of the reasons may be that these children are beyond the pediatrician-focused stages and the mothers forget how much training came from the medical men.

Experience may be the best teacher for many roles, but only 30 of the 571 interviewees claim they owe their accomplishments in the role of housewife to it. This fact again points to a knowledge, rather than a skill, orientation. Urban women list more secondary sources and fewer personal "experts" than the other

Table 14: Percentages of respondents listing secondary sources in answer to "Where have you gotten help in learning how to perform your homemaker role?" by residence, working status, and age decade.

Sources	Suburban Housewives				Urban Housewives					Working Women					
	20	30	40	Total	20	30	40	50	Total	20	30	40	50	total	Total
"Reading"	15	12	3	12	2	6	4	3	4	4				1	7
Books, magazines, and newspapers	8	10	12	10	11		3	3	5	7	11	11	11	10	8
Magazines	19	14	12	15	82	65	67	60	65	7	11	28	18	18	32
Newspapers	2	3		3	20	12	22	19	20	11		3	8	6	9
Books	8	10	12	10	4	6	11	14	10	4		9	7	6	9
Radio — TV	7	10	3	9	11	6	13	16	13		22	22	8	11	11
School	6	4	9	5	2	12	4	5	5			8	11	6	5
Mass communication media in general	14	11	15	13				3	1			3	3	1	7
Other	8	10	12	10	2	12	5	7	5		11	3	11	5	7
No. of respondents	87	158	34	279	45	17	66	64	192	27	9	36	28	100	571
No. of answers				240					243					64	547

The percentage is of the number of people who listed the item. Since more than one answer could be given, the percentages do not add up to 100 per cent.

Table 15: Percentages of respondents listing primary relations as sources of answers to "Where have you gotten help in learning how to perform your homemaker role?" by residence, working status, and age decade.

Source	Suburban Housewives				Urban Housewives					Working Women					Total
	20	30	40	Total	20	30	40	50	Total	20	30	40	50	Total	Total
Mother	28	22	24	24	40	24	44	47	42	59	44	47	39	48	34
Home	6	8	3	6	22	18	4	11	12	15	11	3	7	8	9
Other relative	5	4		4	2		3	2	2		11	8	14	8	4
Husband	7	8	3	7	11	18	4	2	6	4		6		3	6
Friends and neighbors	7	11	9	9	4	18	11	6	8		11	3		2	8
Doctor	17	5	12	9				2	1						5
Experience	8	5	3	6	2	6	6	8	6	4			7	3	5
Other	3	4	3	4	7	11	11	6	7		11			1	5
No. of respondents	87	158	34	279	45	17	66	64	192	27	9	36	28	100	571
No. of answers				194					192					73	459

two populations. Working women average .64 secondary sources per person, suburbanites average .82, and urban housewives 1.36.

Newspapers as Sources of Knowledge for Women

One of the major means by which the separation between the two areas of a housewife's world, "inside" and "outside" of the home, is bridged in modern society is the daily newspaper. It is often delivered to the home, and it contains two major types of information of interest to the housewife: data on what is going on outside of her walls, within the range of various physical and psychological distances from her, and data developed on the outside, but to be used within her home. Suburban housewives were asked a series of questions to determine specifically the type of newspaper items which they find of interest and of use. Only comments relating to the contribution of such media to the role of housewife are discussed in this chapter.

Each interviewer carried with her a copy of the same issue of the daily newspaper, and the respondent was asked to point to the kinds of features which were of special interest to her. The paper was the *Chicago Tribune,* a major one in the area, but some women were obviously not familiar with the format. All were given a limited time to select items, and the answers of the few who claimed unfamiliarity with that newspaper were analyzed separately. Selective perception of items, sufficiently strong to enable rapid identification, points to areas of interest and is made on the basis of general title, assumed topic, or author, in the case of named features. The action of pointing was often accompanied by recorded comments explaining the selection: "I would read anything about child care," or "I like Dr. ———," or "That looks interesting." Twenty per cent of the women state that they are not able to read newspapers with any regularity, and many others imply this, but most were sufficiently aware of what newspapers contain to be able to handle the question.

When asked "What type of, if any, helpful information do you find in your newspaper?" 238 of the 279 suburban women list 577 separate items which fall into the housewife role rather than into involvement outside the home. These are split into the following areas of emphasis: cooking and recipes (38 per cent of the respondents), the whole women's page (22 per cent), child care (19 per cent), household hints (48 per cent), psychology (42 per cent), and medical columns (11 per cent). Only 11 women make any reference to gardening news, although most have gardens. This area of knowledge is undoubtedly where magazines enter the picture for suburbanites and for home-owning urbanites.

Social class differences emerge in the responses. The women in the socio-economically lowest suburb represented in this study are most likely to list specific areas, especially cooking. In spite of a high total number of specific references by the 25 women (60 comments in all), there is no mention of home decorating, home furnishing, fashion, entertaining, etiquette, bridge, book reviews, or recreation reviews. These are listed with relatively great frequency by the higher-class respondents. What is helpful to the role of housewife depends on how the role is conceptualized and the limits of the person's resources, both financially and in breadth of perspective.[12]

Class variations also appear in answers to the next question: "What information do you use (entertainment, cooking, household hints, child care, garden, etc.)?" Lower-class women make very few references to actual use, although they point to many items as "helpful." Out of a total of 570 items listed as used, 141 are to recipes, the highest proportion coming from the communities in which the respondents have the highest level of education. The same response distribution is true of the 122 references to child care, 103 to household hints, 85 to gardening and 50 to entertaining. This is the order of interest. The difference among the social classes is so strong as to again support the inductive conclusion that the educated woman is more open in her ability and courage to experiment with new methods of dealing with her world, at least in the roles of housewife and mother, than the less-educated woman. Two quotations indicate the differences between women in three classes:

Upper-Middle: Help: "Happenings in other countries; politics and economics; financial news if you have investments, learn about people, how they

12. Leon Warshay, "Breadth of Perspective," in Arnold Rose's *Human Behavior and Social Processes,* Boston: Houghton Mifflin, 1962, pp. 148–76.

react; price information on homes, food, clothing."

Use: "Entertainment, household hints, child care, garden."

Upper-Lower: Help: "Health columns, recipes, household hints."

Use: "Child care too modern. I believe in old-fashioned methods."

In-Between (Upwardly mobile, recently entered into the middle-class)

Help: "All I read is the comics and the picture section on Sunday. This, of course, bothers a husband like mine, who is interested in all sorts of things; but it just isn't in me to read or get interested in the world's problems."

Use: "No."

Contrast appears in comments about help in the role of housewife and in that of mother. Many women mention the difficulty in using child-care articles. They are threatening, are based on bits and pieces of several theoretical foundations with which they are not familiar, and involve the translation of abstract principles into actual relations. The more concrete items, presenting a closed-end sequence with a definite product, such as a recipe for a meal or a hint for ironing, are easily transmitted through the mass communication media, because there are few variations in the condition of the objects for which the action is prescribed. Suburban housewives of the lower and middle class are very child-oriented and interested in reading about the subject, especially in reading what experts say, but many state that they do not use newspaper advice. They seem to lack self-confidence in choosing between items, not approaching them in the same manner as they approach recipes, by seeing first if they fit their unique needs and facilities. They are likely to use a book, especially Dr. Spock, if middle-class, or tradition, if lower-class.

When directed to the interviewer's copy of one of the daily newspapers and asked to "Please turn to the women's section and point out articles which are of interest to you," 54 per cent of the interviewees select at least four features and only 4 per cent refuse to point to any. Most references are to cooking or child-care articles, and this time the mother role dominates; 218 selections are made of features dealing with children and only 163 with cooking. Interestingly, 60 of the full-time housewives point to features dealing with working women. Several explain that it reminds them of their working days. Sixty-three women point to fashions, and 50 to advertisements. Thirty-seven different items within that particular women's section draw the notice of at least one woman.

Modern newspapers have become increasingly aware of their female audience, and many have expanded the number of items directed toward them. The women were asked: "Do newspapers provide sufficient services and features of interest to the young suburban wife?" Our interest was not only in the level of satisfaction, but also in the areas in which women found newspapers wanting. Sixty-eight per cent of the women state that newspapers give adequate services; 6 per cent that they themselves do not read the papers often enough to be able to judge. Only 25 per cent answer "no," but they are quite explicit in their answers. The largest number of persons who find some area for criticism of the newspapers are residents of suburbs with a higher educational or income level. Possibly they consider themselves more competent, on a level closer to the experts whom they read, than do the less educated women. Our society of experts may be producing new experts in its housewives, women who evaluate sources of knowledge, rather than automatically accepting "the printed page."

The possibility that the modern woman is able to work with abstract ideas presented by the mass communication media, and that she has the self-confidence to evaluate and to use this help in the performance of her role, was tested through two "role-taking" questions. Ever since the publication of C. Wright Mills's *The Power Elite*[13] and David Riesman's *The Lonely Crowd*,[14] the assumption is often made that members of American society feel powerless, controlled either by a strong and distant minority or by diffused "others out there."

13. C. Wright Mills, *The Power Elite,* New York: Oxford, 1956.

14. David Riesman, Nathan Glazer, and Reuel Denney, *The Lonely Crowd,* New Haven: Yale University Press, 1950, presents a frightening picture of the other-directed man who feels powerless to control even his own children, let alone society outside of the home.

A frequent form of situational control, available to each person even when direct power is lacking, is criticism of another's action. Criticism does not necessarily result in an increase of influence, but it suggests the ability to place oneself in another's shoes and say, "I would act differently," a non-passive evaluation of actions or situations. The degree to which the perspectives of others are actually understood affects the logic of the imaginative exchange, but the development of the personality into broader areas depends first on a willingness to take the role even of influencing others.

The first role-taking question asked: "If you were an editor of the women's section of a newspaper, what articles, features, services would you stress to attract the young suburban wife?" The social role of editor of a major section of a newspaper is a highly ideational one, removed from the life of housewives, and the question also calls for generalizations about the housewife. It could not have been asked of women in many other societies, because they are not trained to judge the performance of people outside the home in roles as powerful and professional as the press.

Only 10 per cent of the women state that they would not change anything, since newspapers are doing a good job. Four per cent of the total say they cannot answer, because they do not know newspapers. The remaining women supply 560 ideas about subjects they would include, or modify, if they were editors of the women's section. The responses are very scattered, showing a great range of interest. The subject of child care brings the greatest convergence of concern: 109 references are made to it. Seventy-seven comments focus on cooking and recipes, with frequent suggestions to include less expensive and complex dishes than currently in papers. Specific ideas about fashion and clothes are given by 56 women, many of whom would include less expensive items than they now find. Twenty-eight would stress information on suburban living, 26 on home decorating, 34 on gardening. Shopping guides, containing information on new products, would be included by 22 suburbanites. The comments are not, except in the case of child care, as much pleas for help in solving personal problems as a search for creative modifications of action or product.

The other side of the role-taking question is: "Which would

you omit?" Twenty-one per cent of the respondents would omit nothing, and another 11 per cent say that "Someone must like it." Thirty-four per cent of all the women, and 54 per cent of those who would change the newspapers by omitting something, would do away with "society news." This high proportion is tremendously interesting in view of the sociological and societal assumption that American women are interested in the activities of the "elite." The convergence of answers and the comments themselves warrant analysis.

Traditionally, information about the activities of the "elite," and of the layer immediately below, performed three functions. It provided vicarious enjoyment for those who did not attempt to duplicate the activities, but who felt in the others an extension of themselves; it educated those aspiring to that status; and, it imparted news. The process of vicarious enjoyment has many aspects; often it is not role-taking in its most precise meaning, because it does not involve imagining oneself in the others' situation.

Three types of women want to eliminate "society" news. One states that she does not know the people in the stories and so she is not interested in what they are doing. The second shows disinterest in any upper-class behavior. The third manifests very strong sentiments of dislike, even hostility. These different reactions may express the changing concerns of American society. Geographical mobility has broken the ties with personally and sentimentally perceived upper-class families. The size of society separates each class from all the others, except those contiguous below and above, so that literally and psychologically the elite moves in a distant sphere of life. Their names may be known in passing, but no bridges of continued identification connect them to those below. Vicarious identification of the sentimental sort becomes impossible.

Social mobility experienced by the new suburban resident and acceptance of democratic principles may have increased unwillingness to see the elite as models, even for imaginative role-taking. Other reference groups have developed in complex societies. Since experts provide easily accessible role-training, a person is not dependent upon role models, even upper-class ones. A literate person has a wide range of information sources available to her, whether they be "confession" magazines or home-decorating journals. Radio programs explain the code of behavior appropriate during deer hunts; TV chefs indicate wines to be served with different courses; and fashion magazines show styles worn internationally or by "people like us."

The depersonalization of the social elite has occurred simultaneously with the emergence of personality-involving national heroes. The same women who answer the question about desirable editorial omissions by deleting "society news" later point to a story about a "national heroine" as the kind of feature they would read. The traditional place of local social elites as sources of identification has been taken over by national event heroes, such as the astronauts and their families. Their lives are followed in detail by the middle classes and their experiences are shared vicariously. Completely fictional characters supply other vicarious contacts, while role-training models are provided by experts who tell the woman how she can act like the popular image of the modern housewife. Testimonials remind her of specific people she can resemble, but most of them are not furnished by upperclass women.

Complete lack of interest in the larger society's "society news" and in the local elite represent only two instances of a desire to exclude information of their activities from newspapers. The hostility contained in the following statements, which are representative of a major category of comments, cannot be ignored.

> Why so much splash on debutantes' pool parties, eh? Who cares except that group—that is, the minority. Of course, money talks, I guess. Stop splashing opinions and happenings of morons and perverse people; put it back and talk about people that make up the majority of nations. Get news of communities sent in some way . . . (Mount Prospect).

> Society news?—don't hold the "400" in awe any more. The average person accomplishes as much good in her activities, sometimes at a bigger sacrifice of time and money than they do, so she is not impressed by the charitable activities of society, for instance (Park Forest).

> There's an awful lot I don't read. The gossip columns mean nothing to me. . . . The Chicago society news is ridiculous (La Grange Park).

Such hostility suggests the importance of "society" to those who feel so strongly about the subject. There seems to be an unconscious "dislike" or envy of the kinds of activities in which the elite engage and even of the presence of an elite. Its existence reminds the newspaper reader of the long way the upwardly mobile still have to go. It might be more comfortable to look back and read of behavior problems of the lower classes rather than to be faced with the unattainable behavior or situations of those above.

The concentration of "anti-society" comments by the first- and second-generation middle-class women leads to the tentative conclusion that the class gap is still great in urban America, but that stories about the life of the upper class perform neither the sentiment-identifying nor the role-taking function for most new middle-class members. A major category of respondents does not "feel good" from knowing that the elite is enjoying itself, nor is it preparing for the same kind of life by seeking hints of appropriate action. Its members want to be left alone to enjoy their own success, with no reminder of the height of the ladder they climb so laboriously.

THE ASSISTING SEGMENT OF THE SOCIAL CIRCLE OF HOUSEWIVES

The modern urban housewife frequently interacts with many different people. As one responsible for running her household, she depends on services brought into her home, as well as on those performed in social spaces controlled by others. The number of services is increasingly large, the choice available to her increasingly demands professional competence, and the rights and duties of the relations are varied and complex. As Gregory Stone points out in his study of city shoppers, women differ considerably in the ways in which they approach their marketing function.[15] The great diversity in the types and qualities of services available to those with increasingly discretionary incomes necessitates flexible behavior based on planned selection and a great deal of knowledge.

The traditional city store catered to a small and steady clientele with whom almost primary relations were maintained. Each

15. Gregory Stone, "City Shoppers and Urban Identification: Observations on the Social Psychology of City Life," *American Journal of Sociology*, 60 (July 1954), 36–45.

store carried limited goods, arranged in a manner known only to the owners, the only people with rights of access. The housewife would enter very frequently, lacking refrigerator and freezer facilities. She tended to develop a daily round, synchronized with her other duties and convergent with the rounds of other women with similar life styles. The butcher or baker knew each by name and by favored types and quantities of purchases. He and the customers tended to live nearby, so that the economic connections among them were reinforced by ethnic, educational, political, and recreational ties. The "mom-and-pop" store carried a variety of items, but it too was run by a small and closely connected unit in a manner similar to the specialty shop. Housewives did not experiment with menus or ingredients learned from secondary or "stranger" sources, for personal talk as well as advice for solving familiar or small new problems abounded during the shopping exchange.

One of the women interviewed in the pilot study, an older Italian widow who moved to a new home in a newly developed neighborhood in a newly booming suburb, complained bitterly throughout her two-hour interview over the loneliness she felt as a result of the change in shopping facilities. She does not drive and cannot get to stores daily; when there "she can't find anything." The whole round of life has been changed. The aura of the large supermarket is so different as to make her feel that its food is foreign and that she is ignorant. Her one wish is to move back to the old neighborhood, where she could again start the morning, after straightening up the house and dressing, by visits to the different stores she knew. She even misses the smells, finding modern shopping centers "unappetizing." Many Broadway plays and fictional portrayals in film and books speak nostalgically of the "old neighborhood," with special emphasis on its businesses in which personal relations were tied into the whole process of home and life maintenance.

Two main trends affecting the social role of urban housewives are the expansion of the service segment of this role and the depersonalization of many of its component relations. Both trends are a consequence of, and in turn contribute to, three other characteristics of modern merchandising: the increasing size of the customer or client segment of a store's circle; the emphasis on quality standardization and other measures of "efficiency"; and consumer sophistication. Mass communication media have increased the customer's knowledge and skill in determining desired items and their qualities. Modern women, doing most of the purchasing for the family, are no longer willing to have the butcher select and judge items to meet their needs. The impersonal structure of the modern store performs new functions for a different kind of housewife. Open counters and their contents are labeled, systems are designed so as to facilitate the "logical" deduction of the probable location of items even in strange stores, and the customer is left free to make decisions. No one questions her selection or recommends anything on the basis of personal knowledge about her and her family.

The depersonalized, large, and competency-demanding supermarket is not the only service center. Most women utilize a great range of places, offering a variety of spatial rights and relational opportunities (see Table 16). They can enter gossipy beauty parlors, small and charge-account clothing stores, or completely depersonalized discount houses. In these places, they can become involved in personal relations, task-focused but individually designed interaction, "just looking," or an in-and-out trip without the exchange of a single word.

The presence of these multiple systems is taken for granted in this society. Members fail to recognize that providing the services needed to run the American middle-class home involves many levels of interaction, knowledge, and skill which are institutionally multidimensional and expansive in social life-space.[16] In shopping, a modern woman must learn to define spatial rights, item characteristics, abstracted combinations of singly purchased

16. The concept of social life-space is important to this study. Based upon Kurt Lewin's work (see Morton Deutsch's "Field Theory in Social Psychology" in Volume 1 of Gardner Lindsey, ed., *Handbook of Social Psychology,* Cambridge, Mass.: Addison-Wesley, 1954, it became an important part of the work of many members of the University of Chicago Committee of Human Development. Generally, it refers to the extension of the person's "being" into social relations and social roles. Elaine Cumming and William E. Henry used three measures to determine the extent of societal engagement in research which resulted in *Growing Old,* New York: Basic Books, 1961. I have found the need to organize the social life-space into sets of roles falling into different institutions. The greater the institutional divergence of the roles of a person, the more multidimensional his life-space and thus the more complex his personality.

Table 16: Percentages of "interaction patterns" respondents using specified services within the home, by frequency of use.

Code: (1) Daily or at least three times a week; (2) often, once or twice a week; (3) once a month, but not as often as once a week; (4) once a year to eleven times a year, not once a month; (5) rarely, less than once a year; (6) used to, at least once a month, but now don't; (7) never; (8) other; (9) other persons do that, not I; (0) no answer.

Services Used in Home	Frequency of Use									
	1	2	3	4	5	6	7	8	9	0
Maid, full-time servant	2	5	0	1	1	3	82	1	0	3
Not live-in, regular help	3	14	7	3	0	5	65	0	0	3
Medical Doctor	0	1	6	34	24	0	30	2	0	1
Babysitter	4	9	10	4	2	14	54	1	0	1
Gardening service	0	5	0	5	3	1	75	2	6	1
Diaper service	1	2	0	0	0	30	64	1	0	1
Service organization, cleans house	0	1	1	5	5	0	85	0	0	2
Window-washing service	0	0	3	18	6	1	64	1	7	0
Snow-shoveling service	2	3	0	3	2	1	68	1	16	1
Mail delivery	89	1	-	0	0	0	3	0	4	1
Milk delivery	26	13	1	0	0	9	47	1	0	1
Bread delivery	1	1	0	0	0	2	92	0	0	2
Other food delivery	0	13	12	7	3	2	59	1	0	2
Laundry, driver comes to home	0	12	18	2	2	6	57	0	0	1
Clothes, cleaning, driver comes to home	0	13	15	2	1	5	61	0	0	1
Other, store, phone order (drug, liquor)	1	6	17	16	10	1	47	0	0	1
Rug, furniture cleaning	0	0	0	24	35	1	38	0	0	0
Painting, inside, outside	0	0	0	15	41	0	28	2	14	0
Special problems: plumber	0	0	2	20	32	1	25	3	15	1
Appliance repair	0	0	2	20	40	1	26	1	6	3
Other problems	2	1	0	4	5	1	25	0	1	58
Newspaper delivery	53	8	1	0	0	5	29	0	0	3
Door-to-door sales, Avon, Fuller	0	1	9	25	14	3	42	0	0	3
Other door-to-door	0	0	1	5	6	2	57	0	0	27
Teacher (piano)	0	6	0	1	0	9	73	0	0	9
Other (specify)	0	1	2	6	3	0	27	0	0	59

Total no. of respondents 205

things, and interaction sequences of great complexity in order to produce a nutritious menu, a color synchronized bedroom, or a set of Christmas presents. She must know if she can expect "help" in the selection of items or if she can serve herself from storage areas. Foreign visitors to American cities are often bewildered by the array of spatial rights and behavioral sequences available to, and utilized by, the modern housewife.[17]

An interplay of services both inside and outside of the home can create irritation in client-professional, customer-service organizations, or buyer-seller relations. This can be verified by a trip to a medical clinic, a crowded store, or any of the variety of service centers. A major difficulty of many interactions between the service- or object-provider and the recipient is a lack of sufficient competence on both sides. Irritation is highest when the pattern is new and those involved are not trained to facilitate the exchange or to creatively adjust to situational changes. Personnel usually handle the lack of institutionalization and of training of all involved in the relation through a client-classificatory system. For example, some patients are "good," but "trouble-makers" are expected in every situation.[18] Those clients or service members who are new to the pattern are labeled as "difficult" or "stupid," because those accustomed to the procedure assume its "naturalness," even when it is relatively new to the other participants. In spite of this, women have developed a great willingness and capacity to utilize a variety of relations with the assisting segment of the role of housewife (see Tables 17 and 18).

A scale of service use was devised to test the hypothesis that the presence of children and variations in family income and educational achievement affect the frequency of use of in-the-home services. Women with low income and without children have the lowest in-the-home service scores, and there is a definite increase in the number of items and in use frequency with increase in income, especially for families with offspring.

17. Helena Znaniecki Lopata, "Of Space and the Housewife," paper given at the meeting of the Society for the Study of Social Problems in Miami, 1966.

18. Howard Becker *et al.* found the *Boys in White,* Chicago: University of Chicago Press, 1961, classifying patients, writing off from full care those they defined as "crocks." The same system seems to exist in all occupations.

Table 17: Percentages of "interaction patterns" respondents using specified services outside the home, by frequency of use.

Code: (1) Daily or at least three times a week; (2) often, once or twice a week; (3) once a month, but not as often as once a week; (4) once a year to eleven times a year, not once a month; (5) rarely, less than once a year; (6) used to, at least once a month, but now don't; (7) never; (8) other; (9) other persons do that, not I; (0) no answer.

Services Used outside home	Frequency of Use									
	1	2	3	4	5	6	7	8	9	0
Food store, large chain	24	60	11	1	1	0	1	0	0	1
Neighborhood grocery	21	36	12	4	5	2	17	0	0	1
Delicatessen	2	24	24	13	8	0	27	0	0	2
Bakery	10	29	24	12	6	6	16	0	0	1
Butcher or fish store	2	28	15	9	7	3	34	0	0	1
Fruit, vegetable store, stand	4	20	11	10	11	3	39	0	0	2
Fancy foods store	0	3	16	11	11	1	55	0	0	3
Other foods	0	4	10	11	3	0	36	0	0	35
Dime store	0	13	51	23	8	0	3	0	0	1
Department store	1	15	57	23	1	0	1	0	0	1
Shoe store	0	0	21	68	4	0	5	0	0	0
Clothing store	0	5	30	53	3	0	6	0	0	1
Hardware	0	3	20	48	19	0	6	0	1	1
Discount store	1	5	23	24	18	0	27	0	0	2
Liquor	1	2	19	25	15	0	34	0	1	1
Take to laundry	0	17	13	2	4	4	54	0	1	2
Laundromat	1	18	8	4	6	6	52	0	0	3
Self-cleaner, cleaning clothes	0	3	22	25	9	1	35	1	0	2
Seamstress, sewing	0	0	5	25	19	0	51	0	0	1
Drug store, pharmacy	5	22	48	16	2	0	3	0	0	1
Other stores (gift, furniture, etc.)	0	3	18	39	27	0	12	0	0	0
Beauty shop	0	26	30	26	6	2	8	0	0	0
Repair shop (shoe, TV)	0	1	13	58	18	1	7	0	1	0
Doctor for children	0	0	12	41	10	5	25	1	0	4
Doctor for self	0	0	9	57	27	1	3	1	0	1
Dentist for children	0	0	6	41	8	2	34	3	0	5
Dentist for self	0	0	8	54	27	1	7	1	0	0
Automobile repair	0	0	7	42	11	1	28	0	6	3
Bank	1	25	40	11	5	0	8	0	6	3
Restaurant	5	21	34	22	8	0	8	0	0	0
Food caterer	0	1	0	5	14	1	72	0	0	6
Other (first mention)	0	2	3	2	1	0	13	0	0	77
Other (second mention)	0	0	0	1	1	0	12	0	0	84

Total no. of respondents 205

Table 18: Frequency distributions and percentages of references to specific objects in answer to "What are the problems peculiar to this role (housewife)?" by residence and working status.

Object	Suburban Housewives No.	Suburban Housewives Per Cent	Urban Housewives No.	Urban Housewives Per Cent	Working Women No.	Working Women Per Cent	Total No.	Total Per Cent
Self	36	10	32	12	4	4	72	10
Husband	16	5	11	4	14	16	41	6
Children	126	36	81	32	20	22	227	33
Family	25	7	51	20	26	29	102	15
Other relatives	1	0	0	0	0	0	1	0
Friends and neighbors	10	3	6	2	0	0	16	2
Community and society	11	3	2	1	1	1	14	2
Object not specified	54	15	47	18	3	3	104	15
House, material possessions	73	21	27	10	21	24	121	17
Number of answers	352	100	257	100	89	100	698	100
Number of respondents	268		200		100		568	

Mean scores for each sub-category of the population show that the highest users are women with some college education and children. The lowest mean is reached by high school drop-outs, with or without children. Income differences provide even more dramatic variations. Women with higher incomes can afford, and desire, services to be brought to them, and they delegate more of the house maintenance work to professional specialists, such as painters or furniture cleaners, than their less affluent counterparts, who do the work themselves. In addition, the wealthier women utilize the telephone more frequently and have goods delivered in addition to going to stores.

However many women use services brought to them in the home, many more enter spaces belonging to others in order to meet their family needs. One-fourth go to a store daily or at least three times a week; another 60 per cent go at least once or twice a week. Thus, 84 per cent enter a large food store in each week and 1 per cent only claims never to use such facilities.

The neighborhood grocery is used several times a week by one-fourth of the respondents, and at least once a week by 57 per cent.

Only food-catering services are seldom used. Even beauty shops are patronized at least yearly by all but 8 per cent of the women, one-fourth going once or twice a week. Five per cent eat in restaurants almost daily, 60 per cent at least once a month, and all but 8 per cent at some time during the year.

The presence of small children within the home tends to keep respondents with lower educational achievement in the house, but it does not seem to affect those in the higher levels. The tendency seems to be for women with lower education to use few types of stores, but very often. Frequent shopping is reminiscent of older styles of purchasing, those utilizing the neighborhood store, bakery, and butcher. Women with a college degree tend to enter a greater variety of places, but to keep down the frequency of such trips. They group their contacts in time rather than repeating them in the same place.

Income and use of outside-of-the-home services are again related. The higher the income, the more the woman uses a variety of facilities, in a near-weekly pattern Women with low incomes simply do not have money to spend on different goods and service centers. The lowest mean score (28) is obtained by young women with under a $3000 income, the highest mean score (61) by mothers who are living on over $20,000. The scores are higher than those for services inside the home.

PHYSICAL TOOLS OF BEING A HOUSEWIFE

Money

Housewives require a certain number of tools for work or life, although their quantity and form vary considerably by society and by social class. In urban areas most of them are selected by the woman, the major ones in co-operation with the man of the house. Modern life makes it necessary to have sufficient amounts of the common denominator of money in order to obtain the objects used in the role. The housewife is dependent upon the ability to convert items obtained from others into ones for family use. The production of items used within the home has become divided into two stages, with the important intermediary factor of distribution binding them together. Initial production is carried out away from the home. Food is grown and often processed away from the home. It is packaged and distributed to centers located sufficiently near the home to enable direct or intermediary selection by the housewife. The frequently heard judgment that the home is only a consuming center ignores the housewife's participation both in the distribution process and in the second stage of production—converting the still unusable product into something which can be consumed by the family in question. It is her function to procure and select the items and to produce them for consumption by the "client" segment of her social circle. The amount of work this stage of production requires varies considerably by item. The importance of the modern woman's desire to feel that she is an essential producer is even built into many products such as cake mixes, which are intentionally left incomplete to increase her chance to place her stamp on them.

Money frees the woman from the need to engage in all stages of production; a need which used to leave the all but upper-class woman physically exhausted, while at the same time enabling the remaining stages to be carried out in expanding and creative ways. Societies in which each family produced all it consumed tend to be limited to repetitive roles and actions preventing any development of new ideas or items. Thus, money earned by the woman or by her husband can provide *freedom to* experimentally build new life patterns. The interviews indicate that this is one of the meanings money has to housewives: a release from past limitations and a means of increasing competence and breadth of perspective. This emphasis may be alienating the very young generation, for which it has a completely different symbolic quality, but the parents speak of it in terms of freedom, as having significance far beyond its character as a logical exchange medium and even beyond the physical quality of the objects it makes possible.

Erich Fromm and others have pointed out that money became at one time a measure of a man's worth in comparison to other men, a rather restrictive consequence of the devaluation of inherited status.[19] As a substitute, his salary or wage indicates how much he is "worth" to status-conferring organizations. One earns as much as others are willing to pay, and the quantity of money easily becomes converted into the quality of self. That it became the first substitute for unchangeable, ascribed self-value is not surprising, because of its easy indication of "achievement." New forms of personal identity are now beginning to emerge in America, but the paycheck serves as an important intermediary symbolic source of rank.

A second meaning of money in America is as a means for the purchase of objects and life styles. Objects have status, due primarily to their traditional symbolic connection with persons in different social classes. An original sculpture by a fashionable artist is a more prestigious purchase than a Kewpie doll, not merely because it costs more, but because such possessions have been identified with different European-based status levels.

As we have seen, one of the reasons the social role of housewife has had low status in American society is that it does not draw a wage or salary, nor is its level of performance rewarded by a monitarily visible and comparatively honorable "raise." If new forms of status brought by life styles or non-occupational roles replace the paycheck, the housewife's status may be more directly connected to her role performance. The housewife has obtained money-connected status in two ways: through the money she has from her family of orientation (inheritance or allowance) and from her family of procreation (family income or allowance) and through the manner in which she converts these funds into home use. Traditionally, she had been guaranteed prestige by being born into a high-status family. Marriage into a "good" family was her second major source. The ideal housewife is now seen by the women interviewed as one who "manages" her selection of items well and converts them into personality stamped prestigeful life patterns. This image fits into recent views of marriage as a partnership, providing a fourth source of prestige to women who are not earning money directly; they can be judged as contributing indirectly to their husbands' economic success. Middle-class women tend to so identify their roles.

19. Erich Fromm, *Man for Himself,* New York: Rinehart and Company, 1947.

Housewives often mention a financial event in talking about their lives and role sequences. Young women tend to feel that it is a major means of solving problems of home maintenance, and all but the very old see the future as economically better. Mothers wishing to meet the societal standard of evaluation of performance express the desire to have greater means for physically maintaining or socializing their young. Even husband-wife relations are assumed to be eased with the help of goods or services which free the wife from energy and time consumption in the role of housewife.

The social background of girls entering marriage affects the degree to which they see their husbands as an economic investment and the way they evaluate the early years of marital life—a period during which the husband's income tends to be relatively small because of newness to his occupation. American culture encourages "complete independence" from parents immediately after marriage, frowning on economic support from even wealthy families of orientation. Recent studies by Sussman, Litwak, and Shanas indicate that such help is more frequent than assumed, conducted under the guise of gifts or the covering of certain types of bills.[20] However, a number of housewives feel that they are unable to maintain their homes after marriage in "the style to which they had become accustomed." "It has changed very much by my move from my childhood home where we had servants; by working, then marrying and having children and now a home." The implication is of a drop in financial status, but she adds: "My husband has progressed nicely in his work and will probably continue to do so." Aged thirty-two, this housewife and home-owner in the suburbs apparently succeeded in rising economically to a position closer to that of her childhood than the one held during early marriage.

"It's totally different. I came from an extremely wealthy family. Right now, to us, we're pinched—not that we're poor, but in comparison. It's a lot different—but I like it a lot better. My husband wants to move to a smaller town, we want more children." This thirty-year-old mother of three children, none over pre-school age, seems quite satisfied with life in spite of the

---

20. Most of the research establishing the facts of kin functionality is summarized in Ethel Shanas and Gordon F. Streib, *Social Structure and the Family: General Relations*, Englewood Cliffs, N.J.: Prentice-Hall, 1965.

financial reverse and the inability to purchase objects and services which her childhood home contained.

Some respondents find the change from residence in a home maintained by others to one which they must run on a limited budget very difficult: "When we began just after marriage, we had to start and fight up from the bottom. All due to the lack of money." Now her children are married, and she wishes that "I could own another house in a better part of the city; I also wish money were there to go places and do things." Life seems less of a struggle now and more of a leisure-oriented vision, but the absence of desired events is defined in terms of the same thing, a lack of money.

Others, however, seem pleased with the means they have for performing the role of housewife: "Came from a large family with very little money; now we have more money to do with." The phrase "to do with" is an interesting part of the American vocabulary, indicative of the fact that money is seen as a means of selectively meeting needs. Specific contributions of money to the role of housewife are mentioned by a number of respondents. "Life is much better than it was in the past. I have a washer and dryer and anything else I want."

Money provides release from worry, security for children, and easing of work. "I would like enough money so that I would not have to think twice before spending a dollar," states one woman. When asked what she would like to change about her present life, one young respondent states: "My husband and I would be finished with school. I would be making money and he would be making more money than he is. My house would be better furnished—telephone, TV, drapes, more chairs, rugs, everything." Thus, the young girl dreams of furnishing her own place, the new home-owner of meeting the mortgage or carrying out expansion plans. Other women would convert the increase of income into help for the care of possessions they already have. "I'd have a maid come in at least once a week. Do ironing, that would be a big help," wishes a thirty-year-old mother of a two-year-old child, reflecting the most frequently mentioned specific direction of spending money. Her whole life definition is seen in terms of financial problems: "When we got married, my husband was a crop-duster, mostly cotton, some corn, and we traveled about. In the spring, he'd get itchy 'cause he could make $4000 or $5000 in a couple of months, so he'd pick up and leave—that's not so good. Now he's given that up; not kidding himself anymore; going slower. He's learning that you can't just pick up and leave whenever you want. We do hope to get into a higher income bracket and have more. Not hard to get ahead in flying; he's thought of being a company pilot." She explains that these are mostly ideas or hopes, rather than definite plans; so it is not very probable that her wish for a maid is realistic. "In the future, things will be better financially—might even have a cleaning woman for the heavier work." "Change? I would like to be a little better off financially; I don't want servants or to belong to a country club. I would just like enough to relieve the constant pressure. I wouldn't want any other changes." This suburbanite does not seem to have a clearly developed plan for getting a cleaning woman, but she is making a definite distinction between such help and "servants," feeling the latter to be part of a way of life not for her.

A maid is the dream of many suburban housewives, the major single item they would include, but it is also the wish of an urban waitress: "I would use more money, but I enjoy life as it is now, more or less. I and my husband enjoy keeping the house up and cleaning. I would like a part-time maid to do ironing and cleaning, but I feel it's too hard to find someone you can count on" (aged forty-two, children twenty-four and sixteen).

"I would like to have enough money to quit work and to be able to go more places and do more things," says a fifty-five-year-old who is far from feeling life is slowing down; and she is joined by a sixty-year-old mother of two adult children who also says: "Travel some, general living conditions,—but I wouldn't change much."

Money is often seen as a release from present restrictions of life. "I'd like to be doing something where I would be doing for someone else, something like social work. Yet, if there is no money connected with it, the cost of transportation and other things would prevent me from doing it," states a forty-six-year-old. Her three children, now twenty-two to fourteen, are above the age in which she feels strong time demands, but she wishes for activities impossible because of finances. The same limitation of money affects many older women, widows, and those whose husbands have retired without a high benefit or pension plan. Even going to club meetings requires funds which cannot be taken away from basic necessities. Interaction with others is not defined as a strong need when compared with food or housing.

Release from paid employment is seen as a possible freedom to be granted by having money. "If there is anything I would like to change, I would like to be home twenty-four hours a day, if I had an income," is the wish for desired change by a forty-nine-year-old widow with two teenage children. Her working does not seem to be a matter of choice. "I would like to stay home and do the things I'm not able to do." "To have more money—to change things so that I wouldn't have to work so hard. If you have money, you could change anything. I would like to live in a home in the suburbs." These comments by mothers who are in their forties indicate a definition of outside employment not as a source of self-expression, but as an imposition brought about by a shortage of money. Some women would relieve their husbands of the need to work "so hard" by obtaining money from other sources, which are often unspecified: "I would like us to have enough money for my husband to retire or, at least, not to work so hard." This woman is forty years old, with two teenage children, and her wish for the husband's retirement is rather premature, especially in view of the fact that he is also in his forties.

Finally, the possession of money can provide a feeling of comfort, of protection against unexpected and feared events. "I'd love to have money in the bank for security." This forty-six-year-old mother of two children, ages twenty-three and nineteen, is surprisingly the only one of the housewives to wish for money in the bank when offered a chance to imagine a change in her life. All other respondents wish for more money in general or as a means of purchasing specific objects and services.

The Home

The home which the housewife is responsible for running takes many forms. Its modifiable aspects include: the size and arrangement of the abode; the type and quantity of items contained in it; the condition in which they are expected to be maintained; the processes required for their care; their relation to each other in terms of space and use; the number and types of occupants within it and the personal rights of each of these people and even of the animals; the relation of the residence to the rest of the community; the connection between its occupants and others in the society; and any other characteristics which affect how it is perceived and the significance it has for those whose relations are influenced by its presence and form. The housewife is not the only one who has rights over its arrangement and use; the whole society is usually concerned with it as part of its life and culture. Social groups vary considerably in the freedom which they allow their members in actions directed toward, or within, their residence.

The traditional Judeo-Christian cultures upon which most Americans build their life patterns maintained ancestral homes in a familistic style. Each designated inheritor of the home and its possessions from prior generations was responsible for transmitting them in the same or better condition to future family descendents. This familistic system, which treats each generation as simply a trustee of family possessions, as temporary occupants of homes owned in perpetuity by a unit of which it is only a link, existed in rural America.[21] The system was non-individualistic and demanded strict conformity with traditional ways of handling things. The small community provided many kin members and neighbors who guaranteed a lack of experimentation by surrounding each resident with witnesses and critics judging action in traditional terms. Often relatives of the patriarchal line were already established in the home the new bride entered, and she had no rights to impose her individuality.

Industrial, urban America has changed the nature of the home. At its extreme of mobility, it is a society of new homes or older dwellings with new owners, of mushrooming suburbs surrounding work centers not only with circles, but also with spokes of touching buildings or lawns. The transition between the ancestral home and the private abode of each nuclear family was the rooming house, which freed the individual from familial and sometimes even communal controls. Russell Lynes says: "During the nineteenth century it was estimated that more

21. This is the main conclusion of Ernest W. Burgess, Harvey J. Locke, and Mary Margaret Thomes in *The Family: From Institution to Companionship,* New York: American Book Co., 3rd ed., 1963.

than 70 per cent of the population has lived in boarding houses at some time in their lives." The migrant, usually a male, came to the city and lived in a boarding house or apartment until he accumulated enough money to send for his family. This unit could not be immediately housed in a permanent home, and assimilation often meant continual movement from the least expensive housing into more comfortable dwellings and more "illusion of luxury." [22] For the new migrant, home was subordinated to work. With upward mobility the pendulum swung back to an emphasis on the home, with its subsequent movement away from work into more "desirable" residential neighborhoods and with changes in appearance created by abundance. As Riesman states, by the time a person moves to the suburbs, he wants to keep home and work entirely separated.[23] Wood found the professionals living farther from work than employees at the lower rungs of the socio-economic ladder,[24] and the housewives explain their selection of the housing unit differently, depending on their education and social class life styles.

The United States has developed an interesting compromise between two systems of official definition of the domicile of the married woman which exist in the modern world. It is one of several countries in which "The domicile of the wife follows that of the husband except in certain specified cases," according to the laws of various states. In this it differs slightly from the more patriarchal societies, such as those in the Arab world, where "The domicile of the wife follows that of the husband until dissolution of the marriage," and the more egalitarian societies of Scandinavia, Poland, and Yugoslavia where the domicile of the wife is independent of that of her husband.[25] Those societies see the woman not "as taking his domicile, but as having the same domicile as he." Thus, the American society sees the home as maintained by the woman in her role of housewife,

22. Russell Lynes, *The Domesticated Americans,* New York: Harper & Row, 1963, p. 39.

23. David Riesman, "The Suburban Dislocation" in *The Annals of the American Academy of Political and Social Science* (1957), 123–46.

24. Robert C. Wood, *Suburbia: Its People and Their Politics,* Boston: Houghton Mifflin, 1958.

25. UNESCO Commission on the Status of Women (December 1953, New York, E/CN6229, p. 11).

but technically under the ownership of the husband. She still is traditionally carried over the threshold, just as when the man stole her from her family to run his house. Although no longer entering the husband's ancestral dwelling she, not he, is the addition to the home.

However, although the husband is considered the master of the first home into which he brings his bride, the modern definition of marriage as a partnership assumes a greater involvement by the wife in its maintenance and a more equal responsibility for insuring its continued ownership or rental. The wife is currently a major consumer, even when she takes the role of the other in selecting items, and the person responsible for converting the "house into a home" by manipulating its form.[26] Its general appearance and even content are seen as a result of her taste; and the husband, newly returned from full-time employment outside its walls, is often felt to be an uncomfortable daytime stranger within it.

26. Robert O. Blood, Jr. and Donald M. Wolfe, *Husbands and Wives*, New York: The Free Press, 1960. See also Janet L. Wolff, *What Makes Women Buy*, New York: McGraw-Hill, 1958.

FOUR

Becoming and
Being a Mother

BACKGROUND

A large proportion of the respondents who have minor children in the home focus their role-cluster upon the functions of being a mother; the others assign it a second place, after the role of housewife or wife. Few ignore it completely in a rank order of roles or during two-hour depth interviews.

Many factors contribute to the heavy emphasis on the social role of mother. The interviews took place during the day: a woman with young children is more likely to be centered around her role as mother then than during the evening hours. This does not invalidate the answers; it simply reflects the fact that young mothers spend the majority of their waking hours in the home with children. A second explanation for the emphasis on this role—often to the exclusion of husband-wife relations, the role of housewife, community participation, and other sets of obligations—is the strong child-orientation of American society. Many observers have pointed to this aspect of the culture, and knowledge of its presence by members of the society increases its importance. It becomes the legitimate explanation of almost any action. Moving to the suburbs, taking a job, leaving employment, joining voluntary associations, or devoting oneself to household tasks can be justified as "good for the children."

A third reason for concentration on the role of mother may be the growing difficulty in learning and carrying out the complex child-rearing procedures. Traditional culture provided formulas for rearing and authoritarian controls over the young. These were easily available to the mother and relatively unchanging. The knowledge currently judged necessary for childrearing, originating in medicine, psychology, the other social sciences, and even the humanities, is not easily obtained or available in total packages that can be consistently utilized by the mother.[1] The methods by which the theories and suggested actions in child-rearing are disseminated result in sporadic, disjointed, and often distorted information. Although each childrearing theory may be internally consistent, most women get it piecemeal, mixed with bits of other theories. The time and space limitations of mass communication media and the immediacy of many problems facing mothers result in darts and dashes into the field of psychology or other sources of knowledge in child development. Pre-parental education is rarely sufficient to prepare future mothers for the competence-demanding world. The media's desire to supply the parent with information is often coupled with the assumption that the reader or listener will not be interested in it or understand what is said unless the ideas are highly simplified and "dramatized." The consequence is a warping of scientific findings. Articles ignore the conditions under which a pattern of behavior can be introduced into a relation—for example, spanking to a child-rearing system. Generalizations are so abstract as to make their application impossible or at least difficult. Many theories do not provide steps by which a specific mother-child relation can be developed in the desired direction. Many women are attempting to rear their offspring in scientifically based or at least "modern" ways, but they find the process very difficult. This can contribute to the importance assigned to the social role of mother.

A fourth explanation for the emphasis of American women upon being a mother is the societal placing of almost total responsibility for the rearing of children upon them. This is one of the few times in recorded history that the mother-child unit has been so isolated from supportive adult assistance. Responsibility for the health and welfare, the behavior and ability of the child is basically unshared. The father is usually not held ac-

1. Helena Znaniecki Lopata, "The Dysfunctional Effects of the Dissemination of Social Science Knowledge," paper read at the American Sociological Association meetings in Washington, D.C., 1962.

countable for what happens to the children, because "he is not home much of the time." The former extended kinship group which lived under one roof or quite nearby has dropped away, each member being geographically isolated and able to provide only stop-gap help and this only after a lapse of time and with no sharing of responsibility for the outcome. The community within which the mother is functioning may easily be hetero-geneous: indifferent to her child, hostile, or ostentatiously carry-ing out different child-rearing procedures. She then lacks an environmental support for what she does and what she demands of the child and of their relation. She faces nothing but criti-cism and possible conflict with her offspring as he learns cul-turally different patterns.

A fifth explanation for the emphasis on the social role of mother lies in the recent revolution in American views about human nature and the potentialities of children. Two basic com-ponents of this ideological redefinition of the situation are of particular relevance to the role of mother. Both are based on the conviction that the environment can and must be controlled by means of the scientific and secular knowledge of each person as he operates in his world. One form of change in the theoretical set of modern society is in the field of illness and health; each adult is now trained in its fundamentals and assumed to con-trol his life in such terms. Medical science has decreased infant and child mortality, but only with the co-operative effort of competent mothers. The ideational change has placed the re-sponsibility for the development of infant health upon the mother working in co-operation with medical experts. Modern doctors continue to have problems with lower-class women's approach to life. Their complex of attitudes and behaviors allows children to engage in unhealthy action, fails to understand and diligently follow a home-care regimen, and assumes that certain children die anyway. Infant mortality has decreased in the homes of more educated mothers.[2] The fact that the whole med-ical institution is dependent upon people who understand the

2. Dr. Herbert Slutsky, of Roosevelt University, worked as a medical geographer with Dr. Samuel Andleman, former Commissioner of Cook County Board of Health, in attempting to control factors contributing to lead poisoning of infants. They found that many mothers simply do not under-stand the whole principle of systematized and scientific investigation and treatment of disease.

nature of disease and who purposely manipulate the environment to prevent or cure illness places a heavy burden on a mother in this society. Cultures which regard disease as inevitable or brought about by gods pacified only by powerful magicians relieve parents of the responsibility for ensuring the health of their children.

The second form of modern ideological redefinition is in the social sciences, and it has had similar consequence upon the role of mother. The idea that human beings are not born with a closed set of personality and ability traits which will simply "evolve" has changed all estimates of the importance of motherhood. Dissemination of this knowledge has developed an awareness of the influence parental behavior has upon children and of the strain of their roles. Traditional culture assumed that once a child was born, or sometimes once he was named after a dead or living relative, nothing the parents did would influence his intelligence, personality, or temperament. This ideology relieved the mother of the responsibility of providing a psychologically healthy environment for her child and helping him to develop his potential. The modern woman does not have this advantage, being aware that she is held responsible for what her offspring "grows up to be."

Two additional characteristics of the social role of mother complicate its competent performance by young American women. One of these is the fact that she has been trained to handle problems rationally, systematically, without a show or even a strong experience of anger; to solve each in order and to proceed to a new situation.[3] School and work teach her to be task-oriented, to measure accomplishment in terms of finished product, and to organize it in blocks of time within a specialized division of labor. The care of infants and the socialization of children are, however, highly emotional processes in this society of cultural change and heterogeneity, and there are no perfect procedures for them. In addition, American youths are expected to be handled emotionally, with "tender and loving care." Parent-

3. The culture of several Anglo-Saxon nations has often been categorized as rejective of a show of emotion. Geoffrey Gorer notes this about British attitudes toward grief in *Death, Grief and Mourning*, Garden City, N.Y.: Doubleday Anchor Book, 1967; and Edward Hall about American feelings of physical closeness in *The Hidden Dimension*, Garden City, N.Y.: Doubleday, 1965.

child interaction, particularly in the pre-adult years, consists of many "episodes" laden with all forms of sentiment and high emotion. Constant interruptions make the work to be accomplished between these exchanges very difficult, and children often disorganize what mothers have just finished doing. The young mother, lacking a consistent cultural base for fitting together mother-child relations and these to other roles, surrounded by anxiety, guilt, and frustration, often finds herself acting in ways she does not like and becoming angry at times when she wants to maintain calm. The emotional level of interaction appears "abnormal" to her when compared to prior life and training, and it often causes negative feelings toward herself.

A second characteristic of the social role of mother, which distinguishes it from the many other roles in this society and which causes much strain, is its dynamic nature. Behavioral, attitudinal, and relational patterns which are developed and judged satisfactory at one stage of the life cycle of the role become ineffective and even dysfunctional within a relatively short period of time. The mother must constantly learn new ways of relating to her offspring as his needs and definitions change, in order to help in the process of growth and development.

Of course, not all housewives feel the significance of the role of mother for the same reasons. Some stress it because of the traditional cultural emphasis, others use it to justify all the actions they wish to undertake. Those who are aware of the increasing responsibility placed upon the mother by the ideological revolution do not necessarily respond by building the role into a creative and experimentally dynamic pattern. There is a great heterogeneity in the significance and forms of "becoming" and "being" a mother assigned by those who are performing this role in the urbanized areas.[4]

4. The role of mother within American society has been described or researched by a number of sociologists. Chief sources are: Robert R. Sears, Eleanor E. Maccoby, and Harry Levin, *Patterns of Child-Rearing*, Evanston, Ill.: Row, Peterson, 1957; James Bossard, *The Sociology of Child Development*, New York: Harper and Brothers, 1948; Guy E. Swanson and Daniel R. Miller, *The Changing American Parent*, New York: John Wiley, 1958. Of course, all textbooks on the family contain summaries of such data, and psychologists as well as social psychologists have long been interested in the effects parental attitudes and guidance have upon children. Two major areas of such research focus on prejudice and motivation and achievement.

BECOMING A MOTHER

The dictionary usually defines a mother simply as a female parent, without explaining how a woman becomes one. Societies differ in the event or sub-event which is used to symbolize entrance into the role. What is common to all systems is some form of official recognition of a bond between a woman and an infant or child, of her functioning in the culturally established way as "his mother." The bond can be assumed to begin with conception, the birth of a live offspring, or only after a set of procedures testing the newborn for qualities needed for future membership in the society. It may be dependent upon a testing of the person wishing to undertake the role of mother, as in adoption cases, and upon a public announcement of her acceptance. In most societies, the official mother is the one who has given birth to the baby, although all known groups have some form of adoption by which another person can take over the role. American society has legalized the right of a woman who has given birth to decide if she wishes to take on the social role of mother. Children can be taken from a mother only through court action proving that she is unfit for the role, that is, that her behavior indicates a lack of ability to adequately fulfill its duties.

Motherhood is thus a social phenomenon, as are all social roles, but one entered into by an act which can be minimally social and be minimally concerned with it as a final result. The Catholic Church solved the problem of making people accountable for parenthood many centuries ago by restricting sexual intercourse to persons deemed suitable parents, who are willing to undertake the roles as a consequence of it, and by symbolically identifying motherhood with conception. This policy was currently reaffirmed by official declaration, although middle-class American Catholics have been using "artificial" birth control for some time according to all reports and birth statistics.[5] Modern norms have expanded sexual intercourse to functions other than that of creating parental roles. "Planned parenthood" is a concept accepting sexual intercourse at certain times as a

5. The August 1968 pronouncement by the Pope that all forms of birth control are contrary to Catholic principles has met with strong public criticism by religious personnel, lay members, and the secular press.

purposeful initiating stage in the process of becoming a parent, while reserving it at other times for purposes of personal satisfaction. Such a planned entrance into the role of mother involves not only timed conception, but the utilization of the extended period of pregnancy for psychological and environmental preparation for the birth and for entrance into the social duties of motherhood. Although middle-class Americans usually prepare for the birth of children, the event may be unplanned and even unwelcome, and the women may not introduce changes in the environment or in themselves until after the baby has been born. Motherhood by adoption involves other sets of planned action.

Thus, entrance into the social role of mother can be defined as beginning with the decision by a husband and a wife that they wish to undertake parenthood roles and by their action to bring about a birth or an adoption. Testing each other for these roles is often not based on criteria relevant to the performance of those duties, but on the romantic love components of modern marriage. Technically, the woman does not start the official societal phase of "becoming a mother" until an announcement of the forthcoming birth or adoption is made to others, who then relate to her in special ways because she will become a mother. In middle-class families the "first to know" is usually the future mother who detects symptoms of pregnancy, the future father, and the obstetrician or general practitioner who confirms the prediction. Close relatives and friends are informed and the physical changes of pregnancy soon spread the announcement to those with whom physical contact is maintained.

In a majority of American families the social circle of the mother is expected to contain a medical man, a hospital staff, a pediatrician, all who supply the services needed in the care and rearing of the offspring, those to whom the infant is considered related through the father or the mother, and any others from whom the mother receives rights or toward whom she has obligations based on the fact that she *is* a mother of that infant. The circle varies according to many factors and changes as the child grows, that is, as his needs and place in society are modified. It thus contains, at different times, playmates, the members of several school systems, teachers of specialized skills, the spouse and the children of the offspring's family of procreation, and any member brought in by the mother or others in the group. It may even contain truant officers, court officials, and corrective home personnel.

Most American girls do not have, by their own admission and by the judgment of trained observers, sufficient knowledge and skill to become effective in the role of mother at any stage of "becoming" or even of "being" in it. Medical men, hospital staffs, more experienced parents, and the mass communication media assist the new parent in acquiring the ever-evolving knowledge and skills needed to fulfill the physical and social obligations of being a mother. Such knowledge is usually sought only after the birth of a child, although some women use the pregnancy period to prepare for that event.

The process of "becoming a mother" has been judged by many observers of the American scene to be a traumatic or "crisis" experience.[6] Urban living complicates this event because of several related factors: the mother moves with approaching completion of pregnancy from full participation in the life of the society through school, work, friendship, and other social roles to complete absorption in being a mother. Sometimes the process is accompanied by an uneasy shift in relations with former associates, especially with the husband; by spatial restrictions during the early years of the child's life which disrupt the prior pattern of mobility; by limitations of social contacts during most of the day, which is a dramatic change from a lifetime of full interaction during those hours; by the need to shift all social roles, causing conflict in the cluster; and by an increase in the level of responsibility which faces the young wife in sudden contrast to the rather carefree pre-parental life in an abundant society which caters to the young.

Becoming a mother is a major goal of most American girls, as reported by numerous studies and reflected in interviews with high school and college students, young working women, and the newly married. Entrance into the role is obtained by the

6. Chapter One contains all references to the "parenthood as crisis" series of studies supporting this thesis. Medical men and psychiatrists are so aware of the depression following role shift upon entrance to motherhood as to assign it a special name, *post partum*. The fact that becoming a mother is a strong change in life patterns, especially for American women, has received very negative comment by most observers, who somehow feel that it is "unnatural."

birth of the first child. Women with several offspring, when listing major events in their past life, tend to focus upon the birth
order rather than upon the sex of the child as a form of identification. Each new infant adds to, and modifies, the existing pattern, not by doubling work but by changing all components of
the mother role. Only 14 of the 205 "interaction patterns" respondents mention the birth of a son and an equal number
mention the birth of a daughter. The sexual identification of
the child is usually made by mothers who already have one or
more children of one sex and who then speak of one more as
a contrast. "My daughter was born, I was thrilled to have a
girl," reports a mother of two boys. In each case of direct sex
identification of offspring, it is the distribution which draws attention to this aspect of the birth event. This does not mean
that this characteristic lacks significance in future years of the
mother-child relation, only that the early stages of infant care
are not heavily influenced by whether it is a male or a female.
One hundred and two of the 175 birth references by the 205
respondents are directed toward birth-order identities. Women
with one child list that event as "My child was born" or as
"That was the year Mary was born."

Although becoming a mother is an event faced by all but
17 per cent of the women in American society, it has a wide
range of meanings for those who have been connected with
the process.[7] Some insight into these variations flows from the
actual language used to describe the birth of a child. Medical
men speak of a woman delivering or being delivered of a child;
mothers use any of a number of terms which imply different
levels of direct or conscious involvement. Respondents, reflecting on past events, tend to think of the child as "appearing," as
if the decision to have it and the carrying and bearing process
were not dependent upon the mother. Children "come," are suddenly "here," "arrive," or "are born"; others "have" them. They
are "wanted," "planned for," "expected"; or present themselves
as a *fait accompli*. Their entrance into the life of a woman is
seen as a consequence of marriage, as an accident, as a major
event in itself, or as the first incident in a whole new phase of
life. The statement, "That was the year Mary was born," implies

7. Robert Winch, *The Modern Family*, New York: Holt, Rinehart and
Winston, rev. ed., 1963, p. 184.

a *post-facto* involvement in the process and ignores the mother's direct participation. "The baby came" is an equally non-responsible phrase.

The birth of a child may be perceived as an introduction to a new relationship evoking sentiments of love or irritation; as a set of fresh duties and responsibilities or as a means of bringing parents "closer together"; as part of the onward flow of life or as a wedge breaking it into two distinct halves. No woman speaks of the birth of her children with hate, but several mention it with irritation. Unplanned-for births do not necessarily produce the same effect on the lives of women. Many definitions of the significance of becoming a mother are mentioned; these influence, or are affected by, the relation which develops between a mother and a particular offspring.

"The change from working to full-time homemaking and, of course, the presence of a child caused great change in me. I hope to have more children." The infant is treated as if his presence came suddenly, without any action on the part of the mother, although she now seems ready to assume direct responsibility for "having" additional offspring. "It changed after the children arrived, and I suppose it will change after they are in school." This definition of life by a twenty-six-year-old pictures children entering and leaving, while she remains stationary. The implication that childbirth is not a planned-for event is obvious in the statement of a twenty-eight-year-old woman: "The first thing I think of is that I'm expecting my fourth baby in four years. I try to remember what my mother tells me, 'remember that when your youngest child reaches school, your life will become much easier, but your husband has to continue to work hard most of the rest of his life.'" Her expectation of the event announces that something will happen to her, rather than that she is making it happen, and her passivity of adjustment fills the whole situation.

Many interviewees define the process of becoming a mother as "having" children in terms of possession, compressing several sub-stages to such role involvement. Definite initiative is implied in one woman's description of the past: "leaving my job and having a child at the same time involved settling down to a home routine." This woman considers the new role reactively or even passively: "And being unable to come and go as you please, that was quite a change." She could have stated that the new form of life requires different behavior and planning on her part. Instead, she sees it as a set of restrictions upon her. She defines the future as follows: "It will get worse with more children. They tell me I'm on a gravy train now with just one. I'd like part-time care of my child and I'd go back to work a few days a week. It would give me a chance to keep up with my career." No definite plan for re-entry into the career is given. One gets the impression of a reactive approach to the role of mother and to the total role-cluster. It is quite possible that the "career" was handled in the same way, but this respondent seems to feel that she had been an initiating person able to "come and go as I please" before the birth of the child.

One woman says she is now occupied "by having children, being home with them. Eventually they'll leave for school and I'll get out to do things I'd like to do and am expected to do." This explanation of past and future life patterns implies that now she is not doing what she likes or what she is expected to do; children are viewed as a temporary constriction preventing desired experiences.

Consequences of "Becoming a Mother"

The event of "becoming a mother" is defined by the women interviewed as having at least one of five major sets of consequences. Many respondents feel that the greatest change produced by the birth of children is in themselves. Two types of self-modification comment appear in the interviews. One refers to what can be called an "identity crisis," the feeling that the whole personality is affected by constant physical work and contact mainly with infants in a small confined space, and resembles the sentiments of a college graduate studied by Mirra Komarovsky:

> When you are married and with small children, you have a lot of things you would like to do but can't; you don't have time and facilities. If I could, if I had peace one-two hours a day, I would continue voice, buy a piano, study. Sometimes I feel lost in the shuffle, confused; not the make-a-meal self, but as if I lost identity. Before, I

worked in an office, was career-minded. I would like to be what I
am a few hours a week. My greatest satisfaction does not come from
"terrific dinner" as much as from "she sings well."

The "identity crisis" is real for those who had participated
in multidimensional social roles and relations before the birth
of the first child. It has been observed by sociologists in both
America and England. It is similar to the effect of retirement
on men and is felt even by those women who did not have
strong identifications with a profession or career.[8] This sudden
narrowing of chances for interactions which call out many different attitudes, behaviors, and skills previously learned and
successfully utilized makes the young mother feel that parts of
the self are "lost in the shuffle" or "vegetating." Thus, the crisis
is a multifaceted thing. The care of infants calls for repetitious
actions, isolation from interaction and intellectual stimulation,
and limitation of occasions to display a wide range of personality behaviors in a variety of social contexts which show the
uniqueness of the self.

A second consequence of the birth of children, also defined
as a change in the self, is experienced as an increase in maturity, in capacities and abilities. Pre-motherhood traits are
judged to be irresponsibility, selfishness, and immaturity; the
post-maternal self to be the model of adulthood. Not that the
shift is necessarily defined as easy: "In the first years and with
the first child things were bumpy; my personality, trouble in
accepting the role of homemaker. Now I have trained myself
to accept things as they come along. Adjusted? Well, a little
to do still. Some temper tantrums at first." When asked what
she would like to change in life, this mother replies: "If I did
it over again, then I would go through college, get an education.
I wanted to, but not enough gumption. My parents did not
realize how much I wanted to. I'd try to develop peace of mind
with myself. Since we've moved from the apartment, there are
less frustrations and I've calmed down; I try not to get as upset
as I used to get." The complexity of her life changes has made
her act in a way which goes against the image she wants to

8. This point is made by Mirra Komarovsky in *Women in the Modern
World,* Boston: Little, Brown, 1953, pp. 127–53.

have of herself; being temperamental and frustrated bothers her, but she experiences a lack of control over her emotions in many situations.

A third major consequence of having children, connected with the first two but not involving self-modification, is inevitably expressed as *"being tied down."* "The biggest change came with the children and being tied down"; "I'm very tied down with the children. I haven't been able to be active socially up to now. Later, when the children are grown up, I'll have more time"; "With young children you're tied down very much. When they are grown up, I would go back to teaching. Later, I'll have some time for my husband and myself to do more things. I would like to help with orphan children"; and, "I used to be on the road singing, and I was always on the go. Now I'm tied down. . . ." The concept of "being tied down" seems to contain not only spatial, but time and activity limitations. It is not just the fact of being constricted to a home by the needs of infants or difficulty in transporting them. It implies the constant presence of the offspring, the unremitting demand for attention, and the very important consumption of time. A high convergence of future changes anticipated by women with small children stresses the release of time as symbolic of *freedom from* the present state of "being tied down."

Not all women feeling that they are tied down after the birth of children express great unhappiness with the arrangement. The women quoted above, in the same order, add: ". . . But the pleasure they have given me more than makes up for the restriction. I look forward to more time and relaxation as the children grow older, but I expect life will still revolve around home"; ". . . I wouldn't change anything, really. There are always minor gripes, but even while grumbling you realize the things that bother you aren't really important"; ". . . I'm quite satisfied, I have a wonderful husband. I don't know what I would change"; and, ". . . Perfectly satisfied, if you're happily married everything else is fine." The singer adds, "But it is satisfying." Thus, being tied down may be seen as a stage of life, a constituent part of having children who of themselves and in the whole complex of relations are a strong source of satisfaction.

Of course, other women who define the consequence of having children as being tied down are not so satisfied with their current life or so unwilling to change anything. "Right now, I have no time for myself. I hope to be able to do other things, like sewing," says a twenty-three-year-old who does not wish for an outside job, but would like a change. "My husband's working late; we'd like to have him home earlier and see more of him." "More tied down now, hope to have more freedom later," is the definition of life given by a North Lake woman who expects a release to come from movement away from that community, where she is not happy. "I would like to move to a suburb where there is more convenient shopping and transportation, and paved sidewalks and streets." Her solution to the problem focuses upon technical means of making contact with the outside. A similar situation is faced by another housewife: "My life is not my own. The demands of the children take time and I have less time for myself. When I worked, there was no nervous strain. I wish I would get out more." This respondent thinks that a change in herself would open doors to a fuller life: "I would like to drive a car, so I could be more independent. I would like to go to night school and learn more about sewing and slip-covering and upholstering."

Special circumstances surrounding the birth of a child are sometimes listed as producing unusual consequences: "Change due to having a late child and raising a grandchild at the same time. Oldest daughter's life somersaulted and brought us into the picture. We pulled up roots and headed for a new home. Change will take place when daughter remarries." "Marriage, having a child, owning a home—all are changes. We hope for another child; our boy is adopted, we want a girl too." One woman explains in detail how her life was changed by the birth of a retarded child:

> Our whole life changed because of our daughter. She's retarded. Our leisure time has been cut because she has to be watched continually. We moved here to be near the school. I don't expect my life to change very much in the future. She'll always be our responsibility. If not for her, we would have been in business together. My husband would like to own a small automobile agency in a small town and I would do the office work. When our boys had grown, we had hoped to travel and do things together. I'm not sure how many of these things we will be able to do.

The mother of a mongoloid child feels much less constricted. "Now easier, I do not have babies. I can come and go as I please. When children are older, housework will be easier." Her statement reinforces the sociological generalization that it is not the particular situation, but how it is defined, which affects a person. A third woman simply wishes she could change her son: "I'd like to be able to alter his handicap, he's retarded." But the rest of her interview is quite ordinary. It is probable that the first mother quoted is especially burdened in adjusting to having a retarded child. She feels her daughter's condition could have been prevented by the doctor; the anger and frustration which she expresses may be interfering with the creation of a realistic, but not so limited plan of life.

A fifth consequence of having children is defined simply as the addition of *work and responsibility*. "I don't think you ever realize just how much responsibility you are going to be forced to accept when you are young." Awareness of an infant's complete dependence upon the mother is mentioned most frequently as a contrast between this role and "outside" jobs. Several less articulate women answer: "The children came, more work." Often the work is resented because it takes time or energy away from other activities. A thirty-eight-year-old hesitantly explains that she would like to change part of her life: "I suppose coming from me, with only one child, this will sound lazy; but I would like to have someone to do the housework—washing, ironing, etc.—just once in a while, so I would have a little more time to do as I choose. I guess that probably sounded lazy. I mean, to do some reading or things to improve myself." "Self-improvement" is a positive American value, providing a justifiable excuse for a woman wishing for less work and more leisure. The combination of being tied down and having a heavy workload leads many women in their twenties to wish for a maid or cleaning help. "I would like to have a houskeeper, so I could get away from the house. Not the children, I love taking care of them." Older women express less interest in decreasing the demands in the role of housewife.

The sixth consequence of the process of "becoming a mother" is the need to *change existing social roles* in order to fit this new set of relations into the cluster. "When I was first married, I was exacting about the house, exact time and spotless; as I had children, I realized that this is not the most important thing; picking on children—vicious circle. The most important thing is that children are happy. I learned not to be exacting. Children are getting older, will have interests of their own, then I'll play a different role. Certain functions I will be called upon to do, new experiences. In time this will change, as children older, husband closer." This respondent sees life as a continued shift of social roles and relations; she is willing to modify the role of housewife with the birth of children, and even, by implication, to push back the role of wife. Sometimes the change is not as easily accomplished. "I've lost a little patience over the years. I had to change my way of life and get used to disorder. When I find the system, everything will be in order." This twenty-seven-year-old defines her loss of patience as due to age rather than to her inability to handle the changes in the role of house-wife brought about by the introduction of the role of mother. Her hope for an easy formula reflects the either-or manner in which she is handling life.

One of the major modifications created by the process of "be-coming a mother" is the role of wife.[9] That the addition of motherhood to a woman's set of relations might produce prob-lems in husband-wife interaction was not difficult to hypothesize. Strain is almost inevitable when a major relation must undergo modifications because of the introduction of anything as im-portant and time-consuming as the role of mother. In addition, the American marriage ideal, focusing upon relational and senti-mental features, is very different from the service-orientation of parental roles. When both are carried on within the same geo-graphical space and by the same total personalities, adjustment will be necessary. The demands of small infants are strong, immediate, and recognized as needing attention more than the demands of adults. Most homes do not have full-time nurses. The husband and wife approach her pregnancy and the birth of the first child in a divergent manner; the man resisting the change which he feels is distracting the wife from total atten-tion on him; she focusing upon herself, as the carrier of the unborn infant, and upon it after birth. Thus, strain between

9. E. E. Le Masters, "Parenthood as Crisis," *Marriage and Family Living,* 19 (1957), 352–55.

them is likely to develop during this time. In the first place, the wife changes in the process of becoming a mother. During pregnancy she shifts her orientation to an introspective concern with what is going on within her. Afterward, her whole attention is focused upon the infant. Many features of the nine-month pregnancy and of the first few months after delivery are rejective of the young husband, especially during times when sexual relations are medically discouraged or when the wife is too tired to pay sufficient attention to his desires. The early months of a child's life require almost constant care, since its hours of wakefulness are unpredictable. Most young mothers are so very uncertain of themselves that the time when the baby sleeps is filled with worry about it or with preparation for the next episode of waking. This means that the mother has less time, energy, and psychological inclination to focus on the role of wife than she had before. In the meantime, the husband is not as directly involved in the care process and often feels left out of the basic mother-child unit. There is, further, a tendency of young mothers to feel that the baby is theirs, a possessiveness that excludes male ownership. Finally, the wife's needs in terms of the behavior and attitudes of the husband change as she becomes a mother, and some period of adjustment is required for them to develop a new relationship, one which now includes participation in a sentimentally distinct set of roles. They must now learn to relate as father and as mother of the child. The situation under which the learning takes place is not conducive to quiet reformulation because of the anxiety and physical exhaustion of the mother while the father's ego is hurt and his sleep often interrupted.

"How is the relation between husband and wife changed by the presence of children?" was included in the "social role of housewife" interviews. Responses draw sharp attention to the degree to which the romantic love, *companionate* marriage ideal is confined to the province of only the upper three classes of American society. This image of young marriage as containing a relatively egalitarian interaction based on the sharing of common interests and preceded by companionate dating, courtship, and honeymoon is usually assumed to hold true for most of the population. But the attitudes of many respondents, particularly of those who never went beyond high school and who live in areas and life styles of the lower class or of the lower segment of the middle class, draw a picture of sex-segregated worlds, even in early marriage. Parenthood roles add an important and meaningful bond to a relatively limited relation, bringing the husband and wife "closer together" through the creation of a common interest. Whether the subculture insists that men and women are brought closer together through the presence of children, rather than through marriage, or whether women do actually experience an increased closeness, the idea that children introduce a common interest otherwise missing in a new marital relation is frequently expressed by this segment of the population. It is contrary to the American marital ideal, which assumes that a strong common bond is developed between husband and wife before parental roles are undertaken and that these add a new dimension to an already strong and multifaceted relation.

College-educated women, living in some city areas or in suburbs like Glenview, Highland Park, Park Ridge, and Park Forest, express mixed emotions about the change in husband-wife relations experienced with the process of "becoming a mother." They often define the change as a decrease of time and attention previously shared with the spouse and as an inability to undertake activities previously companionately enjoyed. "Before we had children we did more things together. You give your husband more attention. You can't go out as much, and probably were more carefree. You can't always get babysitters and, if you go out every night, I feel you're neglecting your children," explains a Glenview mother of several. Women who had participated in relatively companionate relations with their husbands in the pre-parenthood stage are more likely to speak of their present life as requiring planning, task orientation, the adjustment of self and roles. They sometimes express a feeling of increased social distance between themselves and their mates. This is particularly true of younger mothers, who are still experiencing these changes.

It is possible that the male-female interaction pattern of the middle class during the girl's childhood, adolescence, and early marriage camouflages the differences between masculine and feminine viewpoints and life styles which actually exist in the family-rearing stages. American society, although founded on a

patriarchal culture, has dramatically changed the relation between middle-class men and women in the pre-parental stages.
The complexes of wife-mother-housewife and of husband-father-
breadwinner roles are much more deeply rooted in traditional
terminology. The young woman is supposed to be surrounded by
her family immediately after the birth of the child. To the more
traditionally oriented lower-class, European, or farm-based respondents, the movement into traditional mother-father, bread-
winner-housewife relations and into an enclosure of the "woman's
world" seems normal, and child-bearing simply provides a link
with the husband in his world. More egalitarian and societally
involved middle-class women define this shift as decreasing
relations with husbands, because they feel themselves being pulled
away from interaction which they had enjoyed. Rather than view-
ing the process as culturally based they explain the change as one
of time or need to plan. They keep reminding the interviewer
that "as soon as the children grow up" they will again have the
time to devote to their marital relation, with the assumption that
it will return to the pre-parental companionate sharing. Now
they feel unable to share in the husband's life and are frustrated
in trying to get him completely shifted into the role of father.
They experience a shift in themselves, suddenly or gradually
beginning to see the world through the eyes of a mother. The traditional approach to child-rearing does not inculcate in the father
and the mother the same view of the child or of the society for
which they are preparing it. The selectivity of their perceptions
is a consequence of more than their contact with the offspring at
different times and in divergent activities. As the young woman
enters into the traditional mother role, encompassing all the
early years of a child's life, even with a "developmental approach," she changes her values and world orientations. Child-
rearing, as carried on by the new mother, produces more traditional feminine-masculine role segregations than practically any
other social relation in modern American middle-class life.

One of the conclusions of this study, based upon inductive
analysis, is that the event causing the greatest discontinuity of
personality in American middle-class women is the birth of the
first child, particularly if it is not immediately followed by a
return to full-time involvement outside of the home. It is not
just a "crisis" which is resolved by a return to previous roles and

relations, but an event marking a complete change in life approach. All other changes, except widowhood, are more gradual. The degree of modification in husband-wife relations which ensues depends on their original form and on the methods by which the changes in the person of the mother are transmitted to the person of the wife. From this study, we do not know directly how a man responds to the changes in his wife, but the interviewees indirectly present two basic types of husbands: those who themselves become increasingly oriented toward the home, focusing on being father, "family man," and husband; and those remaining oriented toward the outside world of work, sports, participation in voluntary associations, and so forth.

Of course, the relation between husband and wife can remain relatively unchanged if the wife does not allow herself to become very different with the birth of the child or if she segmentalizes the personality modification. It can become limited to that of the mother and the father of the children. Or, after the early years of "becoming a mother," it can develop into more multi-dimensional involvement. Many a middle-class woman tries to make marriage again companionate and more than child-connected, after she feels sufficiently stable in her role as mother. The amount of time and the form of change involved in the "becoming" stage vary. The early modification brought about by the birth of children worries middle-class women, if it is seen as a separation of interest worlds, an increased social distance, and a decreased opportunity for companionship; but it pleases the lower-class woman, if she finds it creating a bridge across sex-segregated social worlds.

"Becoming a mother" results not only in a change of other social relations and social roles, but also in a *redefinition of the physical environment* within which they take place. Now confined to the home, the young woman begins to feel cramped and inconvenienced by the spatial limitations or by the location of the housing unit. It is at this time, with the birth of the first child or soon thereafter, that the parents, if they can afford it, usually decide to change their residence. Peter Rossi examined the whole process by which present quarters or areas become redefined as inadequate and mobility as desirable.[10] Of particular interest

10. Peter Rossi, *Why Families Move*, New York: The Free Press, 1955.

here is the symbolic use of the "because of the children" answer to all questions concerning motivation for suburban migration. Every study which asks women "Why did you move to the suburbs?" reports a preponderance of answers focused on the welfare of offspring. An analysis of the form and timing of such responses by the housewives of this study indicates their symbolic nature, one camouflaging a great range of meanings. The whole definition of housing and of the neighborhood changes with the birth of a child, even before the social characteristics of city areas actually create the problems of physical and relational "dangers" so often pointed to by escaping future suburbanites. Increasing crime rates in central cities, concern over "bad influence" upon one's own offspring, problems from overcrowding in schools, worry about health and safety away from the home, are realistic aspects of life. However, young parents of infants usually lack organized life plans for the future, and it is surprising to see them using problems which will not affect them for years as a justification for immediate exodus to the suburbs. The very answers themselves indicate an even broader area of life covered by the "it's good for the children" umbrella. The move serves other functions besides that of actually benefiting the growth process of children.

The suburbs have become symbolically connected with the American dream of upward mobility and "the good life" in the eyes of many people. "Better for the children" may mean that suburbs offer a chance for such mobility, for starting life on a higher rung than the parent. Second- and third-generation Americans, knowing the value of a home and a "proper" neighborhood in the estimation of social class standing, wish to surround themselves and the new infant with the symbols of success. Having these things themselves is part of their wish, as implied by the Polish toast: "May your children have wealthy parents." Geographic mobility assists social movement up the ladder, and not only because of the addition of symbols; it facilitates the break with the past and the learning of styles of life appropriate to the future. Like "passing" out of the Negro community, it sets up the environment for a new way of living.

The shift to the suburbs by young parents wishing upward mobility can be both a push and pull situation. The desire to "give the children better opportunities" can be used as a rationale for the movement away from old or new residents of a neighborhood. It is claimed by many people acting in ways contrary to the American creed of democracy, as in the attempts to protect white schools or neighborhoods against desegregation and/or "busing" which are currently raising the ire of some of the white housewives. Who can be critical of actions which are explained as "giving the children a good start" or ensuring that they be protected against "the bad element"? "I really don't mind (desegregation, equality of opportunity, changing populations of areas, etc.) but the children. . . ."

Since mothers are supposed to be considering only the welfare of their offspring in making major decisions, this rationale can be used to justify actions which provide a direct benefit to the older generation. Lonely women who wish to develop friendship relations with new neighbors, middle-aged respondents who re-enter and enjoy work roles, parents who find pleasure in home-ownership and barbecues insist on explaining that their actions are done only for the benefit of the children. Such statements imply that the poor parents would really prefer to live in the city, not work, not own a house, etc., but that they are virtuously sacrificing their own desires. The burden of gratitude falls on the children.

When the suburban housewives were asked why they moved to these areas, most answer with that standard phrase, although often explanation of the selection process indicates considerations which have nothing to do with child welfare. One-fourth of the 299 women explain in greater detail what they mean by the "for the children" phrase. A typology of these meanings includes:

1. The children are developing human beings who need the atmosphere of the suburbs in order to bloom.

2. Suburbs provide better facilities for the education and development of children, i.e. schools, playgrounds, than the city does.

3. Children are active and need their own space or they interfere with adult space and make work difficult.

4. Children make so much noise and commotion that outdoor activity is easier on parents since it is further away and less distracting.

5. It is easier to raise children in the suburbs than in the city because they require less supervision, control, and attention.

6. Suburbs provide easily accessible playmates who are from "good" families.

7. We had to move from the old neighborhood because I do not want my children to grow up with "those kinds."

8. The suburbs provide a better "start in life" than most city neighborhoods do.

9. Good parents live in suburbs.

"Being a Mother"

The fact that the American mother enters this role by simply giving birth to a child or by adopting one, without having real competence to carry out its duties or enough power to control its environment to ensure effective performance, is reflected in responses to the interviews as well as in much literature dealing with this segment of the population. The role is evaluated as extremely important, yet preparation for it is very inadequate by most standards. The responsibility heaped upon a mother of meeting the almost contradictory goals of socializing her children into both adjustment and creativity, popularity and achievement, excellence in a specialty and multidimensional ability could possibly be carried out by a highly trained psychologist lacking any personality problems dysfunctional to the attempt. Modern mothers are not that trained nor are most of them so free from neurotic tendencies in their relation with ego-threatening offspring as to act in ways all of which are best for the child's growth. Many respondents complain of emotional problems in child-rearing and of the need to make important decisions without a feeling of competence; most of the educated women are aware of the dilemmas built into the role.

In fact, most of the mothers of pre-adult children list difficulties in child-rearing and worry over the behavior of their offspring when asked to explain the problems peculiar to housewives. The 568 interviews on the "social role of housewife" which are being analyzed list 698 problems, and 227, or 33 per cent, of these skipped over to the role of mother by immediately mentioning difficulties with children. Table 18 (see page 171) contains tabulations of answers according to object-creating problems or

Table 19: Frequency distributions and percentages in answer to "What are the satisfactions of the homemaker's role?" by residence.

		Respondents				
	Urban		Suburban		Total	
Satisfactions	No.	Per Cent	No.	Per Cent	No.	Per Cent
I Children						
Having children	14	3	35	7	49	5
Watching children grow	60	12	69	14	129	13
Bringing up children	7	1	25	5	32	3
See children happy	15	3	42	9	57	6
See children healthy	19	4	16	3	35	4
Proud of children, turned out OK	46	9	24	5	70	7
Total children	161	32	211	43	372	38
II Relations						
Able to satisfy, make family happy	78	16	28	6	106	11
Response, appreciation, being needed	37	7	19	4	56	6
Love	17	3	22	4	39	4
Total relations	132	26	69	14	201	21
III Happy marriage, husband	33	7	51	11	84	9
IV Possessions, home ownership	9	2	37	8	46	5
Make home, pride in, for family	23	5	19	4	42	4
Clean, neat house	28	6	36	7	64	6
Other home	42	8	—		42	4
V See fruits of labor	53	11	32	7	85	9
Get job done, finished	16	3	27	6	42	4
Total comments	497	100	482	100	979	100
Total people	300		268		568	

concerning which problems are created. If we assume that "family" references also include a number of situations concerning the role of mother, and that some of the relevant problems are not object-specified, we can conclude that the concern over this role is very high. Working women focus less on such situations because many do not have children in the problem-creating age bracket and because the others are generally less child-oriented than the women who are full-time housewives. All the suburban-ites have at least one pre-high school offspring and their concentration upon the role of mother as a source of problems is the highest. The urban women, many of whom are older and in more traditional age and cultural groups, are more prone to list "family" problems.

The same distribution of objects, with somewhat similar descriptions of the actions directed toward them, appears in answers to the related question: "What are the frustrations peculiar to the role?" Again, respondents jump over to situations or difficulties which pertain to relations with children or with the husband rather than staying strictly within the role of house-wife, repeating the tendency to use the latter designation as an over-all identification. Many could not distinguish between the concepts of problem and frustration, although the general trend was to explain the latter as a source of irritations, and the former as relevant to more basic and important issues. Many of the problems of the role of mother are centered around the woman's inability to accomplish desired results, either because of her own limitations or because of a lack of power to control the situation. Worry over child-rearing, doubt over decisions, conflicts with family members, emotional tension, and children's sickness appear both as problems and as frustrations.

Specifically, four major areas of problems or frustrations in being a mother are listed by the women. These four include: the way she functions in the role or her personal and sentimental responses to it; the child and his behavior or social relations; the actions or attitudes of others in the social circle of the mother; and role conflicts experienced by her.

The problems facing a woman which arise from her own be-havior in the role of mother are frequently those of self-doubt over her ability to function effectively in the dimensions opened up by the knowledge explosion. Part of the doubt comes from the uncrystallized character of the role orientation: the need to apply cosmopolitan (external to the social circle) standards of judgment and rules of behavior to the local client (the child)

with whom all the identification and loyalty are connected.[11]
The mother usually does not want to use the child's judgment of
what is best for it nor the opinions of the remaining segments of
the social circle with which she is interacting. Secondary and
expert sources are outside of her immediate situation, and the
difficulty of acting as translator and interpreter, plus the uncertainty over which source is best, are baffling. No rewards are
available from such cosmopolitan sources, while the directly
involved circle members are likely to meet her efforts with negative sanctions: "Children are always problems; to know how to
raise kids" is a major concern of mothers. It is expressed over and
over in various ways: "Knowing what to do: the responsibility
of proper child-rearing"; "Never knowing if methods of discipline are proper for children"; "Disciplining children—it's hard
to know what to do at the right time." These statements attempt
to explain the depth of the problem. Related to it is the weight
of the responsibility of meeting the needs of the offspring:
"Trying to understand the needs of children and why they do
things"; "Trying to see that the children get proper training." "I
try to see that their emotional needs are filled, it's been my whole
life." Roles in which the source of judgment and the symbols
of success are clear are simple in comparison to some others.[12]
A unique combination of strains is explained by a Japanese
mother: "Dealing with human nature which is unpredictable.
Guiding children. Balancing the American concept of rearing
children with the idea of filial piety, since I am from another
world."

Sometimes the problem of how to accomplish what seems
right in the role is due to a lack of the tools needed to carry
desires into effect. A very frequent difficulty is one of financial

11. Robert Merton first developed the concepts of "cosmopolitan" and
"local" in comparing role performers oriented toward different segments of
their social circle (Robert Merton, *Social Theory and Social Structure*, New
York: The Free Press, 1957). Alvin Gouldner tested these distinctions further
in his "Cosmopolitans and Locals: Toward an Analysis of Latent Social
Roles, Sections I and II, *Administrative Science Quarterly*, 2, No. 3 (December 1957), 281–306 and 2, No. 4 (March 1958), 444–80.

12. The problem of role strain created by conflicting or competing demands of circle members and its resolution have been best summarized by
William Goode in "A Theory of Role Strain," *American Sociological Review*,
25, No. 4 (August 1960), 483, 496.

limitations: "Not being able to do more for them, get things they need." Many of the expressions of frustration at being unable to give children what is defined as good or necessary come from Negro mothers living within congested city areas: "To train the children well, despite outside influences; to help the family see the lighter side of life as well as the serious"; "Trying to live within your means. Trying to find adequate housing within a given amount, locating schools within a given area for your children and good transportation for your family." In the same interview, the last listed set of problems was accompanied by the following frustrations: "School problems you're not able to solve such as overcrowding, inadequate equipment for children, lack of adequate police protection." The inability to protect the child from physical and social dangers outside of the home is defined as a major problem of life by many mothers, but the neighborhoods within which a large group of Negro women have been confined are specially apt to draw such comments.

A part, or even a sizable proportion, of the set of duties contained in the social role of mother is irksome to some of the persons within it. A few comments are all-encompassing, covering the whole relation, because of its over-all problems or the cumulation of smaller irritations. When asked what problems are peculiar to the role of housewife, some respondents state: "Taking care of children"; "Raising children"; or "Being responsible for others." The task of controlling the actions of children is often specified as a problem: "Children, and disciplining them"; "To train children"; "Taking care of my two children, training them, teaching them right from wrong." Specific duties related to stages in the child's life cycle may be defined by the mother negatively: "Bowel training of children"; "Taking the kid to school"; "Up at night with the kids, not enough sleep"; "Running a bus service for children"; and "Settling squabbles."

A major problem is the woman's worry about her sentimental response to others in the role. The constant need for "trying to have patience with children" is difficult for many mothers, not just in itself, but particularly when accompanied by the assumption that the ideal parent can easily control her emotions. The problem is stated in several different ways, but the word "patience" is frequently repeated. "The children can sometimes be frustrating and the lack of privacy. That's about all. Oh, and holding your temper; you know, keeping your head"; "Children getting on your nerves. I think children is the most frustrating thing about it"; "Having to holler at someone all day long, the constant whining"; "Patience, maintaining it brings tension"; and "Children require patience, you can't reason with them as you can with co-workers." One even states: "The kids get on your nerves and you wonder how you can stand any more of it." This set of problems is mentioned by women who are not used to situations creating strong sentimental responses prior to the birth of their children and who lack the ability to either prevent emotional scenes or to fit them into their perceptions of their own personality as a calm person.

The behavior of children at any particular moment can be a problem. As one respondent states it: "The children, trying to keep them from being a problem is a problem." Situations with "misbehaving children," "children not behaving," or "when children are disobedient" in general, as well as in particular, "seeing how the children mess up the house after I spent so much time cleaning it," "trying to get children to pick up rooms, toys, recreation room is a wreck," "the whining of children," and "daughter diddles in the morning, changes clothes 100 times a day"—these are direct irritations affecting the mother in her other roles and in the way she feels about being a mother. Things that happen to the children, such as accidents and illnesses, can be a major source of worry or a frustration because of their inconveniences: "My baby has exema, we can't leave her with anyone, not even with mother," or "The human element, you plan something and inevitably one of the kids falls down or throws up." Some respondents list the marriage of their offspring as a source of problems because of circumstances or changing relations: "It's selfish on my part, but I did not want him to marry. It's an empty feeling, depressed." That is not the same form of letdown as "My son got married—terrible, her parents were nasty."

The way the "child turns out" worries specially the mother whose ego is deeply involved in the child-rearing process.[13] The generalized "disappointment in the development of children"

13. Bruno Bettleheim, in "Does Communal Education Work? The Case of the Kibbutz," *Commentary*, 33 (February 1962), 117–25, states that the Kibbutzim is psychologically healthier than the intensive mother-child relations of middle-class America.

expressed by one woman is implied by many others worried about the outcome of all their years of uncertain motherhood. The concern is symbolized by specific measures of success or failure. One respondent explains that a major event in her life occurred when "My son graduated high school. He was having so much trouble I was relieved." Academic success does not always guarantee peace of mind for the mother. "My first son graduated college. I was proud of him, but worried about him—no girl friend," states a woman who kept referring to the fact that this son had not married throughout the interview. She lists this as a future major occurrence on which she sets her hopes.

Special circumstances of "being a mother" can create problems. "It's hard to raise two families, it would be easier if they were all my own children," states one woman, and others imply their unique difficulties less specifically. The relation between a mother and one of her children is sometimes a cause of frustration, especially if defined as involving "sassy" behavior, being "rude," or "they don't realize how hard you are working." The relation of children to each other is very frequently mentioned as a problem, especially if it is conflict or daily irritation: "With children, normal amount of teasing, fighting"; "Fighting children, they tease each other"; "Fighting between the two youngest ones"; "Family arguments;" and "Trying to keep peace, keep everyone happy, the woman has to settle arguments." These statements imply two levels of frustration, one over hearing the fighting, the other over having to settle it with some form of decisive action.

The relations of children with others in the neighborhood are occasionally mentioned as sources of difficulty within the role of mother: "To keep on friendly basis with other parents of children in the neighborhood;" "Neighborhood children close together, problem in bad feelings over children. Really have to be careful when so many children play together." These statements expand the source of problems to relations with other persons who are part of the social circle.

Other members of this social circle can affect the woman's feelings about her role of mother. An implied or stated problem can be a lack of co-operation from the father of the child in the rearing process or in relation to the offspring. One woman who frequently made hostile comments about her husband answers this question with: "Boy, they know what to ask, don't they! Having one child that is spoiled. There are others [problems] but we won't mention them. The constant whining." Another states: "Trying to get co-operation from other family members [over disciplining the youngest child]." These comments are less frequent than those discussed before.

The final form of problems in the role of mother focuses upon the role conflict which had not been resolved in the "becoming" stage or which developed later. Many respondents feel conflict between obligations to themselves and the duties of child care, even after they are supposedly adjusted to the shift. "The submergence of one's individual personality to the demands of the family" is a strong expression of this sentiment. Another problem, discussed before, is that "The wife-mother role can be imbalanced. I mean that you have to give proper attention to children without neglecting the husband." Many similar comments indicate that often the role conflict occurring from the presence of small infants is not simply resolved by a logical, agreed upon, role hierarchy. An even stronger strain is felt by a college graduate: "Big problem is being pulled in all directions by all members of the family, so she is often concerned with making a choice of the most important need. Husband-wife relation is often neglected."

The interesting fact about the problems and frustrations found in the social role of mother by the interviewees is their distribution within the population by the characteristic of education. The least educated woman is the most likely to state that there are no problems and that "You know what you have to do and go on and do it." If she mentions problems at all, she usually limits them to house maintenance or other task duties. Life is a round of work, met without surprise, and many members of this group do not even answer the two questions. The high school drop-out or graduate is able to list specific problems, most of them focusing on money, disciplining children, and the fighting among offspring. She wants to control her children and wishes they would be quiet instead of constantly destroying the products of her work by creating commotion.[14] As mentioned in the previous

14. Lee Rainwater, Richard Coleman, and Gerald Handel found the *Workingman's Wife* holding similar attitudes (New York: Oceana Publications, 1959).

chapter, this type of woman does not like specific household tasks, but limits her life to them, and she is highly frustrated when children mess up what she has just straightened out, and dirty what she has cleaned. She is product-oriented, wishing simply for clean, quiet, and well-behaved children and a clean, neat house; so she finds it irritating that these conditions are not present for more than a few fleeting moments. She often speaks of patience but projects an aura of irritation even when not expressing it directly.

The more educated woman tends to be relation-oriented and worried about her ability to be a good mother, defining this role as complex and as requiring developmental socialization.[15] The pattern of her responses is similar to the way she approaches other roles. The respondents who have a college education are the most likely to perceive the role of mother as a complicated set of relations and to stress the creative and influential aspects of it in modern society. They are the most concerned about it. They have mastered or feel competent to solve the tasks or technical aspects of life. They are deeply aware of the emotional and relational responsibilities of child-rearing and of the great potential in the role of mother, while their less educated cohorts are still worried about the daily routine of physical life.

One might assume that women with little education, often living in problem-ridden urban areas, would be the most apt to be bothered by many problems. When this expectation is not supported by the data, questions emerge as to its significance. Possibly problems are admitted only when tentative solutions are perceived to exist or when an initiative rather than a passive approach to life is maintained. It may be that the statement, "There are no problems," is a psychologically healthy one, but this study indicates that this definition not only defeats idealism but also is restrictive in reality. Problems experienced by this segment of the population are feared, not tackled, and best not even mentioned. It takes the confidence of at least partial competence and a breadth of perspective for a person to admit having problems in fulfilling the obligations of a whole complex of

15. Evelyn M. Duvall, in "Conceptions of Parenthood," *American Journal of Sociology*, 52, No. 3 (November 1946), 193–203, was one of the first to find a major difference between lower- and middle-class attitudes toward child-rearing.

changing social relations and social roles. Motherhood without problems possibly reproduces formulas and depends upon a complete disregard of the needs of children within modern urban society. Motherhood limited to control and discipline is carried on exclusively for the convenience of the parent. Motherhood concerned with the development of children's abilities may have more problems, but it attempts to bring the facilities of the society and of the self to the growth process.

CONTRASTS WITH GRANDMOTHER

The same conclusion can be reached from an analysis of a whole set of questions asking the housewives to contrast the roles of modern women to those of "your grandmother's generation." In judging the ease, satisfaction, or problems of the old generation, the more education a woman has completed, the less likely she is to concentrate on house and task-limited aspects of change and the more often she will speak of the complexity of human relations, particularly those with children, and of obligations to the community. For example, women with less than a high-school diploma generally feel that life is now easier because of the abundance of electrical appliances; respondents who graduated from high school agree with the "physically easier" part, but add: "It is mentally harder"; "Now expected to participate in outside activities"; or "It is harder to rear children." College graduates, or those who were close to finishing, place a positive evaluation on the change. Four series of answers from suburbanites will illustrate the difference:

Q: How does the *modern* woman's role contrast to (differ from) that of her grandmother?
A: Lots different, life is different, living is different.
Q: Is her life easier or harder than her grandmother's? Why?
A: Grandmother worked much harder.
Q: What duties and privileges does the modern woman have that her grandmother did not have?
A: All modern appliances and running water.
Q: What frustrations or problems, specifically, does she have which her grandmother did not have?
A: We have more sickness now than they had then.

Q: Is the modern woman's life more satisfying?
A: I think so.
Q: Is the job the modern woman performs more or less important than that of her grandmother?
A: About the same.

This respondent is a resident of a blue-collar suburb south of Chicago in which most men are steel workers. She has an eighth-grade education and two children, aged eight and twelve, whom a more educated woman would have mentioned.

The effect of the change in the life of women can be judged by the values of one's own childhood. In these terms, "the children" are often seen as lacking the "character building" experiences of the past. Women with some high-school education tend to feel that the changes in society are having a bad influence on children who do not conform to older standards of behavior:

Q: How does the *modern* woman's role contrast to that of her grandmother?
A: They didn't have modern equipment. Homemaking ideas weren't so pretty then. Men make more now. Couples couldn't afford things. I work half day, have half day to myself.
Q: Is her life easier or harder than her grandmother's? Why?
A: Easier. They used to have more children. My mother had fourteen. They scrubbed clothes by hand . . . it was a lot harder. More money worries; many on relief.
Q: What duties and privileges does the modern woman have that her grandmother did not have?
A: Nice to have schools and churches nearby.
Q: What frustrations or problems, specifically, does she have which her grandmother did not have?
A: There's more worries now. Maybe families give too much to their children. Years ago we had to work. You shouldn't give a child too many advantages. It's too rich here . . . makes teen problems.
Q: Is the modern woman's life more satisfying?
A: They could have been just as satisfied.
Q: Is the job the modern woman performs more or less important than that of her grandmother?
A: Modern world going so fast; main problem is children; play with them; talk things over with them. Keep them from many temptations.

This respondent, with a tenth-grade education, living in a suburb west of Chicago heavily populated by young second-generation Americans, reacts to societal change by feeling that her main contribution is to "keep them [children] from many temptations."

Another resident in the same community, but one who completed high school, answers the series somewhat differently:

Q: How does the *modern* woman's role contrast to that of her grandmother?

A: Families not as large; they stayed in the home, did not go out as we.

Q: Is her life easier or harder than her grandmother's? Why?

A: Easier. Because of labor-saving devices; supermarkets, washing clothes.

Q: What duties and privileges does the modern woman have that her grandmother did not have?

A: Pretty much the same; still feed, clothe, nurse; get around a lot more now.

Q: What frustrations or problems, specifically, does she have which her grandmother did not have?

A: Automobiles and traffic; children not as well behaved now.

Q: Is the modern woman's life more satisfying?

A: No. They are not as contented; always wanting more than they have; they [grandmother's generation] were satisfied.

Q: Is the job the modern woman performs more or less important than that of her grandmother?

A: No! Both end up doing same thing—raising a family; just go about it differently.

This interview is very interesting in that it exemplifies some of the problems of "the expanding blue-collar" group, which knows the American dream and ventures into an expanded world—but without sufficient guidelines. Life is not controlled, going out is accompanied with discontent over a lack of immediate happiness. The image of "grandmother" as "satisfied" with her life is quite frequently presented by such housewives.

The contrast in attitudes toward the increasing openness of life and toward change in parent-child relations between the former three respondents and a North Shore suburb college graduate is dramatic:

Q: How does the *modern* woman's role contrast to that of her grandmother?

A: She has more influence with her family, source of more education in developing well-rounded people; don't leave it to schools.

Q: Is her life easier or harder than her grandmother's? Why?

A: Easier. Because of conveniences, but more demands. Must train children for more than the present.

Q: What duties and privileges does the modern woman have that her grandmother did not have?

A: Closer contact with her family because of time-savers and smaller families.

Q: What frustrations or problems, specifically, does she have which her grandmother did not have?

A: Grandma was interested in the physical well-being of her family. We must be interested in all needs. Join the PTA, entertain, provide cultural experiences for children.

Q: Is the modern woman's life more satisfying?

A: Yes. More influence in more areas.

Q: Is the job the modern woman performs more or less important than that of her grandmother?

A: More important because of greater influence on children and the community.

The last quoted set of definitions of change in the roles of women in the past three generations is much broader in scope and more relationally-oriented than the former three. It indicates, in the same way as other answers, that a decrease of physically exhausting work, combined with the breadth of perspective provided by higher education, changes the woman's view of the role of mother. It also shifts her major focus from that of a repetitiously performing housewife to a relationally-oriented mother, aware of the complexity of that set of obligations.

SATISFACTIONS OF BEING A MOTHER

The changes in role focus and definition are being experienced in varying degrees and often in different ways by interviewees responding to the question: "What are the satisfactions of the homemaker role?" Although "getting the job done" implies household activity and one-fifth of the comments refer to that role only, the largest proportion of answers (38 per cent) point directly to the role of mother. The importance of motherhood is shown by the fact that the homemaker is seldom defined as having her most satisfying relations in the role of wife (8 per cent). No reference is made to satisfactions drawn from friendship, neighboring, or participation in life outside of the home. These are still not defined as part of the homemaker's basic role-cluster, reinforcing the conclusions of Chapter One.

Besides the third of satisfactions which refers directly to children, there is a fifth which lacks a specified object. Quite probably women with children are thinking of them as well as of the husband when speaking of the pleasure derived from the flow of love, response and/or appreciation, and the feeling of being needed. It is also possible that "seeing the fruits of one's labor" has some reference to the role of mother.

Table 19 (see page 205) gives a breakdown of answers to the "satisfaction" question by urban-suburban residence. It is interesting to note the difference between these two populations. For example, the phrases actually used by respondents in category II of non-specified object relations shows that the urban respondents, many of whom are older with a heavy weighting toward lower grades of learning, are more likely to find pleasure in "satisfying" family needs than the more middle-range suburbanites are. They are happy that they are appreciated or needed and that the family is pleased with their efforts. This is a more traditional assessment of the position of women than that given by the changing woman in the newly developing suburbs. Love, which tends to be defined as a two-way process, although mentioned rather shyly by a very few women, is more of a characteristic of the suburbs than of the city.

Women also vary in the style of being a mother, which is reflected in the kinds of satisfactions they derive from that role. There are qualitative differences in relations whose main pleasure is "having children," "bringing up children," "seeing children happy," or "knowing children turned out well." The first form of satisfaction is one of possession and, as indicated earlier, some women seem to view their offspring as objects they own. The second view is of influential action. Such a mother is pleased over the process of being a mother, a process requiring active leadership on her part. The third, and most frequent, source of satisfaction in the life of homemakers is one of passive watch-

Table 20: Total population of Chicago, Illinois, and of its Standard Metropolitan Statistical Area, 1860-1960.*

Year	Chicago City	Rest of SMSA	Total
1860	112,172	147,212	259,384
1880	503,185	268,065	771,250
1900	1,698,575	386,175	2,084,750
1920	2,701,705	693,291	3,394,996
1940	3,396,808	1,172,835	4,569,643
1960	3,550,404	2,670,509	6,220,913

* Evelyn M. Kitagawa and Karl E. Taeuber, Local Community Fact Book: Chicago Metropolitan Area, 1960.

ing, of standing back and noting the condition or the accomplishments of the offspring. Mothers do not necessarily specify the direction of growth of their children which is their main source of satisfaction: the very fact that they grow seems imbued with a positive affect. The feeling of uncertainty, of doubt and worry, is implied in the relief that "they turned out all right." The phrase "after all" seems to follow in parentheses. The end product meets the criteria applied by the mother.

The distribution of answers and the strong convergence upon certain phrases for expression of satisfaction bring out the fact that the role of mother is approached and performed within American society in several different ways. Like the variations in the process of "becoming a mother," the stage of "being a mother" can be carried on by a wide range of stances vis-à-vis the child. Each stance is caught up in its own form and has deep implications for the relationship. Much of the current sociological literature focuses upon the differences between traditional and developmental forms of child-rearing.[16] Greater research must be devoted to the ways in which changes in these forms are developing into mutiple approaches by women in the role of mother.

16. A study testing the hypothesis of class differences within the Negro community is Constance K. Kamii and Norma L. Radin's, "Class Differences in the Socialization Practices of Negro Mothers, *Journal of Marriage and the Family*, 29, No. 2 (May 1967), 302–10. Zena Blau has two relevant articles based upon a comparative analysis of the ways women use expert knowledge in "Exposure to Child-Rearing Experts: A Structural Interpretation of Class-Color Differences," *American Journal of Sociology*, 69, No. 6 (May 1964), 595–608, and "Class Structure, Mobility and Change in Child-Rearing," *American Journal of Sociology*, 28, (June 1965), 210–19.

Many statements of satisfaction cover greater spheres of life than definitions of problems and frustrations. Although squabbling among offspring may be an irritation, "seeing your family happy and your children growing up as you want them to" expresses satisfaction on a broader level. Many respondents simply state that "having children" is *the* satisfaction; others specify elements of the experience: "It is satisfying when you teach your child to do something and then see the progress." "Watching her children develop and grow—guiding her children, knowing that she is such an important figure to her children and husband" is a statement of many-leveled involvement on the part of the mother. It ranges from direct action to a location in the center of the family circle; but also includes a stance apart from it—one of manipulation and observation. Only one of the 571 respondents expresses a strong form of familistic rationalization, "raising children to be something. When you die, you leave something behind."

Specific events which bring satisfaction to homemakers are mentioned by a few respondents: "Love returned for small things. My biggest thrill was to hear my daughter say 'thank you, mummy' "; "The children, not now, but when they step out of the tub"; and "Children, hearing their joys." These examples pinpoint the incidents which the other responses generalize, but the over-all impression is of a deeper set of satisfactions than of frustrations.

Children are most likely to be mentioned as the main object of pleasure by the women in their thirties who had some college experience, with up to four children (but not more, the drop is great), the youngest of which is one year of age or younger. By contrast, those who place the house before children as the main reference have no youngest child, having only one or none; if they have more than one child, they also have little education and a lower income than those who rank the role of mother or wife first.

THE IDEAL MOTHER

The variations among women in their approach to the social role of mother and especially in their relations with children are illuminated further by answers to the question: "How would you describe an ideal housewife?" Restricting analysis to the role of mother and to relations with "the family," we find an interesting clustering of answers not only by educational level, which again differentiates types of concern, but also by ethnic and/or religious identification. Answers by white Catholic and Jewish women stand at the two extremes from each other, with those by Negro Catholic, Negro Protestant, and white Protestant ranging in the middle areas, without necessarily the same flavor; or standing in different form. The contrast can be illustrated by ten typical responses from each of the two extreme groups.

Descriptions of the ideal housewife by Jewish respondents, by level of education:

A woman who keeps her home tidy and clean; has a system for her work. As a mother has to give more love than she gets in return (8th grade education).

One who caters to the needs of her family and doesn't constantly complain about how much she does, but takes it in her stride as part of the job (12 years).

One who is proud of her family; keeps a clean and comfortable home and makes her house a home (12 years).

One who is very unselfish, but not to the point where she's never considered. To receive respect, she must give respect. She must keep harmony in the family; keep abreast of the times so that she can keep on her level with her husband; she must put herself on her children's level (12+ years).

One who has a happy family. If there is happiness, there is satisfaction, respect, love, and companionship (12+ years).

One who is a warm, efficient person, who enjoys all the phases of her work as a housewife (12 years).

One that keeps her family content and happy by doing the needed things. For example, being around when needed by husband and children (12 years).

One whose family comes first above everyone else. One who is a good manager and uses good common sense and one who takes an active interest in outside activities (14 years, two of them in college).

One who is satisfied with herself—receives recognition from her husband and children and is looked upon in the community with respect (16 years, B.A.).

One with a sense of humor to meet all occasions with understanding and love (17 years, M.A.).

Several interesting facts emerge from the description of the ideal housewife given by many women who identify their ethnic background as Jewish. One is the tendency to speak of her in relation to "the family" in general. The second is a strong emphasis upon the personality of the woman, especially upon her moods and traits of interpersonal relations, summarized as "warm," "loving." A third point is her interest in receiving respect within both the home and the community. The less educated woman has a tendency to see her position as that of a hard worker, catering to the needs of others. There is something of a martyr in this stance, with frequent references to a "willingness to do menial jobs," giving more than receiving," and "not complaining." An increase in education is often accompanied by a decrease in concern with work in the home and an increase in community involvement and in the use of the concepts of understanding, love, and respect.

There was some difficulty in finding matching interviews with Catholic women at the higher educational levels, because the Chicago-area population of that religion happens to be still heavily concentrated in the lower levels of education, being composed of first- and second- and third-generation Europeans with a peasant background and a lack of education for women. The flavor of the comments by women who identify themselves as Catholics is quite different from that contained in the above quotations:

The one who has her house in perfect order and if her children are clean and fed (6 years of education).

Her home is always clean, her children are well dressed and fed; her meals should follow one pattern; she should teach her daughters what she herself was taught or was not, but should be taught; her husband should help when she has a bit of work (8th grade).

One who takes pride in taking care of her family (8th grade).

A woman that keeps her house nice and clean and sees to it that her children are well disciplined and cared for (10 years).

A mother who keeps up her house, herself and properly rears children (12 years).

A man should really answer this. She's a woman who can keep the house in order and children under control, and the budget in line. Be ready to entertain and be presentable when her husband comes home (12 years).

One who does her duty (14 years).

She has to be a good mother for her children by giving them comfort in times of crisis and never approach them in anger, but with love and understanding (14 years).

One with patience at all times; understanding; keeps things interesting for the family; makes a decent home (14 years).

She does a good job of rearing her children; she maintains a presentable home; finds time for outside activities; isn't bogged down with details (16 years).

It is impossible to fully account for the differences between the two sets of answers represented here. The Catholic responses come from women identified with several different national culture societies. The Jewish interviewees have not been here much longer, most coming from Eastern Europe within the past two generations. Yet the Catholic descriptions of "the ideal housewife" focus upon the *duties,* of keeping a clean house, of controlling children, and of doing the right thing. They are less likely to mention relations or sentiments, focusing more on end product and/or the task by which it should be reached. The orientation is toward action rather than mood. The woman is the rearer of children and the worker who maintains a clean and good home, but she is not the center of a set of relations—an image expressed so strongly in the other set of descriptions.

Modern society and the expanding education of women have thus made the social role of mother increasingly complicated and important. Although many women still limit their lives to repetitious tasks in the role of housewife and in the physical care of children, the changes in society are beginning to raise problems because of "children wanting too much" and "lacking discipline." Increased education shifts attention away from rigid control over offspring to an awareness of the mother's potential to assist the development of personality and ability in children. The redefinition of what it is to be a mother does not result automatically in competence in this role nor in satisfactory relations with offspring. In fact, it often seems to broaden the problem of acting effectively in the role, by providing a new image of the ideal without designing steps to approach it. Knowledge is fragmentary but often assumed to produce a set of exchanges lacking conflict and emotion which is rarely available in real life.

The traditional portrayal that children happen to "come" or "be born" without control by the mother is being replaced by planned parenthood, which places on the parents responsibility for the care of the infant in the manner best suited to modern scientific society. The significance assigned the role of mother, combined with uncertainty over the best child-development methods, put strong burdens on a woman with the birth of her first child. These burdens require modifications in existing social roles, as well as a redefinition of the self. Experienced sometimes as an identity crisis or as a drawing away from companionate relations with the husband, the process of "becoming a mother" affects with particular strength the middle-class girl whose background developed multidimensional and egalitarian relations with men. Yet, the satisfactions derived from the children themselves or from the warmth of relations with them provide a woman with more than just the culturally approved emphasis upon the importance of "being a mother."

FIVE ❦ ❦ ❦

Relations with Neighbors

BACKGROUND

The preceding chapters have dealt with the processes of becoming and being a wife, a housewife, and a mother, three roles judged by the respondents to be the most important for women. The depth interviews brought out two other sets of relations in which many women are strongly involved but which, however, have not been incorporated into the ideology of what a member of this sex should be or do. Neighboring has been or is becoming a significant activity for many respondents, helping to solve the problem of loneliness and providing opportunities for the exchange of homemaking knowledge and the alleviation of anxieties felt in the role of mother, bringing the pleasure of adult companionship and leisure-time interaction. Also important to many women is friendship with selected individuals or couples begun in a variety of ways and gradually developed into more intimate and "fun-sharing" relations.

Defined broadly, neighboring refers to any interaction with people defined as neighbors.[1] People differ greatly in the limits they assign to neighborhoods, confining them to a square block, to the opposite sides of a street, to a vague "around here" or "in town." Neighboring also varies considerably in its style and level according to the area and among diverse people of the city and its environs. People may consider only the individuals of a certain

1. Susan Keller has an excellent summary of the literature dealing with neighboring in *The Urban Neighborhood*, New York: Random House, 1968. She points to a very useful distinction between neighboring as a set of activities and the neighbor role. My study has concentrated on the former, since I did not determine the size or composition of the social circle, only the activities carried on in the process of interaction.

social category as candidates for neighboring relations, ignoring other people in the immediate vicinity, as is the custom of professors of neighboring colleges and manor-owners. Not being concerned with the precise delineation of a neighborhood, we allowed the free use by respondents of the term neighbor, focusing our analyses on the forms and levels of the relations which they described in answers to a series of questions on the subject.

TRADITIONAL STYLES OF NEIGHBORING

Neighboring as a form of interpersonal interaction is influenced by four sets of factors: the degree and manner of its institutionalization in any community; the attitudes of a person and his neighbors to each other and to neighboring; the ability and facilities of these individuals to develop interaction patterns; and the competition this activity has from other roles in which they are involved. These sets of factors in turn include many historical and situational components.

Americans have developed several different styles of neighboring as a result of their traditional and current life patterns. Our historical literature indicates at least four distinct pre-urban complexes of relations among people considered to be neighbors. One of these is a result of the manner of settlement of individual American farmers. Anyone driving through, or flying over, much of this country's farm land, expecting to see scenes similar to those of Europe, Asia, or Africa, is struck by the isolated position of each farmstead. In contrast to most of the world, where agricultural workers live in homes huddled together in villages, the New World displays each family's dwelling sitting on its own land in proud isolation, with only a rope of road connecting it to major arteries and finally to distant towns. Such isolation has institutionalized a definition of "privacy" as inevitably connected with geographic separation, with freedom to do as one pleases on fully controlled private property, surrounded by strong trespass notices. Contact with neighbors prior to the automobile era tended to revolve around co-operative work or activity connected with public functions such as worship and market exchanges. Such interaction took place infrequently, and the rest of the time each family worked independently. Though social and physical distance between farm neighbors has decreased with the advent of the automobile, their work rhythm prevents intensive socializing.[2]

Although "rugged individualism" and "inner direction" is often defined as typical of early residents of America west of Washington, D.C., the small town has always been "other directed." [3] In other words, although the farmer looks to himself for standards of behavior, the small-town resident is highly dependent upon his neighbors, developing an insular attitude toward the rest of the world. Different patterns of town and countryside life were developed in each region, influenced by the community's age and economic base, but each community became homogeneous in background, although containing a diversification of economic and political roles greater than that of the farm or the village.

The traditional village pattern of neighboring, to which many immigrants to America had been accustomed, was agriculturally based and highly interactive. The authors of *The Polish Peasant in Europe and America* described the pre World War I neighboring relations as extending to the "okolica" or district which "reaches as far as the social opinion about an individual and a family reaches." [4] The houses and most of the stock buildings were located close together in villages, with fields spread out at varying distances from them. Casual interaction occurred whenever people stepped out of their extended family homes onto the main arteries, on their way to the field, to common work areas, or to ceremonial occasions. Work, tool-sharing, and product exchanges involved men and women in many situations of contact which were interlaced with talk, play, and symbolic hospitality. Central meeting places such as churches and village squares provided daily informal contact, augmented by a highly developed rhythm of visiting and on-the-street gossiping fitted into weekly, seasonal, and holiday schedules.

2. Lee Taylor and A. Jones, *Rural Life and Urbanized Society,* New York: Oxford, 1964.

3. Robert C. Wood, *Suburbia: Its People and Their Politics,* Boston: Houghton Mifflin, 1958.

4. W. I. Thomas and Florian Znaniecki, *The Polish Peasant in Europe and America,* New York: Dover Publications, 1958, p. 144. See also the famous description of the daily round of life within a Polish village contained in Ladislas Reymont's *The Peasants,* translated from Polish by Michael H. Dziewicki, New York: Alfred Knopf, 1924–1925. Each of the four volumes deals with a different season, starting in autumn.

The same general pattern of interaction is still going on in villages of Poland, Italy, France, and other countries, with stores and garages added as meeting places and the new motorcycles joining bicycles, horse-drawn wagons, and human legs as a means of reaching contact situations. The main road through a village becomes filled with interacting people during holidays and on niceweather evenings. This form of neighboring is intensive and provincial in its inward orientation, restricted to people living in a small area, known for generations. It lacks stranger-absorbing rituals.

The fourth tradition of neighboring, of which vestiges still remain in America, has been practiced by the rural upper classes of most societies for many centuries. In this highly institutionalized system, neighbors are not people who live at a close distance, who tend to be peasants or workers, but those who belong to the same upper social class, residing even a great distance away. During feudal times, each manor was located on its own land, much like the American farm, but it involved a style of life more similar to that of the plantation house. Economic affluence facilitated frequent "event" interaction, involving leisure activity in the form of "calling," planned visiting, formal dinners and other activities, or convergence at common meeting places. Courts, summer resorts, or any other areas designated as appropriate for this class would draw people from great geographical distances for designated periods of time. Complex formal rituals maintained the relations of those who could not meet "by chance" and at times when they were not staying at the same place. Correspondence nourished the attitude of neighborliness, even among those whose home locations precluded frequent direct interaction. The three major differences between the upper- and lower-class patterns of neighboring in all but urban centers were: the former's spatial extensiveness, its frequent use of "event" interaction focused on a specified activity and requiring pre-planning, and its institutionalized acceptance of appropriately introduced and positioned strangers.

Immigration of both classes of rural Europeans, in-migration of the American farmer and small-town resident into urban regions, the urbanization of most of the population, and the development of an industrial, secular, mobile, large, and heterogeneous society have combined to create several new and distinct styles of neighboring.

The peasant immigrants came in large waves prior to the 1920's and settled in village-based clusters. The Poles, the Irish, the Italians, the Bohemians, and others attempted to preserve the village form of neighboring and to exclude all non-kin or not long-known neighbors from intimate contact.[5] As the settlements grew and developed increasingly complex economic, political, and cultural systems, they became ethnic communities. Formal social groups were added to community life to expand the residents' identification with others considered part of the same "nationality" or "race."[6] Strangers from the same nation, but not of the same village, were more easily absorbed by such groups, and neighbors became people who were also "Poles" or "Italians." However, most of the formerly rural immigrants, and even many of their descendants, still feel suspicious of outsiders, meaning members of other ethnic groups.

Urban expansion due to in-migration and change gradually began to create large heterogeneous areas with institutionalized or anomic non-interaction with neighbors. The former is based upon a consensus about the undesirability of close neighbor relations; the latter involves a rejection of them because of a refusal to share value systems. The real "normlessness" treats the ideas of people living nearby as simply meaningless, not worth consideration or increased contact.

While the ethnic community has continued to perpetuate its style of in-group neighboring, often bordering on non-interactive areas, a major change in neighboring and in total living patterns evolved out of a revolt of second- and third-generation Americans against the traditional past. Born in ethnic communities, but educated in the "American dream" concepts of middle-class styles of living, those who became adults just before, during, or after World War II moved away from the close supervision and conformity of the village-like areas. Many experimented with being anonymous residents of heterogeneous neighborhoods, joining those who escaped the farm or small town. After the war eco-

5. Herbert Gans, *The Urban Villagers*, New York: The Free Press, 1962.

6. Thomas and Znaniecki, *The Polish Peasant*; Helena Znaniecki Lopata, "The Function of Voluntary Associations in an Ethnic Community: Polonia," unpublished Ph.D. dissertation, University of Chicago, 1954, and chapter bearing the same title in Ernest W. Burgess and Donald Bogue, eds., *Contributions to Urban Sociology*, Chicago: University of Chicago Press, 1964.

nomic affluence and the chance to buy a home combined with the desire for a different style of living and with increased self-confidence born of education and functional competence to encourage ventures out of the city by small family units. The middle-of-the-century adults had become lonely in anomic areas, but unwilling to return to the ethnic community confines; therefore, they moved to newly developed communities and turned them into a peer, "other directed" haven of interaction with neighbors.[7] Here they were joined by other descendants of immigrants who did not stop in the anomic half-way house.

In a very major way, the post-war suburbanization and the styles of neighboring which it developed were a revolutionary attempt to build new relations with new people: age, interest, and socio-economic peers, with whom interaction could be symmetrical and on an equal footing. The *freedom from* ———[8] character of the movement, from the ethnic community, from the small town, from the traditional controls and pressures of older generations, and from anomie, resulted in a gradual and uncertain development of new cultural patterns and of a new type of personality. At its most extreme stage, illustrated by the behavior of the early apartment-renters of Park Forest[9] or the home-owners of Levittown, it was a purposeful and strong involvement with the peer group and a total revolt against past family relations, neighbor contacts and activities. Other-directedness was not a surprising result of the intermediary position of those not yet fully confident of themselves or of the life they wished to create. They knew that they did not want either traditional relations or the non-neighboring life, which was then the only major urban alternative for the upwardly mobile. The current revolt of youth rejecting the new culture created by their parents, which is drawing the attention of many observers, is a third wave. The first rejected farm, small town, and Europe; the second, the ethnic community and anomie. These two revolutions produced great change in the life of America. The second, developed mostly after World War II by the

7. David Riesman, Nathan Glazer, and Reuel Denney, *The Lonely Crowd*, New Haven: Yale University Press, 1950.

8. Erich Fromm, *Escape from Freedom*, New York: Farrar and Rinehart, 1941.

9. William H. Whyte, Jr., *The Organization Man* and Herbert Gans, *Levittowners*, New York: Pantheon Book, 1961.

upwardly mobile, educated middle- class and the white-collar families, is now being increasingly followed by people bordering on or even lodged in the lower-class culture.

The growth of Chicago and of its surrounding area from 1860 to 1960 showed two major trends (see Table 20, page 218).

In the first place, there has been a startling growth of the whole area, from a quarter of a million to six and a quarter, an expansion of almost twenty-four times its 1860 total. The second trend has been in the proportions of the city and of its surrounding area relative to each other. In 1860 the territory now considered suburban was larger in population than the central city. By 1880, however, this proportion was reversed as the city tripled its population, becoming suddenly almost twice as large as its environs. The suburbs grew very little between 1880 and 1900, adding less than half of their earlier population, while the city continued to explode. By 1920 the latter was almost four times as large as the former, but the gap between city and suburb started to decrease in the succeeding decades. By 1940 the central unit was only three times as large as the rest of its Standard Metropolitan Statistical Area, and twenty years later only 58 per cent of the total number of residents were still living in Chicago, the other 42 per cent having moved out to surrounding communities.

Although many of the older suburbs contained people of the highest socio-economic rank, others were in reality relatively independent small towns or locales of service personnel catering to the rich. The exodus of urbanites into the newly expanding suburban areas resulted in the 1950–1960 decade in a drop of the median years of schooling and of the median income of most of the older communities surrounding the city, indicating that this is a new population. The background facts about the participants in the various studies which are being reported here indicate that the new suburbanites are second- or third-generation descendants of European or American rural or small-town residents. The movement of the children of the newest migrants out of the city has been somewhat bottled up by racial prejudice, but there are some predominantly black communities and expansions of minority neighborhoods in older towns, such as Evanston and Maywood, which did not fall into our suburban sample.

As the suburbs expanded in number and size, each developed its own set of neighboring interactions, varied by the composition

of the population. Generally, the styles of neighboring have followed class lines, with the upwardly mobile moving each time to
a community with just higher status than the one in which they
previously resided. New patterns of neighboring are picked up by
them in anticipatory socialization with the help of observation
and mass communication media. Knowledge of neighboring styles
is contained in such formalized sources as Emily Post's *Etiquette*
and the more informal works of such people as Amy Vanderbilt.[10] Daily newspapers offer advice on appropriate behavior
in different kinds of situations and detailed reports of social
events, while local papers reflect the life of the community dependent upon them.

In the meantime, changes have been purposely introduced in
the styles of neighboring in central and other selected areas of the
city. Community problems faced by leaders, loneliness, and the
gradual decrease of suspicion of strangers are encouraging the
growth of "block clubs" in the inner city or near-slums, whose
function is co-operative effort to improve their physical and social
characteristics. "Swinging" or socially active and leisure-stressing
middle-class high-rise apartment buildings are developing, with
the help of builders who have recognized, or are inculcating, the
desire for social interaction with neighbors.[11] Even lower-class
residents of public housing units, who had been traditionally hostile to strangers, are joining in activities designed to break down
social barriers. Informal exchanges, the work of voluntary associations, and the efforts of building managers are thus converting
depersonalized, densely inhabited structures into actual communities. One of the relatively new high-rises has even become a modified modern ethnic community, gradually drawing in residents
with the same background culture and providing many formal
and informal interactions within its walls.

Increasingly affluent, former ethnic community or anomic residents who remained in the city, or who ventured out to suburbs

10. Emily Post, *Etiquette*, New York: Funk & Wagnalls, 10th Edition,
1960, and Amy Vanderbilt, *The Complete Book of Etiquette*, Garden City,
N.Y.: Doubleday, 1963.

11. The high-rise building which was studied as part of this research
project included the following services and opportunities for social contact:
beauty shop, barber, coffee shop, restaurant, drug store, health club, limou-
sine to town, swimming pool, card club, book club, ski club, a chapter of a
religious organization, and several less formal groups.

during child-rearing years, are redefining their lives in a return to urban residence. This population has become leisure- and interaction-oriented, partly due to the influence of retirement and "preretirement" communities. Many older urbanites have either visited or read about the highly neighboring involvement of people their age, and they have themselves become increasingly leisure-oriented. This change in attitudes has resulted in a nation-wide expansion of places such as Sun City, branches of which are now located in several warm-climate states. Developers add common meeting places and activity programs. The fact that neighboring in such style may appeal to those no longer interested in the youth-centered suburbs has led such people as Ross W. Cortese to build a number of "Leisure Worlds" for people fifty-two years of age or older, located even in colder climates and near work centers.[12] The success of his communities is facilitated by a guarantee of "10 new freedoms of living," including freedom from "boredom and inactivity" (a number of club-houses and outdoor recreation facilities are provided) and from "loneliness." It is not hard to predict an increased specialization of apartment buildings in urban areas, some having highly institutionalized interaction, others limiting themselves to informal interaction, while a third type maintains the traditional institutionalized non-interaction.

MODERN STYLES OF NEIGHBORING

The questions which were asked respondents about their style of neighboring included: "What is the type and degree of contact you have with your neighbors in a one-block radius?"; "Do you perform services, such as lending things, babysitting, shopping for and with neighbors?"; "Does your husband have frequent contacts with the neighbors? (how often and for what purpose?)"; "Do you and your husband have social contact, such as visiting, outdoor cooking, and such, with your neighbors?"; and "How would you characterize your neighborhood in terms of friendliness?" Each interviewer was instructed to probe, that is, to ask enough neutral questions to ensure as full a picture of the activities involved in neighboring as could be drawn. There was no

12. "What Makes Ross W. Cortese the World's Largest Home Builder?" *Practical Builder* (May 1966), 82–92.

attempt to determine specific frequencies of contact, only a generalized frequency, the form of activity involved, and a definition of the level of friendliness.

Analyses of the styles of neighboring were made according to *forms of neighboring*, broken down into behavioral content and *levels of interaction*. Each form is based upon responses to the questions about socializing by women, exchange of services by women, socializing and service exchange by men, couple interaction, and definition of neighborhood friendliness.

The content of interaction contributes an important part to the style of neighboring. As we shall see in greater detail, lower-class women tend to depend on spontaneous, seasonally fluctuating contacts, if they interact with neighbors at all. Their activity is described as "gossiping" over the fence, or when passing outdoors, and "exchanging services." Their husbands have little contact, usually less than the wife, but of the same type, limited to the exchange of tools or skills or to casual conversation when outdoors. Upper-class women participate much more often in "event" socializing in a selected neighbor's home, or in their own, or by meeting in, or going to, special events or places. Such contact requires pre-arrangement and a more formal procedure.

The style of neighboring was also analyzed according to *levels of interaction,* which combined stated frequencies in all the forms. The levels are: (1) non-interaction, which includes anomic, institutionalized, and justified non-interaction; (2) low interaction, which includes minimal, little, casual, outdoors only, or seasonal; (3) medium interaction, which includes relatively high levels, but limited to only one or a select few of neighbors, those restricted to one form, those accompanied by institutional controls, and those having personal restrictions; and (4) high interaction, which includes intensive and multiform or "close," and even those lacking comfortable controls (see Chart 2 for a model of these levels).

The five levels of neighboring can be exemplified by quotations from the interviews.

Non-interaction

Anomic non-interaction with neighbors exists in many dense and/or heterogeneous urban areas. "We have no contact with our

Chart 2 : Levels of neighboring interaction.

None	Low	to	Medium	High
Anomic non-interaction	Casual		Institutionalized controls	Multi-form
Institutionalized non-interaction	Seasonal		Self-imposed controls	Close
Justified non-interaction	Restricted to one form		Restricted to a few people, selective	Causing uncomfortable strain in other social roles

neighbors," states a forty-eight-year-old resident of a large city apartment building. Obviously, people living in such a building with a limited number of exits and central service area must have some contact.[13] What the respondent means by lack of contact is not its literal absence, but a lack of personalized interaction and of social relations. She does not know her neighbors and, when asked if the area is friendly, she answers: "I don't know. I guess it is." This attitude is completely devoid of "role-taking," by which people learn enough about others to understand their way of life. "We don't have anything to do with our neighbors. They're not like us," is a frequent attitude in anomic areas.

Institutionalized non-interaction is very similar to the former lack of involvement in neighboring, but it is based on a neighborhood consensus to so live, rather than on a lack of identification with the norms of others. A nineteen-year-old wife and mother describes this type of a non-relation in detail: "About the only contact is the recognition, parent to parent, when one child meets another. I have more contact with the children. I know no one's name. It's superficial. I have a feeling everyone keeps to himself. I don't find myself wishing I had anyone to turn to. I suppose I'd rather not be imposed upon by anyone else. We're here to be alone and unbothered and that's one of the things about the

13. Florian W. Znaniecki developed the concept of "humanistic coefficient" in 1934 (*Method of Sociology*, New York: Rinehart, 1934). Its fullest explanation appears in *Cultural Sciences* (Urbana: University of Illinois Press, 1952). He emphasized the importance of the sociologist's using "the humanistic coefficient" in his research, that is, seeing the world from the point of view of the person who is acting in it.

neighborhood. Everyone sort of lives his own way. Even the poorest don't ask anything of anyone. It's ostensibly integrated. Not like in the neighborhoods that have only one ethnic group." An even stronger statement comes from a slightly older urbanite: "I think that everyone has been friendly by minding their own business. I like it that way. This may sound harsh and horrible, but I can't help it. I just feel that way. Neighbors and friends are two different things. I have a few friends in the vicinity, but I consider them my friends. I think of neighbors merely as people living on the block."

Sometimes people who want close neighboring relations move into an area of institutionalized non-interaction and are very unhappy. A respondent living in a community with very mixed patterns and attitudes explains the disadvantages of her neighborhood: "People are not as friendly as I'd heard; not like a small town where everybody says 'Hi!'" She had hoped for informality and spontaneity from neighbors. "I thought I could go out and sun in the backyard, but I don't feel free or right to do so; I'm really disappointed in that no one 'called' when I moved in; no one to talk to when I'm outside; just one came over, but she wouldn't even come in." This expression of helplessness and loneliness is a result of the mismatch between her expectations and the reality of her neighborhood. An interesting aspect of the answer is that she has a rather lower-class and inner-city background and may have built an idealized picture of neighboring without knowing how to locate the kind of area where it actually is developed.

Justified non-interaction is a category containing responses from women who have no or a bare minimum of social contact with neighbors, but who treat it as an unusual circumstance and seem compelled to explain it. Several respondents feel that the contact is still too new. A respondent living in Park Ridge, a highly neighboring community, and of the age when such relations are frequent (thirty-four years) explains its lack: "Well, everybody is so new. It's not to the point yet where we know each other. There are all ages here. They are not young couples with a lot of kids. So when folks are older, they take longer to meet." Another justification is a recognized mismatch between the person and her neighbors: "I am not close to my neighbors; down the street they are younger, but that is a little far to go." Some women feel they

do not have time to enter such relations: "We [she and her hus-
band] don't have time to socialize evenings. By the time we take
care of the house, his widowed mother's house, and an aging
uncle's house—no time left for neighbors."

Other reasons are given for non-interaction, from a purposeful
avoidance to special circumstances. "My husband doesn't care to
do things like that. He's not very sociable" is a typically lower-
class attitude. A combination of justifications is exemplified by a
Wheaton resident who seems to be surrounded by a lot of neighboring: "Very slight contact, not social. They are quite a bit
younger and have tiny children; their interests are different than
mine. I do not perform services—don't want any of that to get
started. The neighborhood is as friendly as I want it to be; I am
holding back. I don't want to waste time drinking coffee or beer;
I want to do more important things." Her husband also does not
interact with neighbors: "He restrains himself." Several other
women are afraid of developing neighboring relations. A Park
Ridge resident who maintains only minimal contact explains: "Just
a friendly 'Hello' when we see them is all. We're not chummy
with any of them. We have nothing in common with them and
prefer to live a little apart. It could get too friendly. It can become quite difficult. They take to dropping in and you don't want
to hurt their feelings, but you're so busy. . . . We all moved in
here about the same time and we all do our gardening and seed-
ing, so we share that common interest and we'll visit a little in the
yard, but most of them seem to feel like I do." One can only
speculate as to the source of her assumption of problems in being
"too friendly," whether it arose from past experiences or from a
stereotype with which she entered this situation.

Not surprisingly, justified non-interaction exists most often in
suburbs in the urban outer layer in circumstances where other
levels are expected or prevalent.

Low Interaction

Low levels of interaction among neighbors are institutionalized
in some urban and even suburban areas or as a consequence of
the history of the relation. A low level of involvement on the part
of an individual living in a community of high neighboring is
exemplified by the rather pathetic story of a thirty-five-year-old

daughter of immigrant parents who now lives in a highly interactive part of La Grange Park:

> Not much; we talk when we're outside, but not friendly otherwise.
> We have nothing to do with the neighbors on one side of us. They
> have two awful boys. They're awful people. I don't like them. We
> used to borrow and lend occasionally with a neighbor, but I don't
> believe in that. . . . I go around my house and do my work and I
> don't get in any arguments with them. When I'm through outside, I
> come in and watch TV in the afternoon and have a beer or coffee
> alone and enjoy myself. These people around here are independent.
> Maybe I am too. They're not very friendly. It's not a nice atmos-
> phere. If they don't bother with me, I don't bother with them. They
> don't come here. Maybe they're jealous or don't like me. One woman
> behind us was very nice when we first moved here and had me over,
> but she never came to my house, so I don't know what was the mat-
> ter. I have my own family and friends.

A partial explanation of her lack of friendship with neighbors
and even of traditional neighboring relations becomes evident in
her answer to a question eliciting memberships in voluntary associations.

> No. [I don't belong to any.] I was invited to a church association
> luncheon one day, but it was the same week as our anniversary and
> we were going out three days later and it was just too much to do in
> one week. I was too busy with my housework to go. Everybody else
> in the block went.

All these incidents indicate that her background did not provide her with skills facilitating easy interaction with neighbors,
even when all the other circumstances of her residence could contribute to the development of such relations.

A purposefully developed low level of interaction with neighbors is accounted for as a result of both prior overindulgence and
role competition by a Park Ridge resident. Asked about her contact with neighbors, she replies: "Just if I'm in the yard. No social
contact. Just see my relatives." It turns out that her sister lives
two houses away and her mother at only a block's distance. She
also avoids all but very restricted relations. "We lived in South
Park Ridge before and there was too much social stuff. So, when
we moved here, I tried to prevent that starting again." In addition: "There are very rich people behind us" and "mostly older

people around here." This is quite a combination of reasons for a low level of involvement in neighboring.

Some respondents explain that they don't want neighbors to get close because they become too "nosy." "I cut out visiting back and forth; they seemed nosy regarding personal matters, so now I avoid them; I don't encourage too much familiarity." Lower-class women are very apt to limit their neighboring for this reason.

Social interaction between low and medium levels very frequently consists of a limited number of social events shared with neighbors or involvement in one form only with a moderate frequency. In the upper three social classes, such contact can be formally delineated by event-socializing. A Glenview respondent explains: "Limited contact. We have open house for new neighbors. Memorial Day picnic to which all neighbors are invited. We always invite everyone in the block, no picking and choosing." A slightly more varied pattern is that of a Hazel Crest couple. She likes "Occasional coffee together, but we don't run in and out." Her husband "talks to them when they meet outside. Always tries to introduce himself to newcomers, so they can wave a greeting thereafter as they empty the garbage." They see neighbors as a couple "only on special occasions, such as exchanging calls on New Year's Eve."

Lower-class women who engage in some neighboring tend to depend on seasonal contact or on service exchanges. Several residents of Park Forest, which used to be almost entirely white collar in composition, have mixed backgrounds or are experiencing upward mobility, i.e. their fathers had blue-collar jobs but their husbands have moved into white-collar positions.[14] The wives do not have the ability to engage in much socializing, but their husbands are exceptions to the rule that men interact with neighbors less often than women. They have already been socialized into middle-class interaction patterns. The respondent feels out of place in the community because: "In my childhood all the people were of the same working class. I don't think these people are any better than I, but their way of living and thinking is different." She justifies this by defining herself as "Not the friendly type. We speak when we are out in the yard. In the year we have lived here, I have only once been in a neighbor's house." She then adds: "My

14. An influx of blue-collar families occurred also in Levittown, according to Gans, *Levittowners*.

husband talks to the neighbors more, because he's outside more. Talk about women being gossipy!!! Men are more relaxed with each other. They don't pretend and try to be something they're not." She seems to want more contact with neighbors, yet lacks the self-confidence and the means for establishing them, even in Park Forest, so famous for its neighboring.

An Oak Lawn woman describes a similar situation. Her husband has frequent neighbor interaction. "Outside work gives him more contact than I. He's very sociable." In some cases such sociability does not lead to greater family interaction, as it did once in Park Ridge for another respondent. "Well, I don't take time off for coffee breaks with them. But our husbands get us together. Last Saturday, the fellows were out on the lawn and got to talking and it ended up with a big neighborhood picnic of five families. We just enjoyed it thoroughly. The men did the cooking and my husband went off and got rolls. Nobody had planned it and we just had a wonderful time." Dependence upon situational spontaneity is the life pattern of this non-initiative woman, who is typical of the lower-middle-class population. "Well, we see each other more often in the summertime than in the winter. In the winter, I see just the people on Chester Street [faces it] out in front. In the summer, you are all in your backyards, and you meet the people on the other street," states another.

A restriction in the amount of neighboring may be, and often is, a consequence of the husband's rather than the wife's characteristics. An Oak Lawn resident first rejected any idea of neighboring: "I don't bother with any of them and I don't want to exchange too many services, because I don't want people to make a habit of depending on me for what they should handle for themselves." It turns out that her husband has a lot of contact with neighbors, but not of equality: "Because he fixes their phones, he sees more of them than I do. His work is centered around this neighborhood."

The most frequent reason for limited neighboring scores is the lack of male and couple participation. One woman who would otherwise score very high has an unco-operative husband. She was voted the nicest woman on the block and presented with a big basket of fruit and canned goods, but she has a husband who relates with neighbors "not at all. He just sits home, never goes outside even when the neighbors try to interest him in something. They finally gave up. He has no friends."

Medium Interaction

The third level of interaction involves more multiform contact than the low level, often of an organized nature or even on an informal basis, but it lacks the intensity of the high level. Organizationally sponsored contact occurs when neighbors belong to the same group which—through planned, systematic events—involves the co-operative efforts of more than one family. Urban residents often mention consistent contact through "block clubs," which help to break down isolating barriers. Contact is defined by one black woman as "friendly and co-operative; we see each other at the block club, shop with them and babysit." The husband "helps them on the buildings . . . and giving advice, and working on cars," and the couple engages together in visiting. Another woman also ascribes the origin of contact to voluntary associations and adds that they see each other "frequently, bridge or getting together for lunch"; and a third urbanite explains her neighboring as "conversation; block parties once a month; church contacts. We are all Catholics."

"Robinhood Estates Association has picnics, dances and meetings for all of us in the community. We have social contacts all year around," explains a La Grange Park resident who seems happy, if somewhat surprised, that the relations are not merely seasonal. Three of the respondents live in an unincorporated area outside Park Ridge. Though composed of 308 families who are divided into two areas containing homes of different price range, this community is nevertheless held together by many voluntary associations. One of these performs the important function of buying co-operatively the area's water supply from a nearby town. The other groups are primarily leisure-oriented. "There is the 'Park Ridge Manor Women's Club,'" one resident explains. "We don't koffeeklatsch. There are more night-time get-togethers. Of course, being in the Manor, the social life for the Manor is organized. There is a men's and a women's group. There are four dances a year, two parties a year for the children. Women meet once a month and have two luncheons a year. We have projects— just got our own school building." Another respondent explains that they could keep busy every weekend night with regular, organized activity. This guaranteed quality of social interaction, with little possibility of personal rejection, has a great deal of appeal not only to the geographically transient, but to the socially mobile. Both face problems of newness to an area and lack the social skills required to develop an extended "social calendar." [15]

Medium levels of neighboring can be reached through intensive contact with a limited number of people. A home-owner on the west side of Chicago who has only an eighth-grade education exemplifies such contact: "There are three or four women I see once in a while—two or three times a week. Especially the woman next door and the woman across the street. We visit each other, sometimes go shopping together. The others I see only once in a great while. I know most of them by name. I see some of them when they come collecting for charities." She exchanges services with the few she selects for interaction and philosophically comments that "sometimes they come or call at the wrong time" but "You just have to ignore things like that or get used to them." Her selectivity is based partly on the fact that "There are one or two on the block who are crabs. They always yell about the dogs, the children, or something, and they're always telling other people what to do, how to plan their flowers, fix their yards. . . ." This respondent's husband is more limited in his relations with neighbors: "He sees them in the summer out in the yard. He doesn't have as much contact with them as I do. He's gone on a couple of fishing trips with the man across the street." There is relatively little couple-companionate contact: "We visit each other once in a while in the evenings, maybe every couple of months. The women mostly visit back and forth during the day."

High Interaction

A high level of neighboring can arise in any of the development communities or areas. These are, in fact, more likely to go in this direction than toward non-interaction. They involve multiform contact of high intensity and are more likely to occur among young than among older women and among suburbanites than

15. The success of the ballroom dance studios among all but the short-term students is partly due to their complex calendar of events labeled "parties" which guarantee fun and the opportunity of interaction with others. This is a more expensive way of guaranteeing parties than the Manor Association's, but it caters to the unattached. See Helena Znaniecki Lopata and Joseph R. Noel, "The Dance Studio—Style without Sex," *Trans-Action*, 4, No. 3 (January–February 1967), 10–17.

among urbanites. A La Grange Park woman explains the reason for this: "We have quite a bit of contact. There are a million children and that draws us together. All seem to be in the same group." Their interaction includes the lower-middle-class's custom of borrowing and lending. An Oak Lawn housewife, aged twenty-four, is very happy in her new home: "I've never been in a neighborhood like this. We all moved in at the same time and are very friendly." She exchanges not only the services mentioned in the interview schedule (borrowing and lending, babysitting, shopping for or with), but others: "We pass along children's clothes and maternity clothes." Another suburbanite explains her husband's involvement: "They use his plastering services, tools, and he uses theirs; all compare notes on building improvements and yards."

North Lake has an unusually high level of neighboring for a community of blue-collar workers, and the major reason for this is that many people bought their homes as shells and used each other's skills to finish their own and the neighbors' homes. A resident of another town also became involved in a major service exchange. Her neighbors "helped us put up the electricity in our garage and my husband helped one of them lay cement. They all get together and help each other, and it saves a lot of money. I can't imagine what it would have cost us to run electricity from the house to the garage." They "play canasta and poker and visit in the evenings and have barbecues at each other's house in the summer."

Middle-class couples engage less in service and object exchanges, unless the area is very new and has to be put into a more completed condition. Multiform interaction is mentioned by a resident of the rather upper-middle-class area of Glenview. As contacts, she lists the following: "Some belong to the same clubs. We have parties and picnics, charity affairs or parties." But, "With unlimited telephone service, talking on the phone, when you should be working, is a disadvantage. You have to learn whom not to telephone." She defines the neighborhood as having an "easy-going relationship," but her associational connections and couple-activities show a style of interaction somewhat different from that developed in North Lake and Oak Lawn.

A system of extensive neighboring can be embedded in, or can result in the development of, real friendship with one person. A Hazel Crest housewife, who is thirty-three years of age, was engaged in such a complex of relations: "Daily chit-chat on the street with all whom I see. Daily, sometimes twice daily, koffee-klatsching with up to seven or eight of them. I met the closest friend I ever had in this block. She has now moved away." Another explains the growth of such a friendship relation: "I am very close to the gal next door, almost like sisters now. We have lots of coffee get-togethers. Last night she came over at 9:45 for potatoes. You have to be good friends to do that. She almost had her baby in my kitchen last year." Defining her neighborhood as very friendly, "just like paradise," she explains: "First we were the only house in the block, except the two Cape Cods in the back. Then the girl next door moved in, said she was scared to death all alone. Now she wouldn't go back to the city." Their relation is surrounded by other neighbor interactions. Asked if she performs any services for others, she says: "All of it; always take the girl in the back in my car to the store. She does not drive. All of us do lots of babysitting, too. We plan parties; yesterday we all got together, sat on the patio and made favors for a baby shower." Her husband is also involved in many relations: "Heavens. They buy equipment and use it back and forth. For example, all got together and bought a big tree sprayer. Bugs were chewing up trees." Relations were thus built over time and are fulfilling the needs of these evidently satisfied respondents.

Urbanites also can have high levels of interaction with neighbors, as evidenced by the life of a thirty-two-year-old Negro housewife: "We have daily contact; chit-chat over coffee, and we gossip. I have contact because I like them." Her husband also interacts with neighbors, and they engage in couple socializing. Both belong to the block club. A young woman in an outlying area of the city replies: "Very strong. I have some sort of contact with them daily. We get along very well." Of course, many technically urban areas are in life style very suburban, and the statistical probability of high neighboring is greater in the home-owning outer fringe than in the inner city.

The fact that a couple may be embedded in a high level of interaction with neighbors does not necessarily prevent it from moving. One La Grange Park woman has her house up for sale, although she is very satisfied with her close relations with people nearby. She expects to duplicate this level in a new community.[16] On the other hand, some women now very neighboring do not intend to duplicate the pattern after moving, feeling that they are entering a new stage of life which would decrease its importance. Interviewing in areas of high neighboring proved sometimes difficult, when the respondent was continually being interrupted by phone calls or "drop-in" visits.

The styles of neighboring involving different *levels of interaction* in all the *forms of neighboring* are thus highly varied in behavior, attitudes, and evaluations. The matching or mismatching of neighboring patterns with the respondents' wishes or expectations may result in strong statements of satisfaction with the relations or in loneliness and mutual or one-way rejection. It would be a mistake to assume that all women, men, and couples have the same style of neighboring or that there is a closed bundle of social "needs" which different areas either meet or fail to meet. Each woman defines her social needs in terms of her whole view of life and her own position in the world. The patterns of definitions and evaluations, not the patterns of invariant needs, are the subject of this study.

CYCLES OF NEIGHBORING

Three cycles influence neighboring and may or may not converge in any particular case: (1) the life cycle of the roles of the women and their husbands; (2) the cycle of institutionalized relations in a particular neighborhood; and (3) the cycle of neighbor relations. All of these cycles are influenced by a number of factors.

These studies do not cover the period of time in a woman's life before marriage, but social psychologists state that socialization and education have as a major function the broadening of the horizons of personal involvement from a very local one centered on the home and neighborhood to identification with larger and larger social units. At marriage, the young couple is not inter-

16. Robert Dubin found the same to be true of highly interactive workers who do not mind changing jobs, even if they leave friends behind. See his "Industrial Workers' Worlds: A Study of the 'Central Life Interests' of Industrial Workers," *Social Problems*, 3 (1956), 131–42.

ested, as a general rule, in their neighbors. Both husband and wife
are deeply involved with each other and with social roles, such as
school and work, which are not likely to be located in the immediate vicinity. Newlyweds usually settle in transient and densely
settled urban neighborhoods in which anomic or institutionalized
non-interaction prevail, and they are happy with the anonymity
of their life.

The situation changes dramatically, as mentioned in the previous chapter, with the birth of the first child. Most wife-mothers
remain at home with the infant, suddenly cut off from adult companionship during most of the day. It is at this time that many
turn to their neighborhood in a search for compatible women in
similar life circumstances. Some remain lonely, others settle into a
pattern of urban neighboring, but many start wishing for their
own home with a backyard for the children. Though reputedly
desiring a suburban residence "for the good of the children" and
not because of their own needs, such young mothers rapidly develop close ties with neighbors, except during the confinement
months which, in northern climes, follow rather than precede the
birth of each offspring. As the children grow, the parents are less
restricted to the local scene; the mother's interests broaden and
she becomes involved in other time- and energy-engrossing relations away from the neighborhood. Relations with people living
nearby, if broken by mobility, are not duplicated later in the same
intensity. Those with whom a woman shares interests, other than
proximity and the life-cycle stage, may continue to be a source of
contact and friendship, but the general trend is for a reduction of
neighboring. A new trend is appearing in leisure-oriented retirement communities or buildings where, as distance becomes a
problem and retirement frees time, people are again beginning to
turn to their neighbors for social relations. This is only possible if
they can live in the very middle-class communities which are typical of retirement socializing and if they themselves lack hostility
to strangers.

The second cycle relevant to neighboring is that of the community itself. Newly developing towns or their sub-units, even
newly expanding urban neighborhoods, often facilitate neighboring. Owners or renters face common problems, are often isolated
from more established areas, and are involved in fixing up their
own places. Borrowing and lending, getting together to discuss

issues, sharing services, are more common in such situations than in old established areas. As time passes, the community settles down into a routine way of dealing with daily events and crises. Institutionalized procedures take the place of spontaneous interaction, and there is less reason or excuse for it. The institutionalizing process varies by community but, wherever there is mobility of populations in and out, some rituals for introducing newcomers into the neighborhood must be devised or the level of interaction drops off. Cliques form or a completely new style may develop with each population shift, the pioneers and the laggards often experiencing non-interaction.

Whatever style of neighboring is evident in a community, the relation between any person and those living within easy contact distance must develop anew. Strangers, even children, can go through the early stages of establishing contact, becoming increasingly involved in interaction, deepening the relations or redefining needs, withdrawing to more restricted levels, or breaking contact entirely. Some women never get beyond non-interactive or minimal contact with neighbors. Others enter all such relations with a set of institutionalized controls which prevent uncomfortable situations or an increase of interaction beyond the desired level. Few are able to maintain high levels of neighboring in all forms throughout their lives. The greatest likelihood that all stages will be experienced is among the upwardly mobile young people who start on at least an upper-lower-class or a lower-middle-class rung of the ladder but who have not been socialized into the procedures for controlling neighbor interaction or preventing situations which make it undesirable. The level reached and what happens when the peak can no longer be maintained are influenced by many factors.

Awareness of the possibility of having neighboring relations on any level varies by social class. Most established middle-class couples and some anticipatorily socialized aspiring young people tend to be aware of the differences in neighborhoods and to select one which meets their defined needs for social relations. Lower-class women most often select their future residence by the price of the house or the rent and by its location with reference to the husband's work. The higher the social class, the freer the man is to select a residence on the basis of a desired style of life away from work rather than near work.[17] This used to mean in America the settlement of upper-class families far from the inner city, but some changes are occurring in Chicago, due to the expansion of luxury living on the near north side. Lower-class respondents often express surprise if they find themselves among congenial neighbors, not being socialized into such relations and not selecting their residence in those terms.

Four means of *establishing social interaction* may separately or simultaneously be built into neighboring behavior: informal and unregulated local contact, gradually building into closer and more stabilized relations; use of institutionalized rituals for developing such relations; organized interaction within the area, guaranteeing contact; and organization interaction outside the area, which is then extended to single or multiform relations with neighbors who are also participants in it.

The two most frequent chains of informal incidents leading to neighboring revolve around children and new homes, because both require prolonged presence outside, in the vicinity of the area. The climate is an important consideration; Californians reportedly engage in neighboring at a higher level than people limited to being outdoors during only part of the year. When children are small, they need an adult to take them out; when they are larger, they form a link between mothers. Respondents often refer to contact with neighbors while walking babies or watching over the play of offspring. Many new communities lack fenced-in private or safe spaces for children's play, and mothers feel obliged or at least willing to stay out with a child.

Often central locations become meeting places for women with small children, because of their facilities or because of the contact itself. Parks, a school playground, or a beach in the summer become meeting places of informally socializing women. Gradually, the rhythm depending very much on institutionalized class styles, the hospitality of the backyard and even of the house may become extended to neighbors met regularly elsewhere. They are then treated as guests, offered food and liquids, and expected to return the invitation. Many respondents indicate that the stage of being invited into the home of another person is symbolically crucial. Women justify their definition of the neighborhood as unfriendly

17. Wood, *Suburbia: Its People and Their Politics.*

by stating that they have never been invited inside a home. The Mount Prospect housewife quoted before felt hurt because the only neighbor who came over to her property "wouldn't even come into the house." On the other hand, there are areas, mostly lower class, where neighbors are never invited into the home. Work outside the home, particularly gardening, can also lead to informal socializing, involving at first prolonged conversations, then an exchange of ideas or work tools, and finally hospitality.

If all the factors leading to increased interaction are present, the relations can become very "back and forth," with extensive rights of use of each other's property and services. A Skokie interviewer observed one such interchange:

> During the interview, a neighbor dropped in to have a smoke with the interviewee. She sat down at the table, uninvited, and proceeded to give her rather unenlightened views of the questions [the interviewer obviously was irritated by this, as she had been instructed to avoid the presence of other adults]. The interviewee continued to answer them, however. Fortunately, the neighbor left after about ten minutes. Before she did, however, she went to the phone and called her own house without asking permission or making any comments. . . .

Informal seasonal socializing may move into the homes of neighbors during rainy days and even extend itself into the winter months. Since, in Chicago, a chance meeting during winter months is less likely than during other seasons, winter contact requires pre-arrangement. Even women who were unaccustomed to interaction with neighbors before their move may become so involved in it during the summer as to purposely work out new patterns to prevent loneliness in the winter. Gradually, the pattern becomes solidified and each woman plans her day's work around the customary gathering times. One Park Forest home-owner who loves neighboring explains that she gets up two hours earlier in the morning in order to have sufficient time to get her work done before socializing. The young mothers who are not working outside the home or interacting with people during the day in other ways welcome the chance to be with adults, compare notes on subjects of interest and concern to each, and engage in pleasurable activity with peers, while simultaneously providing their children playmates. An additional function of such contact is the communication of knowledge on household and child-rearing matters, much as the business conference helps organizational employees solve their problems.

The daytime socializing by women is sometimes accompanied by a parallel build-up of relations among men. The most frequent contacts of men independently of their wives are: "Visiting while working in the yard, borrowing and lending garden equipment" (Hazel Crest); "Helping to build" (North Lake); "Car pooling" (Park Forest); "Walking to the train" (Highland Park). The informal contacts of both spouses can lead to couple socializing, but not necessarily. One of the reasons that apartment dwellers in buildings which lack centralized socializing contact areas such as a swimming pool or card rooms have a lower rate of interaction with neighbors than home-owners is their lack of opportunity for informal interaction. Many do not have young children, and gardening is obviously out of the question except on penthouses which lack immediate neighbors.

Formal rituals have been developed, mostly among the upper classes, which guarantee at least minimal neighboring. These usually begin with the traditional "calling on" new neighbors, within the prescribed times and with normatively controlled behavior. Etiquette demands a return call, which is often followed by invitations to pre-arranged "events" in homes or other socializing locations. Written or telephoned invitations are extended, and neighbors meet at the appointed time to "do something" specific together. They are invited for cocktails, dinner, bridge, a luncheon or "coffee," or to join the hosts in attending a scheduled event somewhere else. The invitations are returned and the relation is built up by an increase in the frequency and variety of occasions in which all are involved. Many neighboring relations are restricted to this level or to a single category of events. The deepening of selectively chosen friendships among neighbors may involve expansion of the form and an increase in informality. In the long run, such a relation may approach many of the characteristics of informally begun neighboring, except that it always tends to involve some formal events and husband, as well as couple, contact. Couples on the top three rungs of the American social class structure tend to be involved in many-leveled relations with selected neighbors geographically dispersed over a wider area than lower-class women. A Glenview woman complains, for example, that it is sometimes awkward for her to give a party, because each time she does not wish to invite all the neighbors with whom she has a variety of different relations, although the area is honey-combed with people who expect to be invited.

Organized activity within the neighborhood can provide the basis for more multileveled relations. Block clubs are often mentioned by urban residents of areas which have them; "protective associations" and *pro-tempora* groups organized to meet special local problems bring people together and remind them that they have much in common. Organized activity outside the neighborhood may bring together people living near each other. Churches are the most frequent source for building sound relations, but other types of voluntary associations serve the same purpose. The men or women who work together and who are also neighbors sometimes engage in greater interaction with each other during leisure times than with others in the area. It is important here to distinguish whether the contact is basically of work associates or of neighbors, since there is usually some overlap. Middle- and upper-class women are aware of organized groups as a resource for social contacts and future friendships or neighbor relations and usually join voluntary associations upon movement to a new area. Contact at meetings with people who turn out to be neighbors then leads to sharing of rides, invitations to homes, and so forth.

If prior training in patterns of social interaction provides no techniques for keeping them within comfortable limits, if the circumstances which might possibly lead to conflict are not foreseen, avoided, or insulated, and if techniques for resolving them are absent, close daily contact can result in great problems. One of the Skokie respondents gives a whole history of such difficulties. Briefly, two of the women across the street from her, living side by side, became involved in a fight and ended up not speaking to each other. The feud had lasted a year at the time of the interview and the neighbors close to each opponent sided with her, so that the area broke into two opposing camps and feelings were still running high.

One of the most explosive sources of conflict in a neighborhood is the behavior of children or of parents toward the young. The underlying anxiety of most American mothers over their ability to fulfill the self-demands in this role and the ego-extension tendencies of parents combine to create problems when an offspring is being criticized or attacked, while the behavior of the young often goes against local norms. "At the beginning we had a nice relationship with our immediate neighbors. Then we had a problem with one neighbor's children. The other, on the other side, lives on a high scale, and I don't believe in trying to keep up with the Joneses; so we don't have much contact now," explains a Glenview resident of a relatively new area.

Property conflict can also break up relations. "We are all in a project out here, so that there have been problems over landscaping. The lot levels aren't the same at all, but before the quarrel we used to have coffee together. We enjoyed that," says a Park Ridge interviewee who adds hopefully: "It'll blow over, I expect." She shows how important this is to her by explaining: "If you have good contact with your neighbors, you'll have a fuller life than in the city. But if you're in bad with them, then it's worse. There, at least, you ignore each other. Here you can't do that."

Not only dramatic conflict but daily irritations can wear down a neighboring relation. Even in supposedly homogeneous suburbs, once the first "blush" of excitement over the close interaction with people living so conveniently nearby wears off, value differences in basic styles of life begin to be felt. An assumed ease of interaction, or "instant neighboring," often prevents the development of procedures which would make cultural differences tolerable. Personal hurt or irritation can lead to withdrawing stances which make the development of the relation or its shift into more realistic groups difficult. Many of the Chicago interviewees feel "stung" by prior close neighboring, and others refrain from entering intensive interaction for fear of such a situation happening to them.

Sometimes decrease of interaction is not so much the result of the problems as of the inability to retain it in changing neighborhood situations. A Wheaton woman states that she does not see as much of her neighbors now as when the street was a "dead end," at which time they constantly "went back and forth." The development of an area around a previously isolated group of houses opens up new lines of contact. An example was provided by the changes within the pilot group of seventeen housewives who contributed to the early stages of this research and who were reinterviewed later. The seventeen neighbors, forming the young and non-working contingent of a set of twenty-four new homes surrounded mostly by open field, became quite close, even playing volley ball in a vacant lot on summer evenings when the weather was nice. All had moved in when they, their children, and the area were young. Gradually, the neighborhood became built up, the ball court taken over by a home; original owners moved out and new neighbors appeared not only in their place but all around. People began to "improve" their property by adding privacy-guaranteeing hedges and fences. One of the re-interviewees says that she "never sees" and does not even know the names of the third wave of residents in the homes back of hers.

The Skokie example illustrates three factors which contribute to the decrease in neighboring. Many researchers have found that close physical proximity, combined with difficulties in the development of other social relations, contributes to the building of interaction. The fact that an increase in alternative relations may decrease a person's dependence upon a group of neighbors with whom intensive interaction had been developed was mentioned by a number of respondents. Mobility also can decrease the amount of neighboring in a particular area. Those with whom close ties were developed move away, and the relation is not reproduced with the newcomers. That stage of neighboring is easily passed, since the original closeness was influenced by situations no longer present. A Hazel Crest woman defines herself as having "not too much contact, except with three neighbors. Several neighbors with whom we were quite intimate have moved away. We're friendly with all and have no trouble." But their evening social contact has dwindled to "very seldom now that our favorite neighbors have moved away."

The person who moves, of course, breaks ties with former neighbors, unless they are converted into friendship relations. Often, as in the case of the women who were quoted in descriptions of medium-leveled, purposely controlled interaction, the former closeness becomes negatively redefined, and attempts are made not to repeat it. A Park Ridge resident states that her relations remain at the "casual" level because "I never let it get to the point when they are in my hair. We are not really buddy-buddy. I made that mistake in La Grange, not here." Another resident of the same town says her contact is "just asking questions and small talk—no social contact. I don't go for koffee-klatsches. . . ." The reason comes out when she explains why her current level of contact has no disadvantages: "Not now. I learned from before, where I never had a free moment. It was a nightmare. I was forever serving coffee to someone. I never went anywhere to drink it, though." One wonders whether the respondent had actually been unhappy at the previous level of neighboring or whether the move to a new life situation led her to redefine desirable relations.

The older respondents, especially those with grown children, tend to engage in less interaction than the young, and they do not often mention any purposeful withdrawal. This may be a consequence of their never having become accustomed to close neighboring or of the presence of institutionalized controls in the areas in which they now reside. The re-interviews of the pilot group suggest a third possibility: the unconscious falling off of neighboring from a prior high or medium level which accompanies a gradual expansion in different directions in other roles and relations, causing role competition and a decrease in common interests. Two of the re-interviewees verbalized the change in their orientations, but most women were not aware of the process. One says: "My base has broadened. I spend less time in the neighborhood and have gotten active in the medical auxiliary." Another woman moved from the area and now finds herself in more restricted relations with new neighbors, because she spends more time in leisure activities away from home with her husband and growing children. One of the major reasons for her expansion is a higher income than she had in Skokie: "Things are better now; we can do more things away from home." Two side-by-side neighbors who remained in the pilot group area have maintained a close relation with each other, adding some new members to the clique and enjoying the local interaction. Even they, however, have expanded individually into different voluntary associations and role relations and find less time to see each other.

Thus, the seventeen pilot group respondents exemplify the process occurring in new or expanding suburbs. They had been involved in relatively high rates of neighbor interaction when they were the mothers of small children, but the level has decreased over the years gradually, rather than purposely. The original common pattern of life developed while they lived in almost identical houses in the same stage of the life cycle. Their backgrounds actually had not been similar in terms of religion, ethnic identity, occupation, and education of parents and husband, education of self, and future mobility probabilities. After they moved into the neighboring homes, and for a certain period of time before they developed other specialties, before the build-up of the area, before residential turn-over, and while children were small, they developed a strong pattern of informal and, in some cases, event socializing. They are now dispersed geographically, and in terms of neighboring and other life styles becoming increasingly diverse, although once they shared a common world.

The following respondent reminds the reader that not all neighbor relations which develop a high level of interaction eventually go through conflict, purposeful withdrawal, or slacking-off stages; that not all those who move wish to change the former level. When asked what type of contact she has with neighbors, a La Grange Park housewife replies: "None yet. The next door neighbors haven't moved in yet, but we have met them and they seem very nice, about our age. In Park Ridge, the neighbors were very close friends, daily contact. We exchanged services and I intend to do the same here. I am used to it. I'm sure we will do these things again." "The more the better" is her definition of the desirability of interaction. She repeats her wish for closeness: "I think it's going to be nice. The people we've met seem friendly. Only one couple was a little strange. Seemed unused to contact; I'm sure it's only temporary. In Park Ridge we had frequent social contact. It was a new community and we all became close friends, barbecues, card parties, birthday clubs, and so forth."

Factors Contributing to Neighboring

The various styles of neighboring which have developed in the Chicago region have been influenced by many factors. The following is a simplified digest of the characteristics of the society, the community, and the person which emerged from the studies of neighboring patterns and the residential areas of the respondents.[18]

18. Each interviewer was asked to name the suburb or neighborhood in which the interview took place, and to describe the respondent's dwelling, inside and out. She also specified several characteristics of its location: the number of attached units, size of lots, the number of vacant lots in the block,

The Society

American society facilitates the development of personal relations among new neighbors, thanks to a relatively open class system in which the current generation's life style is the main factor of their acceptance; geographic mobility, individuation, and informality of interaction being contributing elements. The emphasis on obligations to the nuclear small family residing in their own dwelling rather than to the extended kin releases time and encourages a search for non-kin relations. Scientific developments and social attitudes have freed women from a constant round of physical labor, which limited their life span to childbearing years and their social life space to the home unless they enjoyed upper-class facilities. The concurrent shortening of both the work time and the physical load of men left them free to socialize after the job. The complexity of the social structure now provides social roles away from home and neighborhood, dividing life into separate spheres with few demands on the man once he returns home and on the woman from outside it. Urbanization and industrialization have separated work, church, kin, play, neighbor, and friendship associations from each other, thus releasing each set of relations from controls imposed by the others. It is easier to develop neighboring when the kin are not around to make demands on emotions or time or to impose their standards of behavior. If work is done in the office or factory, then time away from these places is free for interaction in ways meeting other functions. The "fun morality" may not yet have completely counterbalanced the Puritanical definition of a virtuous life as one of heavy physical work and "no nonsense" family life, but church norms apply less and less to non-Sunday life. Thus, the separation of the societally functional aspects from the home has released its members from constant work, once the remaining tasks of person and house maintenance are completed, and it has removed from constant presence critics using standards from other institutions.

---

distance from the shopping center, and approximate price of the respondent's and the neighboring residences. The price was treated comparatively, since each interviewer handled one whole town or area, and it was checked against the figures of average cost for the area contained in the Northeastern Illinois Metropolitan Area Planning Commission's *Suburban Fact Book, 1960,* published in 1966.

In the meantime, American society has become increasingly relation oriented. This tendency is reflected in the developmental trend in child psychology and the companionate emphasis in marriage, as well as in office and factory. The home has become less task and more relationally focused, facilitating its use of human resources outside the four walls. Mothers are encouraged to find playmates for their children, and "families that play together stay together" is a modification of the original motto.

All these societal trends have been accompanied by a general increase in the educational achievement of the metropolitan population over its more rural ancestors. Slowly, but surely, the descendants of villagers are becoming more knowledgeable about the functioning of social systems. Education, formally derived or obtained from the mass communication media, has begun to broaden understanding of human differences so that people born of varied backgrounds begin to share life styles. The whole set of processes is beginning to free men and women to experiment with new social relations, including neighboring with people not known through generations of testing. At the same time, cultural change which has broken down traditional ways of relating to others is not evenly experienced by everyone, so that gaps or mismatches develop between a person's ability to neighbor and the institutionalized or emerging facilities of his neighborhood. Both isolation and irritation over excessive interaction frequently occur as relations providing comfort and contact in the past are less and less available, while the norms of new encounters are also not at easy reach.

The Region

One of the interviewees, who had been brought up in the eastern part of the United States, pointed to an often discussed difference between that region and the Middle West: "People are friendly in the Midwest." The ease of establishing relations and the informality and spontaneity of interaction among neighbors are reputedly greater as one goes from the East Coast to the West, with southern variations.[19] The northeastern seaboard has institu-

19. *The Ladies' Home Journal* devoted a special issue to "The California Woman" with the sub-title, "What happens when all the old rules are left behind?" (July 1967).

tionalized a more reserved attitude to strangers, whose demeanor and behavior are observed for a comparatively long period of time before friendship overtures are extended—if they ever are. Because of the absence of immediate friendship overtures, the midwesterner settling in these areas frequently complains of neighbors being "cold."

The Community Structure and Culture

Each community, urban area, geographically isolated town, armed service base with personnel placed among local residents, and academia composed of people scattered not only residentially but in their several work organizations, develops its own style or styles of interaction. Fisher Island, a summer resort, mostly composed of wealthy people owning their homes for generations, is different from both Middletown and a Lake Michigan town with predominantly "for rent" cottages. The rituals of recognition, introduction, contact establishment, and relation development are different in each place, and the newcomer must learn them before he is accepted. Several characteristics of the community play a part here. The social-class composition of the area and its distribution; turn-over rates in housing units; size and density; age and rate of growth; distance from the center of the city; and the distribution of socializing facilities all contribute to the life styles and their boundaries. The economic level of the community influences the type of activities which bring people together. The lower the average income, the more restricted are the residents to the local area, with spontaneous contact or special rituals. A resident of the inner city explains: "We see each other on the street. We don't have parties, 'cause we have no room." The interview schedule, which was originally designed for suburban homeowners, included an example of barbecuing as a form of couple socializing. A pre-test of this schedule on the urban population immediately brought out the irrelevance of that example. "How can we barbecue, we have no outdoors?" asked a respondent. She obviously did not refer to a lack of "outdoors" in general, since it exists everywhere, but to lack of rights over any space where the activity could be carried out.

The location of the community, be it in Chicago or Highland Park, in relation to other towns is an important factor in neighboring, not only because of the distance to facilities and local independence, but in the development of a unique flavor in its manner of living and types of residents. The further away a town is from the central city, the lower is the proportion of its male residents who work in that center. Migration to a community is influenced by the stereotype of it in the minds of the surrounding population. Exurbia is famed for being an expensive place to live, and this reputation prevents many people who could change neighboring habits from even trying to locate there.[20] Although a newly developed community may draw a heterogeneous population if the prices of homes and apartments vary, the settling-down process may establish increasing homogeneity, which then is built into a stereotype.[21] On the other hand, the reverse can take place, when a relatively homogeneous town becomes broken up by in-migration, as happened in Park Forest. This community, being a "farm-field development," first drew young middle-class couples willing to experiment with new patterns of living.[22] As they became successful and moved away and as the town expanded, blue-collar families began to move in. Town stereotyping resulted in Skokie's gradually becoming almost 30 per cent Jewish, after the first wave of settlers established it as a non-discriminatory town.[23] Prejudiced non-Jews moved out or did not buy, and young families just moving out of the Chicago ghetto took their place.

The Neighborhood Composition and Culture

Regardless of the heterogeneity of urban centers or smaller communities, each of their neighborhoods is likely to develop a more consistent neighboring pattern. Sometimes the local area is able to carry more than one style, criss-crossing interaction con-

20. A. C. Spectorsky, *The Exurbanites*, Philadelphia: Lippincott, 1955.

21. This happened because foremen moved out, leaving only the workers in this new town, according to Bennett M. Berger in *Working Class Suburb*, Berkeley: University of California Press, 1960.

22. The term "farm-field development" refers to communities built as total units by a building developer in the middle of farm fields where the land is bought in large units.

23. A similar kind of community is described by Robert F. Winch, Scott Greer, and Rae Lesser Blumberg in "Ethnicity and Extended Familism in an Upper-Middle-Class Suburb," *American Sociological Review*, 32 (April 1967), 265–72.

tent and level on a street or randomly selecting clique members.
What often emerges is a dominant style with subsidiary sub-units
and deviants. At least, many respondents describe their neighborhoods in such terms, some positioning themselves in the center of
the main stream with others feeling themselves on the periphery.
It is actually within this very limited geographical area that neighboring occurs, and town stereotyping often ignores the local pattern. One respondent explains that her neighborhood is not "like
I had heard it was here; we don't socialize much." Another is
pleased: "This is a good street; down on the other side, no one
talks to each other." Glenview contains two extremely different
sections, one consisting of very expensive homes located on large
wooded lots, the other of small wooden row homes. One respondent cried when her interviewer left because she was feeling
lonely. Married to a man who inherited money and built her a
lovely house in the expensive section, she is better suited to and
more desirous for life among younger and less wealthy people. A
different style of socializing exists among Highland Parkers who
live in the middle-class development west of town than among
those living in older homes close to the lake.[24]

Several social features of a neighborhood contribute to its style
of interaction. Two basic ones are social class and ethnic composition.[25] As mentioned before, classes and ethnic groups vary in
their styles of neighboring. Lower-class residents usually do not
interact closely with most neighbors because of fear that they may
turn out to be "the wrong people" or because such relations
would victimize them. "Some neighbors take advantage"; "We
are careful; in babysitting somebody always gets gypped, so we
watch it. We don't discuss money or personal matters"; "The
closer you get, the more they want to know what you're doing.
Not that they are nosy; it just comes out in the conversation";

24. The Gold Coast and the slum still exist side by side in Chicago. Harvey Zorbough, *The Gold Coast and the Slum,* Chicago: University of Chicago
Press, 1929.

25. Berger hypothesized that a *Working Class Suburb* would not undertake "middle-class socializing," but found out that women comply more with
the stereotyped suburban pattern of neighboring than men do. The process
was gradual, but the women were able to break down the barriers of social
isolation. One of the reasons may be that this was a very homogeneous community, even as the foremen moved out; so that the women's self-confidence
was not threatened by being located in a town with higher class neighbors.

these quotes come from people residing in the same type of neighborhood, but in several different communities. They reflect the
fact that neighborhoods and residents develop their own concept
of privacy.[26] Some areas where women see each other constantly
and interact in all forms of neighboring are defined as advan-
tageous because "Everyone respects each other's privacy," while
others with little interaction contain women who feel neighbors
are nosy. One gets the feeling from re-reading William H. Whyte
Jr.'s description of Park Forest that he disapproved of its intensive socializing and that the concept of privacy which he and his
research staff brought into that situation contributed to such a
judgment.[27] The interpretations given their neighborhoods by the
almost six hundred Chicago area women indicate variations in the
size of the privacy bubble, in how others encroach on it, in how
both parties withdraw from situations of encroachment, and in
the steps needed to be taken to repair the relation after a *faux pas*
has been committed or to prevent its repetition.[28] Of still stronger
influence upon the relation may be the motivation imputed to a
person who has crossed over the privacy line.

Lower-class respondents are the most fearful of close neighboring relations because of the expectation of privacy invasion. This
suggests two exclusive, yet somewhat overlapping, hypotheses
concerning group differences in attitudes toward interpersonal
privacy. One is that privacy-protecting and acknowledging actions are so institutionalized within each group that only situations bringing together people of different backgrounds create
problems centered around such feelings. The second is that
groups vary in their ability to protect themselves against serious
encroachments upon their privacy. It is possible that the lower
social classes of American society are the least protected against
unpleasant situations, because they have such broad areas of vul-
nerability and diffused identity, such deep fears of being left

26. Edward Hall deals at great length with the concept of privacy in *The
Hidden Dimension*, Garden City, N.Y.: Doubleday, 1966.

27. Whyte, *The Organization Man*.

28. Hugh Dalziel Duncan's review of Hall's *Hidden Dimension* was very
critical of his assumption that space affects privacy automatically, that men
respond much like animals to crowding. Duncan's argument stressing the
symbolic meaning of space is very convincing (*Trans-Action,* 4 [December
1966], 50–52).

defenseless, and so little control over the behavior of others, that the de-institutionalization of life patterns constantly brings situations interpreted as an encroachment upon privacy.

Perceived similarity may contribute to neighboring, in other than hostile neighborhoods. "Very friendly, much more so than Ruby Street [previous residence]. These people are more or less in our bracket." "Most are on the same educational level." These are explanations for close neighboring given by several women. "Nice class of people" is the more direct statement of a Mount Prospect respondent.

However, similarity in background may not lead to extended informal interaction, if it deprives women of contact situations. Hired help may free the housewife of dependence on her neighborhood, and landscape gardeners may prevent a man from needing to "swap tools" or spending extended time at the borders of his property where he would likely to meet other men doing the same thing. "We seldom exchange services, we all have cars and help, so it isn't very necessary," explains a Highland Park resident who has a low level of interaction with people nearby. Thus the factor of the functionality of the relation varies by neighborhood. In North Lake the need for work help, as mentioned before, broke down even lower-class barriers.

The presence of common meeting places or regions of contact within a neighborhood can thus be a factor in developing interaction patterns, if they foster feelings of friendliness and a desire for socializing.[29] Neighborhood leaders, both formal and informal, can create interaction-focalizing centers by building swimming pools, arranging luncheons, or serving as a telephone exchange. Such places become imbued with a special meaning which does not grow out of their physical features alone. One of the Skokie interviewees explained that she joined several organizations and went with neighbors to their events because of the influence of one woman who "rounds everyone up, so we go."[30]

29. Leon Festinger, Stanley Schachter, and Kurt Back, *Social Pressures in Informal Groups: A Study of Human Factors in Housing,* New York: Harper and Brothers, 1950. See also Theodore M. Newcomb, *The Acquaintance Process,* New York: Holt, Rinehart and Winston, 1961, for a study of the influence of spatial arrangements on people living in the same household.

30. Elihu Katz and Paul E. Lazarsfeld deal with the influence of informal leaders in their *Personal Influence,* New York: The Free Press, 1955.

A major factor mentioned by many respondents is the comparative age of the area's adults and children. The young age of offspring decreases geographic mobility and role involvement of mothers, but may not produce neighboring if others are not in the same situation. "It's unusual in that everyone is friendly; we're all approximately in the same age group and have similar interests," explains a suburban respondent. "Primarily the children bring the parents together. They go to school together and there is contact through that. The children go to Catholic school," presents a different aspect of the age factor. Baby-sitting, informally or through an organized pool, becomes part of neighboring in areas where paid sitters are unavailable, expensive, or unacceptable.

The involvement of the neighborhood residents in other social roles may affect their interaction with each other. Local churches and other groups serve as meeting places and any joint activity guarantees prolonged or regular interaction. Outside roles may interfere with neighboring. Work roles shorten the time available for socializing and may focus attention upon the roles of wife, mother, and housewife. Some jobs are exhausting and their very rhythm decreases opportunities for neighboring.[31] Kinship roles may tie a person so closely to relatives as to preclude the formation of competing relations.

The level of interaction among the people in an area may be facilitated or hindered by social events. Illness, death, and institutionalized mourning or a wedding can bring neighbors together to carry out rituals or to help those performing them. A neighborhood extra-marital love relation or a conflict between two residents can create sharp hostility lines. Generalized life styles, including the rhythm of daily work, fixed ways of taking care of property and children, or leisure-time preferences can effect neighboring. A group of families addicted to watching television separately, rather than as a social occasion, can decrease interest in, and opportunity for, non-family participation. Outdoor bar-

31. Howard S. Becker, "The Professional Dance Musician and His Audience," *American Journal of Sociology*, 57 (September 1951), 136–44. Becker points to several barriers separating the musician from others in the community, including his deviating work schedule. Judith Shuval also studied the effect of jobs on interaction: "Class and Ethnic Correlates of Casual Neighboring," *American Sociological Review*, 21, No. 4 (August 1956), 453–58.

becuing in an area of no fences and small lots can end up in casual interaction and even in shared meals.

Neighborhood factors which influence interaction include not only the characteristics of the people, but the symbolic physical traits of the area such as its location in relation to the rest of the community. Geographically outlying regions, isolated from services, goods, and social contact, require either very self-sufficient families or co-operative systems of interaction. Proverbial in suburbs, but also mentioned by urban women, are the car pools used to take men to work or children to school, lessons, movies, swimming pools or any other of the many activities by which mothers now expand the horizons of offspring or by which the young attempt to keep "with it." These involve communication of at least minimal levels.

The characteristics of the dwelling units are also an important factor. Inner-city areas often contain small dwelling units which are rented to highly transient people. The age of the houses, as well as the homogeneity of their condition is influential, because of the amount of work demanded of owners and the similarity of the problems they face. Areas of new houses or of newly acquired homes needing reconditioning are usually more productive of neighboring than settled or heterogeneous ones. Of course, the age or condition is only significant if the owners or renters define the house as needing outside work and themselves as the workers. No contact with neighbors can result if residents ignore the condition of their dwellings or if hired workers carry out the garden or house repairs.

The location of each dwelling in relation to others may facilitate contact, if they are close and if no barriers exist in attitudes. However, as mentioned before, closeness may be considered a reason for non-interaction, as it usually has been in traditional apartment buildings. It facilitates social relations only if the people wish them. On the other hand, the frequent assumption that extreme density, as in high rises, necessitates non-interaction has been proven wrong in the new buildings which have built-in socializing facilities that are used extensively.

Thus, the basic characteristic of an area which has a neighboring effect is the manner in which such relations are institutionalized. Even new blocks may be non-interactive, if their residents do not treat casual contact in yards as a social occasion.

The Person

The person himself or herself is the actual interactor and, no matter what the neighborhood institutionalizes as its style, each individual can deviate from it. Even in American society, in middlewestern and other communities, the personal characteristics of a woman and of her family and how they settle into an area may result in a level of participation which fits or differs from the prevailing one. Some people simply may not wish to take part in the style of neighboring around them and may introduce changes, withdrawing completely, shifting the level, or acting in different ways.[32] Other factors besides purposeful nonconformity may contribute to individual variations in neighboring. One is the person's reasons for moving into the neighborhood. This factor covers such things as his definition of the area and of his present and future position in it. Those who intend to stay for a major part of their lives are often interested in building social relations there. Many immigrants to America, however, made no effort to integrate into neighborhoods which did not contain their fellow national because they had no intention of remaining in this country.[33] A person or family may move into a neighborhood temporarily, because they cannot afford to live where they really want to be. Many occupations result in a transiency of settlement. Town-and-gown conflicts revolve around differences between the temporary personnel and the communities in which they settle for a limited number of years.[34] On the other hand, some communities are purposely organized around transients and demand behaviors facilitating easy social intercourse or "instant friendship."

Generally, however, the "migrant" or "transient" attitude of

32. Whyte calls them "deviants" in *The Organization Man*, particularly in Chapter 26 on "The Outgoing Life."

33. This is one of the major factors contributing to the slow assimilation of the Poles settling in America. See Lopata, "The Function of Voluntary Associations in an Ethnic Community: Polonia."

34. "Town-and-gown" distinctions refer to the existence of a local and an academic community within the same town. Air Force Officers' wives, interviewed at a State-side base during the Korean War, felt great resentment against town people from whom they perceived prejudiced behavior and about whom they often expressed condescending attitudes.

newcomers is feared by the more settled population.[35] It is sensed by the way the transient deals with property, neighbors, the values and concerns of the area. Anomic nonconformity to local norms often accompanies expectations of a short stay in it. A condescending attitude, hostility, or indifference may be expressed toward the local population, if it is considered inferior, rejective, or indifferent. The permanent occupants of the area are often prejudiced toward people who come into it with a manner interpreted as migrant. Thus, either migrant attitudes or resident orientations may prevent neighboring interaction.

The characteristics of people which are most likely to prevent neighboring in America are racial and in some cases religious differences, as well as the strong cultural variations of ethnic groups. Other visible traits which can lead to immediate rejection include manner of dress, house furnishings, and deviating demeanors, such as loud talking, use of language found objectionable, an accent indicating lack of education, etc. Whatever the characteristics of the local population, variation from them may result in refusal to accept the newcomers in neighboring relations. Even the manner of entrance can be judged inappropriate, whether it be by formalized vans arriving at a designated time with hired movers or by an informal U-haul with a kin work-team.

At the same time, the initial behavior of the present residents may influence the direction the relation takes, if it is interpreted by the newcomers as symbolic of basic attitudes toward them. The manner of greeting new neighbors is often institutionalized in the area and must be known by the people moving in in order to be understood. Several Chicago area housewives misinterpreted the behavior of neighbors when they moved to suburbs, judging the lack of certain gestures as rejection or assuming that the ritual of greeting would lead to instant friendship. Many were disappointed in the first contact situation and carried this attitude into future interaction, never feeling warm toward their neighbors.

The matching of person and neighborhood includes the amount and use of income and other forms of wealth. The newcomers are

35. Mabel A. Eliott and Francis E. Merrill discuss some of the problems of migrant workers who enter communities for very brief periods during harvest times in *Social Disorganization*, New York: Harper Brothers, 1951.

judged by what they own and how they take care of their possessions, and they in turn make similar evaluations of the people around them. Many leisure-time behaviors are dependent upon sufficient income, made unavailable by the move. For example, the new neighbor may be expected to entertain lavishly, but be unable to do so. People who are afraid of "nosy neighbors" may be attempting financially strained life styles, while assuming that they are the only ones in the area who are in that situation. One combination of factors affecting neighboring is certainly age and financial status. In America young couples are usually expected by all but the upper classes to have a small income and not to be able to engage in some forms of polite companionship interaction. They are also less sensitive about being "broke" than older people who are afraid that this condition will be taken as proof of incompetency. The "market mentality" shared by some Americans, which equates the individual's worth with the amount of money he is able to command in the labor market, does not affect so strongly the young: they can always expect a greater future income, as the middle aged.[36] The whole neighborhood may make fashionable a consumption style which is beyond the current income of residents and the family that refuses to engage in it may be a deviant. The other side of the income medal, the possession of ostentatious affluence and disproportionately high income can antagonize neighbors.

The dramatic conversion of lower-class Americans into middle-class ones has been facilitated by residential mobility. People become socially mobile by anticipatory socialization and movement into an area with a higher social status and style of life than they previously enjoyed. However, the gap between the newcomer and his neighbors must not be too great or they will be rejected, a circumstance which creates strain.[37] Mobility with

36. Fromm, *Man for Himself,* New York: Holt, Rinehart and Winston, 1947, and *Escape from Freedom.*

37. An interesting variation of this point is brought out by Zena Smith Blau, "Class Structure, Mobility and Change in Child-Rearing," *American Journal of Sociology,* 69, No. 6 (June 1965), 210–19. She uses change in child-rearing attitudes as indices of upward mobility and points up the importance of models. William Dobriner, in *Class in Suburbia,* Englewood Cliffs, N.J.: Prentice-Hall, 1963, characterizes the suburbs as very visible in that life style can be observed. Our interviews indicate this to be true of some suburbs only. Upper-class areas may be purposely organized to ensure privacy.

slight differences provides opportunities for observation and the gradual modification of past behaviors. Homogeneous neighborhoods do not provide upward mobility models; heterogeneous ones with a great gap between the classes develop into cliques which are isolated from each other. Thus, it is the slightly heterogeneous neighborhoods which facilitate upward mobility.

A person's socio-economic background influences neighboring by supplying him with certain kinds of social skills which may or may not fit him to live in a particular neighborhood or give him flexibility of adjustment to new circumstances. Generally, the less educated and the more lower class the individual is, the more he is locked into one form of behaving and the less creative he is in experimenting with new actions. On the other hand, even higher social classes may become so routinized in their rituals as to preclude all experimentation and to reject automatically persons unable to carry them out.

The personality of a person or a family may affect neighboring. Social areas differ in their heterogeneity of personality types and their ability to tolerate deviants.[38] The behavior of a woman, her husband, the children, and even the pets can encourage neighbors to build closer relations or stand off completely.[39]

The social roles of family members may either offer opportunities for contact with neighbors or compete with such relations for time and energy. Special problems facing the family may also prevent neighboring, as in the case of the mother of a retarded child who blames the doctor for this condition and is perpetually angry at the world. The age of the person is also a factor, because of its connection with the life cycle and because of its matching or not with the ages of neighbors. The job which the husband has may lead to the family's rejection by people living nearby. Several of the respondents are married to janitors and feel isolated from the renters. One woman complained that her husband was building houses in the vicinity which were judged by her neighbors as inferior; so they snub her.

In general, deviations from the neighboring styles institutional-

38. Louis Wirth found great personality specialization in *The Ghetto*, Chicago: The University of Chicago Press, 1928.

39. The interviewer who covered Glenview found one respondent's children absolutely unbearable and was not surprised over her answers to the neighboring questions: "Some neighbors don't like the way other children play, and I don't see them."

ized in a social area are due to the attitudes of a person toward those living nearby and to their attitudes toward her and her family, as well as to actual behavior.[40]

SOCIAL CHARACTERISTICS OF WOMEN ENGAGED IN EXTREME LEVELS OF NEIGHBORING

Although neighboring varies by community and by areas, its distribution can be studied by analyzing the characteristics of the women who engage in it at extreme levels. They are, after all, the ones who help select a neighborhood in which to settle and contribute to the patterns developed in it. The assumption guiding us here is that women with certain characteristics are prone to indulge in extreme levels of neighboring. The question we shall try to answer is this: "Who are the high interactors and how do they differ from the women who engage in restricted neighboring or completely refrain from it?" In order to answer this question, the levels of interaction in each form of neighboring were cross-tabulated with a selected number of respondent characteristics. To review, the levels are: (1) non-interaction (anomic, institutionalized, and justified); (2) low interaction (seasonal, casual, one style only, one form only, with a few neighbors only, having institutionalized controls or personal restrictions); (3) medium interaction (increasing the number of forms of involvement or the level of contact); and (4) high interaction (multiform, very close, or those lacking comfortable controls). The forms of neighboring are: women socializing, women exchanging services, men socializing, couples socializing, and estimations of neighborhood friend-

40. The discussion gives a more complex breakdown of the various factors stated or implied by Louis Wirth in his famous article, "Urbanism as a Way of Life," *American Journal of Sociology*, 44 (July 1938), 1–24. Other sociologists have worked with the factor of density. See Sylvia Fava, "Suburbanism as a Way of Life," *American Sociological Review*, 21 (February 1956), 34–37, and especially her "Contrasts in Neighboring: New York City and a Suburban Community" in William M. Dobriner, ed., *The Suburban Community*, New York: Putnam's, 1958. Wendell Bell has worked with social interaction in urban communities. Some of the results are reported in Wendell Bell and Marion D. Boat, "Urban Neighborhoods and Informal Social Relations," *American Journal of Sociology*, 62 (January 1957), 391–98. A very good summary of all the theory and research is in Alvin Boskoff's *The Sociology of Urban Regions*, New York: Appleton-Century-Crofts, 1962.

liness. The characteristics against which these levels and forms
are cross- tabulated include: housing (apartment or house), educational achievement, Negro-white identity, husband's educational achievement, family income, age, number of children, and
age of the youngest child. Other traits proved insignificant. The
three populations, suburban housewives, urban housewives and
urban working women, had to be treated separately because of
the differences among them and the internal similarities within
each one.[41] Only women at the extreme levels, non-interaction or
high interaction, will be discussed.

Type of Housing and Extreme Levels of Neighboring

The suburban respondents, all of whom are full-time housewives and home residents, have the largest percentage of high
interactors on the average of all forms and in each form except
service exchanging (see Table 21). Over half are high interactors.
Their husbands have a high level of contact less often than the
wives (49 per cent to 63 per cent), but more often than the husbands of the other four categories. Only one-tenth of the husbands
have "no contact" with other men but one-fourth have no interaction in the vicinity. Estimations of "very friendly" in descriptions of neighborhoods are significantly more frequent in suburbia
than in the city. Half of the suburban couples are high socializers.

Comparatively, urban housewives are infrequent high interactors, regardless of apartment or house residence. Compared to
suburban home-owners, they have more frequent high levels of
service exchanging. They list this activity at a closer level than the
socializing by women. Only one-fifth of urban housewives have
highly neighboring husbands, but a slightly larger proportion
(28 per cent for home residents, 31 per cent for apartment dwellers) often engage in couple socializing. All who exchange services do not evaluate the neighborhood as very friendly; the proportion is 15 per cent or 16 per cent lower in this form than in

41. The first statistical run-through of the cross-tabulations was done on
the whole group of 571. However, the results showed—by the lack of central
tendencies—that a breakdown of the group into its logical subdivisions
was needed. The subdivisions which proved most significant were suburban
housewives, urban housewives, and urban working women. The differences
among these three groups are strong and consistent, so that they have to be
discussed separately.

Form II. Half of the urban housewives engage in no couple socializing, and around one-third have no husbands interacting.

Working women are divided in their patterns of neighboring by type of residence. Those who live in apartments are much less likely to be high interactors in any form than home-owners are, although 40 per cent of both groups define their neighborhoods as very friendly. The highest proportion (65 per cent) of heavy service exchanging takes place among home-resident working women, a significant difference between them and their counterparts in apartments (49 per cent). In fact, no other group matches their high level.

Working women also have a high personal neighboring score more frequently if they live in houses than in apartments. Only 5 per cent of the former, compared to 30 per cent of the latter, declare a total lack of interaction. Two-thirds of the apartment-residing working women claim to have no couple-socializing relations with neighbors, only one-fourth stating that theirs is close. By comparison, only 46 per cent of the house-residing working women have no contact, while 38 per cent are involved in high levels of couple socializing. The same general tendency operates in husband interaction estimates, 38 per cent of the house dwellers stating that their mates have no contact, and 30 per cent that they interact frequently, compared to 56 per cent and 22 per cent for comparable levels among the apartment residents.

Among urbanites, house-residing working women have higher levels of neighboring than their full-time housewife counterparts, an interesting phenomenon in view of the amount of time available for such relations. Among apartment residents the contrast is less, with housewives having slightly higher rates than working women in all forms except in evaluation of the area friendliness.

In general, only 8 per cent of the women in the five population categories claim to engage in no interaction with neighbors, while 53 per cent define their relations as close; 23 per cent exchange no services, but 55 per cent participate in this form at a high level; 26 per cent list their husbands as non-interactors, and 41 per cent as high neighborers. These averages are contributed to very unevenly by the different categories of women, with suburban house dwellers adding the largest proportions to the high interaction scores, while urban housewives and the apartment-occupying working women pull down the total average.

Table 21: Sum Table A: Percentage distributions of extreme levels of neighbor interaction in the five forms, by housing, residence, and working status.

Residence and Population	I Self		II Services		III Husband		IV Couple		V Friendly		Average Percentages of High Interaction
	None	High	None	High	None	High	None	High	None	High	
House											
Suburban											
housewives	1	63	10	55	11	49	23	51	7	66	56.8
Urban											
housewives	12	47	36	56	30	20	53	28	9	41	38.4
Working women	5	46	32	65	38	30	46	38	16	41	44.0
Apartment											
Urban											
housewives	7	43	29	54	40	23	52	31	13	38	37.8
Working women	30	38	46	49	56	22	67	27	17	40	35.2
Total percentage	8	53	23	55	26	38	39	41	17	40	
Total number of respondents											

Table 22: Sum Table B: Percentage distributions of extreme levels of interaction in the five forms, by education, residence, and working status.

Housewives: Education, Residence, and Working Status	I Self		II Services		III Husband		IV Couple		V Friendly		Average Percentages of High Interaction
	None	High	None	High	None	High	None	High	None	High	
Years of Education											
1 - 4											
Suburban											
Urban	0	50	25	75	50	50	25	50	25	75	
Working											
5 - 7											
Suburban											
Urban	25	63	38	62	38	25	50	25	25	75	
Working											
8 (years)											
Suburban		100		75	50	50	25	50		75	too few cases
Urban	18	27	54	46	64	9	73	9	36	36	25.4
Working	33	67	33	67	33	33	33	33	33	33	46.6
9 - 11											
Suburban	4	56	11	55	22	39	39	28		83	52.2
Urban		47	34	47	30	39	48	21	35	35	37.8
Working		58	33	64	42	16	42	50	58	58	48.0

12 (years)											
Suburban	1	70	13	63	13	48	28	59	5	69	61.8
Urban	7	57	29	62	29	25	46	35	18	36	43.0
Working	15	51	30	61	42	24	54	24	31	42	40.4
13 - 15											
Suburban	3	60	9	54	6	60	23	59	26	68	60.2
Urban	14	28	33	54	38	24	64	23	12	42	34.2
Working	36	20	52	48	64	24	72	28	56	32	30.4
16 (years)											
Suburban	3	75	9	68	6	51	22	63	12	62	63.8
Urban		42	6	59	35	41	47	47	12	35	44.8
Working	17	42	42	50	50	33	50	41	25	33	39.8
16 Plus											
Suburban		67	17	33		84		67	17	50	60.2
Urban	11	33	56	33	56	11	67	22	22	22	24.2
Working	21	36	50	50	43	29	71	28		43	37.2
Ph.D., etc.											
Suburban	100	100	100		100		100	100			
Urban						100	100	100	100		
Working											
No Answer											
Suburban				3		24	14				
Urban			38	100		100				41	
Working											

Educational Achievement and Extreme Levels of Neighboring

Two interesting patterns emerge when the closeness of the suburban housewives' relations with neighbors is cross-tabulated with their level of education (see Table 22). The first is the general tendency for an increase in neighboring to accompany an increase in education. The second is for a larger percentage of women with a "finished" or degree level of education to be involved in high levels of neighboring and to avoid total isolation than of women who did not complete the school they began. The pattern is clear in Table 22 as well as in detailed tabulations not included in this volume. The following proportions of the women with specified years of schooling are high interactors: 56 per cent of those with some high school; 70 per cent of those who completed twelve years; 60 per cent of those with some college; 75 per cent of those who completed college; and 67 per cent of those with some graduate school. This up-and-down trend is startling and needs further testing. It suggests three hypotheses. The first is that women who graduate from the school they started comprise the elite of their neighborhood: they are sought after and their overtures often meet with success. The second is that women who complete a specific educational goal have more self-confidence in social interaction and are better able to be involved in the appropriate style of neighboring than those who drop out in the middle of their schooling. This self-confidence may come from the inner knowledge of having finished what they undertook. The drop-outs may experience a decrease in self-confidence because of dropping out or as a result of subsequent experiences which isolated them from former friends. The third hypothesis is that girls who drop out already have a different personality configuration than the finishers, including an inability to follow through a course of action or to develop satisfactory relations. The same self and other personality defects may be operating to prevent their development of relations with neighbors too. Thus, the grade-school graduate may be more capable of entering into the institutionalized patterns of interaction in her community than the high-school drop-out, because of the latter's combination of an early and a subsequent "chip on the shoulder" interfering with comfortable socializing. With the exception of the black community, most men marry women of equal or lower achievement in schooling. Since their income is connected with their training, they are able to settle in areas of similar male rank. Those who marry women who were drop-outs may be placing them in more difficult socializing situations than the wives who have finished the appropriate level. The increase in the level of interaction with higher education indicates a wish to neighbor, if one assumes that schooling brings a wider horizon for choice and an ability to develop good relations with a variety of people. Neighbor interaction seems to be one of the natural consequences of a formal education which broadens knowledge, increases the breadth of perspective, and gives flexibility of action. The highest levels of socializing are reached by those who finish the highest amount of schooling, which for women tends to be in general liberal arts subjects rather than in the specialized fields which increase inner direction and isolation. Even using institutionalized controls, the educated woman develops a high score for neighboring because of its multiform and situational style. Less educated women are suspicious of neighbors and are apt to be purposeful withdrawers after an experience with high intensity interaction without convenient controls.

An additional piece of evidence supporting one or a combination of these hypotheses about the difficulties of the school drop-out in her relations with others comes from the frequency with which such respondents feel compelled to explain to the interviewer their reasons for school non-completion. The question, "How many years of schooling did you have?" did not call for reasons for obtaining that many and no more, but many answers included such self-justifications.[42]

The relation between educational achievement and the level of service exchanges among suburban housewives follows a similar up-and-down pattern as socializing, but with a reverse of the trend. There are high levels of exchange among 75 per cent of the eighth-grade graduates, 55 per cent of the high-school drop-outs, 63 per cent of the high-school graduates, 54 per cent of the college drop-outs, 68 per cent of the holders of a B.A. degree or its

42. The richness of the data is such that all of it cannot be presented. Anyone wishing to learn of the medium level of interaction need only add the low and high levels to each other and subtract from 100 per cent. Sum tables of only two percentages of the two extreme levels of interaction are discussed fully.

equivalent, and 33 per cent of those who had some graduate work. This reverse trend fits the previously drawn conclusion that neighboring performs a secondary function for lower-class women, while it is more of a leisure-time activity and more primary in quality for the highly positioned. The husband's level of contact with neighbors also varies with his wife's education, but does not follow her rhythm. In fact, his own level of schooling has more influence upon his level of interaction than her schooling, which affects her own contact, her participation in service exchanges, and her definition of neighborhood friendliness. Couple-interaction also increases with the suburban wife's increase in educational achievement, however without the dip pattern. High levels of couple socializing are claimed by 28 per cent of those who went to school from nine to eleven years; 59 per cent of those who graduated from high school; the same proportion of those who had some college; 63 per cent of college graduates; and 67 per cent of the women who went beyond a B.A. The trend indicates that the more likely a woman is to be highly educated, the more she and her husband engage in couple-companionate socializing with neighbors. This supports the conclusions of Chapter Two that increased education on the part of a woman results in her spending more of her leisure time in couple-companionate rather than in sex-segregated interaction.

In spite of the increase of neighboring with expansion of educational achievement, there comes a decrease in the estimation of neighborhood friendliness, once the nine to eleven grade level has been reached. It is possible that the more educated women anticipate interaction before moving in and so do not consider its presence as an unusual sign of friendship, while newcomers from lower-class areas seem to be surprised and pleased to have neighbors acting in friendly ways. The criteria of measurement are likely to be different, and institutionalization of the relations deprives them of spontaneity. The lowest proportion of suburban women to judge their neighborhood as "very friendly" is made up of those with graduate-school training (50 per cent, compared to 83 per cent of the high-school drop-outs). One-quarter of the college drop-outs find their areas "unfriendly," a proportion higher than that of any but the middle-range educated working women.

Urban housewives follow a somewhat different pattern. Interaction among the women tends to involve increasingly high pro-

portions of the respondents as education increases from eighth
grade (27 per cent), to high-school drop-out (47 per cent) and
the high-school finisher (57 per cent); then it drops. Only 28
per cent of the college drop-outs rank their neighboring as high,
while 42 per cent of the college graduates and 33 per cent of those
with more schooling make such a designation. Why the more educated urban housewives should be less likely to participate in high
levels of neighboring than their suburban counterparts or than
high-school graduates is not clear from this table. One can only
speculate that they are more involved in social roles outside the
immediate residential vicinity and that some reside in the Lake
Shore apartment buildings with institutionalized non-interaction.

The highly educated urban housewife is also less likely to
engage in service exchanges (33 per cent) than the high-school
graduate (62 per cent), with the other education categories falling between these two extremes. Such exchanges are frequently
higher than the women's socializing levels for all groups except
the college-plus respondents and the high-school drop-outs; both
of these groups have exactly the same proportions in one form as
in the other. Male socializing is least likely to be high for husbands of women with some graduate training (11 per cent) and
for grade-school finishers (9 per cent), although, one suspects,
for different reasons; it is most likely to be high for spouses of
college graduates (41 per cent). High levels of couple socializing
are reported by 9 per cent of urban housewives who finished
grade school, 23 per cent of those who started college, 47 per cent
of those who finished college, and 22 per cent of those with some
graduate training. As before, we find that urbanites with little
education are not involved in couple-companionate relations with
neighbors, while the unusually highly educated are consistent in
their non-involvement in any form of neighbor activity. Urban
housewives do not fluctuate as much as their suburban counterparts in their definitions of neighborhood friendliness; the largest
gap in percentages (50 per cent) is between the suburban and the
urban high-school drop-outs; the lowest gap is between the college drop-outs in the two populations. The urbanites are generally only half as likely as the suburbanites to find their areas
very friendly, with only about one-third of them making such a
designation.

Urban working women have a pattern of neighboring quite

different from that of suburban housewives. The highest proportion of high interactors is among the grade-school finishers (67 per cent), and it tends to drop steadily to a low of 20 per cent for college drop-outs, rising to 42 per cent for college graduates and 36 per cent for those with extra training. Thus, although some dipping for the non-finishers is present, the contrast of urban working women to suburbanites is due to the fact that the less educated women are more likely to be high interactors than the highly educated. One explanation for the lower level of neighboring by the well educated working women is that their jobs involve them more deeply than those of the less educated respondents and keep them away from the area even after working hours. The high neighboring frequency of less educated women can be explained by another fact: there is a relatively large proportion of black women in this category. Negro working women with minimal schooling are high interactors, as are the very highly educated of this social race. The working women are also on the average older than their housewife counterparts.

Urban working women, however, follow a pattern similar to that of suburban housewives in service exchanging: the higher the educational achievement, the lower the proportion of frequent exchangers. The percentages go from a high of 67 per cent for grade-school graduates to 64 per cent for high-school drop-outs; 61 per cent for high-school graduates; 48 per cent for college drop-outs; and 50 per cent for both college graduates and college-plus respondents. The urban working women's husbands contact is high for both grade-school and college graduates. This indicates probably two elites, that of the blue-collar world and that of the white-collar world. Couple socializing, on the other hand, goes steadily up with an increase of education, except for a drop among college graduates. The highest "none" frequency is found in all forms of neighboring among the college drop-outs, an interesting pattern in view of the suburban figures. Women in this category are the most likely to define the neighborhood as unfriendly, and the least likely to find it "very friendly."

The first conclusion which emerges from averages derived from the percentages in all forms of neighboring is that suburban and urban housewives who finished a particular type of school are more apt to be high neighboring interactors than those who did not complete the same school, and that the higher the degree, the higher the frequency of interactors.

The second fact is that the gap between the proportions of suburban and urban housewives who are high interactors increases with increased education, becoming a significant 36 per cent for those with graduate training. This indicates a different style of life for the educated housewife in the city than in the suburb. The same is true of the highly educated working women, all of whom live in the urban center.

A third fact which emerges from the over-all averages is that the frequency of high neighboring among women with some college or graduate training depends on whether they live in the city or a suburb and whether they work or not; and the contrasts are dramatic. The more highly trained women tend to live in city rather than suburb and to be employed, thus having a relatively low score. If they are in the suburbs as full-time housewives, they engage in couple socializing and "event" interaction sufficiently to produce a high over-all frequency in spite of a low score in service exchanges.

Other Characteristics of Women at Extreme Levels of Neighboring

Racial identification. The stereotype of the "happy Negro" immersed in friendly relations with neighbors, dramatized by "Porgy and Bess," is not maintained in the Chicago area studies. No black women fell into the suburban sample, but members of that social race are represented in the urban housewife and urban working women samples. Their responses indicate that the black women who would have the time for intensive socializing, because they do not work away from the home, are the least likely of all urban groups to have close relations with neighbors. Forty-seven per cent of their white counterparts define their neighboring as high, compared with 32 per cent of the Negro housewives; only 5 per cent of the former declare complete noninteraction, compared with 22 per cent of the latter. In fact, black housewives are very similar to white working women in the likelihood of being at the low end of the levels of neighboring. The only activity in which almost half (46 per cent) of them are highly involved is service exchanging; otherwise only a third are high interactors in the different forms. The average proportion of black housewives who are high interactors is 33 per cent, compared to 36 per cent of the white working women, 40 per cent of the white housewives, 45 per cent of the black working women, and 60 per cent of the white suburban housewives. They are also the most likely of all respondents to complain of loneliness as a major disadvantage of their level of contact with people nearby. The difference between them and white urban housewives is not significant, however, when it comes to their reports of husband interaction and couple socializing. Both are low in involvement with their neighbors.

White working women and their black counterparts are similar in that 21 per cent of the former and 24 per cent of the latter report no interaction with neighbors. Also, their estimates of the degree of friendliness in the neighborhood are similar ("very unfriendly," 18 to 16 per cent respectively; "very friendly," 38 to 40 per cent respectively). However, the contrasts between the white and the black working women in other forms of neighboring are strong. Thirty-nine per cent of the white working women claim high neighboring for themselves, 55 per cent engage in service exchanges, 23 per cent have highly interacting husbands, 27 per cent are involved in couple-companionate interaction, and 36 per cent are high interactors in general. By contrast, 50 per cent of the black working women claim high neighboring for themselves, 63 per cent engage in service exchanges, 32 per cent have highly interacting husbands, 39 per cent are involved in couple-companionate interaction, and 45 per cent are high interactors in general.

The fact that the black working woman interacts with neighbors more than her white counterpart or than the black housewife indicates that they live in different worlds. The Negro housewife is likely to live in a neighborhood which she defines as "unfriendly" and in which she does not have enough trust to build satisfactory neighboring relations. The white urban housewife is more apt to have friendly relations with neighbors but she, too, is relatively isolated. The white working woman's noninvolvement in neighboring can be explained by involvement in her employment for most of the day. However, the same could be true of the black worker, who nevertheless is more apt to be a high neighborer. It is possible that women's work has a different meaning in the white than in the Negro community. Assuming that both types of women have equal time at home after employment, the greater neighboring involvement of the black respondents may be due to community attitudes toward women workers. The white community has frequently expressed disapproval of working mothers, while the Negro subculture favors her working because of necessity. Thus, the Negro wife may actually gain in status and in self-confidence for contributing to her family income and for proving her capacity to function in the broader world. Racial discrimination which hits men more than women of this social race may thus have an important function in justifying work by the female and in making her more acceptable in her neighborhood than a housewife or the white worker in her area. Finally, work supplies the black woman with socializing skills which the housewife may lack. On the other hand, the white worker must justify her employment because of the emphasis on the importance of keeping a home and being a wife and a mother, to the exclusion of relations outside of it.

The education of the husband is a factor in his level of interaction with other men in the neighborhood. Particularly among suburbanites, the higher his education, the higher his neighboring level is, as reported by the wife. Couple interaction is also heavily influenced by the husband's level of schooling, the proportion going up until the professional degree is reached, when there is a strong drop. It is difficult to determine why the suburban professional man engages in less couple socializing with neighbors than the college graduate does in the same location. The possibility that he has less leisure time than the non-professional man and that it is monopolized by associational and colleague contacts is somewhat weakened by the relatively high level of couple neighboring by the urban professional man. It may be that this is purposeful restraint on his part because of his local professional activity. The urban professional is less likely to draw clients or patients from the immediate area in which he lives.

Of course, the educational achievement of the husband is closely tied to that of his wife, and most indications point to the latter factor as the more important of the two, once their life style is established on the basis of the husband's occupation and income.

Income, that is, the annual funds brought into the family by whatever means, has an influence on neighboring, mainly because it forms a basis for the location of residence and the style of living. Women whose family income is low are the least likely to define their own neighboring as close (in the 1960's, 42 per cent of those whose income was $5999 or less, compared with 78 per cent of those within the $16,000 to $20,999 range). In addition, the higher the income, the more the urban husbands will act like the suburban men in regard to their neighborhood socializing, with the exception of a few very affluent men. The atmosphere of friendliness in a neighborhood is perceived more frequently by those with relatively comfortable incomes than by those lacking such, and the lonely people are apt to be living on very low incomes.

The difference extends to the lower levels of interaction. The higher-incomed woman is not likely to claim a complete lack of interaction, in its stead substituting "casual" levels. Anomic non-interaction is less frequent in communities inhabited by the wealthy than in areas containing the poor. Impromptu exchanges occur most often in areas defined as friendly by people with recently expanding incomes than in more stable ones. Women with funds stabilized at a relatively high level almost always engage in some neighboring, defining the level as medium or high and multiform, not because of the neighborhood, but as a consequence of appropriate and organized activity. Upwardly mobile families with high incomes sometimes find the formally institutionalized styles of socializing too stiff and therefore define the area as unfriendly, as was the case of several respondents with blue-collar fathers whose high current income is obtained by husbands in white-collar jobs.

Most young housewives, that is, urbanites twenty-four years of age or younger and suburbanites in their thirties, are likely to engage in informal and intensive neighboring and to be pleased with close relations. Statements of restricted neighboring come from slightly older women who are more settled in their areas and now have reduced daytime socializing, while increasing couple and husband interaction.

Particularly among suburbanites, the proportion of women with high levels of neighboring increases with an increase in the *number of children in the family*, from a low of 20 per cent of those with no offspring, through 58 per cent for those with one child, to a rather steady hovering between 74 per cent and 78 per cent for those with three or more children. No suburbanites with more than three children declare a complete lack of contact with neighbors, while 24 per cent of the working women with one child, 21 per cent of those with two children, and 14 per cent with three children engage in no interaction. One reason for the working respondents' low involvement is the age of the offspring. A disproportionate number of mothers who are employed are in the early stage of the family life cycle or have grown children. However, even the employed women increase the probability of neighbor interaction with an increase in the number of offspring. Full-time housewives with more than one child still at home are much more likely to come into repeated contact with neighbors than those in other stages of life. There is a gap in the proportion of high interactors of almost 40 per cent between suburban housewives with three children and their urban working counterparts.

Couple socializing becomes more frequent also among suburban families as the number of children increases; even the husbands interact more with other men in the area, if they have several children, than if they have none or one. The urban pattern is less clear, often because only one or such a limited number of neighbors are involved that the extremely high levels are not reached. On the other hand, women with no children or with only one offspring not only are low in neighboring, but refuse to even estimate the degree of friendliness in their areas.

The *age of the child* influences how restricted to her neighborhood the mother will be while she is taking care of him. Only 5 per cent of the suburbanites whose youngest of several children is one year or less of age declare complete non-interaction with neighbors, while 74 per cent of them are high interactors. Urban women with a youngest child of the same age are less apt to neighbor extensively, only 28 per cent being located at the high end of the scale; on the other hand, none state that they do not neighbor at all.

Some women in the Chicago area are unhappy with their

neighborhoods. Most of them are poor, and blacks contribute a disproportionate number to this category. Unable to move to a different kind of neighborhood, they feel surrounded by unfriendly people of whom they are sometimes afraid. There are unhappy women even in the suburbs, often because the neighborhood lacks the interaction they wish or because they lack the skills for becoming involved in an on-going pattern. The upwardly mobile lower-class women often lack the self-confidence for informal socializing, and even those who have already acquired the middle-class informal skills and tastes feel uncomfortable in the more formal style of the top three classes. An age gap is equally uncomfortable. The combination of age and education exerts an interesting influence on neighboring. The young and better educated fare well in neighboring out in the suburbs; the community institutionalizes easy absorption, and they are competent to take advantage of the pattern. The older woman socializes with neighbors best, if she is either upper class, very stable in a stable area, or now located in a new interactive highrise or retirement community.

PROFILES OF HIGH NEIGHBORING INTERACTORS[43]

The statistical distribution of the respondents at each level of interaction and in each form of neighboring by their social

43. The reader is cautioned to remember that the profile is simply a generalizing device which does not present a particular woman—like saying that the average family has 2.3 children, it can sometimes settle on impossible combinations. For example, it is unlikely that men with professional degrees will be married to high-school graduates. The fact that these two categories have the highest proportions of close neighborers does not mean that they are related to each other. A concentration of persons in a certain category according to one characteristic does not lead to the inevitable combination of the same people when a new characteristic's distribution is measured. Since not all women with high-school degrees have husbands whose education is the same as theirs, their concentration is dissipated into several categories when the answers are organized by the husband's schooling. New concentrations arise of men at each educational level and it is only partially related to the wife's location, since many men do not marry women of the same achievement. The woman's neighboring competence is heavily based on her own education, but the education of the husband establishes her in a certain type of neighborhood.

characteristics facilitates the drawing of profiles of women who are most likely to be involved in the highest levels of socializing with neighbors. The three populations, suburban housewife, urban housewife, and urban working woman, are again kept separate because of their basic differences.

The *high neighboring suburbanites* are all home-owners, racially defined as white, as is the whole sample from the suburbs. The largest *average* percentages of those with high levels of interaction in all five forms of neighboring are found among the following women.

Characteristics	Percentage
a college degree	64
a husband who dropped out of college	62
a family income between $16,000 and $20,000	65
an age between 35 and 39 years	68
four children	70
the youngest of whom is between 5 and 9 years old	70

The most important factors, judging by the strength of the convergence, are the age of the mother and that of the youngest of her children.

The highest suburban percentages in Form I, or women socializing, are found among the following women.

Characteristics	Percentage
a college degree	75
a husband who has a college degree	78
a family income between $16,000 and $20,999	78
an age between 35 and 39	79
four children	78
the youngest of whom is between 5 and 9 years old	79

Thus, the women-socializing convergence is even higher than the five-form averages. The proportions resemble the profile in the over-all averages with one major exception: the husbands are college graduates.

The highest percentages in the service-exchanging subcategories are found among the following women.

Characteristics	Percentage
8 years of schooling or less	75
a husband with a college degree	71
an income between $6000 and $10,999	64
an age between 35 and 39 years	71
four children	74
the youngest of whom is between 5 and 9 years old	75

Service exchanging thus tends to be engaged in by women with a much lower educational achievement than the other forms of neighboring, who are living on a lower family income than the less task-oriented interactors. The detailed tables from which these highest proportions are drawn show a significant rise in the proportion of women engaged in high levels of service exchanging with the increase in the number of children. This supports previously drawn conclusions that high neighboring is in part a consequence of restrictions in availability of alternative roles.

Husband interaction is highest among the following women.

Characteristics	Percentage
a higher degree than a bachelor's	84
a husband with a professional degree	62
an income between $16,000 and $20,999	64
an age between 40 and 44 years	66
five children	62
the youngest of whom is 1 year or less	62

This is a very highly educated group with a much higher income than that of the high service exchangers, with an older average age, a larger number of children, the youngest of which is lower than average in age. The highest concentration, a very high one, is in the wife's educational level; otherwise the figures are low compared to the other forms. There is a steady men-socializing increase as the education of the husband goes up. Income increases till this high, then drops off.

Couple interaction proportions are highest among the following women.

Characteristics	*Percentage*
graduate training	67
a husband with graduate training	64
a family income between $16,000 and $24,999	64
an age between 30 and 34 years	63
two children	58
the youngest of whom is 1 year or less in age	68

This profile shows a higher than average educational level for the wife and for the husband, a slightly younger age group, a smaller number of children, one of whom is younger than in the high over-all neighboring group. These facts reinforce the conclusion that couple socializing, which often involves event planning and institutionalized activities, is a higher-class phenomena than female neighboring and service-exchanging activities. Couple interaction increases with age till the peak, then decreases slightly. The number of children does not seem to have much effect on this form of neighboring, but their total absence cuts its probability down to a very low 13 per cent.

The definition of "very friendly" is most likely to come from the following women.

Characteristics	*Percentage*
only 9 to 11 years of education	83
a husband with 13 to 15 years of schooling	74
a family income of $26,000 or above	76
an age between 35 and 39 years	74
four children	87
the youngest of whom is between 5 and 9 years old	78

The concentrations are high, above the average convergence figures, the strong factors being the wife's education, which is lower than the average, and the number of children, which is average. The family income is much higher, although the number of cases is small. This combination reinforces the previous conclusion that those who find their neighborhoods most friendly are upwardly mobile suburbanites who are surprised at the high level of social interaction available in their suburb. The proportion of "very friendly" judgments varies directly with the education of the husband until the high point is reached, then drops. It also increases with the number of children up to four, and then drops.

The *high neighboring urbanites* with high interaction averages in all five forms of neighboring are found among the following women.

Characteristics	Percentage
residence in an apartment	40
racial identity as "white"	40
a college degree	45
a husband who is either a high-school graduate	43
or has a professional degree	52
a family income between $21,000 and $25,999	73
an age of 24 years or under	44
or between 40 and 44	45
four children	49
the youngest of whom is between 1 and 4 years old	67

One of the high neighboring urban types seems to be older, highly educated, and with a high family income. One suspects that they live in different kinds of apartments than the other type, which is young with small children. Income and age of child have the highest convergence, but the urbanites are much more scattered than the suburbanites, since most of their percentages of high interactors are much lower than the latter group.

The urban housewives who do most of the women socializing are found among the following women.

Characteristics	Percentage
residence in a house	47
racial identity as "white"	47
a high-school diploma	57
a husband who has a professional degree	70
or who is a high-school drop-out	48
a family income between $21,000 and $25,999	67
an age between 35 and 39 years	61
two children	52
the youngest of whom is between 1 and 4 years old	89

The wives of professional men who are living on a high in-come are the most likely of all women to engage in neighboring, but there are not that many of them. The second sub-group which neighbors are high-school graduates in their thirties. The strongest single factor, one of really high convergence, is the age of the youngest of more than one child. For some unclear reason, urbanites in the latter half of any age decade are more likely to be high interactors than are those in the early years of the decade. A similar trend is observable in the early age decade of the youngest child. The urban housewives who have high scores in Form I are less educated than the high five-form interactors, but their husbands have a higher achievement level. The high interactors have fewer children than those with aver-age high levels. The two sub-populations of Negroes and whites disagree in several factor concentrations, but the age of the child is common.

Service exchanges are highest among the following women.

Characteristics	*Percentage*
residence in a house	56
racial identity as "white"	53
a grade-school education	62
a husband with more than a bachelor's but not a profes-sional degree	63
an income between $6000 and $10,999	59
an age in their early thirties	75
six to eight children	74
the youngest of whom is 1 year old or less	71

The women engaged in the city in high service exchanging are less educated than the socializers and they live on a lower income. In addition, they have many children, the youngest of whom is very young. In these characteristics they resemble the suburbanites who also depend on neighbors to solve immediate needs for objects or other services. They are not, however, the frequent socializers, probably being too busy in the home to "koffeeklatsch."

Husband interaction is highest among the following urban housewives.

Characteristics	Percentage
residence in an apartment	23
racial identity as "Negro"	29
a bachelor's degree	41
a husband with a professional degree	50
a family income between $21,000 and $25,999	66
an age between 55 and 59 years	33
four children	36
the youngest of whom is between 20 and 29 years old	36

This form of interaction presents a strong reversal of the two prior ones. Apartment dwellers rather than home-owners, and Negro husbands rather than white ones, are more likely to interact. The educational levels are split, and the better educated women of both races are the ones whose husbands are the high interactors. This set of percentages indicates that the Negro population is also split; thus, urban housewives are divided not only by race, but also by education and income, and whites and Negroes are included in high and low interaction groups. The male high interactors are older, if the ages of the wife and the children are any indication of their age. In general, they are either professional men or those who are established in their neighborhood with a large family now already grown. Urban men are not very frequently high interactors to begin with, so that the convergence characteristics are confusing.

Couple socializing among urban housewives is highest for the following women.

Characteristics	Percentage
residence in an apartment	31
racial identity as "white"	31
a college education	47
a husband who is professionally trained	60
an income between $6000 and $10,999	31
or $26,000 and over	30
an age between 30 and 34 years	50
four children	55
the youngest of whom is between 1 and 9 years old	44

The wide range of percentages displayed in this form of neighboring again indicates a split population. Men with professional training definitely like couple interaction with neighbors, but

other characteristics such as residence, race, and a high income
show a consistent convergence. The higher socializing group
is better educated, either more or less highly incomed, and is
in the middle-age group with older children, which is not the
case for those who pulled the highest all-form averages. The
educational level is much higher for women than when only
feminine interaction is considered. Negroes are less likely to lead
here than in husband socializing.

Definitions of the neighborhood as "very friendly" are likely
to come from the following women.

Characteristics	Percentage
residence in a house	41
(although the apartment residents come close)	
identity as "white"	40
13 to 15 years of education	42
a husband with more than a college degree	42
an income under $5000	46
or between $16,000 and $20,999	50
an age between 40 and 44 years	46
four children	57
the youngest of whom is between 1 and 4 years old	67

The educationally advanced and high-income group on the one
side, and the economically poorer and older population on the
other side, are most likely to feel their areas as friendly, those
in between seeing their neighborhoods through less positive
eyes.

Those among the hundred high neighboring working women
who are the most likely to have high interaction averages,
though the levels for the whole population are low, are the
following women.

Characteristics	Percentage
residence in a house	45
racial identity as "Negro"	45
9 to 11 years of schooling	48
a husband with a college degree	44
or a high-school diploma	41
a family income between $16,000 and $20,999	57
or under $5999	60
one child	40
or, if more, the youngest between 15 and 19 years old	41

Again, this is a split population, divided between those with a high educational and income achievement and those in a lower socio-economic position. Even the Negro working women are divided between blue- and white-collar jobs and educations, and they contribute to high levels of neighboring at both ends of the status continuum.

The working women's socializing proportions are likely to be high among the following respondents.

Characteristics	Percentage
residence in a house	46
racial identity as "Negro"	50
an eighth-grade education	67
a husband who is a college graduate	55
or a high-school drop-out	46
an income under $5999	57
or between $16,000 and $20,999	50
an age between 45 and 49	50
one child	48
or four children	50
the youngest of whom is between 20 and 29 years old	44

Here again we see that the high interactor is the working woman with little education who is older and Negro, although the second category has a college-graduated husband and lives on a rather high income. The woman who is now working but who has developed strong relations with neighbors has a surprisingly large number of children: four, but all of them are now adults.

Service-exchanging proportions are high for the following working women.

Characteristics	Percentage
residence in a house	65
racial identity as "Negro"	63
an eighth-grade education	67
a husband with a college degree	63
or a high-school diploma	61
a family income either under $5999	71
or between $16,000 and $20,999	67
an age between 35 and 39 years	75
one child	67
or, if more, the youngest between 15 and 19 years old	67

Those who exchange services are younger and have younger children than the high socializers among the working women. The population is again divided between the wives of blue-collar and of the more educated husbands with a higher income.

The husband's interaction percentages for working women are high among the following.

Characteristics	*Percentage*
residence in a house	30
racial identity as "Negro"	32
either a college degree	33
or an eighth-grade education	33
a husband with a college degree	36
or professional training	40
a family income between $16,000 and $25,999	67
an age between 35 and 39 years	50
one child	42
or several, the youngest between 1 and 4 years old	50

Although the presence of the two populations is still evident, the tendency of the highly educated men to socialize with neighbors is so strong as to offset any patterns of the less educated black men. The family income is high.

Families in which the wife works show a high frequency of couple socializing for the following women.

Characteristics	*Percentage*
residence in a house	38
racial identity as "Negro"	39
9 to 11 years of education	50
or a college degree	41
a husband with a college	41
or professional degree	41
an income between $21,000 and $25,999	40
an age between 35 and 39 years	67
only one child	43

The frequency of high couple interactors is again relatively low, and the age of the wife is an important factor. This is a higher-incomed group than the service exchangers, but the pattern generally follows that of other populations.

Definitions of the neighborhood as "very friendly" are made by the following women.

Characteristics	*Percentage*
residence in a house	41
racial identity as "Negro"	40
(although whites came close with 38 per cent)	
an incomplete high-school education	58
a husband who has a high-school	54
or college degree	54
a family income under $5999	57
or between $16,000 and $20,999	50
an age in the early thirties	60
four children	62
the youngest of whom is between 15 and 19 years old	54

The age of the woman is again an influential factor, as is the number of children. The division in the education and income groups is again present, influenced to a high degree by the presence of the less educated black woman.

When all three populations are combined, the total of suburban housewives, urban housewives, and urban working women indicates that residence in houses is more favorable to neighboring than apartment dwelling. Racial differences show that the Negro housewife is the most isolated of urbanites, while the Negro working woman is the least, being more interacting than either white housewives or white workers. A college degree on the part of the wife is a definite plus, if all forms of neighboring are judged desirable, but high-school graduation is the strongest factor for service exchanging. An income far above the average, between $16,000 and $20,999, is most conducive to multiform neighboring, as is the wife's age of thirty to thirty-nine years. The presence of children is an asset to neighboring, with a gradual increase of scores until families with four youngsters are reached. Too many children by American standards, that is, over five, are a detriment to anything but service exchanging. Among suburban housewives the youngest child's age most favorable for bringing parents into contact with those around them is between five and nine; for urban housewives it is between one and four, and for working women between fifteen and nineteen.

CONCEPTUAL AGREEMENT WITH NEIGHBORS

The responses to the neighboring questions, focusing upon the perceived closeness and styles of interaction, left an important question unanswered, one relating to the connection between high levels of interaction and attitude conformity. If Riesman's thesis is correct—that high levels of socializing are a result of, and a contributing factor to, other-directedness and blind conformity—then those who interact most ought to be the women who define their views as being in agreement with peers. According to this hypothesis, both uniformity and closeness of daily contact take time to develop, and neither can exist if attitudinal differences are too high. Only one question in the "social role of housewife" interview throws any light upon this thesis, and it does not provide a distribution of actual, but only of perceptual, consensus. Responses to the question "In what ways does your conception of the woman's role vary with the ideas on this subject of your neighbors?" indicate some interesting complications of the relation between the level of interaction and the felt similarity of conceptualizations of vital areas of life.

The institutionalization of non-interaction among urban housewives and the tendency toward non-involvement in the community by urban working women are brought out by several features of the answers to this question. Although only 25 per cent of the respondents feel that they do not know what their neighbors' ideas about the woman's role may be, this proportion is not evenly distributed among the three populations. Only 10 per cent of the suburbanites admit such ignorance, compared with 32 per cent of the urban housewives and 52 per cent of the working women. This reinforces the difference among their life styles and the reluctance of some segments of the American population to "take the role of the other" in order to find out how their neighbors' views of the world differ from their own. Support for the hypothesis of the working women's isolation from her area of residence and her anomic attitudes toward it comes from the additional fact that only 19 per cent of these women feel strong agreement with those living around them. A similar percentage of all three samples knows, and disagrees with, the ideas of neighbors.

At the other extreme, 45 per cent of the respondents express some form of agreement with neighbors, and this definition of the situation is most likely to come from suburbanites. Sixty per cent of such housewives feel that neighbors share with them many ideas about the roles of women. Thus, the women who engage in relatively little socializing, because they have employment roles outside the home, are the least likely to feel that neighbors have ideas similar to theirs. The group of high socializers is the most likely to be in agreement with neighbors.

However, the distribution of the suburban housewife responses does not indicate such a direct relationship between the level of neighboring and the feeling of solidarity in attitudes. In fact, the more educated, younger, and wealthier women are the most likely to express feelings of strong disagreement with neighbors in one or both of the two important social roles—that of mother and that of housewife—and to speak of basic value and role hierarchy differences. Seventy-five per cent of eighth-grade graduates agree with neighbors, compared with only 50 per cent of those with some graduate training. Those who finished college and those who went to graduate school mention more often disagreement over the relative significance of the housewife role compared to other roles than high-school drop-outs do. Those who did not finish college are likely to specify contrasting views about husband-wife relations, and all the women who at least started college are apt to mention disagreement over parent-child relations than any other group.

A high proportion of high-school graduates whose husbands reached only that level of education agree with their neighbors' ideas about the roles of women. The percentage tends to go down from the high of 67 per cent until it hits a low of 12 per cent for wives of professionally trained men. Interviewees with average family incomes (between $6000 and $10,999) identify much more with their neighbors' ideas than other housewives do, with "agree" statements decreasing in both directions from the high of 66 per cent. Perceived disagreement over children is specified by a relatively high (one-fifth) proportion of those whose family income is under $5000, the low interactors; and by those within the $11,000 to $15,999 range, who are more apt to be in the high interactor group. Finally, disagreement with neighbors is most frequently expressed by the young women who have children, yet they are definitely the most prone to high neighboring.

The figure for agreement with neighbors about the roles of women support some of the insights obtained from prior answers. The lower-class urbanites and the "mismatched women" in any area are likely to feel that the values they hold are in conflict with those of neighbors, and these are the women who do not interact with those who are not connected through family. The new, upwardly mobile suburbanites who move to highly interacting areas within which they are able to develop neighboring relations feel that their ideas are very similar to those of people around them. The more educated women, who are conscious of the complexity and openness of the social role of mother and of the life of women, and concerned with working creatively and competently in all social roles, are the most likely to feel that their ideas are strongly different from those of neighbors, while at the same time being able and willing to relate closely to them. The tentative conclusion is that the better educated women are more apt than the less educated women to develop unique ideas and yet be able to tolerate differences in opinions over vital issues. Those less creative in their roles either assume uniformity or are disturbed by differences and fearful of developing relations with those who appear to disagree.

An example of the fact that women can hold strongly disagreeing views with neighbors and can nevertheless interact highly comes from ten interviews typical of Park Ridge. This community's twenty-five respondents represent a more stable middle-class background and present greater middle-class educational convergence than any other of the twelve suburbs which are included in this study, although several of the others have a higher community economic standing in the Chicago area.

Imagine ten women living in the same block who differ as these:

> The big difference is that I believe the man should wear the pants in the family, not 50–50 but 59–41. I do not want my husband hen-

pecked. It shows up when they go out. If he is to be a success socially or at work, he must be used to respect and responsibility.

Well, one I know is constantly out. She comes over here too much. I'd get more work done if she'd stay home. I don't go there. I wait till I'm asked. But she seems to want to get out of her home.

Mostly they don't plan housework and meals from the point of view of the child. He has to fit their schedule, not she suit his.

I think it varies in that most people don't stress home life as I do. All the teenagers eat their meals on the run; each has his own life. I won't allow that.

I'm a little stricter with the kids. I guess none of them make their children lift a finger. Her children [points next door] run her.

I have found contentment in my home. I stay home more and go out very seldom, except once in a while to a concert or a lecture. Not that I'm an intellectual snob, but I'm more peaceful with my kids. I never go to luncheons.

Well, some of the families out here are too concerned with the Joneses. I don't care about that at all. "Each live his own life" is my motto. They are inclined to feel overburdened. They resent being a housewife. I enjoy it and have contentment in accepting my lot. I guess I'm better adjusted.

They think of their house first and to hell with everything else.

We have more discipline around here than anyone else has in their homes. That's the only big difference.

There aren't too many young families on this block, so it's hard to say. Mostly grandparents.

Certainly each feels that her values and hierarchal arrangement of the social roles in her woman's cluster are correct, and she can easily find areas of disagreement with others.

SIX

Couple-Companionate Friendships and Community Involvement

BACKGROUND-FRIENDSHIPS

The social roles of women which are of particular interest to these studies include those of friend, member of voluntary associations, and participant in a community. As mentioned in Chapter One, none of these roles has been included in the definitions of what is important to women, although all three are significant in the lives of many respondents. Women answering the open-ended questions about roles important to members of their sex did not think of these three sets of obligations, nor did they list them high in forced-choice ranks. Yet, many report having friends and organizing their leisure around couple-companionate activities, belonging at one time or another to voluntary associations, and being aware of the community in which they live. The puritanical background of American society may prevent any outside-the-house, leisure-based roles from acquiring legitimized value, but their presence cannot be ignored.

One of the changes in American society which has accompanied urbanization, industrialization, and mass education has been in the relation of friendship to marriage.[1] A husband and

1. Some of the few studies of friendships of married couples have been

a wife are now expected to find enjoyment in each other's company and to be involved in shared leisure-time activity. Thus, marriage has acquired a companionate flavor.[2] In addition, this leisure-oriented comaraderie has become woven into a set of relations with other couples having the same foundation. Couple-companionate interaction brings the husband-wife team into "polite companionship" contact across marital and sex lines.[3]

Couple friendship relations of modern middle-class Americans resemble the European upper-class model more than the behavior of the classes from which most of our family traditions have descended. Descriptions of life in courts and manor homes of many European societies point to a highly developed pattern of polite companionship interaction.[4] A large proportion of currently fashionable forms of couple socializing, such as dinner parties, card games, dancing, an evening of conversation or music, an afternoon of sports, have for centuries been part of the round of activities of upper-class males and females. A great deal of time and planning went into these events.

The pattern of upper-class couple friendship interaction has not been universal. Some of the world societies have institu-

---

done by Nicholas Babchuk. See his "Primary Friends and Kin: A Study of the Associations of Middle-Class Couples," *Social Forces,* 43 (May 1965), 483–93; and, with Alan P. Bates, "Primary Relations of Middle-Class Couples: A Study of Male Dominance," *American Sociological Review,* 28 (June 1963), 377–84.

2. Robert O. Blood, Jr. and Donald M. Wolfe concluded in *Husbands and Wives,* New York: The Free Press, 1960, that such a change in marital relations was occurring in Detroit (see especially Chapter 6, pp. 146–74). As mentioned before, Ernest W. Burgess, Harvey Locke, and Mary Thomes built the whole of *The Family: From Institution to Companionship* around this theme (New York: American Book Company, 1963 edition).

3. Florian W. Znaniecki defines relations of polite companionship as "culturally patterned relations between individuals who carry on social intercourse regularly for the purpose of common enjoyment" (*Social Relations and Social Roles,* San Francisco: Chandler, 1965, p. 172). Philippe Ariès speaks of many adult "games and amusements [which] extend far beyond the furtive moments we allow them" in *Centuries of Chlidhood,* translated from French by Robert Baldick, New York: Random House Vintage Book, 1965, p. 73.

4. I do not agree with Blood and Wolfe that prior centuries of European history lack couple-companionate relations between husbands and wives. Those authors limit cross-sex companionship to mistresses or hetaerae, ignoring a major part of upper-class life.

tionalized purdah, or the custom of having their women removed even from the view of non-kin males. However, European upper-class cultures generally developed permissiveness in the contacts between men and women not related by blood or marriage. Simultaneously, their lower-class cultures were highly sex-segregated and lacked occasions for either husband and wife companionship or the symmetrical relations of several couples. Part of the leisure-time sex-segregation of families living on a bare subsistence level in agricultural lands may be due to differences in the work rhythms of males and females. Much of the indoor work has been delegated to women and, as the proverb says, "A woman's work is never done." In any case, it outlasts the time that men work in the field, since they must be fed and children put to bed. Extended patrilocal families often provided friendship for a wife with other women and for the husband with the men in or around the home. Each sex had more in common with those performing similar tasks than with people involved in a completely different round of work. Companionship interaction between husband and wife was not expected and their ventures into play were usually woven into activities having other than recreational functions.

The lower classes of Europe and America continue sex-segregated lives during off-work hours even in urban centers.[5] In London, women turn to their mothers, sisters, or daughters for the satisfaction of companionate and intimacy needs. Secondary tasks form the basis of marriage, while men have their friendship cliques begun in childhood in the neighborhood and reinforced by common work locations. Sex-segregated friendships have been found also in America.[6]

However, Americans are increasingly involved in couple-companionate interaction. Three major trends have changed the interaction of men and women in the marital unit. The first of these is a change in the work load and content. One aspect of this modification is the movement of work away from the home

5. Elizabeth Bott, *Family and Social Network,* London: Tavistock, 1957; Michael Young and Peter Willmott, *Family and Kinship in East London,* New York: The Free Press, 1957; and Peter Willmott and Michael Young, *Family and Class in a London Suburb,* London: Routledge and Kegan Paul, 1960.

6. Joel I. Nelson, "Clique Contacts and Family Orientations," *American Sociological Review,* 31 (October 1966), 663–72.

to central locations employing large numbers of people. Once the man leaves the factory or office, he is free from the obligations of work, and the length of time he is away from home has decreased for all but the entrepreneurial professional men. Even white-collar occupations have become decreasingly family connected, "mom and pop" stores and similar businesses being replaced by large employee organizations.[7] The few scientific or professional teams of husband and wife are the exception rather than the rule, and they stand as examples of co-operative companionship.[8] Thus, men and women no longer interact during work hours, but the man is freed from work during time at home. Another aspect of work changes is in the lives of women. Released from farm chores, assisted by modern electric conveniences, made healthier by medicine, and less tied-down because of having fewer children, the metropolitan housewife has much free time and energy. The new economic abundance and a decline in the work orientation of the puritan ethic have produced the second major trend: leisure-time orientation. People are willing to take the time and money to play and to interact with others for no other reason except pleasure in the activity and the contact. This attitude is true of husband-wife relations and of couple-companionate ones.

The third trend has been in the lives of men and women prior to marriage and in the relations between them at that time. Women are being educated in the same way as men, and they share many of the same interests and activities. Companionship is expected and non-erotic friendships across sex lines are tolerated, taken as normal, and even encouraged. These trends lay a foundation for symmetrical and leisure-oriented couple-companionate interaction.

Of course, sex-segregated friendships and couple-companionate interaction can be combined in many different ways in the lives of Americans. Even the lower-class marriage teams attend some social events together. Weddings, christenings, special holiday celebrations, and funerals afford shared experiences and the opportunity to reaffirm marital solidarity as well as line continuity. Examples of such events are mentioned by 74 per

7. C. Wright Mills, *White Collar*, New York: Oxford, 1951.
8. Vance Packard, *The Sexual Wilderness*, New York: David McKay, 1968, as reported in *McCall's*, September 1968.

cent of the "interaction patterns" respondents, who explain that they get together with their husbands and other relatives on holidays. At the other end of the class continuum, formal dinners in Europe or America were traditionally followed by a withdrawal of the gentlemen for cigars and "serious talk." Emily Post assures her readers that no lady would impinge on this custom.[9] The variety of friendship relations in which a modern American couple can be involved includes several combinations of persons and ranges of intimacies. Some of the sub-groups in this society still limit friendship to ascribed, kin-connected people. Others separate the roles of friend and neighbor from those in kin groups, a third group allows the development of first-name relations with personally selected individuals. The friendship relations of a couple can best be explained in model form, showing who originates them, whether they are achieved or ascribed,[10] and if they are sex-segregated or involve the marital partner (see Chart 3).

The model does not portray direct relations of persons of the opposite sex who are not connected through someone of the same sex or through the spouse. It would be possible to show that a woman can have companionate contact with an achieved male friend. The same type of contact could be included on the side of the husband. The exclusion of such relations is simply a matter of arbitrary choice, of an emphasis on the couple and on the rela-

9. Emily Post, *Etiquette,* New York: Funk & Wagnalls, 9th edition, 1959: "Each gentleman then bows slightly, takes leave of his partner, and, with the other gentlemen, follows the host to the room where after-dinner coffee, liquers, and cigars and cigarettes are being passed. At the end of twenty minutes or so, the host must take the opportunity of the first lull in the conversation to suggest that they "join the ladies" in the drawing room. In a house where there is no extra room to smoke in, the gentlemen do not conduct the ladies to the drawing room, but stay where they are (the ladies leaving alone) and have their coffee, cigars, liquers, and conversation sitting around the table" (p. 361).

10. The concepts of "ascribed" and "achieved" social relations or social roles are basic to sociology. An ascribed role is "a role based on inherited status and assigned without regard to individual ability or performance." An "achieved" role is one "reached by individual effort." Paul B. Horton and Chester L. Hunt, *Sociology,* New York: McGraw-Hill, 1964, p. 563. In reference to primary or significant relations, ascribed are those which the social system enforces on an individual, achieved are those based on personal choice.

Chart 3: Model of companionate relations, couple and sex-segregated, by originator and degree of choice.

	Originator			
	Wife		Husband	
	Ascribed	Achieved	Ascribed	Achieved
Participant	Couple		Friend or Clique	
Husband	Matriarchal kin and spouses	Her friend, clique, and their husbands	Partriarchal kin (especially sibling)	Friend, voluntary clique, group
	Friend or Clique		Couple	
Wife	Matriarchal (especially sibling)	Friend, voluntary clique, group	Patriarchal kin and their spouses	His friend, clique, and their wives

tions each partner has with couples or with persons of the same sex. It is also much less likely to occur in this society.

The sources and components of companionate relations of married adults can be combined, within different societies and within our own social system, into:

1. *Sex-segregated* friendship relations in which both the husband and the wife participate *in different groups,* as described in working-class boroughs by Elizabeth Bott, Michael Young, and Peter Willmott. "Men have friends, women have relatives," is the way Bott describes this complex.[11]

2. *Sex-segregated* friendship relations in which the *husband* has a close friend or is attached to a clique, while the wife is relatively isolated; as when the women married to clique members do not form a separate group. An example is the lower-class Mexican pattern described by Arturo and Genevieve De Hoyos.[12]

11. Bott, *Family and Social Network;* Young and Willmott, *Family and Kinship in East London.*

12. Arturo De Hoyos and Genevieve De Hoyos, "The Amigo System and Alienation of the Wife in the Conjugal Mexican Family," in Bernard Farber, ed., *Kinship and Family Organization,* New York: John Wiley, 1966, pp. 102–15.

3. *Sex-segregated* friendship relations in which the *wife* has a close friend or is attached to a clique without a parallel involvement by the husband. Such a relation can prevent couple-companionate relations from becoming of primary importance to the wife, as reported by Joel Nelson in his description of a residentially stable segment of New Haven, Connecticut.[13]

4. *Sex-segregated* friendship relations entirely connected with the male kin line, as exemplified in patriarchal, patrilineal, and patrilocal societies. Both sets of friendship groups are ascribed, the male having been born into one and the wife joining its female counterpart upon marriage. Anthropological literature abounds with these arrangements.[14]

5. *Couple-only* companionate relations in which the husband and wife lack any sex-segregated friendship, engaging only in leisure activities as couples, appear rather rarely in modern literature. The honeymoon period in American marital relations draws the attention of the partners to each other, but other units are not usually portrayed as part of the activity. "Vacations with" another couple may set up such temporary relations. The romantic love ideal assumes that no external friendships are needed, that the relation is "total," but many studies indicate that this is only part of the fantasy woven into this "romantic fallacy." The London professional couples are portrayed by Elizabeth Bott as close to this ideal, since they are supposedly separated from sex-segregated friends, but several discussants have felt this "social network" to be inadequately studied or explained.[15]

6. *Couple-plus, sex-segregated* companionate relations seem to exist among many middle-class Americans, including the Chicago housewives. The form they take, the source for either couple or sex-segregated friendships, and the activities they involve vary by social class, residential area, and idiosyncratic factors. The couple-plus concept refers to relations of modern husbands and wives which include both couple socializing and

13. Nelson, "Clique Contacts and Family Orientations."

14. Margaret Cormack in *The Hindu Woman*, New York: Bureau of Publications, Columbia University, 1953, describes such a system, and Barbara Ward, ed., in *Women in the New Asia*, Paris: UNESCO, 1963, presents several different forms of relations of wives to husbands and to the outside world.

15. The main critic known to me is Nelson in "Clique Contacts and Family Orientations," but he makes references to other studies.

peer friendships developed by each partner out of current life. Lower-class couples are apt to have fewer of these, most contact being limited to sex-segregated or asymmetrical relations. The patterns tend to be dependent on individual selectivity and to be connected with the middle-classes and above. The age and the generation to which the respondent belongs are contributing factors to the form these couple-plus relations take and to the way they are woven into each other.

COUPLE-COMPANIONATE RELATIONS

Couple socializing, as a complex of numerous interaction sequences of increasing importance in America, has been facilitated by the release of time and money from the need to meet basic necessities and by the development of norms of equality between the sexes. Whether formal and reported in the "society" pages of the metropolitan or local newspapers, or a barbecue in the back yard, which Riesman found so symbolic of suburban familism,[16] couple interaction involves at least four people who agree that they like each other or the activity well enough to spend their leisure time doing it together. Occasionally, work organization or other enforced "get-togethers" are reported, but they are often defined as part of the obligation system rather than of leisure. Of course, both positive and negative sanctions of the organization or of the community may operate to keep a relatively uncongenial set of couples in companionate contact. Without having to analyze "ulterior motives," we can safely say that continued socializing among couples performs at least three functions: one, it brings husband and wife together in highly interactive situations; two, it facilitates positively evaluated activity; and three, it meets expectations of sympathetically pleasurable friendship relations. A sociologically interesting set of questions arises about the source of such relations among married couples living in urbanized areas of the society. "How do couples who end up seeing each other more often than they see "outsiders" come into contact?" "Who is the originator of a couple relation, the husband

16. David Riesman, "The Suburban Dislocation," *The Annals of the American Academy of Political and Social Science*, 314 (November 1956), 123–46.

or the wife?" and "Which roles of each are most likely to facilitate the conversion of the original contact into couple-companionate interaction?" Finally, we wonder how the sources of these relations vary at different stages in the life cycle.

Sources for Couple Friendships

Several sociological studies and the Chicago respondents provide background knowledge about some of the sources of couple friendship in America. The childhood peer group is of primary importance to the young in modern small families, assisting in the development of personality, in the testing of sentiments, and in the generalization of moral judgments. Thrasher's *The Gang*,[17] Whyte's *Street Corner Society*,[18] and the mass culture's *West Side Story*[19] have described sex-segregated friendship cliques of relatively young adulthood. The last named source indicates "The Old Bunch" begins to break up as each man gets married and develops alternative loyalties and interests—a somewhat questionable assumption about the Puerto Rican lower class. As mentioned before, many subcultures do not demand such a cutoff of clique contact. The equality-focused middle-class culture does demand it; and the exclusive importance assigned the marital tie often contributes to a strain for the newlywed who had been strongly associated with a clique. The transformation of a former clique into a couple-companionate friendship group is generally impossible until most members are married. Even then, the modification of the former sex-segregated sets of relations into a bi-sexual and couple-based group is difficult. Former loyalties are resented by those who feel as strangers in the friendship group: wives if the clique is male, husbands if the clique is female. Action and attitude patterns built into prior relations are hard to shift, especially if underlined by strong sentiments. Both a clique and a companionate marriage tend to operate on the thesis that each should be the focal point of identity. Thus, the ability to develop an equality of involvement

17. Frederic M. Thrasher, *The Gang*, Chicago: University of Chicago Press, 1943.
18. William F. Whyte, *Street Corner Society*, Chicago: University of Chicago Press, 1943.
19. *West Side Story* was a musical, first a theater play, then a movie.

of both husband and wife in the now married former clique without strain is complicated by the asymmetry and by the content of past relations.

Compromise patterns of transferring childhood, or any other sex-segregated relations, into couple-companionate friendships are explained by several housewives. One of these combines some couple contact with special occasions for "the boys to get together" or for "the girls' night out." Another compromise is described by a respondent in speaking of a social event typical in her group. According to this pattern, the wives of the clique members have become very close, in spite of having their friendship roles ascribed, and couple events end up with the men in one room playing cards or discussing "sports and politics" and the women in another room sharing information on household and child-rearing problems.

Sex-segregated couple socializing seems less prevalent among the upper rungs of the social structure, many forms of institutionalized activity requiring the presence of couples. In fact, women without male escorts report feeling like a "fifth wheel" in most social situations of these groups.

Other roles prior to marriage, besides that of clique member, can serve as sources for couple friendships. The sharing of student experiences at any level of education binds people together, as going through the armed services does for men. College fraternities and sororities are particularly strong contributors to companionate relations of alumni. Work roles and, of course, kin relations can add to the fund from which a couple may draw those with whom it interacts for leisure. In fact, the fund is quite large in modern society. Young men and women come into close contact with many people prior to marriage.[20]

Which of these people continue as friends in married life depends on many factors. The content of the interviews suggests the importance of continued availability of contact as a basic factor in friendship. Young families are likely to move from old neighborhoods, and contact with former friends becomes increasingly difficult because of distance. A twenty-five-year-old Negro woman explains that her best friends, those with whom she and

20. One of the conclusions reached by S. Kirson Weinberg in intensive study of friendships is that they are most frequently made in youth and become more difficult with increasing age (explained in private conversation).

her husband had the closest relation before marriage and during its early years, now live in "Gary, Indiana; Brooklyn, New York; Cleveland, Ohio; Washington, D.C.; New Orleans and California." The last-named state contains many people who migrated after World War II, and a relatively large number of Chicago area interviewees refer to that distant location when naming their closest friends.

Even less distant separation can result in a divergence of life styles. Most urban interviewees restrict their major couple contact to other urbanites; and suburbanites tend to narrow the distance from friends, either by settling together or by dropping too inaccessible relations and substituting others who are conveniently nearby. On the other hand, prior friendships can become a good source of couple-companionate relations even after a break in time, when again "re-discovered" within similar life lines. The underlying warmth of recollection results in a purposeful attempt to convert this contact into companionship. Childhood friends can be again found as community or voluntary association co-members. Some social groups, containing alumni from schools, or fellow veterans, guarantee continued contact over years with those for whom the early experiences are equally meaningful. Newly developed contact lines and the absence of barriers, such as divergent life styles or distance, can assist in the conversion of those early, but discontinuous relations into couple-companionate friendship.

Mutual friends can also be brought into couple contact from any social roles in which the husband and wife become involved together after marriage. Voluntary associations, including church groups, neighboring, and even institutionalized play, may lead to continuing sequences of interaction, even with people who had not started out as personal friends of either spouse. Vacations can be sources of contact with couples, as can "mutual friends." The cycle of parties, dinners, or other events bring together a clique and often the peripheral friends of any one couple. The latter become candidates for replacements in the "crowd" as old members move away. Couple-involving voluntary associations, such as dancing or card-playing clubs, or centers for whole sets of activities, such as country clubs, provide guaranteed and regular interaction. Personal selectivity can result in the formation of cliques, if the parent group is too large, but semi-formalized norms often demand that each member be guaranteed at least some socializing. Neighboring is a major source of couple-companionate relations, woven in varying ways with the sex-segregated interaction, as discussed in Chapter Five.

Work, voluntary associations, and other social groups involving only one of the marital partners can be a source of meeting people who are brought into couple interaction. The husband's work or business is a frequent provider of leisure-time companions. Large work groups may not only interview the wife to determine her degree of mastery of social skills, but they may even "recommend" residential location and membership in voluntary associations which guarantee "being with the group." The Armed Services' Officers' or Non-Commissioned Officers' Clubs contain numerous sex-segregated and couple-socializing groups. Shae describes these at length in *The Army Wife* and other books, recommending strongly that the new bride become involved in them.[21] One of the problems of retiring officers is the complete change in their leisure-time schedule, the fear of which often results in settlement near armed service bases which continue to extend membership in the clubs.[22]

Whether work groups insist on couple socializing or not, they can be a source of companionship for the middle-class couple. Although Dubin found that job relations of blue-collar workers are superficial, there is a strong indication from several studies that friendships at work are likely to be carried home, at least among the non-manual employees.[23] Babchuk indicates that couple-companionate associates are most often brought into the unit by the husband and that his work is a significant source.[24] The housewives often mention this form of contact.

The 571 Chicago women, whose answers to the "social role of housewife" interview form the basis of this report, were asked several questions relating to the general area of couple and individual companionate relations, and the "interaction patterns"

21. Nancy Shae, *The Army Wife*, New York: Harper & Brothers, revised edition, 1941.

22. E. Percil Stanford, "Anticipation of Retirement by Military Personnel," Ph.D. Dissertation, Iowa State University, 1968.

23. Robert Dubin, "Industrial Workers' World: A Study of the Central Life Interests of Industrial Workers," *Social Problems*, 3 (1956), 131–42.

24. Babchuk and Bates, "Primary Relations of Middle-Class Couples: A Study of Male Dominance."

interviews pinpoint the times of such contacts. Minimal information as to the source of couple friendships was tapped through the question: "Where did you originally meet each of the five couples whom you see most often?" and "Where do they live now?" About half-way through the study, a related question began troubling us. We really did not know if the women consider these couples with whom they interact most often as their best friends. Finally we could not resist adding the following questions to the last batch of interviews: "Are they (the five couples you see most often) your best friends?" and "If not, who is?" [25] Additional information about friendships was obtained from all respondents by asking them to contrast their conceptions of women's roles with those of neighbors, friends, and parents.

In all, 1429 couples are listed separately by the 571 respondents, for an average of 2.50 couples in companionate relations with each one (see Table 23). The averages are not distributed evenly in the samples, with younger wives specifying 2.82 couples, while working woman fifty years of age or over list only 1.43. Even the suburbanites vary in the ease with which they can list five separate friends, some pointing out that their "crowd" consists of many more, others listing simply a vague source. Few admit a complete absence of couple friends, although interviewers were often suspicious of the answers, especially in cases in which other statements make no reference to such socializing and the whole life style goes contrary to such husband-wife companionate contact.

Chicago area couples draw their symmetrical leisure-time associates from a variety of sources.[26] The most frequently mentioned contact which is then built into companionate relations is

25. Only 93 interviews of those pulled from the collection obtained with urban housewives and working women contain this question. None of the suburbanites had been given these questions.

26. Answers to the couple interaction questions are analyzed by the source of the contact, as listed by the respondent. Most women did not list five separate couples, even when prodded, and the importance of the originator's identity had not been realized at the beginning of the study, so insufficient probing resulted. A vague answer such as "at work," without specification of which couple was so met, is counted as a single source. However, if a woman distinctly lists several couples met through the same contact point, each reference is included separately in the tabulations. This means, of course, that a single respondent can contribute as many as five references to the same source. Generally, however, the sources are mixed.

Table 23: Percentage distributions of couples seen most often, by source of contact, age, residence, and working status.

	Suburban Housewives				Urban Housewives					Urban Working Women					Total
Source	20	30	40	Total	20	30	40	50	Total	20	30	40	50	Total	
Childhood	36	25	13	27	39	17	20	15	23	43	21	27	23	31	26
Work	14	21	20	19	13	24	8	12	12	26	11	27	30	26	17
Neighbors	21	26	26	24	24	19	39	41	34	10	32	16	28	18	27
Relatives	11	7	5	8	5	5	6	4	5	12	11	9	8	10	7
Voluntary association	4	7	18	7	4	17	18	24	16	3	16	10	10	8	10
Other	15	14	18	15	13	19	10	4	10	6	11	10	2	7	12
Number of couples	245	411	84	740	127	42	160	165	494	69	19	67	40	195	1,429
Number of respondents	87	158	34	279	45	17	66	64	192	27	9	36	28	100	571
Average per respondent	2.82	2.60	2.47	2.67	2.82	2.47	2.42	2.58	2.57	2.56	2.11	1.86	1.43	1.95	2.50

with neighbors, the second with childhood friends, and the third through work roles. The 26 per cent of such associates brought in from childhood and the 27 per cent met through the neighborhood indicate the importance of physical proximity for close friendship.[27] Such relations take time and repeated contact to mature. The only groups to have a high proportion of couple friendships drawn from roles away from the home are working women, wives of professionals, and families with a relatively high income and educational achievement. They are able to maintain contact over distance, and they do not allow the inconvenience to deter them from seeing people they enjoy most. They often use centrally located events as gathering places for couples scattered throughout the city or suburbs.[28]

Although childhood friendships contribute heavily to couple-companionate relations, their proportion varies considerably by the age of the respondents in all three categories. Urban working women are the most apt to list childhood associates, and older workers continue such contacts even more than older housewives, although the percentage drops to just over half of that of youngest workers (43 per cent down to 23 per cent). Families who move to the suburbs are unable to maintain contact with childhood friends, their contribution to the total pool dropping from 36 per cent for those forty years of age or over. Even urban housewives, who also usually move around during their married lives, lose touch with childhood friends as the years go by.

Work roles provide only 17 per cent of the friendships of couples, with urban working women having the highest proportion at all ages except, for some unknown reason, during their thirties. There is no visible pattern to the use of work contacts to draw couple-companionate associates.

Although suburbanites interact with neighbors more often than urbanites do, it is the urban housewives who claim the greatest proportion of their couple friends as current or past neighbors.

27. Every textbook on the family points to numerous studies of residential propinquity of husbands and wives prior to marriage. See, for example, Robert F. Winch, *The Modern Family,* Boston: Holt, Rinehart and Winston, revised edition, 1963.

28. This pattern is reminiscent of the professional families studied by Bott in *Family and Social Network.*

This source provides 34 per cent of their associates, compared with 24 per cent for suburbanites and only 18 per cent for working women. The low use of neighbors as friends by workers is partly explained by their shortage of free time at home and partly by the availability of other sources. The high reference to neighbors by urban housewives, combined with other facts about them, leads to a suspicion that many do not socialize often as couples, but will not admit it. Another segment of this highly heterogeneous population lives in areas of institutionalized non-interaction and draws from the whole city for friends. Suburbanites often clearly distinguish couple-companionate friendships from the informal neighboring or infrequent event socializing with people living nearby.

The contribution made by relatives to couple socializing is so low (7 per cent) as to dramatically point up the significance of this aspect of social change in urbanizing centers. In spite of the help and contact provided by the modified extended family, American urban dwellers do not see their relatives in friendship leisure-time activity. In fact, the proportion of relatives with whom recreational time is spent decreases with age from the high of 12 per cent among young working women for all three populations. That is, as women move away from their families, their relatives are replaced by other couples for leisure-time socializing. Most respondents who list a kin connection as one of their couple-companionate associates refer to their own or their husband's siblings and their spouses. They then explain that these people are "Part of the crowd" or that "We also see a lot of my sister and her husband." The implication behind the last statement is that the sibling is not knit into the other leisure-time group. Some respondents see only siblings, but most list them simply as one of the couples seen most often. The infrequency with which relatives are mentioned as couple-companionate friends is unexpected in view of actual contacts mentioned in other sections of the interviews and the results of other research.[29] Thus, although kin are seen, they are not considered friends. One reason may be that "family" get-togethers develop a different

29. Eugene Litwak, "Extended Kin Relations in an Industrial Democratic Society," in Ethel Shanas and Gordon F. Streib, *Social Structure and the Family: Generational Relations*, Englewood Cliffs, N.J.: Prentice-Hall, 290–323.

form of interaction than typical of non-kin peer groups. It may also be true that the two roles, friend and relative, acquire such diverse rights, duties, and sentiments in middle-class and upper-class America that the conversion of one into the other is impossible. Finally, the fact that relatives are always more closely tied to one partner of a marriage than to the other may prevent symmetrical friendships from developing. The whole history of the relation, based on highly affective bonds, makes the in-law always somewhat of an outsider, and feelings of loyalty and trust may enter the picture. Finally, the factor of status de-crystallization of extended families through uneven upward mobility may decrease the availability of relatives as couple-companionate friends. Each couple may feel more comfortable building its circle of close companions out of people with a similar life style and interests rather than trying to find common activities with differently living siblings. Interaction with relatives who no longer share the same style of life then becomes limited to separate occasions.

The youngest of the respondents in any of the three populations are the least likely to list voluntary associations as a source of couple-companionate friends. The proportion of associates obtained from this source rises among suburban housewives from 4 per cent, when the wives are in their twenties, to 7 per cent for those in their thirties, and 18 per cent for older women. Urban housewives in their fifties have an interesting combination of the most frequent sources: neighbors (41 per cent) and those met in voluntary associations (24 per cent). The groups which they mention are likely to be church affiliates. Other analyses of the data indicate that Negro working women list more associational connections as sources of couple friends than their white counterparts. White working women in their fifties are not apt to mention voluntary associations; so the high total for that age group comes from the black respondents.

The "other" sources which were listed include homes of mutual friends, leisure activities such as trips, children, and more idiosyncratic contacts. Such varied sources are twice as frequent among suburban couples as among urbanites with a working wife (15 per cent to 7 per cent). Among urban housewives the proportion of "other" contacted friends decreases with age after a high in the thirties.

All in all, the sources of couple-companionate friendships tend to follow distinct patterns in the life cycles of each of the three populations. Suburban housewives start with predominantly childhood friends (36 per cent), although neighbors already contribute 20 per cent of couples. Other sources account for between 11 per cent and 14 per cent, except voluntary association contacts, which are negligible. As the women age, childhood friends decrease in proportion, neighboring and husband work-connected roles increasing their frequency. The total average of friends decreases in proportion, neighboring and husband work-connected roles increasing their frequency.

Urban housewives also start with childhood friends converted into couple companions, but with each decade this source and the total number of couples diminishes. The average increases in the fifties, consisting mostly of neighbors and co-members of voluntary associations, such as churches. There is a tendency to decrease the number of friends with increasing age, since new roles are not likely to be added and old ones are less able to provide replacements for those with whom contact is no longer easy or pleasurable.

Working women interact with fewer couples than the housewives do, even in early years of marriage. Their average drops considerably with age, more so than the averages of the other two groups. Couple socializing by young employed respondents is predominantly with childhood friends, the proportion of 43 per cent being met only by the neighbor concentration of older urban housewives. Work roles are second in importance to working women, and neighbors increase as childhood friends decrease their contribution to the total. Of course, many young working women later become suburban or urban housewives, while many of the older working women are returnees, making contact with new people as they and others change jobs.

Contributions of Husband and Wife to Couple-Companionate Relations

One of the subjects of interest to sociologists has been the relative contributions of the husband and of the wife to the pool of their couple-companionate friends.[30] The detailed tables show-

30. See Babchuk, "Primary Friends and Kin: A Study of the Associations of Middle-Class Couples," and Blood and Wolfe, *Husbands and Wives*.

ing which spouse provided the initial contact with marital units later converted to friends show some interesting population contrasts (see Tables 24, 25, 26).

Only half of the couples the respondents see most often who had been known to one of the marriage partners in childhood are designated by the line of original contact. Of course, some women were brought up in the same neighborhoods as their husbands, attended the same schools, or participated in a common courtship interaction group, so that the friendship lines overlap. However, when the specified lines are examined, an interesting pattern emerges which may throw light on the general source. The most likely to be specified as the originator of childhood contact for the couple is the wife. Two factors may account for this alleged asymmetrical contribution of childhood friends to couple-companionate relations. One is the possibility that the wife actually tends to keep more contact with her former girl-friends than her husband with his buddies, especially since our society places more of the burden of relation-maintenance upon a woman. She also has more time than the husband, if she is not working. Thus, the young wife may keep in touch with friends and convert them into couple companions more often than her husband does. This thesis is corroborated by the fact that working women list more couples as their husband's childhood friends than the housewives do. They are busy and involved in other roles from which friends can be drawn, so their effort to maintain their own past relations and to convert them into couple associates may be less intensive than the housewives' is. They may also be more willing to accept their spouse's former friends. However, the fact of selective perception and memory cannot be ignored. It is very possible that the respondent tends to generalize her husband's contributions to their set of companions as "childhood friends" with no indication of the originator of the contacts and without specifying her own lines. Part of this generalizing tendency may be due to the fact that she is the maintainer of the relation, so that she gradually transposes it in her mind to "our friends" met in childhood. Her own friends prior to marriage she remembers distinctly. She may specify as "husband's childhood friends" only those with whom the line of contact is still directly between the husband and that couple, rather than going through her. Whatever the reason, a woman tends either to generalize the source of couple-companionate associates as originally met in the childhood of either marital partner or to credit herself with contributing more people met in their youth than in her husband's. Suburban housewives generalize thus more often than urbanites.

A similar pattern develops when we analyze work roles as sources of couple-companionate relations, specifying the line of contact as husband's, wife's or "generalized." Employment provides 17 per cent of the 1429 couples seen most frequently by the 571 respondents. Working women obviously have two current sources, and they are the more likely to refer to friends met originally at work than the housewives are. Almost all of the housewives worked before the birth of their children, but such contact is hard to maintain over the years, as evidenced by the fact that only 38 per cent of suburbanite couples' work-met friends and 30 per cent of urbanites' were brought in by the wife, compared with 70 per cent of the working women's.

In view of the time gap between work and current life on the part of suburban housewives, the number of couple associates met originally on the job is very surprising; their percentage contribution seems to be increasing with their age. It is, of course, possible that the young suburbanite with small children and a new home is so involved in the mother and housewife roles as not to have time to keep up with past co-workers who live in other places or continue working. She may then be willing to accept people brought into the unit by the working husband. Later she may seek out past co-workers as the demands on her at home decrease. However, it is likely that the same generalizing memory pattern is operating here as in assignment of childhood friends. There are several indications of this. In the first place, only sixty-six work-met couples have a specific designation as originated by her, out of a total of 140 obtained from this source. Secondly, the number for women in their forties and over who have work-met friends is so small that only four women in that category are claiming to maintain contact with friends originally met years ago in a job situation. The generalized sources, we can hypothesize, are more likely to be the husbands', because the working women have very few such loosely designated lines. Most of them know very well whose job is bringing friends into their companionate socializing. Even urban housewives who

Table 24: Percentage distributions of wife and husband connection to frequently seen couples through childhood, and the numbers of couples obtained from this source, by age, residence, and working status.

	Percentages and Numbers of Couples Listed as Met in Childhood															
	Suburban Housewives				Urban Housewives					Urban Working Women						
Originator*	20	30	40	Total	20	30	40	50	Total	20	30	40	50	Total	Total
Wife	62	64	80	64	62	80	75	72	70	58	67	57	100	62	66
Husband	38	36	20	36	38	20	25	18	30	42	33	43	0	38	34
Total	100	100	100	100	100	100	100	100	100	100	100	100	100	100	100
Number of couples	37	53	5	95	39	5	24	17	86	26	3	14	5	48	228
Number of respondents	87	158	34	279	45	17	66	64	192	27	9	36	28	100	571
Total childhood, with and without originator	87	103	11	201	50	7	32	24	113	30	4	18	9	61	375
Average per respondent	1.0	.65	.32	.72	1.11	.41	.48	.38	.58	1.11	.44	.50	.32	.61	.69

* The first four sets of figures refer only to childhood-met couples listed specifically as having been connected with the husband or the wife. The bottom line lists the total number of couples connected with childhood, regardless of originator.

Table 25: Percentage distributions of wife and husband connections to frequently seen couples through work, and the numbers of couples obtained from this source, by age, residence, and working status.

	Percentages and Numbers of Couples Listed as Met at Work														
	Suburban Housewives				Urban Housewives					Urban Working Women					Total
Originator*	20	30	40	Total	20	30	40	50	Total	20	30	40	50	Total	
Wife	21	44	50	38	33	25	36	27	30	64	50	73	80	70	44
Husband	79	56	50	62	67	75	63	73	70	36	50	27	20	30	56
Total	100	100	100	100	100	100	100	100	100	100	100	100	100	100	100
Number of couples	19	33	8	66	12	8	11	15	46	16	2	15	10	43	155
Number of respondents	87	158	34	279	45	17	66	64	192	27	9	36	28	100	571
Total of work references with and without originator	35	88	17	140	17	10	13	20	60	18	2	18	12	50	250
Average per respondent	.40	.55	.50	.50	.39	.59	.20	.31	.31	.67	.22	.50	.43	.50	.44

* The first four sets of figures refer only to work-met couples listed specifically as having been connected with the husband or the wife. The bottom line lists the total number of couples connected through work, regardless of originator.

Table 26: The number of couples brought into companionate relations by the husband and by the wife, by age, residence, and working status.

	Age, Residence, and working status														
Source of Contact	Suburban Housewives				Urban Housewives					Working Women					Total
	20	30	40	Total	20	30	40	50	Total	20	30	40	50	Total	
She	33	60	10	103	32	6	27	21	86	30	4	22	15	71	260
He	35	56	10	101	26	13	20	22	81	20	4	17	4	45	227
Number of respondents	87	158	34	279	45	17	66	64	192	27	9	36	28	100	571

Table 27: The number of couples seen most often who were brought in through neighborhood contact and the average per respondent, by age, residence, and working status.

	Number of Couples and Respondents' Age														
Neighbor	Suburban Housewives				Urban Housewives					Working Women					Total
	20	30	40	Total	20	30	40	50+	Total	20	30	40	50+	Total	
Number of couples	52	107	22	181	31	8	62	67	168	7	6	11	11	35	384
Number of respondents	87	158	34	279	45	17	66	64	192	27	9	36	28	100	571
Average per respondent	.60	.68	.65	.69	.69	.47	.94	1.05	.88	.26	.67	.30	.39	.35	.67

interact with people met in work situations are very specific about whose job provided the contact. It is the suburban housewife, who has a tendency not to name the originator, whose figures are misleading. Her percentage would go down considerably if we added the "generalized" couples to her husband's score.

The process by which a woman ends up answering "at work," without specifying whose work it is, involves identification of her husband's job as the only one for the whole family. She often feels that she contributes to the friendship, if she is the person who sets up the dates for the socializing. Also, if the man works in a large organization, she may identify work friends in general terms because of her part in the selection of a limited number of friends out of many co-workers. Either attitude indicates an involvement in the spouse's work relations to a higher degree than is true of women who designate the source of friends as definitely the man's. The combination supports the Babchuk and Bates conclusion that men contribute heavily to the couple's friends, but the Chicago area wives are much more likely to be the originators of contact than the women in their sample were.[31] The difference among the urbanites who work and who do not work is strong. While the young (less than thirty years of age) urban housewives are willing to credit their husband's job as the source of couple friends (67 per cent) rather than their own (33 per cent), the working women of that age claim 64 per cent of the work-met friends as their own and only 36 per cent as the man's. The same distribution difference exists for the women forty years of age and older. However, the tightness of the fit in the latter years of life is somewhat thrown off by the fact that the women are more apt to be widows.

In summary, if both the husband and the wife are working, her employment role will feed more couple companions into their relation than his will. If the wife is no longer working, her past contacts are not strong enough to offset his current connections. If she is a suburbanite, the respondent is more likely to generalize the work source than to credit either herself or her husband with it.

31. The middle-class Chicago housewives, in fact, report much more influence in bringing couple-companionate friends to the unit than found by those sociologists.

The housewife lists her husband about as often as she lists herself as the originator of contact with couple-companionate friends, whatever the source originally was (see Table 26). The working woman, on the other hand, feels strongly that she has brought more friends into the circle than her husband has (71 couples on her side, compared to 45 couples on his). The figures probably reflect the complexity of social life space. The more complex it is, the greater the pool from which friends can be drawn, and few women limit themselves to only one source. Additional insight concerning couple-companionate interaction comes from comparison of Table 26, listing the originator of all contact as the wife or the husband, and Table 23, containing the sources of these contacts and the average number of listed couples. The working woman, as mentioned before, has the lowest number of couples given as frequent interactors. At the same time, she is the most likely to give herself as the initial contact point. This combination indicates some hypotheses worth testing in the future. It is possible that couple-companionate interaction is dependent upon what we have called "event socializing" so heavily that only people in constant contact and with freedom of time, or those socialized to plan ahead, are able to have an active "social calendar." In fact, there might be two distinct patterns, as with neighboring. The more educated and higher positioned women see friends from a variety of contact situations, through arranged exchanges of dates. Lower-class women are more dependent on constant contact which may evolve into couple interaction. Suburbanites in our sample tend to be more highly socialized to event relations and to draw from many sources. Urban housewives are more heterogeneous, with one segment depending on their husband's contact, while the other segment has a complex social life space. Urban working women do not have the time to keep up with their husband's friends and have easily available relations at work which can be converted to couple associates. If young, they can also convert childhood friendships. However, either their needs or their facilities must be lower than those of suburban housewives, since they do not see as many friends with great frequency as the latter. However, the term, "working women" camouflages differences between the blue-collar women and those skilled in white-collar socializing.

One source of the friends which are not identified as "his" or "hers" is the neighbors (see Table 27). The dependence of urban housewives on neighbors is much greater than that of working women, as mentioned before. In fact, the former average .88 couple friends met as neighbors to a low of .35 for the employed women. Older urbanites are particularly prone to list neighbors. They give 2.58 friends on the average, 1.05 of these as neighbors. By contrast, the older working women list 1.95 friends as an average, and 1.35 of these are neighbors. Even suburbanites forty years of age or over list only .69 as the number of friends who are or were neighbors, out of a total of 2.67 couple associates.

The conclusion that a higher proportion of suburbanites see more couples, obtained from a greater variety of sources, than urban housewives or urban working women do is supported by all the tables in this chapter, in spite of the socio-economic divergence of the suburbs studied. An excellent example of the varied sources from which suburbanites draw their friends is contained in the answer of a twenty-three-year-old respondent: "(1) A buddy from the army Rich [her husband] was stationed with; (2) In school—I knew the husband; (3) Rich met him [the husband] at work; (4) Where we used to live; (5) Rich knew him from the neighborhood, as boys." This example demonstrates the purposeful selection of a few couples from a pool of available contacts within past and current life. It is unusually high in the credit given the husband as the main source of connection. It is typical of the lines drawn by the younger people, who are more likely than their elders to have several distinctly specialized friends and to engage in frequent couple socializing. Except for the socio-economically higher husband and wife teams, such socializing decreases in frequency and formality as age increases. Interaction with other couples decreases, if it is not highly institutionalized in activities and in substitution of new companions to offset those who drop away; or if it is not carried on by persons trained to create new patterns. Such training is available in groups demanding high mobility of its members, such as the armed services or large organizations with many branches. It is also part of the upper-class educational system, which ensures that all stages of increased contact can be built up to couple-companionate relations.

Four sets of factors thus contribute to a couple's symmetrical companionate relations: (1) the presence of social contacts of the husband, the wife, or the unit, prior or during marriage, which can be converted into such relations; (2) the means institutionalized in the culture for the conversion of asymmetrical or casual interaction into such relations; (3) the ability and willingness of the husband or the wife, operating independently or as a unit, to use the established, or create new, means for developing such relations; and, (4) the availability of all these patterns to an extent sufficient to replace former companions with new ones as mobility or other circumstances shift the foundation. The data in the various tables indicate that the social roles which are entered into by the women individually and those which they feel their husbands enter without their participation are likely to be identified by direct line to the contact source Those respondents who feel couple involvement in each other's roles, past or present, are more likely to generalize the source of contact of the five couples they see most often. This is particularly true if they feel that they have had an active part in selecting friends from the total of their husband's work companions or if they feel close to his role. These conclusions imply that a specific identification of the source of couple-companionate relations may be due to original strain in the conversion of asymmetrical interaction into symmetrical relations. Some respondents still continue asymmetrical relations, even within couple interaction. They never develop a common "crowd"; some friends remain "his," others "hers," and socializing is alternated rather than shared.

RESIDENTIAL SCATTER OF COUPLE-COMPANIONATE FRIENDS

When asked for the present residence of couples with whom they interact most often, the women name the same neighborhood or suburb more often as their age increases, regardless of location or working status. However, interesting patterns emerge in the life cycle. The fewest friends living in the same community are listed by the youngest suburbanites. Only 10 per cent of all the couples with whom companionate relations are maintained live in the same suburb. Twenty-six per cent of the interviewees in their twenties report all but one of their five couples completely scattered, and another 29 per cent report no friend in the same town. New home-owners have usually moved away from childhood and work friends and have not developed couple-companionate relations with neighbors to substitute for them. Those friends who are located in the same town may be the people whose movement into it spurred their own search for a home in that community.

During the early thirties the friends of both suburban and urban housewives are likely to be located in the same area or nearby. This can be due either to the movement of prior friends closer to each other as the years go by or to substitution of distant companions by new ones who are more conveniently located. This tendency is reversed among the suburbanites in their late thirties and forties, indicating a second wave of mobility or expansion of contact horizons, but it never reaches the early low. Children are older and couples more mobile. Twenty-six per cent of those in their forties report only one couple friendship in town and an additional one-third list all companions in different locations. This is the same distribution as for all housewives in their twenties.

The urban working women under fifty are not likely to live near the people they see most often as couples. They resemble the professional families studied by Bott in London, but the pattern is a consequence of the wife's, not of the husband's occupational contacts.[32] The oldest workers narrow friendships to geographical convenience, and they resemble the more area-limited urban housewives. Few urban working women and not many urban housewives frequently see couples living in the suburbs. Suburbanites may have friends scattered among different towns, but they too tend not to cross the city-suburb line. Urban housewives restrict their contacts to a smaller variety of neighborhoods than any other group. The upper-class urbanites report a higher geographical scatter than their lower-class counterparts. It must be remembered that almost half of the working women and one-fourth of the urban housewives are Negroes for whom residential scatter of companions is limited by discriminatory practices. Most of the Negro couple friends are located in a restricted number of neighborhoods.

Only 22 of the 93 urbanites whose interviews included the

32. Bott, *Family and Social Network.*

question "Are they (the five couples you see most often) your best friends?" answered "No." Other facts support the thesis that couple-companionate interaction often involves women who consider each other to be friends. Seventy-six per cent of the wives have been able to convert former friends or acquaintances into couple relations or to build the intimacy of interaction with couples sufficiently to meet self-defined needs. This does not mean that the level of the relation is the same in each case. Some American women do not expect sex-segregated friendships because they consider the spouse a friend or because they do not accept non-kin friendships and so are satisfied with casual couple interaction.[33] Only one-fourth of the Chicago area housewives feel that couples seen most often are not closest friends. However, they do not necessarily fall into the sex-segregated clique pattern of the more stable New Haven respondents studied by Nelson. The major reason for their answer of "No" is that the couples considered best friends have moved away and are no longer available for contact as they had been in the past.

Very few women explain that the couples they see most often do not include their best friends because these have not been converted into such companionate relations. Only three women state flatly that they have no best friend. Half of the remaining nineteen are in their thirties, with urban housewives contributing a disproportionate number. Younger women seem more able to transfer prior relations into couple socializing. Three women in their twenties explain that their best friends are girls who are not part of the group, and three that their closest companions have moved away. Three women in their thirties specify that their sisters are the closest and that they do not see them as couples; three more have sex-segregated friends. Those in their later thirties are the most likely to mention inability to keep in contact with best friends; this may be due to recency of moving. Older women seem more able to fuse "best friend" and "couples we see most often" into the same package, either through actual conversion or through memory warping. It is possible that married women try not to develop friends whom they feel their husbands would reject in couple-companionate relations.

33. This is what Blood and Wolfe found to be the attitude of the Detroit couples. *Husbands and Wives*, Chapter 6.

SOCIALIZING WITH FRIENDS

All societies have institutionalized several events during which relatives, friends, and sometimes acquaintances are seen for companionship interaction. For example, in the cities of Poland Christmas Eve is reserved for the immediate family, Christmas Day for kinship visiting, and the day immediately following, which is also a holiday, for exchanges with friends. Holidays, connected with religiously significant events or with dates meaningful to national culture societies,[34] during which work ceases as much as possible without the necessities of life coming to a complete standstill, are the usual times for companionship interaction. Climate and national custom influence the ways in which leisure occasions are spent, sharing a meal being probably the most universal activity. Holiday companionate ceremonials have the important function of re-establishing the group identity and of pleasurable sentimental involvement in it.[35] The specifically puritanical and generally Protestant ethic of "work is virtue" condoned non-work play as a means of preparing people to go back to their labor, "re-creating" their energy for it.[36] Even modern-day American men justify weekend play as psychologically or physically necessary in order to enable continued efficiency at work.

The American weekend, usually including the hours from 5:00 P.M. on Friday to 9:00 A.M. on Monday for both blue- and white-collar workers, is a time for relaxation and companionate

34. The concept was developed by Florian Znaniecki in *Modern Nationalities* and refers to a society "which has a common and distinct secular, literary culture and an independent organization functioning for the preservation, growth and expansion of this culture" (Urbana: University of Illinois Press, 1952, p. 21).

35. According to Emile Durkheim in *The Elementary Forms of Religious Life,* religious ceremonials which bring a community together perform this function of revitalizing beliefs and identities (translated by Joseph W. Swain, New York: The Free Press).

36. The definition is found in Max Kaplan's *Leisure in America,* New York: John Wiley, 1960, pp. 19–20. See also Foster Rhea Dulles, *A History of Recreation,* New York: Appleton-Century-Crofts, 1965, and Sebastian de Grazia, *Of Work Time and Leisure,* New York: Twentieth Century Fund, 1962.

socializing. Even professions such as medicine or dentistry, and occupations requiring continuous activity or the giving of service to the weekending segment of the population, regard at least Saturday night as a time for doing "fun" things. Thus, both holidays and weekends have become times for socializing activity, while non-working hours during the week are properly devoted to rest or to events having more than leisure as their function. Organized play held during the week is often justified by some altruistic goal.

The expansion of companionate relations which are not family or kin-connected has resulted in specialization of times devoted to the two mutually exclusive groups: friends and relatives. Seventy-four per cent of the "interaction patterns" interviewees, all of whom are urbanites, see relatives on holidays, and only 26 per cent see friends at such occasions. Forty-six per cent visit relatives on vacations and only 10 per cent spend them with friends. Sunday is also more likely to be a day for regular contact with kin than for being with unrelated people (42 per cent to 17 per cent). On the other hand, friends are given as sporadic weekend contacts more often than relatives (56 per cent to 42 per cent). Saturday night is more likely to be spent with friends than kin members, 33 per cent of the respondents specifying this type of contact. Several others list activities which are often carried on with people outside of the immediate family, such as going to the movies or "going out" without specifying with whom they do this. Seven per cent of the urbanites play games requiring more than two adults. Twenty-three per cent go "visiting," without indicating their relation to the hosts.

Friday night is less of a companionate socializing time, although 16 per cent of the respondents list visiting; 4 per cent go to club meetings, 6 per cent "go out," 4 per cent go to parties, and 6 per cent go to the movies. Some respondents list more than one activity. In all, 176 separate activities are specified by the 205 respondents for Saturday night, and only 100 for Friday night. Twenty-seven per cent state that they watch TV on Saturday night, and 44 per cent that they stay home on Friday night, 2 per cent specifying that they watch TV. Thus, only 37 per cent of the activities listed for Friday night are likely to involve other people in socializing, while 64 per cent of the activities referred to for Saturday night can easily involve companionate contacts.

In addition, women see or talk to their female friends often during the week. Sixteen per cent list a friend coming over to their homes at some time during a "typical day," or their own venture into the homes of others; 17 per cent see their friends in public places or on property owned by others; and 44 per cent talk daily on the phone. In fact, the schedule of social activities of some respondents sounds so full as to allow little time for work or any other tasks. The greatest frequency of contact with people other than friends is with the mother and mother-in-law (36 per cent and 37 per cent, respectively). Most of these are telephone communications. Direct contact is most frequent with neighbors, 30 per cent of the metropolitan-area women specifying that they go to the home of or are visited by people living nearby almost daily.

AGREEMENT WITH FRIENDS OVER CONCEPTION OF WOMEN'S ROLES

One other question contained in the "social role of housewife" interview relates to the subject of friendship. All of the respondents were asked: "In what ways does your conception of the woman's role vary from the ideas on this subject of your neighbors, your friends, your parents?" Space was left for answers to each of the three categories of relations. The distribution of agreement and areas of disagreement with neighbors were discussed in Chapter Five. The following, very abbreviated summary will indicate the different degrees to which the respondents feel they have developed consensus with these three groups of significant others (see Table 28).

As one interviewee explains, "Your friends are those with whom you agree." This statement seems to be representative at least of the suburban women. Eighty-two per cent of them feel that their ideas on the role of women are similar to, or the same as, those of their friends. Only 16 per cent feel a strong disagreement, while 82 per cent state agreement. By contrast,

20 per cent of the urban housewives and 20 per cent of the workers differ from their friends in opinions about women's roles, only 64 per cent of the former and 55 per cent of the latter finding similarities. This is a significant contrast between suburban housewives and urban working women. It is possible that the latter have friends who do not work, so that their views may really vary. The second possibility is that working women are more conscious of role strains and spend more time discussing attitudes. The third possibility is that they may be more independent and more vocal in expressing divergent opinions.

Another significant difference in the responses of women in the different residential areas and working statuses is in the "don't know" category. Suburbanites seem to be very aware of what their friends think, only 1 per cent of them claiming that they do not know their friends' ideas on the woman's role, compared to 14 per cent for the urban housewives and a high 25 per cent for working women. Thus, working women are more prone than the other two groups are to feel their ideas differ from their friends' opinions. It is possible that they avoid related subjects or that they have no interest in them, but the answers imply a rather strong rejection of discussion in this area. It is hard to imagine how people can be friends and never broach topics of such current interest.

Details of the answers indicate that the most frequent area of disagreement among friends is the same as among neighbors: children and child-bearing. Eleven per cent of all respondents state this to be the subject on which they do not agree, a relatively large proportion, considering how many state they agree or find no differences of opinion. Some explain the contrasts with a great flourish. Those who are most likely to list this area of disagreement are urban housewives (15 per cent), while working women who have older children make relatively little mention of the mother role. In spite of the scarcity of disagreement on the part of suburbanites, an aggregate of ten women living in Park Ridge produced so many typical statements as to be worth quoting. The same ten respondents were quoted at the end of Chapter Five, in explanation of areas of disagreement with neighbors. These are relatively highly educated women with above-median incomes, living in new homes within a rapidly expanding and quite middle-class community.

Table 28: Percentage summaries of answers to "In what ways does your conception of the woman's role vary from the ideas on this subject of your neighbors, your friends, and your parents?" by residence and working status.

	Category of Significant Other, Residence and Working Status								
	Neighbors			Friends			Parents		
Agreement or Disagreement	Suburban	Urban	Working	Suburban	Urban	Working	Suburban	Urban	Working
Differ	30	31	29	16	22	20	49	38	29
Agree, similar	60	37	19	82	64	55	46	46	41
No answer, don't know	10	32	52	1	14	25	4	15	31

Table 29: Percentages of suburban housewives who belong to voluntary associations, by the last year of completed schooling.

Years of Schooling	Number of Voluntary Associations					Total Who Belong	None	Number of Respondents
	1	2	3	4	5			
8 grades, or less							100	4
9-11 grades	6	11	17	—	—	34	67	18
12, finished high school	25	24	10	9	4	72	29	114
13-15, college	32	14	20	5	9	80	20	65
16, B.A. degree	16	22	9	9	31	87	12	31
Over 16	17	17	—	—	33	67	33	6
Number of respondents	61	46	30	18	22	177(74%)	61(26%)	238(100%)

They try to direct their husbands too much, try to run their lives. I will talk things over with my husband and make suggestions, but I will never tell him what to do.

I'm not a perfect mother. Most are trying to do things like I am —the best they can. The day isn't long enough. We all need more time.

They give too much freedom to their kids. They go constantly. Parents don't know where they are half the time. They give them money or whatever they want. We let our children earn money, just as we have to. We all pitch in and do our share and we have lots of fun together, too.

Some are different from me. Just how, I couldn't say. Maybe I'd be smart not to.

They don't think youngsters should have too many responsibilities. Think school is enough. I don't agree.

I'll tell you frankly. I'm happy to be a woman. They resent being tied down. They resent the physical act of child-rearing, won't nurse their kids, etc. I never was like that.

My husband and I are more or less homebodies. Some of our friends are much more socially inclined than we are. I enjoy being home with my family.

My attitudes are a little different because of my religious values. They seem to seek excitement and glamour. They worry about not being invited out on New Year's Eve. There is too much emphasis on running around. It only makes them more miserable when they have to stay home.

My husband and I are not so dedicated to making money. To us money isn't so all important. We are extremely different in our sense of dedication. Of course, many of our friends are in church work.

I'm happier to be home, and my husband and I are more content to be just ourselves. Sometimes too much so. We are not as socially minded.

These ten interviewees are not representative of the whole sample, because they are very aware of differences in the ideas held by them and by their friends about the role of woman and because they are very articulate in explaining these. It is very probable that a concentrated probing of attitudinal differences, specially in the role of mother (although maybe also in the roles of wife and housewife) would provide more complex answers from other respondents. What this general question brings out is that more women feel they agree with friends than with neighbors or with parents, and that the working urbanite is the least likely of the three populations to claim agreement with her friends on topics related to the woman's role. Answers also offer clues as to the significance of the role of mother, in which anxiety and the desire for competence cause the greatest possibility of conflict with friends and neighbors.

The expressed agreement with ideas of others may be due to selective perception of the relation or to the process of friend formation. It is doubtful that complete agreement actually exists, and this whole area simply needs more study. The question which is raised is significant. It makes a difference whether women feel that they agree with friends as a result of a basic, original, other-directed homogeneity among them; because of a willingness to accept daily and general differences without classifying them as strong disagreements; or because of selective perceptions of the relation.

SUMMARY OF COUPLE-COMPANIONATE RELATIONS

In summary, most of the housewives either interact in couple-companionate relations or feel that such contact is so common that they cannot disclaim it. Some leisure-time comrades have been known from childhood or they are a result of adult residential and work proximity. Continued contacts are attempted even after movement to a new location, but they are gradually replaced by ones that bridge fewer barriers. Couple interactions tend to be with people considered as best friends by the wife and to involve people living nearby or temporarily scattered over the metropolitan area at different times during the life cycle. Women engaged in multiple roles feel that they contribute more than their husbands to the fund of couple-companionate relations; women relatively housebound and isolated from childhood contacts which have not been converted into symmetrical friendships tend to depend more upon their husbands to originate contacts at work. Many housewives, however, feel so identified with the work role of the spouse, or with the process by which such asymmetrical relations were converted into couple-companionate friends, as to generalize the contact without tracing direct lines to the husband. Most respondents feel that friendship involves knowledge of, and agreement over, conceptions of the role of woman. Perceived differences in child-rearing techniques break the uniformity of this pattern among housewives, and a lack of knowledge of what friends think on related subjects decreases feelings of consensus among urban working women.

VOLUNTARY ASSOCIATIONS

Much has been written about the voluntary associations of urban dwellers, and the Chicago area housewives generally reflect the conclusions drawn by others.[37] The main factors contributing to differences in the frequency of memberships among the interviewees are: the education of the respondent, place of residence, working status, and race. The last two factors have been studied less frequently than the first two.

A higher proportion of suburban housewives than of urban housewives or working women belong to at least one voluntary association. A total of 346, or 64 per cent of the 539 respondents whose answers are being analyzed in this section, belong to at least one organization, with suburbanites contributing 77 per cent of their total to this figure, while 63 per cent of the urban housewives and 61 per cent of the workers are members. The contrasts in membership figures among the three samples are not as dramatic as the differences in the populations might suggest.

Two tendencies are visible among the suburban housewives when their membership is cross-tabulated by education (see Table 29). In the first place, there is a clear rise in the percentages of women who belong to at least one such group as the level of education increases, until the post-B.A. level, when there is a

37. Mirra Komarovsky, "The Voluntary Associations of Urban Dwellers," *American Sociological Review* (1946), 686–98, is a classic in this field. See also Wendell Bell, "Social Structure and Participation in Different Types of Formal Associations," *Social Forces*, 34 (May 1956), 345–50; Wendell Bell and Maryanne T. Force, "Urban Neighborhood Types and Participation in Formal Associations," *American Sociological Review*, 21 (February 1956), 25–34; Wayne C. Gordon and Nicholas Babchuk, "A Typology of Voluntary Associations," *American Sociological Review*, 24 (1959), 22–29; Carol Slater, "Class Differences in Definitions of the Role and Membership in Voluntary Associations Among Urban Married Women," *American Journal of Sociology*, 65 (May 1960), 616–19.

drop. Secondly, women with higher educational levels are more likely than the less educated ones to belong to more than one group. Starting with high-school drop-outs, the percentages read: 28, 47, 48, and 71. College graduates are particularly prone to hold multiple memberships in voluntary associations. Post-B.A. housewives are not as active in such groups as those with a slightly lesser achievement, a difference hard to explain through available data. This group has shown unusual tendencies throughout the study.

Urban housewives display different trends in the distribution of their organizational involvement. Although their numbers are small (twelve), the very uneducated urbanites are the most likely to belong to at least one social group. One hundred per cent of the women who never finished grade school are members of associations, 33 per cent of them being involved in more than one organization. It turns out that these women are first-generation European immigrants belonging to ethnic groups or lower-class Negroes belonging to church-affiliated clubs. The proportion drops to 54 per cent for grade-school graduates and then to 42 per cent for high-school drop-outs. The high-school graduate has the second highest frequency of at least single membership (68 per cent), followed by the college graduate (66 per cent). No category reaches the high of the suburbanites who finished high school, had some college, or graduated from it. Thus, the total of 63 per cent for urban housewives having at least one membership is comparatively heavily contributed to by the less educated woman, who offsets the tendency of the more educated urbanite to be a less frequent joiner. Part of the frequency of memberships by the less educated respondents is a direct influence, as mentioned above, of the presence of Negro housewives. Although 50 per cent of that segment of the population do not belong to any group, those who are members are concentrated on the first three rungs of the educational ladder. The fact that fewer Negro than white homemakers belong to some group reinforces the conclusion reached during the discussion of neighboring, that these are the most isolated women in the five populations formed by residence, working status, and race cross-tabulation. (No Negro suburbanites fell into that sample). Factors other than education seem to differentiate the joiners and the non-joiners of that racial housewife aggregate.

Table 30: Percentages of urban housewives who belong to voluntary associations, by the last year of completed schooling.

Years of Schooling	Number of Voluntary Associations					Total Who Belong	None	Number of Respondents
	1	2	3	4	5	Belong		
1-7 grades	67	25	8	—	—	100	—	12
8 grades	18	27	9	—	—	54	46	11
9-11 grades	17	17	—	4	4	42	56	23
12, finished high school	20	20	11	17	—	68	33	55
13-15, college	17	14	19	7	5	62	38	42
16, college graduate	18	18	18	—	12	66	35	17
Over 16	10	20	—	—	30	60	40	10
No answer	—	—	—	—	—	—	100	1
Number of respondents	36	32	19	8	8	108(63%)	63(37%)	171(100%)

Table 31: Percentages of working women who belong to voluntary associations, by the last year of completed schooling.

Years of Schooling	Number of Voluntary Associations					Total Who Belong	None	Number of Respondents
	1	2	3	4	5			
8 grades	33	33	—	—	—	67	33	3
9-11 grades	33	8	—	—	—	41	58	12
12, finished high school	33	30	6	3	3	75	25	33
13-15, college	36	8	8	—	—	52	48	25
16, college graduate	17	—	17	8	17	59	42	12
Over 16	29	7	14	14	—	64	36	15
Number of respondents	31	15	8	4	3	61(61%)	39(39%)	(100%)
Total number	128	93	57	35	33	346	193	539
Total per cent	24	17	11	7	6	65*	36	

*Rounding accounts for the difference between 64 per cent and 65 per cent when computed the two ways.

Working women are less likely than housewives to be members of a voluntary association, but their proportions in the different educational levels are highly different from those of suburbanites. High-school graduates (75 per cent), grade-school graduates (67 per cent), and those with more than a B.A. degree (64 per cent) have a higher than average (for this group) proportion of members in at least one voluntary association. It must be recalled that these urban working women are located more frequently at the higher extreme of educational achievement level than the urban housewives are. Twenty-six per cent of them, compared with 9 per cent of the housewives, finished college or went beyond. The high membership figures for the uneducated women are partly a result of the presence of twenty-eight Negro working women, almost three-fourths of whom belong to at least one organization. The more educated of this social race are active participants. The white working woman is low in such involvement, resembling more the black housewife than any other group; only 52 per cent of them belong to at least one group. The difference between the white and the black workers in terms of organizational participation reflects the contrasts in neighboring patterns and again points to the possibility that working has a different meaning in these two communities. The Negro female employee may obtain sufficient prestige and self-confidence from that role to become a community leader. It is equally probable that both work and participation in other groups may be undertaken by the Negro women who are the most skilled in interpersonal relations, so that both attract the elite of the community. The white woman, on the other hand, may be working against, or at least without, community approval. A third possibility is that the black and the white workers feel different levels of obligation to the community in which they are living. The contrast is significant and needs further research.

One other comment is warranted here. Despite the popular image of the woman "joiner," which assumes that involvement in one association inevitably leads to multiple memberships, the respondents most often belong to only one organization. Of the 64 per cent who joined at least one group, 24 per cent limit themselves to a single membership; only 17 per cent listing two, 11 per cent three, 7 per cent four, and 6 per cent five or more.

THE COMMUNITY: PERCEPTIONS AND SENTIMENTS

Definitions of, and feelings about, the community in which women maintain their homes were tapped through a series of questions. Some reference to the results has been made in Chapter Five in relation to neighboring, but additional discussion may round out the picture of metropolitan area women. The respondents are scattered in 58 of the 75 local community areas delineated by the University of Chicago Community Inventory and described periodically since 1938 in the *Local Community Fact Book*.[38] The suburbanites are clustered in 12 of the 147 municipalities containing 2500 or more persons, as of 1960, which lie within the Chicago Standard Metropolitan Statistical Area.[39]

The urban housewives and the working women were asked the following series of questions about the community: "How would you describe life in the city?" "How would you describe life in your neighborhood?" "Why did you choose this neighborhood to rent (or buy)?" "What advantages of the neighborhood have you discovered after moving here?" and "What disadvantages of urban living have you discovered after moving here?" Suburbanites were asked: "How would you characterize suburban living?" "What were the reasons for your move to the suburbs, in order of importance?" "Why did you choose this particular suburb?" "What advantages of suburban living have you discovered after moving here?" and "What disadvantages of suburban living have you discovered after moving here?"

A comparison of the answers to questions listed above and the responses to neighboring queries indicates that women who explain their search for a residence in community-oriented terms are more likely to develop close relations with those living nearby than women who restrict their conscious descriptions of the selection process to the price, physical features, or geographical location of the home. The relational emphasis is more typical of the

38. Evelyn M. Kitagawa and Karl E. Taeuber, eds., *Local Community Fact Book, Chicago Metropolitan Area, 1960,* Chicago: Chicago Community Inventory, University of Chicago, 1963.

39. Northeastern Illinois Metropolitan Area Planning Commission, *Suburban Factbook, 1960,* published in 1966.

better educated women than the latter is. Several questions are raised by this fact: Are women who develop good neighboring relations more likely to retrospectively claim original community interest? Does such a selection process lead to better matching of neighbors to the self in class traits, and those to easier contacts? Or, are both tendencies reflective of greater interest and ability to interact with others? Lower-class women tend to concentrate all their answers on physical features of the home and neighborhood, being impressed by space, cleanliness of air, "healthy environment," etc. The more educated women speak of community atmosphere, composition, and relations. Those experiencing upward social mobility into the various layers of the middle class most frequently state that they originally chose the home for its characteristics, but that they have found the social relations within the community to be an unexpected advantage. They are the most likely not to have been socialized into an expectation of "polite-companionship" relations, acquiring them in adulthood within the middle-class subculture. The more stable women of the latter class, who chose first the community or a limited number of similar towns before trying to locate a home within that area, are the most likely to list physical features of the town as disadvantages not anticipated prior to movement into it.

Definitions of city and suburb are strongly influenced by the style of life the respondent is now leading and by her satisfaction with it. A relatively large proportion of urbanites refer to the city in "pace of life" terms. Those who are very active and pleased with their life speak of this center as "exciting" and full of "things to do." They are more apt to be older working women or young housewives than other segments of the population, 36 per cent of the former and 34 per cent of the latter converging on such a definition. Those who do not like the pace call it "hectic" and "rushed." Twenty-one per cent of the residents so define the city.

Interestingly enough, although many women define the city as hectic or rushed, only 2 per cent so characterize their own neighborhood. In fact, the area of residence is usually described as "slow," "relaxed," or "casual." The city is seen as noisy, but the neighborhood is seven times as likely to be defined as quiet. The city is "exciting," but few use that term to define their local area. The city is perceived as unfriendly by twice as many as feel it to be friendly; one-fourth of the urban respondents mention that their neighborhood is friendly and only 4 per cent that it lacks this quality. Working women are half as likely to define their area as friendly than the housewives are in answer to questions about residence. This tendency reinforces the conclusions reached from the answers to neighboring questions. Few respondents mention that the city has a high density of population, a trait deemed to be one of its three basic characteristics by Louis Wirth.[40] Comments about the heterogeneity of the city usually refer to population shifts. Both white and black respondents become more conscious of differences in residents in contact situations, but evaluations vary. Some among the Negro respondents purposely selected integrated areas for living, while others express a wish for homogeneity. One respondent answered the question "Why did you choose to rent here?" as follows: "Because it was a nice, quiet neighborhood. The neighbors are all Negroes. Being that, it is a homogeneous group; there are no racial tensions here, no name-calling or brick-throwing."

Several women speak of the neighborhood in terms of ethnic composition when explaining the selection process or the advantages of a new location, pointing to the presence of fellow nationals. Many of the lower-class suburbanites explain their movement away from the city as an escape from a race or ethnic group. Middle-class suburban women are not as likely to make such specific comments for two reasons: their culture does not contain open prejudice to the same degree and their previous residence had less chance of bordering on areas of Negro expansions.

Location near family members or old friends is not given as a reason for the selection of a town or neighborhood as frequently as might be expected from reading other segments of the interviews. Many suburbanites and urbanites mention at some point that they knew some people prior to moving into the area, but for some reason this link is not given as a major factor in the selection process. Since no respondent examined each of the 75 metropolitan areas and 249 communities outside Chicago in selecting a new residence, some method of narrowing the range must have been operating. Yet, most respondents are either unaware of the proc-

40. Louis Wirth, "Urbanism as a Way of Life," *American Journal of Sociology*, 44 (July 1938), 1–24.

ess by which large chunks of the Chicago Standard Metropolitan Statistical Area[41] were eliminated from consideration or they are accustomed to compressing their explanations. In either case, the items which are selected for mention, although varied by class, neglect personal influence. The fact that original contact with an area may have occurred when visiting friends is not remembered as part of the decision to try a similar life style.

Whatever the reasons given for the move to the suburbs in general or to a specific community or neighborhood in the city, most respondents list more than one factor. Generally they express satisfaction with the choice, indicating that at least temporarily they are not engaging in the process of redefinition which precedes a decision to move again.[42] Such satisfaction is particularly evident in the suburbanites, but it does not preclude definite statements about the disadvantages of the house, neighborhood, or community. Many suburbs experienced a dramatic increase of population, often accompanied by a shortage of facilities for convenient living. Half of the 147 communities which in 1960 had a population of 2500 or over were relatively new towns: 50 per cent or more of their homes had been added in the preceding decade.[43] Some, like Park Forest or Hoffman Estates, were "farm-field" developments, rising as whole communities in a previously unpopulated location. Some included planned facilities, meeting the needs of new residents better than the towns which had grown like Topsy.

The combination of reasons for the selection of a community, descriptions of it and of the general style of living typical of such an area, and judgments of advantages and disadvantages not anticipated before the move, produce interesting "ideal-typical" profiles of residents. The use of ideal types facilitates the classifi-

41. The U.S. Bureau of the Budget has "delineated 'Standard Metropolitan Statistical Areas' (SMSA's) around each large city. Each SMSA includes at least one city of 50,000 inhabitants or more, the countries in which that city is located, and continuous countries which are essentially metropolitan in character and are socially and economically integrated with the central city." Kitagawa and Taeuber, *Local Community Fact Book, Chicago Metropolitan Area, 1960*, p. xv.

42. Peter Rossi, *Why Families Move*, New York: The Free Press, 1955.

43. *Suburban Factbook, 1960*, Table 3, "Township Population Growth and Density, by Sectors, Suburban Northeastern Illinois."

cation of women into five basic categories of suburban and six categories of urban residents.[44] The types represent varying dimensions of emphasis along three lines: (1) the degree of satisfaction with the community; (2) the source of satisfaction with the community; and (3) the form of identification with the community, ranging from a concern with their own residence only, to interest in the physical traits of the area, to involvement in interpersonal and organizational activity with others inhabiting the town.

A TYPOLOGY OF HOMEMAKERS

The "Ideal-Typical" Suburbanite

THE RELUCTANT SUBURBANITE is not too happy over living in the suburbs. She is rather rare among the home-owning respondents with pre-high school children. Least frequent is sub-type A who complains against suburbia as a general phenomenon; sub-type B, who is unhappy with her particular town, is much more likely to be found.

A. *The reluctant suburbanite in general.* There is only one pure case of the first sub-type of reluctant suburbanite among the 268 full-time housewives who are included in this analysis. This Park Ridge resident answered the series of questions as follows.

Description of suburban living: "Oh, a woman in a station wagon, full of kids on her way to meet the train. There's a lot of chauffeuring to be done. Guess I'm down on suburban life—the prerequisite seems to be knowing how to play bridge and golf. You belong to little "do-well" groups—a lot of gardening. It's not too stimulating because you get so involved in a home and diapers and dandelions."

Why moved to suburbs? "We never considered life in the city, we couldn't take that." (They are both from a small town.)

Why chose particular suburb? "It was convenient for a driving

44. For an explanation of ideal types, which are a sociological tool for the analysis of "historically unique configurations or their individual components by means of genetic concepts," see Max Weber, *Selections from His Work*, edited by S. M. Miller, New York: Thomas Y. Crowell, 1963, pp. 27–31. Extreme cases of phenomena are used to delineate outside limits of continua.

pool to husband's work. I prefer it over Des Plaines, where we were before, because their section was all post-war transient kids, all so temporary feeling. Here there are no taverns, there is more cultural life here. It's wonderful for the kids."

Advantages? "I knew them all, being from a small town."

Disadvantages? "All the above is not the fault of the suburban people only. I guess I'm not prepared for the homemaker life in the suburban community. I need outside outlets. Transportation to the Loop is a problem."

B. *The reluctant resident of a specific suburb.* The second sub-form of the reluctant suburbanite is the person who does not object to this form of life in general, only to the community in which she now finds herself. A Wheaton woman exemplifies attitudes of this type.

Description of suburban living: "Good for children; lots of room to play, nice way of life."

Why moved to suburbs? "Business transfer, bought home in one weekend. My husband has never felt settled in Wheaton, never put down roots here."

Why chose particular suburb? "House and lot. Hope we can take more time and more things into consideration next time we buy."

Advantages? "Very friendly, good school."

Disadvantages? "None. Our house is too small."

How long expect to stay? "We are looking for a larger house now. Have been for several years; I was against starting over, but husband would like to be further out." *Where?* "Glen Ellyn, roots more out there; our church and friends are there; we prefer Glen Ellyn to Wheaton."

THE ENTHUSIASTIC SUBURBANITE is very pleased about living in the suburbs. There are four different types of women who fall into this general category: the mother, the neighbor, the community participant, and the class-conscious resident.

A. *The enthusiastic mother* is happy about suburban living because of what it does for her children and because of the way it assists her in her role of mother. "It's good for the children" is her persistent motto.

Description of suburban living: "Informal living, feeling of relaxing, healthier. Some day we might like to live on a farm. Children are happier. We like to wear shorts and live and cook out, informal."

Why moved to suburbs? "We were looking for a place to live and saw a sign that said, 'Children Welcome.' "

Why chose particular suburb? "What I just said. The type of house we wanted before was too expensive. We didn't want to put everything we had into a house and we didn't want to try to keep up with the Joneses."

Advantages? "There are not too many ways for children to get into trouble. The town is small and you get to know your children's friends. Healthier way of living. Meet different types of people and different races and it is broadening." (Park Forest has some Negro and some Oriental families, but not many.)

Disadvantages? "None for myself, but my husband gets tired of the train ride."

How long expect to stay? "Until the three-and-a-half-year-old gets through high school."

B. *The enthusiastic neighbor* enjoys particularly her relations with neighbors.

Description of suburban living: "It's quieter than the city, cleaner, much happier, friendlier atmosphere. We are close friends with our neighbors, a relationship you can't have in the city."

Why moved to suburbs? "There was a death in my husband's family and my mother-in-law wanted us to move back to Chicago to be closer to her. We decided to buy a home and thought the suburbs were the best place to raise children."

Why chose particular suburb? "It was the first house we found that we could afford and we thought it was a nice suburb."

Advantages? The same as in Answer 1.

Disadvantages? "If I had to do my own grocery shopping I would find it difficult, as the stores are too far away, especially hard when you have children. I was lonely here at first before I met anyone, but I'm not now. The children get more bumps and bruises here than in an apartment because they roam around the neighborhood and you can't watch them all the time."

C. *The enthusiastic community participant* has a broader identity with the town.

Description of suburban living: "There is more community-
mindedness in Park Forest than in Chicago, especially among
women." (She gives examples of a parade and a "Pow Wow"
in which parents participate, costumes are judged, etc.) "The
PTA is much more active in Park Forest."

Why moved to suburbs? "We planned to have a child, wanted
play space and fresh air, resented slum areas of our own childhood."

Why chose particular suburb? "Had friends here, commuting
was good, houses at a reasonable price."

Advantages? "More community-mindedness than I expected. I
have joined the League of Women Voters and am delighted
with it."

Disadvantages? "Commuting time mostly; also wish community
were more heterogeneous; don't want child to grow up with
all one kind of people, but should have broader experience."
(She intends to join the PTA *before* her child enters school.)

D. *The enthusiastic class-conscious resident* is particularly
pleased over the "type" of people her community contains,
although she may be hesitant to admit social-class prejudices.
A LaGrange Park resident was finally helped by the interviewer, who supplied the sentences without quotation marks:
"I like it very much—clean living—and I think you tend to
gather more with people of your own, what should I say? How
will I put that? I know what I mean, but I don't know how to
say it. Isn't that awful?" No, sometimes it's hard to put things
into words. Do you mean people of your own economic level?
"Yes, that's it. You know when we lived in the city there were
some hot rocks and some who had a hard time making a go
of it."

A Glenview woman gives similar sentiments a more middle-
class expression.

Description of suburban living: "Husband commutes, there is a
small business section, unusual neighborliness and friendliness.
Homogeneous society with everyone on the same level."

Why moved to suburbs? "For the sake of children, we like spa-
cious lots and trees and quiet. Most like California."

Why chose particular suburb? "Quality and culture without being snobbish. Looked like California."

Advantages? "Children in a town where everyone is comparatively neighborly and safe to ask information of. No fear of kidnappers or rapists."

Disadvantages? "No part-time help."

A third basic category of suburbanite includes two types of blue-collar suburbanites, the tight blue-collar suburbanite, who defines her life with traditional workingman's values, and the expanding blue-collar suburbanite, who is modifying the pattern.

The blue-collar suburbanite

A. *The tight blue-collar suburbanite* answers as follows.

Description of suburban living: "It's a lot better for children. Communities nicer, fresh air. Spread out more. Children get in the wrong crowd sometimes in the city. There's no colored here. I don't like to live with the colored. I will say, though, that it was more friendly in Cicero than it is here. Most people aren't so nice here. My boy liked the children in Cicero better. There are only two neighbors here I enjoy. They're 'Bohunks' too. The others are all for themselves. I don't give a hang for any of them."

Why moved to suburbs? "We used to live in tight quarters, right by an alley. Homes are prettier here and it's healthier. Had only one bedroom in the apartment and needed more room as the boy got older."

Why chose particular suburb? "We went all over looking. The lots were more expensive in other places. We got this one pretty cheap. And it's close to my husband's work."

Advantages? "Outdoor life, schools and shopping centers close and nicer."

Disadvantages? "I miss the stores along Twenty-second Street. I used to walk every day with the baby and shop in all the stores. Now I have to take a bus to the village market."

B. *The expanding blue-collar suburbanite* is introducing openness in relations and definitions, and presents a positive picture of life.

Description of suburban living: "We have peace and quiet out here that we never had before, people more friendly, life more informal."

Why moved to suburbs? "For the children—healthier environment; more educational. They have more privileges and freedom than they would in the city."

Why chose particular suburb? "Near my husband's work; it seemed so quiet and peaceful, and we found that it was."

Advantages? "I have my own vegetable and flower garden—enjoy it very much. I can keep the house cleaner; you don't have the smoke and grime of the city."

Disadvantages? "I have not found any."

THE WHITE-COLLAR SUBURBANITE also comes in two sub-types, depending on how strong she builds the norm complex around herself.

A. *The tight white-collar suburbanites* are explained by a young woman.

Description of suburban living: "I like it, as ideal as you can have, friendly, casual, hectic. Work too hard at being casual, always inviting people to 'drop in.' Everyone has to be an extrovert in suburbia or is looked at queerly."

Why moved to suburbs? "Increased space; more room for the dollar for children; relaxed type of living—we thought. Actually, city dwellers are more relaxed."

Why chose particular suburb? "We liked the size; had a feel for it. We liked the idea that they had homes on all income levels."

Advantages? "Friendlier, more community spirit, interested in community projects."

Disadvantages? "Transportation."

B. *An expanding white-collar suburbanite* explains her town in terms of freedom in social relations.

Description of suburban living: "Casual, social, very pleasant; small-town atmosphere is nice for growing children; life is freer from tensions, away from the noise of the city."

Why moved to suburbs? "We wanted our own home; play area for the children, rooms of their own; to feel part of the community; to have roots, feel settled, and secure."

Why chose particular suburb? "Friends lived here; pretty town, more trees, more settled than some of the newer suburbs."
Advantages? "Space to expand; happier atmosphere; children seem less tense and less argumentative."
Disadvantages? "Crowded parking, poorer shopping."
How long expect to stay? "About six years; will move to larger home, same suburb."

THE ATYPICAL SUBURBANITE is, to some extent, every suburbanite because each one combines characteristics of past and present life into a unique pattern, different from that of other women in her neighborhood, from that of many persons in her town, and from that of most other suburbanites. However, some women seem to combine the various points of difference into a style of life which makes them strikingly atypical. What makes the following suburbanite unique is her residence in a rather prestigious community, in a relatively expensive home, at a very young age, and her lack of both a job and offspring.

Description of suburban living: "Own garden and flowers. So many things you can do if you want to. I am not a church or club woman, but probably more women in suburbia do belong than in the city."
Why moved to suburbs? "The rent we were spending; we could put it into a home as a security investment. Many advantages that apartment living hasn't got. Though the house is not built exactly to our specifications, almost everything is here." (Interviewer's comment: beautiful corner ranch, looks professionally decorated.)
Why chose particular suburb? "The builder was a friend of ours and said if we bought a lot near his he would put his house and ours together. Near a park, if we had children."
Advantages? "I enjoy daylight coming in the windows all day. At night, I can go for a walk if I like. Enjoy my dogs. Learn about insects, bugs, worms, etc. I have an encyclopedia, I look them up."
Disadvantages? "None."

The "Ideal-Typical" Urbanite

Two urban ideal types can be added to the categories of suburbanites developed from the interview with residents of twelve

Chicago area communities: the inarticulate urbanite and the indifferent urbanite. It is sometimes difficult to separate one from the other, in any specific manner, but the moods are very different. Both types show a lack of sentiment, but one is due to an inability to conceptualize life, the other to a lack of interest in the process.

THE INARTICULATE URBANITE. The interview schedule was designed with the middle class and the upper segment of the lower class in mind. Questions asking for descriptions of urban or suburban life can be answered only by those people who have an abstract idea of what urbanism or suburbanism is, a set of criteria for each, and a way of comparing them. Some women simply do not have these. Interviewers were reporting more difficulty with this part of the schedule than with any other. All American subcultures have conceptual frameworks for the roles of woman, mother, man, husband, etc. Many of our respondents lacked such constructs for "city," "neighborhood," and "suburb." One session which frustrated the middle-class interviewer resulted finally in her having to rephrase the question asking for a description of life in the city to: "Is it bad or good?" The answer was not very rewarding: "It's what you make of it anywhere." The respondent stuck to the same vagueness when describing life in her previous neighborhood: "It was in between good and bad, but it was bad when so many people started moving in." Asked about life in the suburbs, she said: "OK, I guess." However, the query as to her reason for moving to the present residence brought a concrete answer: "Well, Thirty-ninth Street was worse than Sixty-third, and the place was too bad and dirty and torn down." What is good about her present neighborhood? "All the stores are right here; the children don't have to go too far." The bad things? "Well, the taverns in the block make it bad, so the children must stay in the back all day or in the house. They go to the playground about three blocks away sometimes, too." Abstract concepts are meaningful only when translated into the daily experiences of living. Their absence makes for inarticulate responses and coping behavior based on short-range plans. Problems are solved with stopgap measures.

THE INDIFFERENT URBANITE is typified by the following exchange.

Description of life in the city: "Satisfactory to me."
Life in the neighborhood? "Less tendency to know neighbors."
Life in the suburbs? "I don't know."
Why chose this neighborhood? "Close to transportation."
Advantages? "Transportation really good; near bowling alley."
Disadvantages? "None."

THE RELUCTANT URBANITE included one rather brief, but strong, rejection of the city in toto.

A. *The reluctant urbanite in general*

Description of life in the city: "It's pretty impersonal, and it's dirty as hell; it's incredible."
Life in the neighborhood? "The same. It's not as noisy as some, but there's as much dirt."
Why chose this neighborhood? "It's not a bad one, and the rent isn't too high, and we've got friends nearby."
Advantages? "I knew the area before."
Disadvantages? "We've got some psychotic neighbors."

B. *A reluctant urbanite* objecting to a particular neighborhood answered as follows.

Description of life in the city: "I've always lived in a good-sized city. Physically you don't have as much space to live, or privacy in high-rise buildings. Still it has a lot more to offer in business, education, and culture."
Life in the neighborhood? "I don't think we have much of a neighborhood. It's too transient in that few consider this permanent. There are not many activities, community-wise. I feel more danger in this area, since it's so close to a slum."
Why chose this neighborhood? "The rent for the amount of space was reasonable, and it's a convenient area."
Advantages? "In comparison to other neighborhoods, none. In a lot of respects there are common things, as income."
Disadvantages? "The shopping area is very bad. Services are worse, prices are higher, lack of freedom of going out at night alone. There's a need for police and police dog protection."

THE ENTHUSIASTIC URBANITE does not include, in our 200 house-wives and 100 working women, many of the first type, A.

A. *The enthusiastic mother.* A larger number of urban than suburban housewives do not have children of an age which would bring to mind this role; some have no children at all. It is possible that there is an additional factor of cultural institutionalization. Middle-class people with children tend to move to the suburbs, if they are strongly child-oriented; if not, remaining in the city, they do not justify their selection by reference to offspring. When people think of the city, they think of features other than child-rearing facilities, unless they think of these negatively. Lower-class people do not plan their lives as consciously around their children. Many urbanites state that it is not a good place to rear children because of the danger, "Lack of outdoor space for children to play, or closeness of housing." "Not healthy for children" was the summary comment of those who still live in the city because they must or because other values outweigh the implied desire to have healthy children. "Very nice for adults, bad for children," defines one urban dweller.

B. (1) *The enthusiastic neighbor* can live in the urban area, but she is more likely to define the neighborhood and not the city in terms of these relations.

Description of life in the city: "Hustle and bustle; activity: people coming and going to work; people don't know each other and don't care; apartments; lack of warmth."
Life in the neighborhood? "Warm and friendly; people interested in each other and in their homes."
Why chose this neighborhood? "Originally this was my mother's home. She wanted to live in an area where her children could feel their identities."
Advantages? "Feeling of individual importance because there are fewer people here; seeing growing things, more social life."
Disadvantages? "Feeling of community, that they are not affected by the outside world." (Located far south, but in city, middle-class home, Negro area.)

B. (2) *The enthusiastic non-interacting neighbor* abounds in the city, as evidenced by the answers to the neighboring questions, and she tends to define the city in impersonal terms.

Description of life in the city: "One can lead an easier life in a city, because there is hardly any inter-connection between neighbors, and thus you are practically lost in the crowd."

Life in the neighborhood? "It is typical of just about any city neighborhood. It is sort of friendly, but hardly anyone knows his immediate neighbor."

Why chose this neighborhood? "We chose to buy and because of our national population."

Advantages? "The business district isn't far."

Disadvantages? "None up to this time."

The enthusiastic urbanite is often a devotee of certain features of the city which she thinks are not duplicated in the suburbs. The urban culture enthusiast feels that "Chicago is a city that gets in your blood." One young Negro gives a description of city life in great detail: "When I have problems or just want to be alone, I find it very refreshing to take a nice walk in the Loop, and I watch the people, look at the buildings. When my husband and I were going together, we would sometimes take a walk in the Loop at night, when the neon lights were on. It seemed almost as if we were the only people in the world, but it was a peaceful feeling. Away from the personal side, life in the city offers you many opportunities to meet many different kinds of people; also it has many cultural advantages. Besides, the hustle and bustle and fast life."

C. The following section from an interview with a nineteen-year-old *urban culture enthusiast* illustrates her attitudes.

Description of life in the city: "Exciting, I enjoy the section of the city where I live. We have our shop here. Therefore, it becomes not only enjoyable, but profitable as well. I like the feeling of the city. I think I'm too young to live in the suburbs. The only thing I don't like about living in the city is the dumb, miserable heating system in the winter, and I think I would enjoy seeing a few more trees scattered around. Other than that, I love the city."

Life in the neighborhood? "It's fun! There's a lot to do. Most of the people I know are other shop-owners. There is such a variety of people. It's very integrated here and all kinds of crazy people are here. We have tourists that come and bother us, but they buy things from our shop, so they make us happy.

There's a surprising amount of co-operation for all the different types of people who live here. Like the people who are trying to rehabilitate the neighborhood. That's nice."

Why chose this neighborhood? "I think the homes around here are some of the nicest in the city for the price. It's a different neighborhood from all the others, because it has such a variety and you don't have to know your neighbors. I don't. I don't care to. I like the way it looks. I like a lot of the people and if I don't like the people, I don't have to see them. The whole neighborhood has an atmosphere which is nice. It is close to everything downtown—the lake—you don't even need a car. Also, it's close to our shop. But I'd rather live on Dearborn Street in a duplex." (Same neighborhood, Old Town.)

D. *The enthusiastic class-conscious resident* is just as pleased with the city neighborhood, because it has a "nice" class of people, as was her counterpart with the same trait in the suburb.

Description of life in the city: "Excess of all sorts of culture; museums, minimized money spent for pleasure. Parks, beaches, organized play for children, low-cost entertainment for members of the family."

Life in the neighborhood? "A very nice, middle-class neighborhood, closeness of schools, parks, and organized activities. Block clubs and community activities."

Why chose this neighborhood? "Because it was far enough removed from the center of the city; close enough for its advantages."

Advantages? "Close to schools and churches, and close to some long-term friends."

Disadvantages? "Before so many people moved into the neighborhood, not much police protection was needed. Need more bus service and improvements in alleys."

THE BLUE-COLLAR URBANITE who still accepts lower-class values is illustrated by the janitor's wife in a family earning less than $5000, who is now sixty years of age and who answers as follows.

A. *The tight blue-collar urbanite*

Description of life in the city: "City living is faster, easier because of transportation, shopping is closer; you don't have to have a car."

Life in the neighborhood? "It's a typical city neighborhood; very noisy, streets are busy, a lot of people moving to work and back; noisy when near a factory; seems like someone is always around."

Why chose this neighborhood? "Mainly because of his work."

Advantages? "Shopping close by, didn't have to wait for transportation. Church was close."

Disadvantages? "A lot of dirt; factories too close; factories too noisy, the people working near here too noisy." (Five years of education, has worked making cigars and light bulbs.)

B. *The expanding blue-collar urbanite*, whose horizons are broadening, is exemplified by a high-school-graduate wife of a service manager in a garage. She is very insightful in her description of the city.

Description of life in the city: "It provides more conveniences. You are closer to everything. There are more activities, more advantages, more and better schools, churches. But it's more crowded, living is not relaxed. I guess people aren't as neighborly. At least, that's what they say."

Life in the neighborhood? "We are friendly. Of course, there are a few I don't like too well, who cause trouble; who interfere; always barge in when not wanted. We talk to each other if we see each other outside. Occasionally I invite one or two neighbors, couples over for an evening."

Why chose this neighborhood? "We liked the house, thought it would serve our needs. It is handy to my husband's work; he can come home for lunch. We thought mainly about the house rather than the specific neighborhood."

Advantages? "It's convenient to shopping, but then I always have a car. But still it's nice not to have to go too far. It's nice looking, well kept up, if this could be called an advantage. Not too crowded or busy as some areas. There are two or three very friendly, helpful neighbors. I guess this is the main advantage."

Disadvantages? "Taxes have gone up so much, but they are

higher everywhere. And there is a lot of work keeping up the house. But I wouldn't like a small apartment. Even when the children leave, I still want a house."

THE WHITE-COLLAR URBANITE is also represented among the respondents by both the tight and the expanding types.

A. *The tight white-collar* pressures are felt thus by women in the city.

Description of life in the city: "I would say it is extremely complex, sometimes hectic, but interesting. I wouldn't move out." *Life in the neighborhood?* "Extremely dull, it's kind of a typical middle-class block. You know, the bridge clubs—that kind of nonsense." *Why chose this neighborhood?* "I didn't." *Advantages?* "It's a lot quieter than where we moved from; more space for the children to play, people aren't as friendly, though housing is better, no rats, roaches. Socially, I don't think the children have to face as much, as many bad influences, and I think there are more things for an educated person to participate in, clubs for instance; some enjoy it, I don't. You don't find this in the other neighborhoods." *Disadvantages:* "None."

B. An example of the *expanding white-collar urbanite* states the following.

Description of life in the city: "The men are active in different organizations, whether it's politics or church organizations." *Life in the neighborhood?* "Women are more relaxed—live in shorts—neighborly. I notice this out here more than right in town where I lived. They seem to be freer, active, clubs formed in the neighborhood, barbecues, etc." *Why chose this neighborhood?* "We liked this location, it was the coming location, the price was right, we bought the lot and built." *Advantages?* "Cleanliness, much cooler living in the summer—people." *Disadvantages?* "Bus service, if you don't have two cars in the family, you are out of luck; we have one car. My daughter has her own car and needs her car."

These ideal types have been drawn to represent the respondents as they vary in the basic criteria, attitudes toward, and perception of, the community of residence. Many suburbanites and an even higher proportion of urbanites do not involve themselves or their homes in the community; they have not developed the more upper-class feeling of obligation or sentiment connecting them with the communities in which the homes they maintain are by their choice located. Some women have ventured out of their four walls only to feel uncomfortable, unwelcome, or awkward in meeting the life-style demands of the town. These are the most likely to experience the community as an outside force pressing upon them and demanding depersonalizing conformity. The more involved respondents feel that they are part of the community and they define life within it as facilitating their free and creative contributions. The form of community life institutionalized in each social area is an important factor in how a resident identifies with it, but so is her total orientation toward the world outside her home. Suburbs seem to provide women with an identifiable unit for involvement, because of their size and often because of their newness, offering opportunity and reward for active participation. The more educated the woman is who lives in such an environment, other roles not commanding her attention, the more likely is she to have the skills and self-confidence for active involvement in the community and in its many levels of interpersonal relations. Her orientation brings her to such a town anticipating or at least willing to become an active part of the unit. The less educated woman, socialized into a concern with her immediate world, suspicious of the outside, and lacking relations-initiating skills, who moves to a suburb often as a means of escaping the changing urban scene, is less likely to direct her attention toward the community and its voluntary associations.

The urbanite either identifies with the total urban culture and its sets of activities, selecting from a wide range of facilities provided by such a center, or restricts herself to her own residence, street, and lines of repeated movement to a limited number of work or house-maintenance places. Neither city nor suburb guarantees a decrease of isolation, specific lines of contact, or an opportunity to open the home to societal life. Fear, suspicion, lack of self-confidence, absence of interpersonal skills, and a restricted view of the role of housewife and of the home can tie a woman down into a routine task-oriented rhythm in a limited life space, whether she lives in the city or in one of the outlying towns. Suburbanites are generally more actively involved than urbanites. It is possible that those who move out of the city have more "pioneer" spirit, greater self-confidence, or more facilities for expanding than those who remain, so that the suburbs end up by having more people willing to be involved. The great range of responses given by women living in socio-economically divergent communities indicates that this is not necessarily the case. Rather, the opportunity for adult socialization into broader involvement in the community is more likely to be available in rapidly expanding, but relatively small towns whose residents share the same problems.[45] Those places may be more able to socialize the non-upper-class woman into a broader view of life and interaction than the city is. It takes the more educated and multidimensional personality to perceive and take full advantage of the complex living conditions provided by the urban center. For those lacking such social, psychological, and pragmatic skills, the city may be a stifling residential location, as indicated by many women in their definitions of urban life.

A striking feature of the traits chosen through selective perception as typical of the city, neighborhood, and suburb is their dependence upon the respondent's own style of life. As freedom of residence expands for women, who no longer enter the ancestral home of their husbands, but who help select several locations during their life cycle, and as the areas offering different styles proliferate, community relations will develop greater variations.

Residential mobility is a crucial factor of change in social status and in life style. Social mobility is facilitated by geographical movement, and each step requires redefinition of living needs. Selection of a new residence involves "anticipatory socialization": a woman must visualize herself as living in a certain place and, consciously or not, must prepare to act in what she judges to be an appropriate way. The lower-class woman restricts her view to the limits of her new property. The upper-class woman incorporates the whole community, including its formal and informal activities, into her view of herself in a new situation. The perspec-

45. Both Orville G. Brim, Jr. and Stanton Wheeler have excellent essays on this subject in *Socialization After Childhood*, New York: John Wiley, 1966.

tives of the women in between depend on their background and the stage in their life cycle. A young and upwardly mobile wife learns through living in several neighborhoods to look at the community from different points of view.

In general, the women living in the many areas of metropolitan Chicago vary greatly in their perceptions of the community and in their involvement with people outside the home. It may be that the behavior which Riesman defined as other-directed and concerned with peer judgments provides the suburbanite a foundation which later enables individualistic life styles and a full utilization of societal facilities. Thus, it may be a functional step in the life changes of women, leaving behind restrictive lower- and lower-middle-class backgrounds and gradually becoming part of a neighborhood, a friendship group, a voluntary association, and a community in a way that previously was possible for none but the very upper-class wife.

❦ ❦ ❦

Conclusions

COMMENTS

The basic conclusion of the Chicago studies is that modern women are becoming increasingly competent and creative in their social role of housewife and in the manner in which they combine different roles within their life cycle. This result should not be surprising in view of the American ideology of democracy and the emphasis on education for all its members. Yet, all the literature dealing with the modern woman of this society describes the role of housewife and the women who carry it on in quite different terms. Culturally embedded assumptions about the housewife, which make women object even to the title, focus upon the supposed impossibility of creativity in the role on the part of persons "limited" to it. House-maintenance is pictured as routine, unrewarding, lacking in mental stimulation, and unconnected with mental ability; as either physically exhausting or insufficiently tiring. Women who are housewives are visualized as basically passive, unimaginative, uninterested in events outside their walls, chained to routine tasks, and unable to understand the work their husbands and children perform away from the home. Simultaneously, they are not trusted in major decisions because of "masculine protest" or their emotionality. This combined stereotype is present not only in Betty Friedan's *The Feminine Mystique*, which evaluates work for money as the only worthy effort, but in the pronouncements of most feminists and anti-feminists, men and women.[1] They even label other-than-in-the-home activities of women, such as community participation, artistic effort, educational or child-oriented actions, not challenging to anyone with intelligence. The only source worthy of intellectual identity is the "job" or "career."

1. Betty Friedan, *The Feminine Mystique*, New York: Norton, 1963.

Yet, increasingly, although all jobs outside the home are viewed as stimulating, requiring intellect and imagination, important and highly rewarding, especially when compared to being a house-wife, girls are not encouraged to seriously pursue occupational careers.

In addition to labeling what women do as inferior to what men do, the current view of the life cycle of the female in this society is outlined in very non-flexible stages. Her life is portrayed as a sequence of definite and irreversible states. She is expected to move from birth and home-centered childhood into school at-tendance for a time sufficient to find a husband, but not so long as to waste valuable youth on knowledge used only for a short time. The next appropriate stages are work before and after marriage, giving birth to a limited number of children, rearing children, caring for the retired husband, widowhood, and death. This de-scription does not take cognizance of new trends in education: of interruptions, a return to school at a later date, continuous need for new knowledge; nor does it recognize discontinuous work ca-reers and shifts in life interests. The basic personality is supposed to be early developed, then continuously the same. The young girl is expected to be boy-clothes-and-popularity focused. Mother-hood brings maturity. The more educated the woman, the more dissatisfied she is expected to become in middle years. Even the "labor-saving devices" which the society has provided her are dysfunctional to the housewife, because they leave her with "nothing to do" in the "full-house plateau" and "shrinking circle" stages. By past standards of virtue, she is defined as increasingly useless with each decrease in physical work. The expansion of her time and energy has been equated with inevitable boredom and licentious behavior. Women and the lower classes are not trusted to use leisure well, although a similar prediction of the dire con-sequences of the lack of physical exhaustion does not seem to apply to the upper-class male. De Toqueville's fear of the masses, which assumed that a change in work patterns cannot be accom-panied by changes in interest and perspective, is echoed in de-scriptions of the middle-aged, middle-class American woman.[2] The last stage of her life is pictured as even less functional, with

2. Alexis de Tocqueville, *Democracy in America,* New York: Alfred Knopf, 1945. See also Max Lerner, *America as a Civilization,* New York: Simon and Schuster, 1957.

travel funded by the late husband's estate as her main occupation.

At the most extreme, the woman is seen as a parasite, passively taking economic goods from her husband and unable to make decisions without an "other-directed" search for values. Equally current, but opposite stereotypes present her as a "smothering" mother who emasculates her husband and male offspring because of her own feeling of inferiority and wish to dominate.

American homes are portrayed by "observers" as devoid of all grace, operated by buttons, with tasteless meals and lamps in front of the picture windows. They are drawn as identical units in mass-produced suburbs, containing people stamped in the same mold, an idea which does not occur when descriptions of apartment dwellers are given.[3] Their owners are described as increasingly alienated, passive or withdrawn, and as that way inevitably because of technology, size, urbanization, and television. Television is always brought in as the *bête noire*.

These images of Americans are not isolated, nor does this presentation exaggerate the content of much of the commentary. The images have been woven into dramatic fabrics of critical rejection by those who selectively perceive items in the culture and in societal behavior which indicate either social disorganization or thoughtless conformity. They are available to any reader of the public press or even social science literature and seem to be believed by the American housewife, who does not counterbalance them by a defense of even her own behavior. Other commentators, eulogizing the opposite side of the picture, also draw great fabric designs of already achieved "democracy" and "progress," the mottos of fully happy and adjusted people. None of these definitions of American society deal with its actual heterogeneity or with the trends in the social roles of its members, certainly not in those performed by housewives.

3. The heterogeneity of background of persons undertaking "other-directed behavior" indicates that it may not be an outgrowth of suburbia, but of early life in urban areas. This orientation may fill the need to find new patterns of action and to allay feelings of insecurity produced by geographical and social mobility. See Helena Znaniecki Lopata, "Conformity in Suburbia," *Free: The Roosevelt University Magazine* (Spring 1964).

Factors Contributing to the Stereotypes of Housewives and of the Home

A number of historical factors have combined to create the highly negative stereotypes of American home life and of its women. These include the constriction of the home into a privacy-seeking isolated unit, the acceptance of lower-class definitions of the housewife, and the cultural lag which has prevented women from taking full advantage of the opportunities for multidimensionality offered by the modern urban centers.

One of the very dramatic changes that has occurred in family life within the past few centuries of European history has been in the location of the home in relation to the society. As Philippe Ariés points out in his *Centuries of Childhood*,[4] the manor homes of Europe had been the center of societal life prior to the eighteenth century. This was particularly true of societies which had not developed important public meeting places for the transaction of political and economic affairs. A variety of people lived within these manor homes or came into them often from the outside, and the common rooms contained simultaneous or sequential patterns of activity reflecting much of the culture. The eighteenth century, according to Ariés, changed the significance of the home, which became a closed-off, privacy-ensuring place of residence for family members. Rather than being the focus of social life, it was purposely withdrawn from the major institutions of the society. Work and politics moved to specially designated physical spaces, followed by the men and children judged old enough to participate in a less restricted life than the one available in the home. Only the women remained in it, especially if they were part of the lower and less educated social classes. The upper-class females were educated by tutors or interested relatives, and they went out of the home to participate in various societal activities or brought some of the life back into it through social events and their own companionate relations.[5]

European societies have differed from each other and still vary in the manner and degree to which women contribute to the func-

4. Philippe Ariés, *Centuries of Childhood*, New York: Vintage Books, 1965.
5. Mary Reynolds, *The Learned Lady in England, 1650–1760*, New York: Houghton Mifflin, 1920.

tioning of their social systems. Some have institutionalized the seclusion of the upper-class females in a way similar to the Muslim, Chinese, or Indian nations. But most depend upon women to help carry out their activities in many areas of life.[6]

In America, the isolation of the home from the rest of the world was reinforced in pioneer years. The farmer built his house in the center of privacy-stressing property, preventing frequent contacts, and often rejecting life outside the narrow belt needed to maintain him within it. The creation of a farmstead required hard physical labor, and poverty resulted in a dearth of content within the dwelling. Puritanical tradition honored a lack of embellishment and a disdain for "earthy belongings." Plain furnishings, plain food, and plain clothing were the best contribution a woman could make to her family; and hard physical work was judged a vital feature of honest life. Even the man did not have much interest outside the home and the farm; the whole family was restricted to a minimal involvement in society. The economic and family institutions formed the focus of life; commitment outside the home was certainly not expected of the woman and she was not trained for it.

6. William Goode states in *World Revolution and Family Patterns,* New York: The Free Press, 1963, that upper-class women have much less freedom of action than the lower classes. This conclusion applied in cases of societies practicing purdah, or the seclusion of women. In these the top strata were particularly strict in preventing women from participation in outside life. However, societies lacking such restrictive ideology define conformity to norms and the practice of setting a good example called *noblesse oblige* as taking an active part in societal life or various segments of it. Ariés reports women so active in early Europe. India, which restricted its upper-class women severely after about 200 A.D., had in early centuries given them "considerable freedom. Girls were educated like boys. . . ." (S. C. Dube, "Men's and Women's Roles in India: A Sociological Review," in Barbara Ward, ed., *Women in New Asia,* Paris: UNESCO, 1963, p. 183.) See also P. Thomas, *Indian Women Through the Ages,* New York: Asia Publishing House, 1964. According to Ward, Indian women have experienced great changes in the degree to which they have been allowed a breadth of perspective and involvement in society, from one of great freedom to purdah, and recently to increased multidimensionality. Other societies experimenting with changes in the involvement of women are those within the communistic block. For example, see Magdalena Sokolowska and Krystyna Wrochno, "Women's Social Position," mimeographed, Warsaw: Institute of Philosophy and Sociology, Polish Academy of Sciences, June 1965, and Jerzy Piotrowski, *Praca Zawodowa Kobiety a Rodzina,* Warsaw: Ksiazka i Wiedza, 1963.

The norms of the pioneer country were reinforced in their restrictive influence on the home by the culture and life style of most immigrants to this country. The foundation of America is the lower-class, agriculturally trained, rurally reared, and culturally divergent immigrants. Their definitions of the home, of the woman, of the city, of large organizations, of paid employment, of political obligation, of experimentation, of creativity in human relations are still embedded in a non-literate culture of scarcity.[7] Although life has changed and descendants of immigrants are entering initiative-demanding occupations and professions and living complex lives, the peasant view of the world has not been significantly modified in the non-technological spheres of existence.

The upper-class educated woman did not become the ideological model of Americans in the role of housewife, although most middle-class wives and mothers have adopted many patterns of her behavior. It is not her home, run with complexity of interaction and knowledge, which comes to mind when that role is discussed. It is not the person who has opened her home to free movement in and out who is the stereotype of "the housewife." That term connotes all the characteristics of lower-class, uneducated non-involvement: ignorance, passivity in relation to self and to others, hostility or apathy toward neighbors, lack of involvement in the life of the society, and willingness to have the elite run the world. Restricted by her lack of tools, by the demands of work and culture, and by traditional ritual, the peasant woman maintained her home at a minimal level. The modern American woman has available to her a completely different set of demands, sanctions, objects, and tools. Many utilize these in building creative action and societal involvement, but even they are not explaining what they do in freedom to———terms.

The ideological lag in definitions of the home and the housewife does not represent the changes in actual behavior and abilities of the Chicago-area women. The major revolt of lower-class families who were willing to leave European communities and the

7. Robert Thobald points out the need for a change from the values of scarcity in *The Challenge of Abundance,* New York: The New American Library's Mentor Book, 1962. John Galbraith has often spoken of this cultural lag in the American philosophy of life, as in *The Affluent Society,* Boston: Houghton Mifflin, 1958.

security of a known way of life to come to this society was followed in the post World War II years by the anti-tradition and
anti-ethnic revolt of the next generations. The late 1950's and the
1960's witnessed a movement of young adults out of the American
farm, small town, ethnic community, and anomic neighborhood in
a dramatic attempt to change the style of life. Freedom from
———became the cry, explained by Erich Fromm and recorded
by many others.[8] The young marrieds, equipped with horizon-
broadening education or armed services experience, confident
of economic prosperity and job opportunity, left their parents,
literally and figuratively. The depth and significance of the revolt
has been glossed over by many observers of the American scene
who assume it to be a "natural" outgrowth of assimilation, requiring no conscious decision-making and having none but "success"
consequences. The descendents of Poles, Italians, Germans, Bohemians, Irishmen, Armenians, French Canadians, southern farmers, and of many other groups forming the numerical majority of
the American population moved from where they had been reared
and where their parents still lived to cities, urban fringes, and
suburbs. Purposely rejecting the culture of their parents, they
forged for themselves a new life.

The relational and normative patterns they started creating,
with hesitations and problems, as well as with excitement and
pleasure, were easily available to societal observation. Rejection
of prior dependence upon parents, in-laws, older siblings, and
whole communities which had supported strict superordinate-
subordinate relations and personality-limiting interaction of family members resulted in "other-directed" concern with peer-group
values. The removal of traditional foundations of knowledge and
the new self-confidence did not automatically produce easily
available new guides. Attempting completely new styles of life,
the post World War II housewife-revolutionary turned to two
sources of knowledge. One was her peers, women going through
the same experiences. A major feature of such other-directedness,
which was so critically described by the authors of *The Lonely
Crowd,* is its equal-power base. The woman, freed from traditional controls over her behavior, turned to those like herself,
women who were also revolting and who did not know the an-

8. Erich Fromm, *Escape from Freedom,* New York: Farrar and Rinehart,
1941.

swers to life's problems. Through the telephone, outdoor "sunning," koffeeklatches, and "brain-storming" sessions, modern women exchanged information and solutions to problems, sharing both anxiety and competence-building feelings. Their grandmothers had tradition, the revolutionaries had each other. The pattern still continues in any community and for any group of women who are experiencing the same revolt against a completely different ethnic or social-class style of life.

The second source of knowledge for the modern American woman attempting to build new life patterns has been the depersonalized mass communication expert. The scientific or technical expert is used in different ways than the community sage or family member. The difference is one of choice and, again, of power. Medical doctors or mass communication advisers can be selected and rejected; they transmit knowledge which increases competence and which does not demand passive or reactive stances. The relation of the woman to them increases her knowledge and skill as a decision-maker. The revolt against traditional patterns of behavior has combined with the results of modern education to demand of the person rational selection from many alternatives of action.

CONCLUSIONS

American metropolitan housewives do not form a homogeneous group. Far from it. The metropolitan area of Chicago contains a diversity of women performing the housewife and related roles, ranging from the very restricted to the highly competent, from the ritualistic to the creative, from the task- to the relation-oriented. They vary in each role and as total personalities. Some are single-dimensional, concerned with only their home and with the role of housewife or of mother. Others are highly multidimensional throughout life or at different stages of its cycle. In conclusion, only three general types will be discussed, the restricted, the uncrystallized, and the emerging competent or multidimensional modern.

The restricted housewife, who is usually relatively uneducated and lower class, limits herself to passive stances, task-orientation, home-bound interests, and minimally creative performances in the roles of housewife, wife, and mother. She often experiences a feeling of inadequacy in a world in which she thinks "other women" have much more influence. Her children do not obey, fall under "bad influences," and are not "happy," no matter what she does to please them. Lacking power to control them through traditional methods, she does not have the ability to use other means of relating to them, so she restricts the mother role to physical care.

The restricted housewife remains resentful of the male, as a consequence of the former strongly patriarchal control of fathers and husbands, even when she gets some "rights." Her world is peopled with strangers whom she fears and toward whom she has no means of building relational bridges. As her extended kin group disperses, for much of the day or week she is often deprived of really close contact with anyone she can trust and with whom she feels comfortable. If she is a Negro living in a slum area of the city, she is the most isolated of women, not having many neighboring relations, or continuous family contacts, or identifications with the community to sustain her self-identity and feeling of worth. The white urban working woman is also likely to be isolated from her community, anomically un-involved in its life, although having a tie with the outside through her work. Pockets of lower-class ethnically close groups carrying out multiple relations in the community still remain in the city, but many white urban housewives are also relatively restricted to their homes and to a minimal view of the role of housewife.

The housewife with a bit more education and some skills for interacting with others is happier about her community, although still feeling powerless in relation to the society. If matched to her neighborhood, she can develop strong levels of interaction, although sometimes hurt by her lack of skill in preventing uncomfortable situations. She shows an interest in the ideas in newspapers and magazines, which could bring creativity into her role of housewife, but she is still hesitant about experimentation in behavior. She expresses a desire to organize life around her rather than just passively adjusting to it, but she still lacks sufficient knowledge to anticipate the consequences of various lines of action and then to act in accordance with long-range plans. She is changing her life style, although often wishing for formulas to solve emerging problems.

Basically, this kind of a woman is typical of the city middle-class which is still "uncrystallized" in its life patterns, engaging in a variety of mutually inconsistent behaviors supported by ideologies often dysfunctional to the goals. Most Americans older than twenty-five have not been socialized into sufficient self-confidence and competence to enable full expansion of the self into creatively developed roles in the community and in the society. The lack of competence is a consequence of cultural change, of weakness in societally institutionalized training sequences, and of the person's own movement from one life style to another. Not only women, but also men, face strains and conflicts from these factors, and different sub-groups are more prone to experience them than others are. However, the demands and duties facing the woman are especially difficult because of the criticisms directed toward her. The volume of literature devoted to her, in comparison to books depicting "The American Man," witness this concern. Fear of societal criticism is more strongly built into the socialization of girls than of boys, who are encouraged to experiment with life plans and to take the initiative.

The lack of crystallization of the recently middle-class woman is evident not at only one period of time, but in the whole life cycle. The young girl is encouraged to limit her interests to popularity and boys. She becomes multidimensional because of the general trend toward work, school, clubs, etc., without building this into a personality pattern that can withstand the sudden collapse of these roles into home-bound ones during the early life of her children. Lacking an ideology which considers her as part of the community and the society, she must build a new life with relatively few skills. Having had companionate relations with her new husband before the marriage and the birth of the first baby, she feels the shift as pulling her away from their multileveled involvement into a more sex-segregated world. Lacking the ability to initiate neighboring, she is often lonely. She usually lives in a community with anomic or institutionalized non-interaction, in a society which has not solved many of the problems of young mothers through co-operative effort. She is unable to see this stage of life as one which is temporary and whose difficulties could be partially solved through co-operative effort. However, if she is fortunate enough to move into a suburb or an urban area housing those in a similar situation and containing some institutionalized form of neighboring which she is able to carry out, or at least to learn, she may use such relations to help make life more enjoyable and to expand her competence. In addition, having been educated at least partially into abstract knowledge, she may turn to secondary sources of information to creatively modify her roles. She is not likely, however, to change her basic ideology which restricts the home and the role of housewife to traditional lower-class minimal levels, no matter how she actually expands the multidimensionality of her own life.

The uncrystallized woman also faces problems during the "full-house plateau" and "shrinking circle" stages of the role of house-wife. Not having been socialized to plan for a long life beyond the role of mother to young children, when she is freed from the engrossing stages of that role, she often finds time and energy she does not know how to use. Unaccustomed to feeling part of the community and society and accepting much of the stereotype of American women, she becomes concerned and worried over the gap between freedom from——— and freedom to———.

Some of the previously uncrystallized housewives are, however, using the period when the mother-housewife roles decrease in significance to develop themselves into human beings with a more multidimensional involvement. They are experimenting with new training and educational systems for learning or updating role knowledge or they are developing skills to be used in expanding sets of relations already within their role-cluster. Others more passively await events which will force or justify undertaking new roles, as when widowhood is followed by re-entrance into the labor market. Problems arise for one sub-type of uncrystallized woman for whom traditional or lower-life limitations are no longer satisfactory, yet for whom new expansions in the complex are seemingly out of reach: this is exemplified by the Park Forester who stands behind the curtain of her window, watching her husband socializing with neighbors, afraid to go out herself. Problems also arise for a different type of woman who acquires self-confidence and competence, but not self-control, resulting in an overbearing manner which suggests that no one else knows anything. The newly competent woman has difficulties in situations of polite companionship which are still organized traditionally with males dominating the discussion. The "society of experts" which is developing may make social intercourse very difficult during the intermediary years, as each person tries to prove his or her newly acquired competence. One of the respondents feels awkward in many situations which she and her husband attend together, explaining that she now knows more about the polite companionship conversation subjects than her mate, who is too busy in his profession to read material she has time to cover. She thinks that it is unfeminine for a woman to dominate the discussion, but she hates to hear him express ignorant views. Thus, strains are experienced in many ways in a society changing as rapidly as ours. The frequency of humorous and more veiled comments about the alleged American matriarchal trend is interesting to note in view of the complexity of role definitions and attempts to solve the daily problems experienced by women.

The lack of crystallization in the life style of any one woman may not be due just to discontinuity in her life stages, but also to the fact that her education may outdistance, or be insufficient for, the income with which the family has to work, the cultural background of her husband, the patterns of her community, and the demands she or others make upon her in her roles.

While the lower-class woman expresses her feeling of change as simply a removal of controls by others, that is, as freedom from dominance, and the newly mobile respondent expresses pleasure over her freedom from work and over her neighboring relations, the third type of housewife expresses attitudes which may represent a new personality trend, possibly the final consequence of some of the other changes. Increased education, income, and freedom of life styles are facilitating an expansion of role conceptualizations beyond the prior restrictions. The modern housewife is very likely to define homemaking as extending into the community, mothering as utilizing all societal facilities to expand the world of the young, and wifehood as many-leveled involvement in the various social roles of the husband. In spite of the complexity she assigns to these three roles, the same woman is the most likely to think of self-expressive and creative roles for herself and to feel obligations to the society and the community in which she functions. She gives the impression that the role of housewife provides her a base for building a many-faceted life, an opportunity few other vocational roles allow, because they are tied down to single organizational structures and goals. In fact, working women, that is, those who are carrying on paid employment roles, are less likely, particularly if they are not Negro, to define life in such complex and multidimensional terms because they restrict women to more traditional life styles.

The newly developing competent housewife is utilizing multiple sources for the acquisition of knowledge and skill in the performance of that role, building unique patterns of action from items selected out of the large fund of interpersonal and secondary material she now has available to her. The higher her education, the more convinced she is that the role calls for a great deal of knowledge and the more able she is to bring new ideas into the home and to go out in search of them. The training in the home or obtained later from "mother" is supplemented by organized bodies of data contained in secular and scientifically based sources. Magazine and newspaper information is adjusted to fit individual needs, and items are modified through the intermediary production process in the home. The woman has thus returned some of the production function to the household. The knowledge she obtains is informally shared with neighbors and friends.

The home the modern housewife maintains is no longer the restricted, closed-off area which Europeans made of it in the eighteenth century. The woman, with the help of architects and builders, has brought the home physically and psychologically back into the world. She has brought the world into the home through the use of glass instead of brick and through her open-door policy of neighboring and child-rearing, of entertaining friends and work associates of her husband, and of holding League of Women Voters research meetings. She has simultaneously brought the home into the community by looking and going out into it, protesting the way others are running the town or the school, if she feels it wrong, going to service centers in order to maintain her house, and entering public and private spaces as a representative of her family. In the process of running a home, of adequately functioning as the mother of a spatially non-restricted child, of assisting her husband in his roles, and of satisfying her own self-expressive needs, she has extended the life of housewives into the world even beyond her immediate area. The home no longer contains wall-bound people, but functions as part of the ideological and social world. In addition, the housewife has become flexible in the manner in which her activities and interests fit into the different social roles she performs, as relations in them are redefined.

As a wife, the newly competent woman relates to her husband in a multileveled manner based upon the ability to "take the role of the other" and to give her mate the opportunity of doing the same. She defines the role in relational terms, regarding tasks as significant only in their contribution to the home. She expresses an interest in her husband's roles outside the home through direct help when needed, or encouragement and discussion. She sees husband-wife relations not as a struggle for authority, but as a process of developing interpersonal depth suited to the unique needs of both personalities. She defines the three-generation changes in the roles of family men as a shift from authority into full and personal participation in the unit. A division of labor within the home is generally maintained by such a housewife, but it is modified by emergency situations and joint activities, explained in rational terms as needed for the welfare of the unit. Couple-companionate relations are brought into the marriage by either spouse having the opportunity for contacts which can be transformed into symmetrical friendships. Wives contribute childhood friends or those met prior to marriage or their various roles, as well as neighbors, with whom they usually have a higher level of sex-segregated interaction than the husbands do. Work roles of the male combine with, and finally substitute for, his childhood friends, as contact with the latter becomes increasingly difficult to maintain. Such relations enable the husband and the wife to engage in symmetrical leisure-time activities.

The social role of mother does not produce many women who express full confidence in their ability to perform it at desired levels. In fact, the more educated the American metropolitan woman, the more conscious she is of the complexity of this role and of the difficulties involved in competent child-rearing. The relational emphasis of this type of mother, combined with a societal focusing of responsibility on her and awareness of the importance of the home for child development, make for worry over actions designed to best meet the goals of the relation. The physical care of the offspring is no longer a major source of concern, as it was for the lower-class antecedents of the modern woman; she quite competently handles preventative and curative situations of child health. It is her desire to provide the offspring with the best available resources for the development of their personality and potentials, coupled with the inadequacy of the sources of knowledge which she can utilize, which creates the greatest degree of concern for the new American woman.

Even the competent woman has not fully modified her ideological explanation of the role of housewife to fit the actuality of her behavior and other definitions. *The Feminine Mystique,* which holds that "a woman's place is in the home," and Betty Friedan's restriction of the home to an uncreative and limited function, both seem to be operative. The limited view of the life of women is presented by those who work, as well as by those who are full-time housewives; by those who have small children and by those who have no offspring remaining in the home; by those active in complex kin relations and those who have no living kin; by those who have withdrawn behind the physical and psychological walls of their own homes and by those who maintain them as part of the on-going life of society. The pervasiveness of the ideology which limits all women to constricted family roles and the home to a closed-off cloister unconcerned with what goes on outside, even when husbands and children are involved away from it, and the simultaneous negative evaluation of the housewife role around which the complex is clustered, are interesting and significant phenomena of American society. This restrictive ideology contributes to the self-effacing meaning of the statement, "I'm just a housewife," in answer to identity questions, often offered with a coyness which leads the partner in the interaction to say, "Oh, no, you are obviously much more than that."

Subject Index

Age, 175, 206
  and community orientation, 342, 361
  and friendship, 282, 311, 313–15, 325–26
  and housewife training, 146, 149, 155
  and marriage attitudes, 75, 82–84
  and neighboring, 235, 241, 246, 253, 262, 266–67, 278, 282, 284, 285–95
  and relationship to husband, 103, 106–7, 111–12
  and women's roles, 38–39, 49, 61, 66–67, 217, 219, 296
  of respondents, 14–15
  of the uncrystallized housewife, 371
  See also Life cycle
American women
  literature on, 7–8, 8n
Anomic neighboring, 228, 233, 245
  See also Non-interaction
Anomic non-conformity, 265
Apartment. See Housing type
Artist role, 51–53
Atypical suburbanite, the, 351
Authoritarian husbands, 76
Authority in the family, 108n

Beauty shops, 172
"Becoming"
  definition of, 32n.8
  stages in, 77–78
"Becoming" a housewife, 32–33, 43, 138–65

"Becoming" a mother, 187–204
"Becoming" a wife, 77–88
Best friends, 327, 335
Block clubs, 231, 240, 242, 250
Blue-collar suburbanite, the, 349–50
Blue-collar urbanite, the, 356–58
Budgeting, 154

Career role, 51–53
Career-oriented woman, 66
Careers, 13, 30–31, 362, 363
  See also Employment
Catholics, 123–24
  and attitudes toward men, 95, 98, 122
  and the "ideal" mother, 220–22
  in the sample, 12
Chicago, 230, 247
Chicago Standard Metropolitan Statistical Area, 341, 344n.41
Child, first, 200–201
Childbirth, 191, 195
Child care, 184–85, 218n
  in American society, 114, 120–21, 182–86, 374–75
  knowledge of, 154, 159–62, 331
  major problems of, 206–13
Childhood friends, 307, 313, 316, 317
Child-orientation
  and attitudes, 112
  and life styles, 201–4, 346–47, 354
  description of, 182
  in American society, 59, 59n.28, 63, 160
Child-oriented woman, 60, 65

Name Index